D1726924

European Yearbook of International
Economic Law

EYIEL Monographs - Studies in European and International Economic Law

Volume 17

EYIEL Monographs is a subseries of the European Yearbook of International Economic Law (EYIEL). It contains scholarly works in the fields of European and international economic law, in particular WTO law, international investment law, international monetary law, law of regional economic integration, external trade law of the EU and EU internal market law. The series does not include edited volumes. EYIEL Monographs are peer-reviewed by the series editors and external reviewers.

More information about this subseries at http://www.springer.com/series/15744

Suhailah Akbari

The WTO Transit Regime for Landlocked Countries and its Impacts on Members' Regional Transit Agreements

The Case of Afghanistan's Transit Trade with Pakistan

 Springer

Suhailah Akbari
University of Passau
Passau, Germany

ISSN 2364-8392   ISSN 2364-8406   (electronic)
European Yearbook of International Economic Law
ISSN 2524-6658   ISSN 2524-6666   (electronic)
EYIEL Monographs - Studies in European and International Economic Law
ISBN 978-3-030-73463-3   ISBN 978-3-030-73464-0   (eBook)
https://doi.org/10.1007/978-3-030-73464-0

This Springer imprint is published by the registered company Springer Nature Switzerland AG.
The registered company address is: Gewerbestrasse 11, 6330 Cham, Switzerland

Acknowledgment

The present research is a doctoral dissertation submitted to Passau University in partial fulfillment of a doctoral degree in law.

A lot has changed for me both professionally and personally since I started my doctoral research in the small, beautiful city of Passau. I came here as an inexperienced young woman with very little knowledge about my research topic. My choice of conducting a doctoral study in a specialized subject of international trade law has been inspired by the fact that there has been very little expertise and academic knowledge of trade law in general and international trade law in particular in the Afghan academia. Lack of female expertise is particularly obvious motivating me to fill the gap by conducting my doctoral research in the mentioned field. However, I was not aware of the challenges I would face along the way. In addition to challenges that PhD students face commonly, my challenges have been tougher and so have been my fights to overcome them, given that I come from a different life, culture, language, and educational background that would demonstrate enormous struggles and difficulties, particularly for girls. Takhar Province in the north of Afghanistan where I was born, raised and completed my high school education is a very conservative least progressed society for girls.

During my stay in Passau, at points, I felt inferior to others around me in the academic sphere. Most PhD researchers were ahead of me in the way they were conducting their research. In comparison, I had to struggle a lot, read two or perhaps a few times a topic to comprehend it. The struggles rose at their peak as I got married and soon expected my baby with extremely depressive pregnancy and post-partum and with bearing the responsibility of raising a baby. There were times I was almost giving up, trying to convince myself that I was still not ready for an advanced education and that it was extremely difficult to meet the western educational standards, especially those required for a PhD research. However, there was this prominent motive that saved me. I NEED TO SET A GOOD EXAMPLE FOR AFGHAN GIRLS and that I should not waste the chance that other Afghan girls dream about, that the Afghan society needs female law experts, and that it was my moral duty to contribute to my country's academic enrichment by bringing my doctoral skills home. Thanks to those struggles for making me stronger. I am writing this acknowledgment from the beautiful city of Kabul, I now teach at university and work in a senior position with the government. In my new role, I am leading Afghanistan's technical negotiating team for conclusion of a new transit trade agreement with Pakistan. This is a dream come true for me as I am applying my professional expertise in practice and I am looking forward to a new Afghanistan–Pakistan Transit Trade Agreement which effectively regulates transit trade and deepens the bilateral transit ties between the two countries.

I wholeheartedly thank my supervisor professor Christoph Herrmann who was my major source of support and encouragement and I am in awe of him for the successful completion of this study. I am grateful of my husband who has been there for me through ups and downs, lifted me when I fell, found me when I was lost, and made me see my potential strength and talent when my self-confidence was dying. I am equally grateful of my parents and siblings for their immense support. My mother and father have gone through a lot because of my rebellious character and have borne harsh behavior of our traditional community so that I achieve my dream of pursuing advanced education and becoming an independent capable woman who will be part of positive changes for Afghan women. If it were not for them in the first place, I would have not been where I am today.

Finally, I would also like to express my appreciation to the German Foreign Office which financially supported the early stage of my research through Hamida Barmaki PhD project at the Max Planck Foundation for International Peace and Rule of Law. Likewise, I thank those at Passau University including the Frauen Office who made it easier for me by providing social and financial support.

I dedicate this work to all Afghan girls who are talented, resilient, hardworking and are fighting every day for their basic rights including education.

List of Least-Developed Countries[1]

- Afghanistan
- Angola
- Bangladesh
- Benin
- Benin
- Bhutan
- Burkina
- Burundi
- Cambodia
- Central African Republic
- Chad
- Comoros
- Dem. Republic of Congo
- Djibouti
- Eritrea
- Ethiopia
- Equatorial Guiana
- Gambia
- Guiana Bissau
- Guiana
- Haiti
- Kiribati
- Lao People's Democratic Republic
- Lesotho
- Liberia

---

[1]UN Committee for Development Policy, List of Least Developed Countries (as of December 2020), https://www.un.org/development/desa/dpad/wp-content/uploads/sites/45/publication/ldc_list.pdf.

- Madagascar
- Malawi
- Mauritania
- Mali
- Mozambique
- Myanmar
- Nepal
- Niger
- Rwanda
- Sao Tome and Principe
- Solomon Islands
- Senegal
- Sierra Leone
- Somalia
- South Sudan
- Sudan
- Timor Leste
- Togo
- Towaco
- Uganda
- United Republic of Tanzania
- Veneto
- Yemen
- Zambia

List of Landlocked Developing and Least-Developed Countries[2]

- Afghanistan
- Armenia
- Azerbaijan
- Bhutan
- Bolivia
- Botswana
- Burkina Faso
- Burundi
- Central African Republic
- Chad
- Ethiopia
- Kazakhstan
- Kyrgyz Republic
- Lao People's Democratic Republic
- Lesotho
- Malawi
- Mal
- Mongolia
- Nepal
- Niger
- Paraguay
- Republic of Moldova
- Rwanda
- South Sudan
- Swaziland
- Tajikistan

---

[2]UN, World Economic Situation and Prospects (2016), 163; see also UN Statistics Division (2014), http://unstats.un.org/unsd/methods/m49/m49regin.htm.

- The Former Yugoslav Republic of Macedonia
- Turkmenistan
- Uganda
- Uzbekistan
- Zambia
- Zimbabwe

Contents

Acronyms

ADB	Asian Development Bank
ANDS	Afghanistan National Development Strategy
ASYCUDA	Automated System for Customs Data
ANTS	Afghanistan National Tariff Schedule
ACD	Afghan Custom Department
ACCI	Afghan Chamber of Commerce and Industry
AISA	Afghanistan Investment Support Agency
APTTA	Afghanistan–Pakistan Transit Trade Agreement
ATAR	Afghan Trade and Revenue
ATTA	Afghanistan Transit Trade Agreement
BMM	Border Management Model
CAREC	Central Asian Regional Economic Cooperation
CBTA	Cross Border Transit Agreement
CBR	Central Business Registration Office
DSB	Dispute Settlement Body
DSU	Dispute Settlement Understanding
ECO	Economic Cooperation Organization
ECOTTA	Economic Cooperation Organization Transit Trade Agreement
EC	European Communities
EU	European Union
GATT	General Agreement on Tariffs and Trade
IMF	International Monetary Fund
ITLOS	International Tribunal for the Law of the Sea
ITO	International Trade Organization
MFN	Most favored nation
LDC	Least-developed country
MoIC	Ministry of Industry and Commerce
RTA	Regional Trade Agreement
TFA	WTO Trade Facilitation Agreement

TBT	Technical Barriers to Trade
TIR	Transport Internationaux Routiers (United Nations International Road Transport)
SAARC	South Asian Association for Regional Cooperation
SAFTA	South Asian Free Trade Area
SOE	State-owned enterprises
SPS	Sanitary and phytosanitary
TRIPS	Trade Related-Aspects of Intellectual Property Rights
UNCLOS	United Nations Convention on the Law of the Sea
VLCL	Vienna Convention on the Law of the Sea
WTO	World Trade Organization

Chapter 1
Legal Challenges Facing Afghanistan's Transit Trade with Pakistan

In order to compete successfully in international trade, a country needs to establish simple and convenient routes to access world markets. Looking at different trade routes, trade by sea is a preferred option providing short and economic means for the shipping of goods. Nearly 90% of the world's trade accounts from trade by sea. Its popularity arises from the fact that it is not only cheaper in terms of transaction costs but also shorter in terms of transit time compared to overland trading.[1] Therefore, the lack of direct access to the sea impedes the growth potential of landlocked countries in international trade. This particularly affects least-developed countries (LDC), as the majority of them are landlocked.[2] If one wants to ensure, that overall goals such as international trade growth and development of LDC economies are achieved, freedom of transit and free access to and from the sea plays a vital role.

Taking the landlocked LDC Afghanistan as a particular case study, this doctoral thesis examines the World Trade Organization (WTO) regime of freedom of transit for landlocked members, particularly landlocked LDCs to discuss, whether and to what extent the special transit needs of these countries are recognized. For the same reason, this dissertation provides a comparative study of the United Nations Convention on the Law of the Sea (UNCLOS) provisions on freedom of transit of landlocked countries. In the context of Afghanistan, the key questions this research examines are the extent Afghanistan can benefit from WTO transit rules in demanding freedom of transit through the territory of the coastal neighboring country Pakistan, how those rules influence the transit agreement concluded between Afghanistan and Pakistan, and finally how useful a WTO challenge under the WTO dispute settlement system for violation of Pakistan's WTO obligation to provide Afghanistan freedom of transit and free access to and from the sea is. In

---

[1]UNESCAP, Transit Transport Issues in Landlocked and Transit Developing Countries, Landlocked Developing Countries Series 1, UN Doc. ST/ESCAP/2270 (2003); see also *Jayanta* (2005).

[2]See for example *Huarte Melgar* (2015), pp. 10–14; *Bayeh* (2015), p. 27.

doing so, this dissertation determines the interaction between WTO law and other multilateral agreements to explore whether or not WTO landlocked members can invoke transit rules from other multilateral agreements, such as UNCLOS, in support of their special demand for freedom of transit in WTO dispute settlement proceedings.

1.1 Context of the Dissertation

Worldwide a total of 44 landlocked countries exist, 32 of them are developing countries—15 in Africa, twelve in Asia, two in Latin America, and two in Central Europe. 17 of the 32 landlocked developing countries are LDCs.[3] According to a 2016 report by the United Nations Conference on Trade and Development (UNCTAD) the overall trade share of landlocked developing countries amounts only to 1.04% of total world trade with their main export products being primary commodities.[4]

With regard to landlocked countries one distinguishes between single and double landlocked ones. A single landlocked country is a country that is bordered by a country having direct access to the high sea. Afghanistan, in Asia, is for example a single landlocked country, as it is separated from the sea in the south by the coastal State of Pakistan and in the north by Iran. Double landlocked countries in contrast are only surrounded by other landlocked countries and therefore removed from seacoast by two or more countries.[5] Uzbekistan and Liechtenstein are the only two double landlocked countries in the world.

All landlocked developing countries are facing similar transit trade challenges. These rest not only in their distance to the sea that is directly affecting time and cost of trading, but also on weak infrastructure, poor institutional capacities, strict cross-border regulations, and fragile political relationships with their neighboring transit countries.[6] According to a 2013 report by the UNCTAD, transport and insurance costs of landlocked developing countries are on average two times higher than the average cost of transport and insurance of coastal developing countries and three times higher than the average cost of a developed country.[7] In comparison, most landlocked developed countries do not face these difficulties. Lichtenstein, for

---

[3]UNCTAD, The Way to the Ocean, Transport and Trade Facilitation Series 4, UN Secretariat, 1 (UN Statistics Division, 2017); For list of landlocked developing countries see UN Website, http://unstats.un.org/unsd/methods/m49/m49regin.htm.

[4]See generally UN, World Economic Situation and Prospects (2016).

[5]See UN Website (note 3); see also *Uprety* (2003), p. 202.

[6]See generally UNESCAP (note 1); UNCTAD (note 3); see also *Tuek* (2015), p. 339; Faye et al. (2004), p. 31; *Depoorter and Parisi* (2003).

[7]See UNCTAD (note 3); see also *Francois Arvis* (2005), pp. 243–264.

example, enjoys the benefit of free movement of goods and services across the European Union, just like other European landlocked developed countries.[8]

Additionally, some of these countries carry the supplementary burden of having tense political relationships with their coastal neighboring countries. Throughout history, coastal States have used their strategic location as a means of political and economic leverage against landlocked states. Political disruption may also affect trade and transit negatively, for instance when a transit country suspends or blocks, as means of political leverage, the transit of goods and persons of their landlocked neighboring countries, or imposes tariff and non-tariff charges or restrictions.[9] These restrictions particularly injure those, whose main export consists of agricultural products such as fresh fruit or vegetables as these products perish easily when delays are caused by suspension or blockage. For instance in 1958, Pakistan blocked the passage of Afghan goods through its territory to reach the sea. This severe injury created by the restriction brought both countries to the negotiation table to agree on a legally binding transit agreement. They finally reached a consensus that resulted in the 1965 Afghanistan Transit Trade Agreement (ATTA).[10] However, Pakistan often modified the Agreement unilaterally and the Agreement could not resolve the ongoing transit problem between the two countries.[11] Nepal faced similar problems with India in 1979.[12]

Landlocked countries, especially landlocked LDCs, have fought for decades for international recognition of their right to freedom of transit and access to and from the sea. They have been able to conclude regional agreements such as bilateral agreements with their coastal neighboring States to facilitate transit and access to and from the sea. History has, however, highlighted the failure of the bilateral approach as the only legal means of guaranteeing freedom transit to landlocked countries. To defend the countries' special position and to secure their right to access to the sea effectively a broader international legal platform needs to be established.

Therefore, Landlocked LDCs collectively struggled to obtain global recognition for their special needs to freedom of transit and free access to and from the sea. At global level, a number of international conventions and multilateral agreements

---

[8]*Gabriel et al.* (2010), pp. 39–73.

[9]See *Faye* (2004), p. 43. Similarly, during 2016 and 2017, Pakistan closed the Wagah land port several times, each time for several weeks, to Afghan exports. Afghan exports, which were mainly fresh fruits including grapes perished and Afghan traders claimed high financial losses. DAWN, Poor Kabul-Islamabad Ties affect Afghan Fruit Exports (January 2017), https://www.dawn.com/news/1305951; see also *Arwin Rahi*, A Counterproductive Afghan-Pakistan Border Closure, The Diplomat Magazine (March 20, 2017), https://thediplomat.com/2017/03/a-counterproductive-afghan-pak-border-closure/.

[10]Jaridai'i Rasmi Jumhuri'i Isla'mai Afghanistan 57 [The Official Gazette of the Islamic Republic of Afghanistan], Mo'afiqatna'mi Tejarati Transit Bain Jumhuri'i Isla'mai Afghanistan wa Jumhuri'i Isla'mai Pakistan [Afghanistan Pakistan Transit Trade Agreement] (ATTA), 11 Hoot 1343 (Mar. 2, 1965).

[11]See GA, Conference on the Law of the Sea, 29th Sess., 11th mtg, UN Doc. A/Conf. 13/43 (1958).

[12]*Sarup* (1972), p. 294; see also *Kumar Rana* (2010).

recognize the special need of these countries to freedom of transit and access to and from the sea. These multilateral agreements include the Barcelona Statute on Freedom of Transit (1921), the General Agreement on Tariffs and Trade (GATT 1947), the Havana Charter (1948) and the New York Convention on Transit Trade of Landlocked Countries (1965). These conventions and multilateral agreements were however replaced by future conventions and multilateral agreements such as the United Nations Convention on the Law of the Sea (UNCLOS 1982), the United Nations Convention on International Transport of Goods under the Cover of TIR Carnet (TIR 1975), General Agreement on Tariffs and Trade (GATT 1994), and the recent WTO Agreement on Trade Facilitation (TFA 2016).[13] These conventions and multilateral agreements now govern various aspects of international trade including freedom of trade transit. Some of them specifically emphasize the right to freedom of transit and free access to the sea for landlocked countries and some agreements have further granted special and differential treatment (SDT) for the benefit of landlocked LDCs.

Looking at Afghanistan as a landlocked LDC, one can find its struggles to obtain freedom of transit and access to the sea in the countries' history. The conclusion of its first transit agreement with Pakistan in 1965 was influenced by its efforts within the UNCLOS negotiations process. In other words, the UNCLOS negotiations influenced conclusion of the first transit trade agreement between Afghanistan and Pakistan.[14] It will be discussed throughout chapter. 6 that while Article 125 UNCLOS grants freedom of transit to landlocked State parties, it requires coastal and landlocked State parties to negotiate and determine the terms and modalities of exercise of that freedom under bilateral and regional agreements.

Afghanistan has signed and ratified a number of multilateral treaties. For example, it signed the UNCLOS in 1983.[15] It acceded to the TIR Convention in 1982 and reactivated the TIR system in 2013 after several years of domestic war.[16] By obtaining the permanent membership to the WTO, Afghanistan automatically became a member of the WTO multilateral covered agreements including the

---

[13]See generally GATT; UNCLOS; Statute on Freedom of Transit adopted by the Convention of Barcelona (Barcelona Statute), Apr. 20, 1921, 7 L.N.T.S. I (Entry into force: October 1922); Convention on Transit Trade of Landlocked States (New York Convention), done at New York, July 8, 1965, 597 U.N.T.S. 42 (Entry into force: June 8, 1967); Customs Convention on the International Transport of Goods under Cover of TIR Carnets (TIR Convention), Nov. 14, 1975, 16 U.N.T.C. 16510 (Entry into force: Mar. 20, 1978).

[14]*Sultana* (2011), pp. 21–28.

[15]UN, Treaty Collection (UNTC), https://treaties.un.org/pages/ViewDetailsIII.aspx?src=TREATY&mtdsg_no=XXI6&chapter=21&Temp=mtdsg3&clangn.

[16]See International Road Transport Union (IRU), IRU 2014, Annual Report 73 (January 2014), https://www.iru.org/sites/default/files/2016-01/en-ar-2014-web.pdf; see also UNTC, https://treaties.un.org/PAGES/ViewDetails.aspx?src=TREATY&mtdsg_no=XI-A16&chapter=11&clang=_en.

GATT 1994 and subsequently ratified the WTO Trade Facilitation Agreement (TFA) in July 2016.[17]

At regional level, Afghanistan continued to conclude more transit agreements with neighboring countries. Currently, Afghanistan has a bilateral transit agreement with Pakistan (APTTA 2011), and a Trilateral Transit Trade and Transportation Agreement with Iran and India (Chabahar 2016).[18] Afghanistan is also a party to the Central Asian Cross-border Transit Transport Agreement (CBTA 2011) and the ECO Transit Transport Framework Agreement (TTFA 1998).[19] Recently, Afghanistan signed the Lapis Lazuli Route Agreement that allows Afghan goods to reach Europe through Turkey.[20] Although these regional transit agreements are legally binding and in force, the compliance with and the transparency of some of these agreements, along with an overlap in the obligations arising from regional and multilateral agreements, remain a core challenge for Afghanistan.

For instance, some of the substantive provisions of the Afghanistan-Pakistan Transit Trade Agreement (APTTA) lack effective implementation mechanisms and transparency. APTTA grants Afghanistan free transit for its exports to India and other South Asian markets through seaports and land ports in Pakistan. In exchange, it allows Pakistan to use Afghanistan's land ports for its exports to and imports from Central Asia. Although the Agreement allows free transit of both Pakistani exports and imports through the territory of Afghanistan, it does not allow transit of Afghan imports from India through Pakistan. Since conclusion of APTTA, its contracting parties, particularly Afghanistan, have raised continuous complaints about the violation of the Agreement provisions. In particular the tense political relationship between Pakistan and India and between Afghanistan and Pakistan has often affected

---

[17]WTO, Protocol on the Accession of the Islamic Republic of Afghanistan to the Marrakesh Agreement Establishing the WTO (Afghanistan's Accession Protocol), Dec. 17, 2015, WLI/100 (Nairobi. Dec. 17, 2015).

[18]The Official Gazette of the Islamic Republic of Afghanistan 1063, Mo'afiqatna'mi Tejarati Transit Bain Jumhuri'i Isla'mai Afghanistan wa Jumhuri'i Isla'mai Pakistan (Afghanistan Pakistan Transit Trade Agreement) (APTTA), 10 Aqrab 1390 (Nov. 1, 2011); The Official Gazette of the Islamic Republic of Afghanistan 1250, Mo'afiqatna'mi Ejadi Dahliz Haml wa Naql wa Transit Bain-ul-milali Miani Jumhuri'i Isla'mai Afghanistan, Jumhuri'i Hind, wa Jumhuri'i Isla'mai Iran (International Transport and Transit Agreement between the Islamic Replublic of Afghanistan, Republic India and Islamic Repoublic of Iran) (Chabahar Agreement), 25 Hoot 1395 (Mar. 5, 2017).

[19]Central Asian Regional Economic Cooperation (CAREC), Kyrgyz Republic, Tajikistan Welcome Afghanistan into Cross-Border Transport Accord, Press Release (Oct. 18, 2011), https://www.carecprogram.org/?feature=afghanistan-cbta-accession. CBTA was signed and ratified between Kyrgyz Republic and Tajikistan in 2010 in Dushanbe. See CAREC, First Cross-Border Transport Agreement Signed under CAREC, Press Release (Dec. 6, 2010), https://www.carecprogram.org/?feature=first-cbta-signed-under-carec-december-2010; ECO Transit and Transport Framework Agreement, (Almaty, 1998). (Ratified. 2006), http://www.eco.int/parameters/eco/modules/cdk/upload/content/general_content/3758/1515303370972om85qvdt 8gggqsf9ed3ss6q4e5.pdf.

[20]Transit and Transport Cooperation Agreement (Lapis Lazuli Route Agreement), Ashgabat. Nov. 28, 2017, Türkiye Büyük Millet Meclisi Baskanligina (Grand National Assembly of Turkey), No. 2/1195 (Oct. 30, 2018), available at: https://www2.tbmm.gov.tr/d27/2/2-1195.pdf.

the successful implementation of APTTA. According to Afghanistan, Pakistan allegedly imposes unnecessary restrictions, closes its borders to Afghan exports and adopts unexpected unilateral measures that challenge the implementation and transparency of the Agreement.[21] An example of these restrictions by Pakistan is the imposition of quantitative restrictions (QRs) on specific Afghan transit goods. Pakistan is claiming necessity of these restrictions by arguing that those goods are sensitive to Pakistan's domestic markets and therefore precautionary measures are unavoidable to mitigate the risk of smuggling of those goods into its markets. According to Pakistani officials, two third of Afghan exports transiting through Wagha land port to India are smuggled into Pakistan and have harmed its trade domestic revenue and national industries.[22] The imposed unilateral QRs measures on sensitive goods violate APTTA provisions on smuggling trade and transparency. APTTA provides that when the contracting parties allege a smuggling of transit goods into their markets, they should bring the issue to the Afghanistan Pakistan Transit Trade Coordination Authority (APTTCA) for discussion and adoption of appropriate measures.[23] Similarly, APTTA requires that all laws, regulations and measures taken by one contracting party should be announced to the other contracting party and published prior to their application.[24]

Additionally, border closing has been another main challenge for Afghanistan's trade and transit relationship with Pakistan. For example, in 2014, the number of Afghan containers transiting through Pakistan decreased from more than 75,000 containers to 35,000 containers.[25] During the summer of 2016 Pakistan closed Wagah border to Afghan exports for several weeks, because Afghanistan sought alternative transit routes to India and South Asia through Iran. Afghan exports, which mainly consist of fresh fruits perished because of the border closing and Afghan traders experienced high financial losses.[26] After the Afghan President Ashraf Ghani announced reciprocal action warning that his Government will ban transit of Pakistani goods and vehicles to Central Asia, Pakistan reopened the Wagah

---

[21] An example is the 2016 clash between Afghanistan and Pakistan on the Wagah port closing. See *Khairullah Rasuli*, Daad wa Sita dba Hind Shamil APTTA nist (Trading with India is not within APTTA) Voice of America (Sept. 21, 2016), http://www.darivoa.com/a/pakistan-rejected-afghanistan demand-for-opening-wagahto-afghan-trade/3502129.html; see also Afghanistan Chamber of Commerce and Industries (ACCI), Call for APTTA Cancellation, TOLO News (Mar. 6, 2016) , https://www.youtube.com/watch?v=JSYpvAM3Npc.

[22] *Hussain* and *Elahi* (2015).

[23] Art. 3 APTTA.

[24] Ibid., Art. 29.

[25] Telephone Interview with Mohammad Rahim Momand, Former Director General, General Directorate of International Trade, Ministry of Industry and Commerce of Afghanistan (MoIC) (Nov.15, 2015).

[26] Pajwak News, Kandahar's Grapes Fall; Alternative Route Sought (Oct. 24, 2016), https://www.pajhwok.com/en/2016/10/24/kandahar%E2%80%99s-grape-exports-fall-alternative-route-sought.

border in late summer of the same year.[27] However, the same incidents reoccurred on multiple occasions during 2017 and 2018.[28] In contrary, according to Afghan officials, while Pakistan continued to close its border at several more occasions, Afghanistan kept its doors open to transit of Pakistan's transit goods.[29]

Another main challenge within the transit relationship of Afghanistan and Pakistan is created by the transit ban on Indian exports to Afghanistan through Pakistan's territory. The transit ban not only hurts Indian exports but also has a negative impact on Afghan imports by increasing the cost and length of Afghan trading with India which is resulting in relatively higher prices of those imports in the Afghan domestic markets.

In a nutshell, the transit challenges between Afghanistan and Pakistan can be categorized into three main challenges: 1. imposition of QRs on certain transit goods of sensitive character; 2. application of frequent border closure measures by both countries; and 3. transit ban on Indian exports to Afghanistan through the territory of Pakistan.

These challenges persuaded Afghanistan to seek alternative transit routes to access to and from the sea for its trade with India and other South Asian markets. Therefore, Afghanistan, seeking alternative transit routes for its trade with India and other South Asian countries, concluded in May 2016 the Chabahar Transit Trade and Transportation Agreement [hereinafter Chabahar Agreement] with Iran and India. The conclusion of the Chabahar Agreement raised numerous economic and political debates in Afghanistan as to whether the Agreement could present a viable alternative to APTTA.

In the meantime, due to failure of a bilateral approach to resolve Afghanistan's transit and access to the sea problems with coastal neighboring countries, particularly Pakistan, the need for a multilateral approach has surfaced more than any time. Therefore, when Afghanistan obtained WTO membership in 2016, a major perception was that it will help Afghanistan overcome its transit challenges with Pakistan; perhaps by holding Pakistan accountable before the WTO dispute settlement body to provide Afghanistan freedom of transit through its territory as part of its WTO obligations.[30] Given the WTO's ability to enforce its rules through a rigorous dispute settlement system,[31] it was expected that the WTO could provide a feasible platform

---

[27]Wasdam, Wagha Border Open for Afghans: Pakistan's Foreign Affairs Ministry (Sept.11, 2016), https://wadsam.com/afghan-business-news/wagah-border-open-afghans-pakistans-foreign-affairs-ministry-232/.

[28]Pakistan Afghanistan Joint Chamber of Commerce and Industries (PAJCCI), Pak Afghan Trade (2018), 2; see also Geo TV, Closure of Pak-Afghan Border Building into Humanitarian Crisis (May 4, 2017), https://www.geo.tv/latest/133250-Closure-of-Pak-Afghan-border-building-into-humanitarian-crisis-says-Imran.

[29]In-person Interview with Sayed Yahya Akhlaqi, Director, Directorate of Transit, MoIC (Kabul, Apr. 18, 2018).

[30]World Bank Group (WBG), Pakistan@100 Regional Connectivity, Policy Note 22 (May 2019).

[31]*Jackson et al.* (2000), pp. 179–180.

for this purpose. Moreover, the WTO is the only multilateral forum in which both Afghanistan and Pakistan are its permanent members.

1.2 Methodology

This study primarily looks at the WTO transit rules and APTTA. The research contains a doctrinal analysis of Article V GATT on freedom of transit coupled with the transit provisions of Article 11 TFA and provisions of APTTA. Moreover, it provides a complementary comparative study of the UNCLOS provisions on freedom of transit and access to and from the sea of landlocked State parties. In doing so, the research assesses whether the UNCLOS transit provisions can support a transit dispute in the WTO that is brought up by a landlocked State, which is a member to the WTO and a party to the UNCLOS.

In addition, the study also relies on a comparative analysis of the transit disputes of WTO members in order to assess their implications for landlocked Afghanistan. It provides some prospects for the settlement of Afghanistan transit challenges if Afghanistan opts to bring a dispute to the WTO. In addition to a substantive analysis of above mentioned international agreements and case law, the present research also looks at the range of scholarship involved, which either critically analyses or considers the connection between transit trade agreements and the WTO system more broadly.

The study further relies on interviews. It has conducted in-person and electronic interviews with Afghan policy makers, government relevant bodies as well as Afghan representatives in the WTO and WTO Secretariat officers concerned with Afghanistan's accession. Moreover, the study also made an unsuccessful attempt to interview relevant officials from other concerned States, including Pakistan and India, in order to maintain an impartial balance and benefit of views and concerns of these States regarding their transit relations with Afghanistan.

1.3 Significance of the Research

Due to its distant location from the sea, Afghanistan depends on its coastal neighboring countries for access to the sea. Political instabilities between Afghanistan and its neighboring countries often challenge Afghanistan's regional trade and transit regime. Although there are some transit agreements in place to support Afghanistan's freedom of transit, these have not been successful so far. In order to effectively address its external transit problems, Afghanistan needs to seek international multilateral legal guarantees. With its recently acquired permanent membership to the WTO it can invoke the freedom of transit that the WTO grants to its members. To examine the extent Afghanistan can benefit from the WTO rules on freedom of transit for its transit relationship with Pakistan, a legal assessment of

APTTA and the WTO rules is required. Although the topic has been discussed from an economic perspective, until today no research has assessed its legal implications.

This dissertation provides a valuable study of Afghanistan's transit problems by applying a regional and multilateral approach and lays down prospects for future transit negotiations and conclusion of agreements Afghanistan may benefit from. The findings are particularly helpful for Afghanistan and Pakistan in their negotiations on the modification of APTTA or replacement of it through a new agreement that is compatible with WTO rules and which has the ability to resolve the current problems.

1.4   Structure of Chapters

This dissertation is divided in nine chapters. Chapter 1 gives an introduction to the dissertation providing an outline of Afghanistan's international transit challenges imposed by its coastal neighboring States through rigorous regulations and restrictive measures.

Chapter 2 contains a historical review of the right to freedom of transit and the need of landlocked countries to access to the sea in light of past and present international legal instruments, by focusing on the struggle these countries faced throughout history to secure these rights under international agreements.

Chapter 3 provides an overview of the Afghan foreign trade legal regime. It starts by giving an introduction to the economic development of Afghanistan since the 2001 fall of the Taliban regime and continues with an assessment of foreign trade laws, regulations and legal reforms carried out. In doing so, it discusses Afghanistan's route into international trade by reviewing its concluded RTAs, multilateral transit agreements, as well as its accession to the WTO.

Chapter 4 reviews Afghanistan's transit regime and provides a selective study of Afghanistan's international transit agreements. The chapter particularly provides a comparative analysis of APTTA and the Chabahar Agreement to examine which of these agreements offers broader legal transit trade opportunities for Afghanistan's access to the sea and answers the question whether the Chabahar Agreement is a viable alternative to APTTA.

Chapter 5 examines the WTO rules on freedom of transit contained in Article V GATT and Article 11 TFA and discusses the legal status of landlocked members thereunder. It specifically seeks to answer whether, and if so, how the WTO rules on freedom of transit can shape the transit relationship between coastal and landlocked members under transit agreements and outside of them.

Chapter 6 explores the relationship between WTO law and other sources of public international law, specifically focusing on the interaction between the WTO rules on freedom of transit and the UNCLOS rules on freedom of transit of landlocked State parties. In doing so, it aims to assess the possibility of WTO landlocked members to invoke the UNCLOS rules on freedom of transit in WTO dispute settlement proceedings.

Chapter 7 reviews the relationship between the WTO rules on freedom of transit and the GATT general and security exceptions contained in Articles XX and XXI. The chapter also provides a case study of the implications of the relationship between these rules for the transit relationship between Afghanistan and Pakistan.

Chapter 8 assesses the implications of a WTO challenge against Pakistan for transit ban provisions and border closure measures imposed on traffic in transit of Afghanistan. In doing so, it seeks to answer whether these measures can be justified under the GATT security exceptions and tries to set out the role APTTA security exceptions can play in the proceedings. For this purpose, the chapter relies on the assessment carried out in *Russia – Measures Concerning Traffic in Transit (Russia – Traffic in Transit)*, a recent WTO case presenting some similarities to the transit situation between Afghanistan and Pakistan. The chapter also tests the relationship of APTTA security exceptions with the GATT security exceptions and other regional trade agreements in force between Afghanistan and Pakistan, to examine how a dispute involving a transit challenge could be resolved under those other regional agreements.

Lastly yet importantly, Chap. 9 provides final conclusions for this dissertation and presents some policy recommendations.

References

Bayeh E (2015) The rights of land-locked states under the international law: the role of bilateral/multilateral agreements. Soc Sci 4(2):27

Depoorter BWF, Parisi F (2003) Fragmentation of property rights: a functional interpretation of the law of servitudes, Policy Research Working Paper 284. John M. Olin Center

Faye ML et al (2004) The challenges facing landlocked developing countries. J Humanit Dev Capabil 5:31

Francois Arvis J (2005) Transit and the special case of landlocked countries. In: De Wulf L, Sokol Jose B (eds) Customs modernization handbook, World Bank, pp 243–264

Gabriel M et al (2010) Free movement of goods. In: Gabriel M, Trone J (eds) Commercial law of the European Union. Springer, pp 39–73

Huarte Melgar B (2015) The transit of goods in public international law. Brill, pp 10–14

Hussain I, Elahi A (2015) The future of Afghanistan-Pakistan trade relations. Institute of Business Administration, Karachi

Jackson JH, Hudec RE Davis D (2000) The role and effectiveness of the WTO dispute settlement mechanism. Brooking Institute, pp 179–180

Jayanta R (2005) Key issues in trade facilitation, Policy Research Working Paper 3703. World Bank

Kumar Rana R (2010) Right of access of land-locked states to the sea by the example of bilateral agreement between land-locked state Nepal and Port State India. Published Master's Thesis, University of Troms

Sarup A (1972) Transit trade of land-locked Nepal. Int Comp Law Q 21:294

Sultana R (2011) Pakistan – Afghan economic relations: Issues and prospects. Pakistan Horizon 64:21–28

Tuek H (2015) Landlocked and geographically disadvantaged states. In: Rothwell DR et al (eds) The Oxford handbook of the law of the sea. Oxford University Press Oxford, p 339

Uprety K (2003) From Barcelona to Montego Bay and thereafter: a search for landlocked states' rights to trade through access to the sea – a retrospective review. Singapore J Int Comp Law, p 202

Chapter 2
Freedom of Transit of Landlocked Countries in Light of International Multilateral Agreements

Transit is understood as the movement of goods and persons and freedom of transit is the unrestricted movement of goods and persons.[1] Freedom of transit finds its legal roots in the natural law and the Roman principle of 'servitude'. Advocates of natural law see freedom of transit in light of free access to the sea and believe that access to the high seas is a natural right of all nations and therefore landlocked States should enjoy the freedom of transit in order benefit from it, as free access to the sea can only be established where freedom of transit exists.[2] Similarly, the ancient Roman legal principle of 'servitude' provides that the owner of property could enjoy all kinds of rights and actions on the land unless their exercise harmed the fundamental rights of the neighbor's land.[3]

Throughout history, landlocked States used these principles as legal basis in their fight for acknowledgement of their fundamental right to free access to the sea, which was eventually recognized by international law.[4] For example, the 1921 Barcelona Statute on Freedom of Transit was the first international legal instrument that granted landlocked States a formal legal guarantee of their right to free transit.[5] The efforts of landlocked States for international recognition of their freedom of transit and access to the sea have been further addressed in a number of international conventions and multilateral agreements that were concluded after the Barcelona Statute.[6] This chapter provides a brief overview of freedom of transit of landlocked States under the provisions of the 1921 Barcelona Statute, the 1948 Havana Charter, the 1965

---

[1] See *Melgar* (Ch.1, note 2), p. 300, 325.

[2] *Grotius* (1916), pp. 9–10; see also *Pounds* (1959), pp. 257–59.

[3] *Livesey Burdic* (2007), pp. 360–364; see also *Parisi* (Ch.1, note 6); *Yianopoulois* (1983), p. 520.

[4] See for example *Lesaffer* (2005), *Castellino and Allen* (2003), *Lauterpacht* (1927), *Zhou* (2003), pp. 126–179.

[5] See generally Barcelona Statute.

[6] See generally (Ch.1, note 13).

© The Author(s), under exclusive license to Springer Nature Switzerland AG 2021
S. Akbari, *The WTO Transit Regime for Landlocked Countries and its Impacts on Members' Regional Transit Agreements*, European Yearbook of International Economic Law 17, https://doi.org/10.1007/978-3-030-73464-0_2

New York Convention on Transit and Trade of Landlocked States, the 1982 UNCLOS, the 1975 TIR Convention, GATT 1947 and GATT 1994 and the TFA.[7]

2.1 The 1921 Barcelona Statute on Freedom of Transit

The 1921 Barcelona conference was the first initiative to respond to the continuous demands of landlocked States to recognize their right of freedom of transit. The resulting Convention and its annexed Statute recognize free transit of goods and persons of contracting parties based on the principles of Most-Favored Nation (MFN) and National Treatment (NT) and oblige parties to remove any transit charges and duties that did not occur through services rendered.[8] The MFN principle means that countries are required "not to discriminate between goods on the basis of their origin or destination".[9] Similarly, the NT is the principle of treating goods and services of other countries the same as national goods and services.[10]

Although the Barcelona Statute generally recognizes the freedom of transit based on the MFN and NT principles, it leaves room for exceptions. For instance, the Statute allows contracting parties to refrain from applying provisions of the Statute in relation to States that were underpopulated or lacked proper system of rule of law and governance.[11] In addition, it allows the contracting parties to disregard provisions of the Statute in time of war.[12] Further, the Statute recognizes the right of its contracting parties to implement temporary transit and trading bans on certain goods, in times their security was jeopardized.[13]

Retrospective the Barcelona Statute was not successful in granting landlocked States the full right to the freedom of transit. This is partially owed to the fact that the Statute only covers means of water and rail transport. The exclusion of road transport from the scope of application made it difficult for landlocked States to benefit effectively from the Statute as the majority of landlocked States in Africa and Asia depend on overland roads for access to the sea.[14] As a result, landlocked States sought for alternatives to cover the freedom of transit in a more preferable and comprehensive context and correspondingly the United Nations adopted the Havana Charter two decades later.

---

[7]For a detailed list of all international conventions, treaties and agreements governing transit of landlocked countries see *Glassner* (2001); see also UNCLOS, Question of Free Access to the Sea of Land-Locked Countries, A/CONF.13/29 & Add. 1 (Geneva, 1957).

[8]Art. 2 Barcelona Statute.

[9]WTO, Glossary of Terms.

[10]Ibid.

[11]Art. 14 Barcelona Statute.

[12]Ibid., Art. 8.

[13]Ibid., Art. 7.

[14]*Makil* (1970), p. 40; see also *Uprety* (1994), p. 432.

2.2   The 1948 Havana Charter for Establishing an International Trade Organization

The Havana Charter was generated through a series of negotiations aiming to establish an International Trade Organization (ITO) during the 1948 United Nations Conference on Trade and Employment (UNCTE) in Havana.[15] The Charter recognizes among the variety of trade topics covered by it the right of freedom of transit of landlocked countries and accords special treatment to landlocked developing countries.[16]

Article 33 of the Charter governs the freedom of transit of its contracting parties. The Article contains provisions on traffic in transit, freedom of transit, transit charges and fees and a contracting party's obligation to accord MFN and NT treatment to traffic in transit coming from or going to another contracting party. Article 33 gives a detailed description of when traffic is considered to be in transit and unlike the Barcelona Statute recognizes all kinds of means of transport. Paragraph 1 of the Article provides:

> Goods (including baggage), and also vessels and other means of transport, shall be deemed to be in transit across the territory of a Member country, when the passage across such territory, with or without trans-shipment, warehousing, breaking bulk or change in the mode of transport, is only a portion of a complete journey beginning and terminating beyond the frontier of the Member country across whose territory the traffic passes. Traffic of this nature is termed in this Article "traffic in transit".

Paragraph 2 provides for freedom of transit and the sets the primary obligations of contracting parties. These include the obligation to facilitate freedom of transit via routes that are most convenient for international transit, the obligation to refrain from any kind of discriminatory treatment on the basis of, *inter alia*, nationality, departure, entry, or destination of traffic in transit. However, the paragraph does not define what constitutes freedom of transit and subsequently routes most convenient for international transit. The paragraph provides:

> There shall be freedom of transit through each Member country, via the routes most convenient for international transit, for traffic in transit to or from other Member countries. No distinction shall be made which is based on the flag of vessels, the place of origin, departure, entry, exit or destination, or on any circumstances relating to the ownership of goods, of vessels or of other means of transport.

As for transit charges, paragraphs 3, 4 and 5 of Article 33 provide that a traffic in transit shall be free of all charges and duties in respect to transit except for reasonable charges rendered for transit services. Further Article 33 contains interpretative notes on paragraphs 3 and 4, which exclude transport charges from charges rendered on transit services. The Interpretive Note to Paragraphs 3, 4 and 5 provide that

---

[15]UNCTE, Final Act and Related Documents, UN Doc. E/CONF.2/78, U.N. Sales No. II.D.4 (1948); see also UNCTE, Interpretive Note, Annex P to the U. N. Charter, UN Doc. E/CONF.2/78 (1948).

[16]For the text of the Havana Charter see UNCTE, Final Act and Related Documents, note (15).

"'charges' as used in the English text of paragraphs 3, 4 and 5 shall not be deemed to include transportation charges." This means that transit States are allowed to apply their domestic fees and charges in connection to transport and use of transport infrastructure such as roads and ports.[17]

Paragraph 6 of Article 33 recognizes for the first time in the history of international trade and transit the principle of Special and Differential Treatment (SDT) concerning transit trade of landlocked countries. In general, the SDT principle gives special and more favorable treatment to developing countries in relation to their trade with developed countries for example by providing longer periods to comply with their obligations, or by granting them more lenient obligations.[18] The Interpretive Note to Paragraph 6 of Article 33 provides that developing countries should be treated more favorably compared to developed countries, as they are in a weaker position looking at their economic, financial, and technical developments.

Although the Havana Charter marked a turning point in the recognition of special right of transit for landlocked developing countries, it never entered into force because the minimum number of signatories to ratify the Charter was not fulfilled.[19]

2.3 The 1965 New York Convention on the Transit Trade of Landlocked States

The UNCTAD adopted the Convention on the Transit and Trade of Landlocked States in 1965 in New York.[20] Prior to this, several multilateral negotiations on the freedom of transit of landlocked States took place. In 1963 the urgent need for a convention to recognize the special needs of landlocked States to freedom of transit was addressed at the UN Economic Commission for Asia and the Far East (ECAFE). Later in the same year, the ECAFE incorporated this demand in its Ministerial Conference resolution and submitted a request, which included a note by the landlocked LDCs of Afghanistan, Laos, and Nepal for SDT provisions, to the UNCTAD for further discussion.[21] Following the request the UNCTAD established a subcommittee to work on a draft of the Convention on the Transit and Trade of landlocked countries, which was finalized in 1965 and singed by UN members later in the same year.[22]

The New York Convention governs the transit relationship between coastal States and landlocked States and embeds provisions similar to those of the Havana Charter

---

[17]Ibid., 111.

[18]WTO, Glossary of Terms.

[19]See *Uprety* (1994), pp. 441–42.

[20]See generally New York Convention, chp.1 (note 13).

[21]See UNCTAD, UN ESCOR, 35th plen. mtg. UN Doc. E/CONF. 46/141, Vol. VI, 3 (1964); for literature review see *Uprety* (1994), pp. 441–42.

[22]See generally New York Convention, chp.1 (note 13).

but in comparison to it on a larger scope. Not only does the Convention recognize the special rights of landlocked States to free transit but also allows a UN non-member landlocked State to invoke the facilities and special rights provided by the Convention for its landlocked contracting parties.[23] Non-member landlocked countries can invoke this special entitlement under the condition that it has an agreement with a contracting party of the Convention.[24]

Nevertheless the success of the New York Convention was impaired by the fact that its provisions were applied on a reciprocal basis according to Article 15 of the Convention.[25] The reciprocal nature was troublesome as it was difficult for landlocked States to return the same benefits to their coastal counterparts. It eventually led to conflicting interests between the landlocked States who requested excluding the term 'reciprocity' from the Convention and the transit States, who insisted on keeping the term as a precondition for granting freedom of transit to landlocked States.[26] The conflict of interests stalled the operation of the Convention and the Convention was later superseded by the UNCLOS.

2.4   The 1975 United Nations Customs Convention on the International Transport of Goods Under the Cover of TIR Carnets (TIR Convention)

The 1975 United Nations Convention on the International Transport of Goods under the Cover of TIR Carnet (TIR Convention), which is in force since 1987, aims to harmonize and simplify the customs procedures and administrative formalities for road transit and transport.[27] Currently, a large number of landlocked States including Afghanistan are member to the Convention. These countries govern their road transit transport procedures in accordance with TIR procedures and are extensive users of TIR Carnet.[28]

Although the TIR Convention does not directly address the freedom of transit of landlocked States, the Convention is the first of its kind to recognize the needs of road transit and transport of landlocked countries as most landlocked countries in Africa and Asia rely on road routes for access to the sea.

The TIR Convention contains five main principles in relation to road transit transport that contracting members shall comply with. These principles are 1. secured

---

[23]Ibid., princ. VII & Art. X.

[24]Ibid.

[25]See *Uprety* (1994), p. 449.

[26]Ibid., 485–86.

[27]See generally TIR Convention.

[28]See UNECE, TIR Handbook, UN Doc. ECE/TRANS/TIR/6/REV.11 (2018); for more information see also UNECE Website, http://www.enece.org/trans/conventn/legalinst_43_bcf_tir_1975.html.

vehicles/containers; 2. international guarantee; 3. TIR Carnet; 4. mutual recognition of customs controls; and 5. controlled access to the TIR system.

The principle of secured vehicles/containers provides that vehicles or containers that are ready for transit departure at customs borders shall receive a TIR seal or stamp from the customs office of their departure border. Such seal or stamp must be obvious in the body of the vehicle or container. Sealed and approved vehicles and containers are not subject to physical examination by customs offices of transit countries and country of destination.[29] The TIR Convention allows customs offices to only check seals and the external conditions of such vehicles and containers. Nevertheless, customs offices are allowed, in exceptional cases, when there is reason for suspicion of a potential irregularity or inconsistency of the sealed vehicles and containers with TIR standards, to physically examine goods inside vehicles and containers. Those instances of examination are, however, limited by the Convention to three percent of the total goods.[30]

The principle of international guarantee provides that one competent valid agency in each member state undertake the responsibility for all transit guarantees.[31] As such, a member State shall introduce competent guaranteeing agency (ies). Customs authorities of a member State can authorize several agencies to guarantee all duties and charges arising from TIR operations. The TIR Convention provides for a minimum guarantee amount of 50.000 USD per TIR Carnet.[32] In the event of an irregularity or default, the guaranteeing agency is responsible to cover all charges incurred.[33] In addition to the liability of the guaranteeing agency, the TIR Convention allows Customs offices to collect, if necessary, administrative fines or other pecuniary sanctions from TIR Carnet holders.[34]

The principle of TIR Carnet provides that the competent guarantor agency in the departing country issues a customs control document that is valid throughout transit journey of a road vehicle or container and which contains the necessary customs information and a TIR verified reference code. The information contained in the Carnet includes names, stamps, and signature of the guaranteeing agency, start and end date of the Carnet, departure place, transit locations and final destination of transit goods, vehicles or containers. Each vehicle must carry a TIR Carnet.[35] However, several combined vehicles can carry only one single Carnet. In that

---

[29]Art. 5 TIR Convention.

[30]Ibid.; see also Ibid., annex 2 & annex 7.

[31]Ibid., Art. 6 & annex 9.

[32]See UNECE, Explanatory Note to Article 8, paragraph 3, The TIR Convention 1979, 9 REV. 50, http://www.unece.org/fileadmin/DAM/tir/handbook/english/newtirhand/TIR-6Rev9EN_Con vention.pdf. [hereinafter Explanatory Note to TIR Article 8(3)].

[33]Art. 8 TIR Convention.

[34]Explanatory Note to TIR Article 8(3), (note 32).

[35]Art. 9 TIR Convention.

case, the Carnet shall contain separate information about the content of each vehicle.[36]

The principle of mutual recognition of customs controls means that customs offices in transit countries and the country of final destination must accept the TIR customs control measures that the country of departure has applied to transit goods carried in sealed vehicles or containers.[37]

The principle of customs control access to the TIR system comprises specific requirements for guaranteeing agencies and transport operators' access to TIR procedures including access to the International TIR Data Bank. In order to be authorized as a guarantor and to issue TIR Carnets, a national agency is required to be operating for least 1 year and in a sound financial status as well as compliant to any tax or financial laws of the resident country. Transport operators have to meet the same conditions. In order to prove its sound financial condition, the guaranteeing agency has to provide national customs authorities with a financial proof.[38] Currently, several countries, including a large number of landlocked countries, practice the TIR system for road transit and transport purposes. The TIR Convention has been successful to help its member states to simplify their customs procedures, increase mutual customs cooperation, reduce transit time, facilitate cross-border transport, and lower trade and transport costs.

2.5   The 1982 United Nations Convention on the Law of the Sea

After several long and extensive rounds of negotiations, the third United Nations Conference on the Law of the Sea (UNCLOS III) adopted the United Nations Convention on the Law of the Sea (UNCLOS) in 1982.[39] UNCLOS entered into force on 16 November 1994.[40] As of June 2016 with the accession of the landlocked state of Azerbaijan, UNCLOS has 168 State parties including 27 landlocked States,[41] and the landlocked LDC Afghanistan signed the Convention in 1983 but

---

[36]Ibid., Art. 17.

[37]Ibid., Art.5.

[38]Ibid., annex 9, part I.

[39]UNCLOS III 1973-1982, UN. Code. Div. Office of Legal Affairs, http://legal.un.org/diplomaticconferences/lawofthesea-1982/lawofthesea-1982.html.

[40]Art. 320 UNCLOS.

[41]See UN, United Nations Oceans and Law of the Sea: Chronological List of Ratification of, Accession and Succession to the Convention and Related Agreements, https://www.un.org/Depts/los/reference_files/chronological_lists_of_ratifications.htm; see also UNOHRLLS, UNCLOS and Landlocked Developing Countries: Practical Implications: Summary Report, 2 (2012).

has not ratified it yet.[42] No data tackles the question as to why Afghanistan has not yet ratified the Convention.

Between 1973 and 1982, the UNCLOS III conducted eleven meetings to negotiate and discuss the Convention Draft and established three seabed committees to finalize the Draft Convention. The Second Committee was tasked with drafting provisions related to matters such as territorial sea, contiguous zone, exclusive economic zone and the freedom of high seas including freedom of transit and freedom of transit of landlocked countries.[43] The Committee was composed of both transit states and landlocked States.[44] The landlocked States submitted a proposal to the Committee that requested provisions on free and unrestricted transit rights and facilities for landlocked States without any discrimination among them.[45] This proposal also contained recognition of all means of transit routes including rivers that would provide landlocked States with transit facilities for access to the sea.[46] In addition the landlocked States also proposed the inclusion of SDT provisions for landlocked LDCs' access to the sea and their right to freedom of transit.[47]

UNCLOS governs four fundamental activities relating to freedom of high seas. These activities are navigation, resource exploitation, scientific research, and environmental protection.[48] Among them, freedom of navigation is the oldest activity recognized by customary international law[49] and defined by UNCLOS as the freedom of passage including freedom of transit.[50]

The provisions on freedom of transit of landlocked States are articulated in Part X UNCLOS, which excludes the principle of reciprocity and application of the MFN principle while dealing with transit rights of these States, and grants their vessels equal MFN treatment in accessing maritime ports.[51] However, the Convention is subject to terms and modalities of freedom of transit of landlocked States that are to

---

[42]UNTC, https://treaties.un.org/Pages/ViewDetailsIII.aspx?src=TREATY&mtdsg_no=XXI6& chapter=21&Temp=mtdsg&clang=_en#4.

[43]Ibid.

[44]UNGA, 28th Sess., Supple No. 21 & corr.1 & 3, vol. II, annex VI, sect. 5, Draft Articles Relating to Landlocked States, UN Doc. A/AC. 138/93, A/CONF.62/C.2/L.29 at 1 (1973); see also UNCLOS III, 2nd Comm, Revised Draft Articles in keeping with the Declaration of Developing Land-Locked and other Geographically Disadvantaged States, Doc. A/CONF.62/C.2/97 (1974).

[45]UNCLOS III, Revised Draft Articles, (note 44), draft Art. III.

[46]Ibid., draft Art. II.

[47]UNCLOS III, Informal Single Negotiating Text, Official Records 137, 168, UN Doc. A/Conf.62WP.8/Part 11 (1975).

[48]Art. 87 UNCLOS.

[49]See *Melgar* (Ch.1, note 2), 171.

[50]Art. 18(1) UNCLOS.

[51]Arts 124, 125, 126 & 131. The equal treatment to vessels flying the flag of landlocked States put an end to traditional understanding of nationality of vessels through port of registration. Previously, since landlocked States did not have any ports under whose names they could register their vessels, their flag flying over their vessels could not present their nationality to coastal States and, therefore, vessels belonging to landlocked States were not allowed to fly flag from these States. See *Donald and Stephen* (2016), p. 214.

be decided by regional agreements between them and transit States, which limits in practice the non-reciprocity of the right of freedom of transit for landlocked States.[52] Similarly, the special recognition of freedom of transit of landlocked States by UNCLOS does not preclude transit States from taking necessary measures to protect their security and other legitimate interests.

With this said, UNCLOS gives broad authority to transit States in determining the extent of freedom of transit they would provide for landlocked States. Moreover, Part X UNCLOS sets out the provisions regarding freedom of transit of landlocked states for all landlocked States regardless of whether they are developed, developing or LDC States and does not provide for the particular transit needs of landlocked LDCs. Although Article 48 UNCLOS provides for special consideration of interests and needs of landlocked developing States in relation to activities under the regime of high seas including their free access to and from the sea, the exercise of freedom of transit is still governed by regional agreements between coastal and landlocked States, which again gives the coastal States the power as to whether or not and to what extend they give special consideration to the transit needs of landlocked LDC parties. A substantive review of provisions of Part X UNCLOS is provided in chapter 6 of this study.

2.6   From GATT 1947 to GATT 1994: Article V GATT on Freedom of Transit

The GATT 1947 recognizes freedom of transit across the territories of the contracting parties. The GATT 1947 provisions on freedom of transit are contained in Article V GATT 1947. The GATT 1947 was replaced by GATT 1994. The GATT 1994 which is one of the WTO agreements covered by the Uruguay round (the initial negotiating round for establishing the WTO) governs trade in goods between WTO members. GATT 1994 has incorporated most of it rules from GATT 1947 including Article V on freedom of transit. The provisions of the GATT 1947 in Article V were incorporated without any modification in the same Article of the GATT 1994.[53] While chapter five explores Article V GATT 1994 on freedom of transit, this section only sheds light on the historical development of Article V within both the GATT 1947 and GATT 1994.

Taking into account the importance of freedom of transit for international trade, the contracting parties of the GATT 1947 recognized the right to freedom of transit. The provisions on freedom of transit were heavily influenced by the transit provisions of previous international multilateral agreements, in particular by the Barcelona Statute (Arts. I and III) and the Havana Charter (Art. 33). While transit provisions of the Barcelona Statute set the basis for drafting Article V GATT

---

[52]Art. 125(2) UNCLOS.

[53]See Herrmann et al. (2015), pp. 48–49.

1947, the Havana Charter was the corresponding multilateral agreement tin the drafting process of the GATT 1947.[54]

As mentioned above, the Havana Charter never entered into force but instead established international trade rules in the area of commercial policy. Since both the Havana Charter and GATT 1947 were negotiated and drafted at the same time by UNCTE preparatory committees, the committee tasked with the drafting of the GATT 1947 often consulted Havana Charter works, particularly the commercial policy draft rules of the Charter.[55] Originally the GATT 1947 was concluded to serve as a provisional agreement governing multilateral trading relationships between the contracting parties until the Havana Charter entered into force and to establish the ITO. Article XXIX(2) GATT 1947 stipulates that: "Part II of this Agreement shall be suspended on the day on which the Havana Charter enters into force". Paragraph 3 and 4 of the same Article require a consultation between contracting parties on whether the GATT 1947 shall be suspended, amended or maintained if the Havana Charter would not enter into force by its due period. When the Havana Charter failed to establish the ITO, the GATT 1947 contracting parties agreed to maintain the GATT 1947 until it was replaced by GATT 1994 under the auspices of the WTO.[56]

Article 33 of the Havana Charter on freedom of transit, except for paragraph 6 and interpretive notes, was incorporated in the same context as Article V GATT 1947 and subsequently in the GATT 1994.[57] Unlike the Havana Charter that recognizes special transit needs of landlocked LDC member States under an interpretative note to paragraph 6 of Article 33 of the Charter, Article V GATT only grants WTO members freedom of transit in general and does not make a distinction between landlocked and coastal members. It also does not recognize special transit needs of landlocked LDC members, including the special need to free access to the sea.

Although the GATT 1947 was a milestone in the history of modern international trade and framed the first fundamental movement for establishing a world trade organization, it nonetheless did not establish an ITO. It remained a provisional Agreement until the GATT 1994 replaced it during the creation of the WTO. Currently in the WTO, Article V GATT is the primary legal regime providing for

---

[54]ECOSOC, Preparatory Committee of International Conference on Trade and Development, Committee II, Report of the Technical Sub-Committee, UN Doc. E/PC/T/C. II/54/Rev/1, 7–8 (1946); see also Analytical Index of the GATT, Article XXIX, 996–998, https://www.wto.org/english/res_e/publications_e/ai17_e/gatt1994_art29_gatt47.pdf; *Uprety* (1994), pp. 42–45.

[55]See generally UNCTE, Final Act and Related Documents, (note 15. For list of all GATT documents and its preparatory committees see also the WTO webpages, https://docs.wto.org/gattdocs/q/1946_50.htm & https://docs.wto.org/gattdocs/q/1946_50.htm; for literature review see for example *Neumann* (1970), pp. 63–78.

[56]See Analytical Index of the GATT, Article XXIX (note 54).

[57]For more information on differences between Article 33 of the Havana Charter and Article V GATT see UNECAFE, Problems of Trade of Landlocked Countries in Asia and the Far East, Report by Secretariat, UN Doc. ECAFE/I & T/Sub.4/2 (1956), paras. 6–16.

freedom of transit and granting equal MFN based freedom of transit to all WTO members, be it a landlocked, coastal, developed or developing member.

2.7   WTO Trade Facilitation Agreement (TFA)

The WTO defines trade facilitation as "removing obstacles to the movement of goods across borders".[58] As one of the recent WTO multilateral agreements for trade in goods, the TFA was signed at the Bali Ministerial Conference in December 2013,[59] and entered into force in February 2017.[60] The Agreement finds its negotiating roots in the Doha development agenda of 2001.[61] The TFA aims to simplify customs procedures by improving certain aspects of the GATT 1994 including Article V on freedom of transit, Article VIII on fees and formalities connected with importation and exportation, and Article X on publication and administration of trade regulations. In doing so, the TFA recognizes the particular needs of developing and LDCs members with regard to trade facilitation by including a large number of SDT provisions granting developing and LDC members a range of flexibilities and facilities from transitional periods in carrying out their TFA obligations to technical assistance and capacity building programs to enable them to implement their TFA commitments.[62]

The TFA SDT provisions are the result of extensive discussions on the implementation practicalities of the Agreement in particular with regard to trade facilitation needs of developing and LDC members. For instance, paragraph 2 of Annex D on the Modalities for Negotiations on Trade Facilitation of the 2004 General Council Decision called upon WTO members to take full account of inclusion of SDT provisions in drafting the TFA text.[63] Similarly, the 2005 Hong Kong Ministerial Conference considered the TFA implementation issues a priority with regard to

---

[58]WTO, Glossary of Terms (note3); see also WTO Secretariat, Speeding up Trade: Benefits and Challenges of Implementing the WTO Trade Facilitation Agreement, World Trade Report (2015), 35.

[59]See WTO, Ministerial Declaration of 14 November 2001 (Doha Declaration), WT/MIN/(01)/DEC/1, 41 I.L.M. 746 (Nov. 20, 2001); WTO General Council Decision, WT/L/579 (Aug. 1, 2004); WTO, Ministerial Declaration of 7 December 2013 (Bali Declaration), WT/MIN/13/DEC/36 (Dec. 13, 2013); for literature review see *Melgar*, Ch.1 (note 2), 285; *Serra Ayral*, TBT and TFA Agreements: Leveraging Linkage to Reduce Trade Costs, WTO, Working Paper ERSD-2016-02 (June 2016), 4; *Nora Neofeld*, The Long and Widening Road: How WTO Members Finally Reached a Trade Facilitation Agreement, WTO, Working Paper ERSD-2014-06 (April 2014).

[60]See WTO Website, https://www.wto.org/english/news_e/spra_e/spra157_e.htm.

[61]WTO, General Council Decision on Doha Agenda Work Program, Annex D, WT/L/579 (2004), para. 2.

[62]WTO Agreement on Trade Facilitation (TFA), Feb. 22, 2017, WT/L/940, section II.

[63]WTO, Doha Agenda Work Program (note 61), para. 2.

SDT.[64] During the 2009 TFA draft review meeting, the Committee on Trade Facilitation reiterated that LDCs should not be obliged to implement any commitments unless developed members would answer their request for technical assistance and capacity building support in a timely adequate manner.[65]

Although, the TFA provides an extensive set of SDT provisions, it does not, like Article V GATT, recognize any specific SDT for the transit needs of landlocked developing and LDC members and rather grants an equal right to freedom of transit to both WTO coastal and landlocked countries under Article 11. Chapter five of this dissertation provides a further substantive discussion of provisions of Article 11 TFA.

2.8 Conclusion

Landlocked States struggled throughout history to secure a right to freedom of transit and free access to sea under international agreements. Although they have been successful to some degree to receive specific international recognition of their transit needs, the granted SDT does not sufficiently address their particular needs for access to the sea. It is particularly true in the context of the UNCLOS and the WTO regal regimes of freedom of transit. While both the UNCLOS and the WTO accord SDT to developing and LDC countries, any accorded SDT is articulated in a rather general context and does not directly relate to the special needs of landlocked LDCs. With little in their plate, landlocked LDCs continue to struggle for a special recognition of their need to freedom of transit and access to the sea.

References

Castellino J, Allen S (2003) Title to territory in international law: a temporal analysis
Donald R, Stephen T (2016) The international law of the sea, 2nd edn. Hart, p 214
Glassner MI (ed) (2001) Biography on Land-locked States, 5th enlarged & revised edn
Grotius H (1916) The freedom of the seas. Oxford University Press, Oxford, pp 9–10
Herrmann C et al (eds) (2015) Trade policy between law, diplomacy, and scholarship. European yearbook of international economic law. Springer, pp 48–49
Lauterpacht H (1927) Private law sources and analogies of international law
Lesaffer R (2005) Argument from Roman law in current international law: occupation and acquisitive prescription. Eur J Int Law 16:25–58

---

[64]WTO, Ministerial Declaration of 18 December 2005 (Hong Kong Declaration), WT/MIN/05/DEC (Dec. 18, 2005).

[65]Negotiating Groupe on Trade Facilitation, WTO Negotiations on Trade Facilitation Compilation of Members' Textual Proposals, TN/TF/W/43/Rev.19, part F-LDC Provisions (June 30, 2009); for TFA implementation challenges in developing and LDC countries see WTO Secretariat, Speeding up Trade (note 58), 108–132; for literature review see *Melgar* (Ch.1, note 2), 292–296.

Livesey Burdic W (2007) The principles of roman law and their relation to modern law, 3rd edn. Lawyers Co-operative Publishing Company, pp 360–364

Makil R (1970) Transit rights of land-locked countries: an appraisal of international conventions. J World Trade Law 4:40

Neumann P (1970) The relationship between GATT and the United Nations. Cornell Int Law J 3:63–78

Pounds NJ (1959) A free and secure access to the sea. Oxford University Press, Oxford, pp 257–259

Uprety K (1994) Landlocked states and access to the sea: an evolutionary study of a contested right. Penn State Int Law Rev 12:432

Yianopoulois AN (1983) Predial servitudes. West Publishing Company, St. Paul, p 520

Zhou Y (2003) History of international law. Foundation of international law. Source of international law. Law of treaties. Elsevier Science Publishing Company, Netherlands, pp 126–179

Chapter 3
Current State of the Afghan Foreign Trade Legal Regime

This chapter offers a descriptive analysis of the current state of the general pillars of Afghanistan's foreign trade legal regime since the post-Taliban era.[1] Section 3.1 provides a brief review of the Afghan economy and foreign trade development since the fall of the Taliban in the end of 2001. Section 3.2 focuses on laws and regulations governing the foreign trade of goods, mainly in the areas of export-import, customs procedure and other customs regulatory measures such as standards and technical regulations, sanitary and phytosanitary measures (SPS), rules of origin (RoO) and anti-dumping and countervailing measures. Section 3.3 examines laws and regulations governing foreign trade in services, primarily in areas of foreign investment, competition and State enterprise ownership (SEOs). Section 3.4 describes Afghanistan's commercial dispute settlement regime. Section 3.5 describes Afghanistan's route into international trade. Section 3.6 concludes the chapter.

---

[1]The reason that this period is chosen for this study is because it was after the fall of the Taliban regime that Afghanistan experienced a democratically elected Government, a liberal market based economy and speedy integration with regional and international economies. Since there is little legal literature on Afghanistan's foreign trade regime for the chosen period, the study has relied mostly on official reports and governmental data. Such reports and data could be problematic due to statistical discrepancies.

© The Author(s), under exclusive license to Springer Nature Switzerland AG 2021
S. Akbari, *The WTO Transit Regime for Landlocked Countries and its Impacts on Members' Regional Transit Agreements*, European Yearbook of International Economic Law 17, https://doi.org/10.1007/978-3-030-73464-0_3

3.1   The Post-2001 Afghan Economy and Foreign Trade in a Nutshell

3.1.1   Economic Outlook

Generally known as the '*Heart of Asia*', Afghanistan is a landlocked agrarian LDC located between Central Asia, South Asia and the Middle East.[2] The 2019 Doing Business Report by the World Bank (WB) ranks Afghanistan 167 out of 190 economies in ease of conducting business.[3] The report shows a better business environment for Afghanistan than the 2017 and 2018 WB Doing Business reports, which ranked Afghanistan at place 183 out of 190 economies in ease of conducting business.[4]

Afghanistan's latest Gross Domestic Products (GDP) stands at nearly 20.8 billion US dollars (USD) and its GDP per capita stands at 613.6 USD as of 2018.[5] The Afghan Government expects a growth of 5.2% in GDP in 2019 making it 21.8 billion USD and an average growth of 3.8% in GDP per capita raising it to 677.3 USD until 2030.[6] These figures are slightly different from those statistics presented by international organizations such as the WB, the International Monetary Fund (IMF) and United States Agency for International Development (USAID).[7] Nevertheless, all the available statistics indicate a slight annual growth of above 2% in the Afghan GDP since 2015. The country's national revenue stands at an average of 2 billion

---

[2]Aldosari (2007), p. 341.

[3]WBG, Doing Business 2019: Economy Profile 2019: Afghanistan (16th edn., October 2018); WBG, Doing Business 2018: Economy Profile 2018: Afghanistan (15th edn., April 2018).

[4]Ibid.; see also IMF, World Economic Outlook (January 2017). Between 2009 and 2013, the WB ranked Afghanistan 164 out of 189 economies in ease of doing business. WBG, Doing Business Economy Profile 2014: Afghanistan (11th edn., 2014).

[5]See The Government of Afghanistan, Afghanistan National Peace and Development Framework 2017–2021 (ANDPF), (2016), 6, http://extwprlegs1.fao.org/docs/pdf/afg148215.pdf; MoIC, Afghanistan National Export Strategy 2018–2022 (2018), 9 [hereinafter NES 2018–2022]; see also WTO, Afghanistan Trade Profile: 2015–2017, https://www.wto.org/english/thewto_e/countries_e/afghanistan_e.htm; WB, Afghanistan Development Update (August 2018), 38.

[6]ANPDF (note 5), 6; NES 2018–2022 (note 5), 9; see also WB, Afghanistan Development Update (2018), (note 5), 15.

[7]For example, according to the IMF, Afghanistan GDP per capita stood at 726 USD in 2015 and 576.3 USD with total GDP of 19.3 billion USD in 2017. IMF, World Economic Outlook (October 2014); IMF, World Economic Outlook (October 2016). Similarly, according to the WB, Afghanistan's GDP stood at 20.4 billion USD in 2015. WB, Afghanistan Economic Update (April 2015). Moreover, the 2018 Report by the IMF suggests that Afghanistan's GDP had an average 2.5% growth in 2018. The GDP growth was expected to raise to an average 3.6% in 2019, making it from 21.7 billion USD in 2018 to 22.9 billion USD in 2019. IMF, Islamic Republic of Afghanistan, IMF Country Report, No. 18/127 (May 2018).

USD, which accounts for a 10–11% share of the total GDP.[8] Similarly, more than 50% of the national budget depends on foreign aid.[9]

Until the collapse of the Taliban regime in late November 2001, Afghanistan's economic system was shaped for several decades as a 'war economy'.[10] The private sector played no or little role in the economy and there was hardly space for investments. The major contributing factor to the economy was agriculture, accounting for 72% of the total GDP.[11] During the time of the Soviet Union invasion (1980–1990), Afghanistan enjoyed a mixed economic system where the Government played a major role in controlling the market and only few domestic small and medium sized enterprises were doing business in the country.[12]

With the commencement of the Afghan Transitional Administration in 2002, the legal, political and economic systems began to evolve and Afghanistan shifted to market economy.[13] Although the Bon Agreement[14] paved the way for the market economy in the country, the 2004 Constitution sets the fundamental legal basis for the market economy. Article 10 of the 2004 Constitution forces the Government to protect and support the private sector and to encourage capital investment in accordance with Afghan laws and market economy norms.[15] Since then, with technical and financial support from the international community, the Afghan Government has made significant legal and institutional reform of its economic system. In 2007, for example, with support from the United Nations Development Program (UNDP), Afghanistan adopted a five-year National Development Strategy (ANDS) that aimed at reducing poverty, enhancing social and economic growth, strengthening good governance, and maintaining peace and security in the country.[16]

---

[8]IMF (May 2018), (note 7), 11, 20, 40–43.

[9]Ibid., 1–6; NES 2018–2022 (note 5), 9; see also MoIC, Afghanistan National Trade Policy 2018–2023 (2018), 4; MoIC, Afghanistan 2009–2013 Trade Review (2014), 22; WB, Afghanistan Economic Update (April 2015), 5–6.

[10]Dowdy and Erdmann (2013), pp. 261–281; see also Goodhand (2004), pp. 155–160.

[11]Eltizam (1996), pp. 95–103.

[12]Maxwell (1974), ch. 3.

[13]Afghanistan Business Law Handbook (2013), pp. 29–30.

[14]After the fall of the Taliban in late November 2001, the international community held a conference comprising international allies and prominent Afghan leaders in Bonn, Germany to discuss establishing a new democratic government for Afghanistan. In the conference, international allies signed the Bonn Agreement under which they pledged to provide financial, technical and legal supports to Afghanistan. Although the Bon Agreement does not contain any explicit provision on free market economic system, it has a provision on the adoption of necessary legislations and law reforms based on the needs of the modern economy, which can be implied for market economic system. For the Text of the Bonn Agreement see http://www.afghanistanembassy.no/afghanistan/government/core-state-documents/bonn-agreement.

[15]Art. 10 Qanuni Assassi Jumhuri'i Isla'mai Afghanistan [The Constitution of the Islamic Republic of Afghanistan] 1382 (2004).

[16]Islamic Republic of Afghanistan, Afghanistan National Development Strategy 2008–2013 (ANDS), vol. V (2007), https://www.wto.org/english/thewto_e/acc_e/afg_e/WTACCAFG18_CD_1.pdf.

The economic growth objectives of the ANDS focused on trade and sustainable development through an enhanced private sector-led market economy.[17] Furthermore the objectives included reforming the Afghan legal and institutional trade systems, facilitating a conducive environment for the attraction of foreign investment, strengthening regional economic cooperation and accelerating Afghanistan's accession to the WTO.[18] Motivated by its membership proposal to the WTO in 2004, Afghanistan began to reform its old trade laws and passed a number of new commercial legislation. Currently, Afghanistan has 28 new and amended trade laws and regulations.[19]

Moreover, over the past couple of years, Afghanistan has launched a number of new strategies and policies relating to economic development. The strategies and policies include the 2016 five-year Afghanistan National Peace and Development Framework (ANPDF), the 2018 National Export Strategy (NES) and the 2018 five-year Afghanistan National Trade Policy (ANTP). The ANPDF aims to enhance economic growth through comprehensive development of the private and agricultural sector.[20] Similarly, the NES aims to promote the Afghan export competitiveness in world markets by enhancing the capacity and quality standards of Afghan exports. Given that the Afghan economy highly depends on agriculture, the NES brings its focus to boosting agricultural exports and strengthening the agricultural sector.[21] To this end, the Government launched numerous agriculture development programs within the framework of the NES and the ANPDF.[22]

The agriculture sector remains the traditional key driver of the Afghan economy accounting for more than 50% of the total GDP.[23] Following the agriculture sector, the services sector plays another major role in the Afghan economy accounting for 30–35% of total GDP. Currently, amounting to a nearly 70% share within services sector, foreign investments lead the services sector.[24] Foreign investments include mostly telecommunications, hotels, industry, banking, construction, media courier and postal services, environmental services and education. UAE based companies,

---

[17]Ibid., 73–76.

[18]Ibid.; see also ibid., 143.

[19]See MoIC Website, http://moci.gov.af/fa/page/7565.

[20]See generally ANDPF (note 16); for a comprehensive review of the ANPDF see The United Nations in Afghanistan, One UN for Afghanistan (Mar. 27, 2018).

[21]See NES 2018–2022 (note 5).

[22]See ANDPF (note 5), 18.

[23]See Afghanistan 2009–2013 Trade Review, (note 9), 22; see also Ministry of Agriculture, Irrigation and Livestock of Afghanistan (MAIL), Comprehensive Agriculture Development Priority Program 2016–2020 (August 2016), 6–7; WB, Islamic Republic of Afghanistan Agricultural Sector Review: Revitalizing Agriculture for Economic Growth, Job Creation and Good Security, Report No. AUS9779 (June 2014), 5–10.

[24]See Afghanistan National Trade Policy 2018–2023 (note 9).

Indian and US investors are the main foreign investors.[25] However, the growth of the services sector, particularly for foreign investments, has not been steady. Between 2013 and 2015, for instance, foreign direct investment slowed down by approximately 50% and major investors withdrew from the country.[26] Particularly in 2014, the Afghanistan Investment Support Agency (AISA), did not register any new investments and the country experienced the lowest investment rate so far. The decrease in international aid, the withdrawal of international forces, the uncertain and volatile security and transition of political power to a new national unity government, which many believed would not be capable of maintaining the stability in the country, all contributed towards the uncertainty and distrust in doing business and investing in Afghanistan, and consequently slowed down the investment activities in the country.[27] Likewise, since the beginning of 2013 the rapid depreciation of the Afghani currency vis-a-vis the USD resulted in decreasing imports of products and causing inflation.[28] Unlike the services sector, the agricultural sector remained stable during this period and it continues to be the leading economic sector of the country.[29]

Although Afghanistan experienced economic growth and trade progress since 2002, it continues to suffer from legal and institutional challenges as well as obstacles at both national and international levels. At national level, the challenges include policy implementation, poor administrative skills leading to mismanagement and poor implementation of rules and measures including their transparency, and corruption coupled with political volatilities and security threats. At international level, Afghanistan faces challenges in relation to governance, effective implementation of international aid and compliance with obligations arising from its commitments under international agreements. In September 2019 the US Government, alleging that corruption existed within certain bodies of the Afghan Government, cut its 160 million USD aid that was originally granted to support the development of the Afghan energy sector through implementation by USAID.[30] The Afghan Government refuted that the corruption came from international agencies implementing aid projects in Afghanistan and argued that the lack of report on expenditure and implementation of aid by those international agencies such as USAID added another challenge to the already existing corruption within the different layers of the Afghan

---

[25] Working Party on the Accession of the Islamic Republic of Afghanistan, Report on Accession of the Islamic Republic of Afghanistan—Derestriction of Documents, WT/ACC/AFG/38. WT/MIN (15)/6 (Nov. 13, 2015), para 256 [hereinafter Working Party on the Accession of Afghanistan].

[26] Afghanistan 2009–2013 Trade Review (note 9), 23 & 28.

[27] Ibid.

[28] Ibid.

[29] Ibid.

[30] *Lara Jakes*, U.S. Cuts $100 Million in Aids to Afghanistan, Citing Government Corruption, The New York Times (Sept. 19, 2019), https://www.nytimes.com/2019/09/19/world/asia/us-afghanistan-aid.html.

Government.[31] To help overcome its economic development challenges, at least on the national level, the Afghan Government started launching capacity building trainings for its officials and adopted anti-corruption policies, implementation strategies and action plans. At international level, it lies within the hands of the international community to rethink some of their approaches and to include the Afghan Government within the implementation process of international aid in order to mitigate corruption, maintain transparency and to effectively coordinate between the Afghan Government and international communities.

3.1.2   Foreign Trade and Customs Reform

Although Afghanistan's foreign trade has experienced since 2002 growth due to extensive reforms of its customs, it has been unsteady. Between 2002 and 2003, the Afghan official trade volume stood below 4 billion USD with an exports volume of 100 million USD and imports volume of 3.6 billion USD,[32] the country's current annual trade volume accounts for nearly 8 billion USD.[33] However, the gap between exports and imports is still huge—exports contribute less than a billion USD, while imports contribute to more than 7 billion USD to the total trade volume[34]—showing an average trade deficit of 6 billion USD or a negative trade balance of 75%, which is one of the highest trade deficits in the world.[35]

Afghanistan heavily relies on imports. Since 2002, albeit the export rate has continuously risen, the import rate has also been rising at an average of 11% making up 90% of the consumption goods at local markets.[36] However, since 2013 the 2009–2013 Trade Review Report by the MoIC shows a slight decrease in the rise of imports and a 40% dramatic increase in exports.[37] Again, this statistic is different from the figures that international reports present.[38]

---

[31]Radio Azadi (Radio Liberty), Abdullah and Nabil Should be Held Accountable, https://www.youtube.com/watch?v=vztEU5cUEsE (Mins 22–23:20).

[32]IMF, Emergency Customs Modernization and Trade Facilitation Project (November 2003); see also United States Department of Commerce, Doing Business in Afghanistan: 2011 Country Commercial Guide for US Companies (2011), 2.

[33]WTO, Afghanistan Trade Profile: 2015–2017, https://www.wto.org/english/thewto_e/countries_e/afghanistan_e.htm.

[34]Afghanistan 2009–2013 Trade Review (note 9), 23; Afghanistan National Trade Policy 2018–2023 (note 9), 4; IMF (May 2018), (note 7), 18.

[35]Afghanistan National Trade Policy 2018–2023 (note 9), 4; NES 2018–2022 (note 5), 9.

[36]NES 2018–2022 (note 5), 9.

[37]See Afghanistan 2009–2013 Trade Review (note 9), 6 & 23; see also MoIC, Report of Imports and Exports 2014–2017, http://moci.gov.af/Content/files/Afghanistan%20Trade%20Statistics%20 (2014-2017).pdf.

[38]For instance, a 2013 report by the USAID shows an increase from 5.7 billion USD to 7.6 billion USD in trade volume between 2009 and 2013. USAID, Trade and Accession Facilitation for

Afghanistan imports different types of products but exports basic commodities. The top importing products include petroleum, machinery and equipment, food products, metals and similar items. Imports primarily come from Pakistan, Iran, China, the Central Asian Republics, Japan, India, Turkey, and the United Arab Emirates (UAE).[39] Afghanistan's national commodity exports include dry fruits, tropical fruits, spice seeds, saffron, carpets, cotton and wool, and mineral stones including marbles.[40] Carpet, saffron and dry fruits are among the exports of high comparative advantage, particularly in regional markets. Afghanistan's top export markets are Pakistan, India, Iran, Iraq, the UAE, China, and the Central Asian countries.[41]

Customs, being the main institution facilitating export-import process and implementing export-import regulations and procedures, have been at the focus of the Afghan Government's foreign trade objectives and received substantial technical and financial reform supports from international donors and. In 2003, with the technical and financial support from the WB, the Government launched a five-year Emergency Customs Modernization and Trade Facilitation Project to improve the customs system. The project focused on digitalizing customs procedures including procedures related to goods clearance, tariffs, and valuation mechanisms.[42] The project also covered institutional arrangements and administrative reforms such as the establishment of an office of standards and quality, an upgrade of customs warehouses and industrial parks, and the creation of digital communications at domestic level between customs offices as well as at cross-border level with neighboring trading customs partners.[43] To further advance reforms in Afghan Customs, the WB launched the 2010 'Second Customs Reform and Trade Facilitation Project'. The project aimed at advancing the customs automation system, installing customs information systems to enhance data exchange and cross-border customs cooperation, providing technical assistance, and developing more customs facilities such as industrial parks.[44]

Similarly, USAID launched the Trade and Accession Facilitation for Afghanistan projects (TAFA I, TAFA II) between 2009 and 2013 and their successor the

---

Afghanistan, Final Report (August 2013). Similarly, a 2018 report by the IMF shows an average 7% increase in exports between 2015 and 2018. IMF (May 2018), (note 7).

[39] Afghanistan 2009–2013 Trade Review (note 9), 29.

[40] Ibid., 28–40; see also WB, The Overall Exports and Imports for Afghanistan in 2014, http://wits.worldbank.org/CountrySnapshot/en/AFG/textview; WB, Afghanistan Development Update (2018), 19; for literature review see Parto et al. (2012), p. 15.

[41] See for example Afghanistan 2009–2013 Trade Review (note 9), 39; WB, Afghanistan Development Update (2018), (note 40), 20.

[42] See generally WB, Emergency Custom Modernization and Trade Facilitation (November 2003).

[43] See ibid.

[44] See Ministry of Finance of Afghanistan (MoF), Afghanistan Customs Department (ACD), Annual Progress Report 2016 (2016), 54–55; WB, Afghanistan Second Customs Reform and Trade Facilitation Project: Restructuring, Report No. RES30675 (Dec. 18, 2017).

Afghanistan Trade and Revenue project (ATAR) between 2014 and 2017.[45] USAID supported projects that focused at advancing reforms for four trade and customs priorities: customs reforms, trade policy reforms, improving the climate for private sector and investment, and finally enhancing trade facilitation and global economic integration of Afghanistan including its accession process to the WTO.[46]

The mentioned projects have had some successes in modernizing and simplifying the Afghan customs system. Lengthy border checks of trucks decreased from 3 days in 2003 to a maximum of 40 min in 2012 followed by 20 min in 2018. Customs procedures decreased from 33 to twelve steps at major customs borders.[47] Marking a milestone in the history of the Afghan customs system, the ACD was able to launch an Automated System of Customs Database (ASYCUDA). The ASYCUDA is an international automated module for national customs offices and enables them to control and track exports-imports and movement of goods, including those being in transit online. The launch of the ASYCUDA has helped the ACD to develop further customs modules and management systems. These modules and systems include a border management module, ASYCUDA TIR module, a Trade Logistics Impact module, a risk management module, a valuation module, an e-payment module, a declaration process system, a customs information system, and a National Single Window and Information Portal.[48]

The border management module is a customs guideline for internal joint management of border activities and provides customs information to agencies working at customs borders.[49] The ASYCUDA TIR module ensures that movements of goods into and out of Afghanistan, including goods in international transit, comply with the TIR procedures. The Trade Logistics Impact module is designed to reduce customs clearance time. The application of this module reduced the inland clearance time from 3 days to 1 h and the border customs clearance time to 20 min in most Afghan customs offices.[50] The valuation module enables national customs offices to calculate import-exports customs values electronically and provides consolidated customs valuation data that is accessible for all customs offices.[51] The e-payment module replaces cash payment of customs tariffs and duties with an online payment

---

[45]USAID, Trade and Accession Facilitation for Afghanistan (TAFA), Final Report (August 2013); see also ACD, Annual Progress Report 2016 (note 44), 51–53; USAID, Response to the Inquiry Letter on Afghan Customs Revenue, USAID Memorandum (Mar. 19, 2015).

[46]See for example TAFA (note 45).

[47]See MoF Website, http://mof.gov.af/en/page/421; see also WB, Afghanistan-Second Customs Reform and Trade Facilitation Project (note 44), 4; see also Special Inspector General for Afghanistan Reconstruction (SIGAR), Analysis of TAFA Final Report (April 2014), 16–18; UNECE, Strengthening Regional Cooperation in Central Asia: A contribution to long-term stability and sustainable development of Afghanistan (SPECA Economic Forum (2010).

[48]ACD, Five Year Strategic Plan 2014–2018 (2014), 32; see also SIGAR (note 47).

[49]ACD, Five Year Strategic (note 48), 36–37.

[50]See WB, Afghanistan-Second Customs Reform and Trade Facilitation Project (note 44), 4.

[51]ACD, Five Year Strategic (note 48), 49.

method through Afghan banks.[52] Currently, the Da Afghanistan Bank (The State Central Bank) is in charge of the customs e-payments.[53]

Likewise, the declaration process system enables customs offices to track the movement of goods in and out of Afghanistan online and subsequently expedites the clearance of goods, calculation and collection of customs duties and charges. The information system connects national custom offices and expedites customs documentation process through electronic collection of customs data. The system further provides a text message (SMS) alert option, which sends message alerts to traders with regard to their customs duties and other obligations. It further accelerates cross-border exchange of data and customs to customs cooperation. Recently, data exchange between Afghanistan and Tajikistan has been implemented through the information system, a Memorandum of Understanding (MoU) on Customs cooperation through data exchange has been signed between Afghanistan and China and an interface system between Afghanistan ASYCUDA and Iran ASYCUDA has been developed.[54] The ASYCUD, in particularly the valuation and e-payment modules help reduce trading time and in-person contact between customs officers and traders, which ultimately helps decreasing corruption and maintaining transparency between national customs offices and cross-border customs in neighboring countries.

According to domestic and international reports, customs reforms have helped customs revenue to increase.[55] The customs revenue rose up from 77 million USD during 2003–2004 to more than 900 million USD during 2009–2010, contributing more than 50% of total domestic revenue.[56] However, between 2012 and 2014, due to security challenges and political instabilities affecting the export-import and investments, the customs revenue decreased to 700 million.[57] From 2015 onward, the customs revenue has again experienced an average growth rate of 5.5%, counting for more than 40% of the total domestic revenue.[58]

Although as a result of the carried out customs reforms, technical, institutional and infrastructural gaps substantially subsided, some challenges such as poor state of rule of law, poor coordination between Customs and other relevant governmental bodies, inadequate energy power especially electricity, corruption and security threats remain. For instance, the Afghanistan Customs Department (ACD)[59] has

---

[52]See ACD, Annual Progress Report 2016 (note 44), 30.

[53]Ibid.

[54]Ibid., 28–53; see also ACD, Five Year Strategic (note 48), 32–52.

[55]Ibid.; see also SIGAR (note 47), 2.

[56]WB, Second Customs Reform and Trade Facilitation Project: Project Information Document: Appraisal Stage, Report No. AB5364 (Apr. 14, 2010), para. 5.

[57]ACD, Five Year Strategic (note 48), 48; SIGAR (note 47), 2.

[58]ACD, Annual Review on Revenue and Trade (2016), 6–7.

[59]The ACD which falls within the authority of Ministry of Finance, is the responsible body for the overall legal, administrative and technical activities in customs. Its main responsibilities, *inter alia*, include monitoring the overall border activities concerning imports and exports, collecting customs tariffs and other relevant duties and charges, processing customs valuation and administering customs administrative dispute settlement including administrative appeals. Parallel with the

not been able to activate and use all the ASYCUDA designed modules and digital systems such as the information system, valuation system and e-payment system due to inadequate electrification.[60] As a result, procedures and information are not as transparent, customs tariffs and duties are still paid in cash at most customs, and there is a high potential for corruption.[61] Moreover, at most customs offices, officers do not acquire the required technical skills to run the technical facilities. Similarly, the Da Afghanistan Bank, which is the only Bank in charge of customs duties, has only a limited number of branches in few major cities and in cities where there is not a Da Afghanistan Bank branch, traders have to pay their custom duties in cash at customs offices.

3.2 Laws and Regulations Governing Foreign Trade in Goods

3.2.1 Rules Governing Customs Procedures: Import-Export Documentation and Customs Valuation Methods

Since 2002, Afghanistan has significantly reformed its customs laws and adopted several new customs regulations and policies. The laws include the 2005 Customs law with its latest amendment in 2016 (hereinafter the 2016 Customs Law), the 2016 Customs Administration Law, the 2005 Regulation on Customs Valuation and the 2006 Regulation on Determining Price of Goods in Customs. These laws and regulations are modern and intend to fill the previous regulatory gaps. For instance, they contain provisions on customs control and track systems, WTO consistent valuation methods, post-release checks, facilitation for selective examinations, electronic filing, customs brokers, deferred payment and e-payment.[62] The new laws and regulations simplified customs procedures substantially, particularly documentation and business registration processes.[63]

ACD, the Afghanistan Chamber of Commerce and Industries (ACCI) was established to represent the private sector and undertakes duties and responsibilities concerning tariff classification, customs valuation, registration of business invoices and issuance of customs documents such as certificate of origin and certificate of value. ACCI Website, http://www.acci.org.af/about-us/about-acci.html.

[60]See Afghanistan Customs Tariffs Handbook: Strategic and Practical Information, vol. 20 (International Business Publications, DC., 2016).

[61]The ACD has been ranked one of the top three corrupt financial institutions in the country. See WB, Eliminating Customs of Corruption: New Approaches in Cameroon & Afghanistan (2012); see also SIGAR, (note 47), 2.

[62]For comparison, see for example Qanuni-i Gumrukat'i Afghanistan (Afghanistan's Customs Law) 1321(1982); Qanuni-i Gumrukat'i Afghanistan (Afghanistan's Customs Law) 1384 (2005).

[63]Afghanistan adopted a Single Administrative Document (SAD) that aimed at harmonizing codification and simplification of customs procedures. See for example ACD, Annual Progress Report 2016 (note 44); see also ACD, Five Year Strategic (note 48).

For example, the customs law lowered the total number of import-export documents from 33 documents to ten documents.[64] The generally required documents for import of all products include an import license, customs declaration, quality certificate, consignment notes or bill of lading, certificate of origins, packing list, authority letter for handling goods, certificate of value, and a proof of transaction cost of goods (commercial invoice).[65] For import of medicine and medical equipment, importers are further required to present a separate medicine import license.[66] The failure to present one or more of these documents leads to enforcement measures such as extra charges. For example, customs offices apply an additional customs duty of 25% ad valorem to goods that do not have a certificate of value.

In addition to the documents required for imports exporters have to present a phytosanitary certificate for plants, a veterinary certificate for animals, a certificate for seeds for the export of seeds, an export approval for films, an export approval for handicraft, and an export approval for printed materials such as books and brochures.[67] Since 2019, exporters are not obliged to obtain and present a certificate of origin at customs borders. However, exporters can voluntarily request from the government a certificate of origin.[68] Similarly, to simplify the facilitation of the export procedure, the government plans to remove the requirement for some other certificates such as quality certificates and SPS certificates and to make those voluntary for exports.[69] Likewise, the MoIC has recently launched the Export One-Stop-Shop, which aims to speed up export documentation procedures and to provide improved export facilitation.[70]

Afghanistan applies its customs value on imports based on four valuation methods using the CIF (Cost, Insurance and Freight) indicator.[71] The CIF indicator adds insurance and freight to the transaction cost of consignments subject to the customs value.[72] The four customs valuation methods are the transaction value of

---

[64]USAID, Doing Business in Afghanistan (2014), 4–6; MoIC, An Inventory to Exporting Goods from Afghanistan (2013); In-person Interview with Mir Saeed Saeedy, Director General, International Trade Directorate, MoIC (Oct. 2–4, 2018); see also Parto et al. (2012), p. 15.

[65]Arts. 15, 31, 38 Afghanistan's Customs Law of 2005 [hereinafter 2005 Afghanistan Customs Law]; see also Working Party on the Accession of Afghanistan (note 25), 89.

[66]Afghanistan Regulation on Production and Importation of Medicine and Medical Equipment of 2017.

[67]Working Party on the Accession of Afghanistan (note 25), 89.

[68]Afghanistan National Trade Policy 2018–2023 (note 9), 45.

[69]Ibid.

[70]See MoIC Website, http://customs.mof.gov.af/Content/files/OSS%20One%20Pager%20English. pdf.

[71]Art. 9 Afghanistan Regulation on Determining Price of Goods in Customs of 2009 [hereinafter Regulation on Determining Price of Goods in Customs]; see also ACD, Customs Valuation, http://customs.mof.gov.af/en/page/1034/customs-valuation.

[72]Afghanistan Regulation on Customs Valuation of 2006, Ministerial Regulation No. 38 [hereinafter Regulation on Customs Valuation]; see also MoIC, An Inventory to Exporting Goods from Afghanistan (note 64), 13.

goods, transaction value of identical goods, transaction value of similar goods, and customs value of specific goods. Afghan customs offices apply the customs valuation of imports based on transactional value of goods. In the absence of transactional value proof of imported goods, the transactional value of identical products sets the basis for customs valuation.[73] Identical goods are in this context products, which are alike to another in all respects including physical characteristics, quality and reputation and are produced in the same country by the same producers. In the absence of transactional value of identical goods, the transactional value of similar goods sets the base for customs valuation. Similar goods are in this context goods that closely resemble other goods with respect to their component materials and physical characteristics, which can be commercially interchanged and come from the same country by the same producer of the goods. The customs valuation method of specific goods is different from other methods and is only applicable to some specific goods. In the absence of all these methods Afghan laws allows custom offices to determine the customs value of imported goods based on other reasonable means using data available in the originating country of imported goods.[74]

Afghanistan's customs regulations, particularly those concerning customs valuation reflect the many features of the modern customs system and are compatible with the principles of GATT 1994 on customs valuation. GATT Article VII on customs valuation provides that WTO members shall determine the customs value of imports based on the transaction value of goods. The Article further states that in the absence or doubt of transaction value the transaction value of like products shall be the basis for customs valuation.

3.2.2 Products Prohibited from Importation into Afghanistan and Products Subject to Prior Permission for Importation and Exportation

Afghanistan's import regulations prohibit the importation of certain products as well as their transiting through the territory of Afghanistan for religious, health, environmental and security reasons.[75] These products are mainly:

1. Alcoholic drinks (both import and transit);
2. Living pigs and all pig products (both import and transit);
3. Cottonseeds, gypsum (import);
4. Narcotics/drugs (both import and transit);

---

[73] Arts. 23, 24, 2005 Customs Law; Arts. 3, 4, 5, 6, 7 & 8 Regulation on Determining Price of Goods in Customs.

[74] Ibid.

[75] Arts. 3, 4, 5, 6, 7 & 8 Regulation on Determining Price of Goods in Customs.

5. Chemical fertilizers including Ammonium Nitrate (both import and transit);[76]
6. Plastic bags (carrying bags) (import) and;
7. Gases destructive to the ozone layer (import and transit).

Among these products, the embargo on import of cottonseeds was applied temporarily on MFN basis and the Government removed it in 2018.[77] The Government originally banned the import of cottonseeds after finding out that they carried some type of disease.[78] The 2016 Customs Law embodies security and general exceptions that allow ACD to impose temporary bans or restriction measures on imports for the protection of security, national treasures, commercial and industrial policies of the Government, public interests, health and environment.[79] In terms of export, there are certain products that are subject to prior permission, strict control or ban of export. Archaeological relics, antiquities and works of traditional arts are among those goods prohibited to export.[80] To ensure preserving cultural and historical heritage of the country, the Government strictly controls these goods and prohibits their export. Mines and mineral products are export-restricted goods that require prior permission by the Government and are subject to relatively higher export tariffs.[81]

3.2.3   Customs Tariffs, Preferential Customs Tariffs and Other Duties and Charges

Afghanistan applies relatively low import tariffs and does not currently impose export tariffs on most export products.[82] It applies its import tariffs based on MFN and preferential tariff rate basis. MFN tariffs are applicable to imports from all countries and preferential tariffs are applicable to imports from the South Asian Association for Regional Cooperation (SAARC) member states in accordance with tariff rates agreed upon by these member states under the South Asian Free Trade Area (SAFTA). The Government applies each import tariff based on *ad valorem* (transaction value of goods) and non-*ad valorem* methods using CIF (cost, insurance and freight). For export tariffs, it applies FOB (Free on Board) indicator.

---

[76]Qanuni-i Gumrukat'i Afghanistan (Afghanistan Customs Law) 1395 (2016); ACD, Schedule of Tariffs (2014), www.customs.mof.gov.af; Presidential Decree, No. 28/Jan. 2010; Ministerial Cabinet Act, No. 1/Mar. 2011.

[77]See Ministerial Cabinet Act (note 76).

[78]Telephone Interview with Mir Saeed Saeedy (note 64), (Mar. 12, 2019).

[79]Ibid.; see also Working Party on the Accession of Afghanistan (note 25), para. 28.

[80]Art. 53 2016 Afghanistan Customs Law.

[81]See generally 2004 Afghanistan Law on Preservation of Historical and Cultural Heritage; see also MoIC, An Inventory to Exporting Goods from Afghanistan (note 64), 8–9.

[82]MoIC, An Inventory to Exporting Goods from Afghanistan (note 64), 8–9.

Afghanistan's current national schedule of tariffs[83] contains twelve different tariff rates and is compatible with the International Harmonized System of Coding.[84] The twelve different tariff rates are 0, 1, 2.5, 3.5, 5, 8, 10, 12, 16, 20, 25 and 40%. Different average tariff rates are applied for agriculture and non-agriculture imports. For agriculture imports a 6.9% average tariff rate is applied and for non-agriculture, a 6.7% average tariff rate is applied.[85] This average tariff rate is two times lower than the average bound tariff rate for imports that Afghanistan undertook as part of its accession commitments to the WTO. The bound average tariff rate for all products that Afghanistan undertook in the accession process to the WTO stands at 13.5%. For agriculture products, the WTO average bound tariff for Afghanistan stands at 33.6% and for non-agriculture, the average rate stands at 10.3%.[86]

In addition to import tariffs, the government applies a 2% fixed tax, a 4% specific tax called the Business Receipts Tax (BRT) and a 0.2% Red Crescent tax on imports.[87] While the fixed tax is applicable only to imports and does not extend to domestic like products, the BRT is applicable to both domestic businesses and imports. The BRT rate for domestic businesses is different from the BRT rate for imports. For domestic businesses, the BRT is calculated based on the total gross income of the businesses per quarter. This means that all natural and legal persons who conduct business in Afghanistan (whether business in goods or services) whose total gross business interest amounts for 750,000 AFN per quarter, are obliged to pay 4% BRT.[88] For incomes exceeding 750,000 AFN per quarter, the BRT increases to 5 and up to 10% depending on the increasing amount of the quarterly business gross income.[89] However, imports are subject to only 2% BRT based on transactional

---

[83] Schedule of Tariffs (note 76). Prior to the 2014 Tariffs schedule, Afghanistan introduced its first post-Taliban tariff schedule in 2012 and was designed in a way to be in line with tariffs schedule of the South Asian Free Trade Agreement (SAFTA). SAFTA requires member States to lower their tariffs rate to 0–5% from their existing tariffs line within a transitional period. Although Afghanistan received a transitional period until 2021 for a final reduction of its tariffs rates, the Afghan government brought its tariffs rates in line with SAFTA tariffs rates in 2012. See ACD, Schedule of Tariffs (2012); for information about SAFTA tariffs rates see SAARC Website, www.saarc.gov. org.

[84] Harmonized System (HS) is a unified system of tariffs coding and classification adopted under the International Convention on the Harmonized Commodity Description and Coding and Classification System of the World Customs Organization (WCO). WTO members and members of other international organizations apply the HS as coding method for their tariffs schedules.

[85] Schedule of Tariffs (note 76); Afghanistan 2009–2013 Trade Review (note 9), 8–9; see also Working Party on the Accession of Afghanistan (note 25), 22.

[86] See WTO Secretariat, Overview of Afghanistan's Commitments to the WTO (2018), https:// www.wto.org/english/news_e/news15_e/afgancommitmentsmc10_e.pdf.

[87] The fixed tax on imports with a trade license is 2% and for imports without a trade license is 3%. Arts. 69, 70 Qanuni-i Maliat bar Aáidat'i Afghanistan (Afghanistan Income Tax Law) 1388 (2009).

[88] Previously the BRT was 2%. In order to increase domestic revenue, the government increased the BRT to 4% in 2015.

[89] Arts. 64, 66 Afghanistan Income Tax Law; see also generally MoF, Afghanistan Revenue Department, Business Receipt Tax (BRT) Guide 03 (2012).

value of imports. The customs offices calculate and collect the BRT on imports when they calculate and collect the import tariffs.[90] The Afghan government, however, has committed to the WTO that it will substitute or remove these three additional taxes. It has committed to substitute the BRT prior to 1 January 2021 with the value added tax (VAT), a tax most countries apply to sale products nowadays.[91] A VAT is a consumption tax levied on the sales price of a product and its amount stands in the purchase invoice of the buyer.[92] To this end, the government has passed the 2016 VAT Law which will enter into force by January 2021.[93] This law provides for 5% VAT on consumption products and services.[94] In the same time Afghanistan has committed to remove the Red Crescent Tax within 15 years from the date of its accession to the WTO and the Fixed Tax by 1 January 2021.[95]

Moreover, Afghanistan applies some import tariff exemptions. The 2016 Customs Law exempts a specific category of goods, which includes books, magazines and items for the official use by Government and international organizations, from import tariffs.[96]

While Afghanistan exempts a large number of export products, including agricultural products, from tariffs,[97] it nonetheless applies export tariff rates of 2.5, 5, 10 and 20% along with a 2% fixed tax on all exports. The average export tariff stands at 3.8% and export tariffs are mostly applicable to mines and mineral products.[98]

The Afghan Government grants a limited export subsidy to agricultural products. However, it has committed to the WTO to remove its agricultural exports subsidies and apply any export exemption in conformity with WTO rules.[99] The Government has currently drafted an anti-subsidy law that, once passed, will govern the government's overall subsidy measures and actions.[100] In addition, the Government grants

---

[90]Art. 64 (3) & (4) Afghanistan Income Tax Law.

[91]See Overview of Afghanistan's Commitments to the WTO (note 87). The WTO agreements do not contain an explicit provision on VAT nor do they define the term. However, the OECD defines VAT as "[g]oods and services Tax". In other words, VAT is a tax on consumption paid. OECD, OECD International VAT/GST Guidelines: Guidelines on Neutrality 3 (OECD, Center for Tax Policy and Administration, June 2011).

[92]Article 2(1) of Afghanistan Law on Value Added Tax defines the VAT as an indirect tax levied on the supply of goods, services and taxable imports. Qanuni-i Maliat bar Arzush-i Afzooda'i Afghanistan (Afghanistan Law on Value Added Tax) 1395 (2016) [hereinafter Afghanistan VAT Law].

[93]See for example Art. 33 Afghanistan VAT Law.

[94]Art. 4 (2) Afghanistan VAT Law.

[95]Chp. 11 Afghanistan Income Tax Law; see also Working Party on the Accession of Afghanistan (note 25), paras. 94–100.

[96]Art. 27 2016 Afghanistan Customs Law.

[97]WTO, Committee on Agriculture, Export Subsidy: Afghanistan, G/AG/N/AFG/2, Notification Doc No. 16-4244 (Aug. 8, 2016) [hereinafter WTO, Export Subsidy: Afghanistan].

[98]MoIC, Exports Tariffs List of Goods (December 2012); see also WB, Afghanistan Development Update (2018), (note 40), 18.

[99]Overview of Afghanistan's Commitments to the WTO (note 87).

[100]In person Interview with Mir Saeed Saeedy (note 64).

domestic support to research activities particularly in connection to environment, agriculture and advisory business services and to infrastructural services including electricity reticulation, water systems, roads and transport infrastructures.[101]

3.2.4   Non-tariff Customs Procedures Affecting Foreign Trade in Goods

3.2.4.1   Trade Licensing

According to the amended 1955 Commercial Code, and other Afghan trade rules and regulations, all imports and exports shall be licensed, and their required documents have to be carried across customs borders. Importers and exporters are obliged to obtain a trade license, from the MoIC prior to the start of trading. The Afghanistan Central Business Registry of the MoIC is in charge of registering traders and issuing tax identification numbers.[102] In addition to registration with this agency, importers and exporters must complete a criminal dossier[103] and publish their registered business in Afghanistan's official Gazette. Until 2018, a trade license was valid for 1 year and required annual renewal. Recently, as part of its trade facilitation reforms, the MoIC has extended the period to 3 years.[104] In addition, Afghanistan committed to the WTO to implement its laws and regulations concerning business licensing in line with the WTO provisions on import licensing procedures.[105]

3.2.4.2   Rules of Origin

Rules of Origin (RoO) are laws, regulations and administrative procedures that determine a product's country of origin.[106] Currently, Afghanistan does not have a separate law on RoO. However, many other trade regulations and policies including the 2016 Customs Law and the 2018 National Trade Policy regulate matters related to RoO and oblige importers to carry a certificate of origin while importing into Afghanistan. For exports however, a certificate of origin is not mandatory as of 2019 but exporters may request one from the government. The Afghan Chamber of

---

[101]WTO, Export Subsidy: Afghanistan (note 98); see also Working Party on the Accession of Afghanistan, Domestic Support and Export Subsidies in the Agricultural Sector, WT/ACC/SPEC/AFG/2 (Oct. 29, 2012).

[102]See Afghanistan Central Business Registry Website, http://www.acbr.gov.af/index.html.

[103]In Afghanistan, to start any business, besides other official registrations, a person needs to obtain a verification certificate from security bodies verifying that the person does not carry criminal background.

[104]Afghanistan National Trade Policy 2018–2023 (note 9), 45.

[105]Working Party on the Accession of Afghanistan (note 25), 28.

[106]WTO, Glossary of Terms.

Commerce and Industries (ACCI) is the responsible authority to issue such a certificate of origin for exports upon request.

The existing rules and procedures on RoO comply with WTO Agreement on Rules of Origin.[107] Chapter 9 of the 2016 Customs Law provides for provisions on RoO and the 2017 Procedure on Advance Ruling on Binding Decisions sets out procedural rules for application, processing and administration of those provisions including advance ruling on origin and provides for the implementation of the advance ruling on origin provisions of the WTO Agreement on Rules of Origin.[108]

The ACD is responsible for binding decisions on matters concerning RoO and publishing those decisions within 30 days.[109] The publication and notification of decisions should provide reasons for issuing those decisions, define conditions that could revoke or remove the decisions, and clarify procedures for applying, revoking or removing the decisions. The decision is valid for 3 years. In the event of a doubt in the authenticity of a certificate of origin for an import product, the ACD contacts, via electronic correspondence, the competent authority of the issued certificate of origin in the origin country of the concerned import product for verification.

Additionally, the 2016 Customs Law grants exporters, importers or other interested groups the right to request the ACD to assess the origin of an import. The ACD can carry out such an assessment during customs clearance of the concerned import. Accordingly, imports for which no certificate of origin or a defect certificate is presented can still be released if the importer submits a security guarantee to the Afghan customs along with a declaration guaranteeing a later submission of the required certificates within a certain period of time which is specified by customs authorities.[110]

3.2.4.3 Standards and Technical Measures

Standards are non-tariff measures ensuring the quality and safety of products. The WTO Agreement on Technical Barriers to Trade (TBT) defines a standard as a "[d]ocument approved by a recognized body that provides for common and repeated use, rules, guidelines or characteristics for products or related processes and production methods, with which compliance is not mandatory."[111] Similarly, it defines a technical measure a "[d]ocument which lays down product characteristics or their related processes and production methods, including the applicable administrative

---

[107]See Working Party on the Accession of Afghanistan (note 25), paras. 122–129.

[108]See ibid.; see also MoF, Procedures on Advance Ruling on Binding Decisions (August 2017). For WTO provisions on advance rulings on origin see Art. 3(b) & Annex 2, para 3(d) WTO, Agreement on Rules of Origin, 1868 U.N.T.C. 397.

[109]Art. 17 2016 Afghanistan Customs Law.

[110]Ibid., Art. 56 (a).

[111]Annex 1, para 2 WTO, Agreement on Technical Barriers to Trade, 1868 U.N.T.S. 120.

provisions, with which compliance is mandatory."[112] The International Organization for Standardization (ISO) provides similar definitions for standards and technical measures.[113]

Afghanistan suffers from low quality of import products and until recently did not have a national standardization system. In 2013 the Government adopted a National Standard Law for the first time.[114] However, already in 2007, a National Standard Authority (ANSA)[115] was established to carry out activities related to national standards and technical regulations. The ANSA is an independent agency responsible for adopting measures and carrying out activities related to standardization, conformity assessment, accreditation and metrology, and other technical regulations.[116] One of its main responsibilities is to adopt and when necessary revise governmental standards and technical regulations and ensure their transparency.[117] For this purpose, the ANSA has established an information center for standards and technical regulations.[118] Since its commencement, the ANSA has adopted 51 national standards for 13 different types of products. These products are food and agricultural products, oil and lubricants, petroleum, cosmetics and pharmaceuticals, textiles, construction materials, electrotechnical products, metrology, environmental and infrastructural codes.[119] Nevertheless ANSA still does not have its own developed technical regulations and the Government continues applying regional and international standards and guides as a basis for its technical regulations and conformity assessment measures.[120]

In 2017, the government passed a new law on Standards and Technical Regulations to make its standards regulatory system conform to WTO and ISO relevant norms. The 2017 Law on Standards and Technical Regulations recognizes the compatibility of national rules on standards and technical measures with international standards and grants the supremacy to international rules on standards and

---

[112]Ibid., Annex 1, para 1.

[113]According to ISO, a standard is "a document that provides the requirements, specifications, guidelines or characteristics that can be used consistently to ensure that materials, products, processes and services are fit for purpose." International Standard Organization (ISO), http://www.iso.org/iso/home/standards.htm. The Standards and Technical Regulations Law of Afghanistan provides a similar definition. Art. 3 (2) Qanuni-i Standard wa Muqararat'i Takhnik'i (Afghanistan Law on Standards and Technical Regulations) 1396 (2017), [hereinafter Afghanistan Law on Standards and Technical Regulations].

[114]Art. 14 Qanuni-i Mili'i Standard'i Afghanistan (Afghanistan National Standard Law) 1392 (2013).

[115]Islamic Republic of Afghanistan, Ministerial Council Resolution, No. 20 (September 2007).

[116]Art. 5 Afghanistan Law on Standards and Technical Regulations.

[117]Ibid., Arts. 6, 7, 10, 24, 27.

[118]Ibid., Art. 37.

[119]MoIC, Afghanistan National Standards Authority (ANSA), Standards Adopted by the Afghan National Standards Authority (December 2012), http://moci.gov.af/Content/files/ANSA%20standards%20EN.pdf.

[120]Articles 9 and 13 of the Law on Standards and Technical Regulations recognize international standards and guides for adopting and applying technical regulations and conformity assessment.

technical measures.[121] The law also recognizes national technical regulations of other WTO members provided that they are compatible with Afghan laws and equivalent to national technical regulations in objectives.[122] Further the law recognizes results of conformity assessment carried out on import products by an exporting WTO member with which Afghanistan has an international agreement, even if the results are different from those carried out by Afghanistan.[123]

The 2017 Law on Standards and Technical Regulations differentiates between voluntary standards and mandatory standards. Imports and exports have to comply with mandatory standards and will otherwise be prevented from importing in or exporting out of Afghanistan. Imports failing to comply with mandatory standards are either pending at customs borders for conformity assessment or are directly rejected and send back to their origin.[124]

The 2017 Law on Standards and Technical Regulations excludes certain types of products from its scope of application without specifying by which law they should be governed. These products include products related to Government specific procurements, legal and educational services, medications and medical equipment and food safety.[125]

The 2017 Law on Standards and Technical Regulations provides that adoption and application of standards, technical regulations and conformity assessment should not be more trade restrictive than necessary to fulfil a legitimate objective. The Law obliges the Government to remove its standards, technical measures or conformity assessment when the objective or reason for implementation no longer exist or could be addressed in a less trade restrictive manner.[126] Similarly, the Law provides for the MFN and national treatment of all import products in connection to standards, technical regulations and conformity assessment.[127] It also ensures MFN and transparent application of equivalent foreign technical regulations and conformity assessment. These non-discriminatory provisions fill the gaps of the previous 2013 National Standards Law, which did not incorporate MFN and national treatment provisions.

The 2017 Law on Standards and Technical Regulations grants licensed natural and legal persons the right to voluntarily adopt standards and further recognizes the intellectual property right of their standards. Such standards should however be compatible with national, regional and international standards.[128] The Law also provides for the engagement of individual experts, institutions and interested groups

---

[121]Ibid., Arts. 5(2), 13, 14(2).

[122]Ibid., Art 11.

[123]Ibid., Art 22.

[124]Ibid., Arts 11, 12, 13.

[125]Ibid. Art. 4.

[126]Ibid. Art. 9.

[127]Ibid. Arts. 7, 9, 13, 14(1)(2).

[128]Ibid. Arts. 11, 14.

including the private sector in standardization process to include their views and comments in adopting standards and technical regulations.[129]

Although in theory, Afghanistan now has a standards, technical control and conformity assessment regime which is broadly in line with WTO technical regulations requirements and is equivalent to those of developed countries, in practice, the country still maintains low quality imports and with the basic standardization and quality control technological facilities. The primary reason for this is that Afghanistan does not have technical measures of its own and therefore has not been successful in controlling the standard and quality of import products.

3.2.4.4 Sanitary and Phytosanitary Measures (SPS)

Sanitary and phytosanitary measures (SPS) deal with food safety as well as animal and plant health.[130] Afghanistan's SPS regime only recently evolved and is governed by the 2016 Law on Plant Protection and Quarantine, the 2016 Law on Food Safety, the 2017 Law on Animal Health and Veterinary and the 2018 Law on Plant Variety Protection.[131] Nonetheless, Afghanistan still does not have rules and regulations in place to ensure the safety of food products produced by biotechnology.[132]

Afghanistan's SPS rules and regulations are in line with internationally recognized SPS standards, particularly those of the WTO. However, Afghanistan has a WTO transitional period until the end of 2019 to implement the WTO SPS Agreement.[133] Afghanistan recognizes and applies Codex Alimentarius (food codes) and is a member to the World Organization for Animal Health (OIE) and International Plant Protection Convention (IPPC).[134] Furthermore, Afghanistan recognizes the application of SPS measures of other countries—provided that such SPS measures

---

[129]Ibid. Arts. 11, 13.

[130]WTO, Glossary of Terms.

[131]Qanuni-i Hefazat'i Nabatat wa Qaranti'i Afghanistan (Law on Plant Protection and Quarantine of Afghanistan) (1395) (2016) [hereinafter Afghanistan Law on Plant Protection and Quarantine]; Qanuni-i Amni'a t'i Ghazai'i of Afghanistan (Law on Food Safety of Afghanistan) (1395) (2016) [hereinafter Afghanistan Food Safety Law].

[132]Biotechnology is a specific technology that ensures the safety of those food products such as agricultural products and animal products that their production process is escalated by biological scientific methods such as genetic changes. In broad sense, biotechnology refers to "the use of living systems to develop products" such as improving "selected attributes of microbes, plants, or animals for human use by making precise genetic changes that were not possible with traditional methods." *Kevin Keener & Thomas Hoban*, Biotechnology: Answers to Common Questions, vol. 1, North Carolina State University, Department of Food Science, https://fbns.ncsu.edu//extension_program/documents/biotech_QA.pdf; see also Hoban et al. (2002), pp. 1384–1385.

[133]Working Party on the Accession of Afghanistan (note 25), 44.

[134]See for example Law Art. 18 Afghanistan Food Safety Law; Art. 16(1) Afghanistan Law on Plant Protection and Quarantine; see also Working Party on the Accession of Afghanistan (NOTE 25), paras. 172–183; for Afghanistan's membership to the Codex Alimentarius, OIE and IPPC

are comparable to Afghanistan's SPS measures or demonstrate the same level of protection that Afghanistan's SPS measures provide.[135]

The Ministry of Public Health (MoPH) is responsible for developing, administering and enforcing sanitary measures, and the Ministry of Agriculture, Irrigation and Livestock (MAIL) is responsible for developing, administering and enforcing phytosanitary measures. Each of these two ministries has an SPS directorate and an Enquiry and Notification Point (ENP) that carry out the overall activities concerning SPS measures. The responsibility of the ENPs is to provide information to enquires and receive comments and views from interested groups, and the SPS directorates are on the other hand obliged to consider those comments and recommendations when drafting SPS measures.[136]

Afghanistan's SPS regime incorporates various risk assessment methods for circumstances arising through the adoption and application of SPS measures. The methods include examination of available scientific evidence, product quality including physical inspection of products, prevalence of specific diseases or pests, ecological and environmental conditions, and quarantine. The quality examination method particularly applies to agrochemical, chemical fertilizers and non-processed agricultural import products, except live animals and live plants and importers are required to present phytosanitary quality certificate for these products.[137]

Afghanistan requires an international sanitary certificate for processed food products. After testing the sanitary certificates and the quality of all these products Afghan customs offices will issue a release certificate. Customs offices test the quality of products based on samples using organoleptic examination, appearance, scent, texture, taste and sound test approaches. For pharmaceuticals, Afghanistan uses the Codex Alimentarius pharmaceutical standards, European pharmacopeia, British pharmacopeia and US pharmacopeia as basis for quality examination.[138]

Exports from Afghanistan are also subject to SPS certificates. The required certificates include a phytosanitary certificate for export of plants and plant products, a quality certificate for export of all non-processed agricultural food products, except living animals and plants, and a sanitary certificate for export of processed food products.[139] Domestic products produced and sold within domestic markets are also subject to the same import-export SPS procedures. The ENPs are responsible to oversee, on a regular basis, the compatibility of these products in domestic markets

---

consult their official websites, http://www.fao.org/fao-who-codexalimentarius/about-codex/mem bers/en/; http://www.oie.int/; https://www.ippc.int/en/countries/all/list-countries/.

[135]Art. 20 Afghanistan Food Safety Law; Art. 16(3) Afghanistan Law on Plant Protection and Quarantine.

[136]See for example Law Art. 21 Afghanistan Food Safety Law; Arts. 38, 40 Afghanistan Law on Plant Protection and Quarantine.

[137]Working Party on the Accession of Afghanistan (note 25), paras. 175–177.

[138]Ibid.

[139]Art. 31 Afghanistan Food Safety Law; Art. 12(5) Afghanistan Law on Plan Protection and Quarantine.

with the SPS requirements.[140] However, the Government does not subject domestic products produced and sold in domestic market to SPS certificates.

Afghanistan's SPS legal regime includes non-discriminatory and less-trade restrictive SPS measures and further provides for their modification or removal when the circumstances that generated their adoption change or end.[141] Moreover the regime requires that the SPS test, control and assessment procedure should be reasonable and necessary and should avoid unnecessary delays and negative effects on trade. It grants importers whose products are subject to SPS examination the right to complain against procedures and activities inconsistent with SPS laws and regulations. The responsible ministries are then obliged to review the complaints appropriately and take corrective actions when a complaint turn out to be justified.[142]

Although Afghanistan has an internationally compatible SPS regime, technical shortcomings challenge the practical implementation of its SPS rules and measures as well as transparency of its SPS mechanisms. Besides suffering from poor technical equipment, the testing laboratories struggle of low quality of technical skills required for their personnel. With regard to transparency, the ENPs do not yet have an information system or online platform to exchange and extend SPS relevant information. The limited webpages that MAIL and MoPH run for SPS procedures lack sufficient regulatory and procedural information. In order to implement its SPS laws and regulations effectively, Afghanistan needs to implement technical and capacity building improvements.

3.2.4.5 Countervailing, Anti-dumping and Safeguard Measures

Countervailing, anti-dumping and safeguard measures are interrelated protective measures taken by governments to protect their domestic markets from unexpected harmful trade incidents. Countervailing measures are "actions taken by an importing country, usually in the form of increased duties, to offset subsidies given to producers or exporters in the exporting country or to combat dumping actions."[143] Similarly, anti-dumping measures are countervailing actions against a dumping action.[144] A product is considered dumped if "it is exported to another country under a price lower than its normal value price and lower than the comparable price

---

[140]See for example Law Art. 4 Afghanistan Food Safety Law.

[141]See for example ibid., Arts. 19, 31; Arts. 16, 12(5) Afghanistan Law on Plant Protection and Quarantine.

[142]Art. 31 Afghanistan Food Safety Law; Art. 12(5) Afghanistan Law on Plant Protection and Quarantine.

[143]WTO, Glossary of Terms.

[144]Ibid.

for like products in the exporting country."[145] Safeguard measures are "actions taken to protect a specific industry from an unexpected build-up of imports."[146]

Currently, Afghanistan does not have a separate law on anti-dumping measures, nor does it have any rules and policies in place governing dumping practices. The 2010 Law on the Protection of Competition includes a limited provision on anti-dumping, which obliges the government to prevent dumping practices.[147] Also, Afghanistan has not carried out any anti-dumping investigations until to date.[148] Regarding its WTO obligations concerning the application of anti-dumping measures, Afghanistan will not apply any anti-dumping until it has adopted and notified appropriate laws in conformity with the WTO relevant rules.[149]

However, Afghanistan has few laws and regulations that provide safeguard measures for domestic production and other commercial activities of high national interest. The 2017 Law on Safeguards Measures for Domestic Production and Article 9 of the 2016 Law on Foreign Trade in Goods[150] set out safeguard measures provisions for domestic production.

Article 3(1) of the 2017 Law on Safeguards Measures for Domestic Production defines a safeguard measure a measure "imposed on investigated products for protection of domestic industry". The law provides that safeguard measures adopted to protect domestic production shall be necessary, less-trade restrictive and comply with Article IXX GATT on safeguard measures and the provisions of the WTO Agreement on Safeguard measures.[151] Moreover, the law requires transparency of all adopted safeguard measures through publishing those measures and notifying the WTO and all other interested parties prior to their application.[152]

The 2017 Law on Safeguard Measures for Domestic Production provides for safeguard enforcement measures which include customs duty and non-customs duty enforcement measures. The law does not define which specific types of customs duty and non-customs duty enforcement measures should be taken but Article 9 of the 2016 Law on Foreign Trade in Goods contains a list of safeguard enforcement

---

[145]Ibid.; Art. 2(1) WTO Agreement on Anti-Dumping Measures.

[146]WTO, Glossary of Terms.

[147]Art. 2 Qanuni-i Hemayat az Mostahlik'i Afghanistan (Law on Consumer Protection of Afghanistan) (1395) (2016).

[148]See WTO, Committee on Anti-Dumping Practices, notifications under Articles 16.4 and 16.5—Afghanistan, G/ADP/N/193/AFG/1 (June 6, 2018).

[149]Overview of Afghanistan's Commitments to the WTO (note 87). Afghanistan has committed to notify the WTO on the status of its ongoing activities in this regard. In June 2018, Afghanistan notified to the WTO that it did still not have any relevant law. See WTO, Committee on Anti-Dumping Practices—Afghanistan (note 149).

[150]Qanuni-i Tijarat'i Khariji'i Kala'i Afghanistan (Law on Foreign Trade in Goods of Afghanistan) 1395 (2016) [hereinafter Afghanistan Law on Foreign Trade in Goods].

[151]Arts. 2(3), 21, 45 Qanuni-i Hemayat az Sana'ai Dakhli'i Afghanistan (Law on Safeguards Measures on Domestic Production of Afghanistan) (1396) (2017) [hereinafter Law on Safeguards Measures on Domestic Production].

[152]Arts. 27, 28 Law on Safeguards Measures on Domestic Production.

measures that includes anti-dumping duties and anti-subsidy duties, compensating duties, compensating tariffs, other charges and fees for customs duty safeguard enforcement measures and preventive measures, quotas, technical regulations, and permissions for non-customs duty safeguards enforcement measures.

The 2017 Law on Safeguards Measures for Domestic Production provides for institutional arrangements for implementing the provisions and carrying out activities related to safeguard measures. As such, the General Directorate for International Trade of the MoIC is responsible to implement the provisions of the Law Safeguards Measures on Domestic Production and adopt and apply safeguards measures. Similarly, the law establishes a National Board on Domestic Production Safeguard that is responsible for ratifying safeguards policies, strategies, plans, and all other activities and decisions carried out by the General Directorate for International Trade.[153] The ACD is responsible for applying safeguard financial enforcement measures such as collecting countervailing customs duties.[154]

3.2.4.6 Export Subsidy Rules

An export subsidy is "a benefit conferred on a firm by the Government that is contingent on exports."[155] Such benefit to exports can injure the domestic market of the importing country by awakening, disabling or slowing down production process of that good in the importing country.[156] To offset such subsidy injury, countries adopt anti-subsidy measures. Afghanistan does not have a law governing subsidies in force and does not grant or maintain a subsidy or any other support measure that may result in increasing exports or reducing imports.[157] However, Afghanistan has drafted a law on anti-subsidy measures for domestic industries that, once passed, will protect domestic markets from unfair trade and subsidized imports and will further facilitate free and fair competition in the Afghan domestic market through the adoption of anti-subsidy measures.[158] The draft law provides that the adoption and application of anti-subsidy measures should be fair, less trade restrictive, equal to the level of inflicted injury, and applicable on MFN basis.[159]

The draft law contains three main conditions for subsidized imports to be subject for investigation and application of anti-subsidy measures. First, the subsidy needs to

---

[153]Ibid.

[154]Ibid.

[155]WTO, Glossary of Terms.

[156]Ibid.

[157]See WTO, Committee on Subsidies and Countervailing Measures, Notification of Laws and Regulations under Article 32.6 of the relevant Agreement—Afghanistan; G/SCM/N/1/AFG/1 (June 4, 2018); see also Committee on Subsidies and Countervailing Measures, Notification under articles 25.11 and 25.12 of the Agreement on Subsidies and Countervailing Measures—Afghanistan, G/SCM/N/202/AFG (June 11, 2018).

[158]MoIC, Draft Law on Anti-Subsidy Measures for Domestic Industries of Afghanistan (2019).

[159]Ibid., Art. 61.

be specific. Second, the country of origin/exporting country needs to provide direct financial supports such as state non-refundable aids, credits, loans, finance shares, reduced customs duties, and export tariff exemption to the subsidized imports. Third, the subsidy needs to be granted to bring more commercial benefits and advantages to subsidized imports and harm the domestic market of Afghanistan. In case these three conditions exist, the draft law allows the Government to adopt and apply anti-subsidy measures to prevent or offset any expected or inflicted injuries.[160]

Furthermore the draft law differentiates between two types of subsidy injuries (a) tangible injury, and (b) prejudiced injury.[161] A tangible injury is one that actually occurred and is measurable (e.g., a lack of sale or drop of price and volumes of other imported products and domestic products or strong reduction in demand for domestic products prevails in the domestic market as a result of subsidized products).[162] In contrast, a prejudiced injury is an injury that has not yet occurred but the Government, based on evidence, considers certain imported goods will if not prevented, injure the domestic market, i.e., when the Government notices an increase of unfair competition.[163]

The draft law contains two types of anti-subsidy measures in form of customs duties (a) provincial countervailing measures, and (b) definitive countervailing measures. While definitive countervailing measures are applied when an investigation is completed, the provisional definitive countervailing measures are applicable when a subsidy is found during the investigation process.[164] The purpose of provisional countervailing measures is to minimize adverse effects of the subsidized imports on the Afghan domestic market during the investigation process. Such duties are applicable for 4 months and are only enforceable after the 2nd month of the investigation process. The investigation should not take longer than 12 months but can be in exceptional situations, extended to 18 months.[165] If a subsidy causing an injury is found upon the completion of the investigation, the Trade Defense Authority[166] applies the definitive countervailing measures. The time period of a definitive countervailing measure is 5 years.[167]

The draft law on anti-subsidy measures for domestic industries is compatible with WTO rules on subsidies and grants supremacy to WTO rules. The draft law also

---

[160]Ibid., Arts. 14, 15, 16.

[161]Ibid., Art. 20.

[162]Ibid., Arts. 20–22.

[163]Ibid., Arts. 20–25.

[164]Ibid., Arts. 53, 57.

[165]Ibid.

[166]The draft law provides for a Trade Defense Authority to be established within the MoIC and carry out activities related to investigation of subsidy and adoption, revision, extension, suspension, and removal of countervailing measures.

[167]Ibid., Art. 65.

obliges the Trade Defense Authority to notify the WTO about any anti-subsidy measures that were taken by the Afghan Government.[168]

3.3 Laws and Regulations Governing Foreign Trade in Services

Except for a few national treatment exceptions, Afghanistan generally has a non-discriminatory legal regime for its services sector and provides equal opportunities for domestic and foreign services providers. Article 10 of the 2004 Constitution of Afghanistan recognizes equal investment opportunities for national and foreign investors, with the only exception that foreign investors are not allowed to acquire property in land. Other exceptions to national treatment in the services sector are priorities given to Afghan services suppliers in the mining sector and different minimum amount of capital required for an investment registration. This section discusses the current legal status of Afghanistan's investment and competition regimes, and the role of State-owned businesses within the services sector.

3.3.1 Investment Regime

Article 10 of the 2004 Constitution and the provisions of the 2005 Afghanistan Private Investment Law, which was amended in 2012, set out Afghanistan's legal investment regime. Article 2 of the Private Investment Law defines an investment as a currency or non-cash contribution used to acquire shares of stocks or other ownership interests in a legally registered enterprise in Afghanistan. It, similarly, defines a foreign investment as an investment that is freely convertible to international currency or is a non-cash contribution by a foreign investor transferred into Afghanistan. Non-cash contributions include, but are not limited to, licenses, leases, machinery, equipment, and industrial or intellectual property rights.

Afghanistan's investment regime is non-discriminatory providing MFN and national treatments to all investments whether domestic or foreign.[169] Notwithstanding, few exceptions are applicable to foreign investments. As mentioned above, one of them is that foreign investors are not allowed to acquire property in land but can lease it only. Previously, the Private Investment Law provided foreign investors a land lease period up to 50 years, which was extended to a period of to 90 years with the possibility of extension by the 2012 amendment of the law.[170] In practice however, foreign investors seek local partnerships in order to avoid leasing

---

[168]Ibid., Arts. 103, 104.

[169]Art. 16 Afghanistan Private Investment Law (amended 2012).

[170]Ibid., Art. 43.

payments and extension procedures.[171] Another exception for foreign investments is the minimum capital required for investment registration. The Private Investment Law requires foreign owned companies to have minimum capital of six million Afghani AFN (around 100,000 USD) to start an investment in Afghanistan. This minimum capital requirement is applicable regardless of whether the investment is independent or takes place through joint venture. The minimum capital required for Afghan owned companies is, however, 70,000 AFN (around 1000 USD).[172]

A further exception is that the Private Investment Law authorizes the Government only to grant support and subsidy to Afghan investors in industrial sector.[173] Nevertheless, the Government has till today not granted any of such subsidies and supports, except subsidy supports for the development of Afghanistan's infrastructural systems.[174] Moreover, procuring companies providing procurement services in Afghanistan are obliged to give priority to goods and services of Afghan nationals in the mining sector—provided that the goods and services provided by Afghan suppliers are identical and equivalent in quality, quantity and price with foreign goods and services.[175] However, Afghanistan has committed to the WTO to remove this requirement so both national and foreign investors will receive the same treatment for their investment in the mining sector.[176] As of January 2021, procuring companies will have the autonomy to choose between domestic and foreign goods and services related to mining and hydrocarbons.[177]

In order to invest in Afghanistan, both national and foreign investors must fulfil certain administrative procedures. They are required to submit an investment application and obtain an investment license from the Afghanistan Investment Support Agency (AISA) and a business license from the Business Licensing Directorate of the MoIC.[178] Foreign investors are not required to be physically present in Afghanistan in order to submit an investment application.[179] However, to start their

---

[171]See for example WB, Investment Climate in Afghanistan (2014).

[172]Working Party on the Accession of Afghanistan, Initial Offer on Specific Commitments in Services, WT/ACC/SPEC/AFG/1 (June 13, 2012), 2; Overview of Afghanistan's Commitments to the WTO (note 86), 2.

[173]Working Party on the Accession of Afghanistan (note 25), 8–13.

[174]Working Party on the Accession of Afghanistan, Memorandum on the Foreign Trade Regime, WT/ACC/4 (2009), 39.

[175]Qanuni-i Ma'adin'i Afghanistan (Afghanistan Mining and Hydrocarbon Law) (1393) (2014).

[176]Art. 7 Qanuni-i Tadarikat'i Afghanistan (Afghanistan Procurement Law) (1395) (2016); Art. 98 Qanuni-i Mineral'i Afghanistan (Afghanistan Mineral Law) (1393) (2014); see also Afghanistan Overview of Commitments to the WTO (note 87), 1; Working Party on the Accession of Afghanistan (note 25), paras. 279, 280, 283.

[177]Art. 7 Afghanistan Procurement Law; Art. 98 Afghanistan Mineral Law; see also Overview of Afghanistan's Commitments to the WTO (note 86), 1; Working Party on the Accession of Afghanistan (note 25), paras. 279, 280, 283.

[178]Ch.3 Afghanistan Private Investment Law; for more information see also ASIA Website, http://www.aisa.org.af/en; MoIC Business Licensing Directorate, http://moci.gov.af/en/page/6926.

[179]Overview of Afghanistan's Commitments to the WTO (note 86), 1.

business, they need to obtain a business visa. For foreign investors with commercial presence in Afghanistan the visa period is 1 year with possibility of extension, and for foreign investors and other foreign services providers who do not have commercial presence in Afghanistan but request temporary stay, the temporary stay period is 180 days per entry.[180]

The AISA is in charge of approving applications with an investment capital up to three million USD while an investment application above this amount requires an approval from the High Commission on Investment.[181] The High Commission on Investment reviews and decides on investment applications on a case-by-case basis. In doing so, the Commission has the authority to require additional requirements for applications.[182] The Commission exercises such authority in exceptional cases of very large investments. Until now, the Commission has not exercised this power.[183] The Commission was established under the Private Investment Law as the highest Authority responsible for adopting investment policies and overseeing the implementation of the Private Investment Law. The Commission is composed of one representative of each ministry of MoIC, MoF, MAIL, Ministry of Foreign Affairs (MoFA), Ministry of Mines and Petroleum (MoMP), and the Executive Director of the Da Afghanistan Bank and the AISA Chief Executive Officer. The AISA Chief Executive Officer acts as an observer and as the Secretariat of the Commission.[184]

The 2018–2023 National Trade Policy envisages carrying out reforms in the area of foreign direct investment till 2023. The planned reforms include escalating the investment registration process, granting automatic visa extension rights upon registering a foreign investment, removing annual visa extension, and supporting and facilitating property lease for the purpose of investment. The Automatic visa extension right will grant a company (whether domestic or foreign) that applies to invest in Afghanistan, an unlimited visa for a specific number of its foreign staff. These will automatically be confirmed during the investment registration process and the visa will be valid until the investing company is validly active in its business and operates in Afghanistan.[185]

Moreover, the Private Investment Law recognizes equal employment opportunities for both Afghan nationals and foreign nationals in domestic and foreign investment enterprises. However, the law encourages investment enterprises to grant priority of employment to competent Afghans in order to improve technical skills of Afghan nationals.[186] If a foreign citizen wants to be employed in Afghanistan

---

[180]Ibid.; see also Working Party on the Accession of Afghanistan, Initial Offer on Specific Commitments in Services (note 173), 2.

[181]Arts. 8, 9 Afghanistan Private Investment Law.

[182]Working Party on the Accession of Afghanistan, Initial Offer on Specific Commitments in Services (note 172), 2.

[183]Working Party on the Accession of Afghanistan (note 25), 9.

[184]Arts. 6, 7 Afghanistan Private Investment Law.

[185]Afghanistan National Trade Policy 2018–2023 (note 9), 26.

[186]Art. 20 Afghanistan Private Investment Law.

he/she needs to obtain a work permit from the Ministry of Labor and Social Affairs. Work permits are granted for a period of 1 year with the possibility of extension.[187] Foreign citizens are also required to present two health certificates, one from their home country and one from the Ministry of Public Health of Afghanistan.[188]

3.3.2   Competition Regime

Article 11 of the 2004 Constitution and provisions of the 2010 Law on Supporting Competition, as amended, [hereinafter the Competition Law], set out Afghanistan's legal competition regime. Article 11 of the 2004 Constitution obliges the Afghan Government to support fair competition in the Afghan market and adopt competition protective measures when necessary. Article 3(8) of the Competition Law defines competition as a situation in the market during which producers, purchasers and sellers compete for producing, purchasing or selling goods or services and none of them have a controlling power to determine the quantity and price of such goods and services. The Competition Law defines the opposite of this situation as a situation of monopoly or unfair competition where businesspersons, whether natural or juridical persons, carry out anticompetitive practices in order to control and restrict the price and quantity of trading goods and services in the market.[189]

The Competition Law prohibits monopoly and unfair competition and provides enforcement of countervailing measures against anti-competitive practices. The Competition Law provides a list of practices that are considered anti-competitive practices that include (a) setting up the price and quantity of trading goods and services directly or indirectly and establishing a monopoly over those goods and services in the market, (b) controlling and restricting the quantity of goods and services in and outside of the market, (c) applying discriminatory conditions on like products and like services, and (e) taking monopoly of the market by few traders by imposing unilateral requirements, forces and sanctions and forcing other traders to agree with their terms.[190] The Competition Law also recognizes the predatory pricing of the market as an anti-competitive practice. Article 3 of the Competition Law defines predatory price as the "sale of goods or provision of services by an enterprise below the average variable cost of production of the goods or provision of services." The Competition Law contains enforcement measures against these anti-competitive practices. The responsible enforcement bodies will first stop the unfair competitors from repeating their anti-competitive practice and subsequently seize

---

[187]See Qanuni-i Istikhda'mi Atba'i Khariji Afghansitan (Afghanistan Law on Foreigners Employment) (1394) (2005); see also Working Party on the Accession of Afghanistan (note 25), 60.

[188]Ibid.

[189]Art. 3(9) Qanuni-i Hemayat az Riqabat'i Afghanistan (Afghanistan Law on Supporting Competition) (1389) (2010).

[190]Ibid., Arts. 18, 19.

their investment or trading shares that they earned as a result of the anti-competitive practice. Furthermore, enforcement bodies may, under specific conditions, subject unfair competitors to pay fines and compensation or suspend their business activities for up to 90 days.[191]

The Competition Law establishes institutions in charge of implementation of the Competition Law and administration of activities concerning market competition. The MoIC is the responsible ministry for the implementation of the Competition Law. The Competition Support Authority that is established within the MoIC is specially tasked to administer, adopt and apply competition activities and competition enforcement measures.[192] The Competition Law also establishes a National Board of Competition, which is responsible to give the necessary guidance to the Competition Support Authority, review and assess the progress of enforcement measures, and resolve competition complaints.[193]

The Competition Law further provides for an administrative dispute settlement mechanism for competition complaints. Individuals, traders, enterprises and other persons who are subject to an enforcement measure or have been affected by an enforcement measure in the past may register a written complaint before the National Board of Competition against an administrative resolution. The Board is responsible to settle the dispute within 30 days from the registration date of the complaint and to issue a decision. The complaining party who is not satisfied with the Board's decision can appeal to the commercial court for judicial settlement. Individuals who are affected by anti-competitive practices can also set a complaint to the court and request compensation.[194]

3.3.3 State Ownership and Privatization

To follow its constitutional commitments of increasing the role of the private sector in trade and investment, the Afghan Government designed a new privatization policy in 2004 and amended its companies' laws. The 2004 privatization policy aimed at developing the privatization process, corporation and liquidation of SOEs.[195] The implementation of the new policy resulted in a dramatic decrease of SEOs from 140 in 2003 to 65 in 2015 and finally to 36 SOEs today.[196] Currently, 36 SOEs,

---

[191]Ibid., Art. 20. The old version of the provision does not specify the activity prevention period, while the amended version determines it 90 years. See Official Gazette of the Islamic Republic of Afghanistan, Addition to, Amendment and Omission of some Articles of Law on supporting Competition, 1259 (2017), Art 1.

[192]Art. 4 Afghanistan Law on Supporting Competition.

[193]Ibid., Arts. 14–17.

[194]Ibid., Arts. 21, 24.

[195]MoF, Privatization Policy (2004).

[196]Working Party on the Accession of Afghanistan (note 25), 13; see also IMF (May 2018), (note 8), 8–10; WB, Investment Climate in Afghanistan (2003), 113.

16 State-owned corporations (SOCs) and three State-owned commercial banks operate in the country.[197] Afghanistan's privatization programs has been also one of the main commitments Afghanistan made to the WTO as part of its accession obligations.[198]

The Afghan Government amended its old State-owned Enterprises Law (the 1955 SOEs Law) in 2004 in order to provide more rights to the private sector to participate in SOEs and SOCs and to improve investment climate for private enterprises.[199] The SOEs amended Law recognizes, *inter alia*, the right for the private sector to share the ownership in SOEs and SOCs.[200] SOEs and SOCs do not receive any governmental subsidy or any other kind of supports and enjoy autonomy in their decision-making and activities.

3.4 Trade Dispute Settlement Regime

Afghanistan has extensively reformed its commercial dispute settlement regime by enacting new dispute settlement rules and recognizing rules and procedures of international conventions governing the resolution of commercial disputes. The 1955 amended Commercial Code, the 2007 Commercial Arbitration Law, the 2007 Law on Commercial Mediation, and the 2016 Customs Law set out Afghanistan's commercial dispute settlement regime. In addition, each trade law provides specific dispute settlement rules and mechanisms.

Afghanistan's commercial dispute settlement regime contains both adjudicatory and alternative means of dispute settlement mechanisms including customs administrative dispute resolution. It also grants the right to administrative appeals including customs administrative appeal.[201] It also grants the right to choose the applicable law to a given dispute including foreign law and obliges national courts to apply the law the disputing parties have agreed upon. For example, Article 2 of the 1955 amended Commercial Code provides that disputing parties to a commercial dispute have the autonomy to choose a foreign law as the law to govern the settlement of their dispute. Such an arrangement however has to be demonstrated through a binding commercial contract that is already enforced between the disputing parties. The Commercial Arbitration Law provides similar provisions obliging national courts to recognize the right of disputing parties to an arbitral award including foreign arbitral award that they have previously agreed upon under an arbitration

---

[197]IMF (May 2018), (note 8), 10.

[198]Working Party on the Accession of Afghanistan (note 25), paras. 42, 45.

[199]See generally Qanuni-i Sherkat ha'i Dawlati'i Afghanistan (Afghanistan State-Owned Enterprises Law) (1334) (1955), amended 2005 [hereinafter Afghanistan SOEs Law].

[200]Ibid.

[201]Arts. 45, 46 2016 Afghanistan Customs Law.

agreement enforced between them.[202] It further recognizes the right of disputing parties to select arbitrators and choose a preferred language for the arbitral proceeding—especially when one of the disputing parties is a foreign national and does not speak one of Afghanistan's national languages.[203]

As for customs administrative appeals, the 2016 Customs Law provides administrative appeal procedures and further grants the right to appeal against customs administrative decisions before commercial courts. A trader can request a customs appeal in writing against a customs decision at the General Directorate of Customs of the MoF within 10 days from the date that the trader is notified of a customs administrative decision. The General Directorate of Customs has developed an online platform for online registration of appeal requests. The Directorate is responsible to issue its appeal decision within 20 days from the date of receipt of the request and failure to do so will automatically result in favor of the appellant. If the appellant is not satisfied by the Directorate's decision, he may appeal before the Customs Arbitration Committee of the MoF or register a complaint with a commercial court.[204]

Afghanistan recognizes application of international rules and procedures concerning dispute settlement. Afghanistan is a member to the Convention for the Settlement of International Investment Disputes (ICSID Convention) and a member to the Convention on the Recognition and Enforcement of Foreign Arbitral Awards (1958 New York Convention).[205] Afghanistan has agreed to recognize and apply the principles of these conventions and accept arbitral awards rendered in other member States in investment and commercial disputes arising in Afghanistan.[206] Afghanistan has particularly committed to the WTO that its dispute settlement regime complies with WTO dispute settlement regime. Afghanistan's trade dispute settlement regime recognizes the right to appeal of administrative rulings that concern WTO provisions before courts or other independent tribunals.[207]

Enactment of new laws and the process of joining international conventions governing the resolution of commercial disputes are part of the significant legal reforms Afghanistan has made within its commercial dispute settlement regime. However, challenges remain in terms of transparency in application of these laws and poor legal skills of commercial courts and tribunals to carry out commercial

---

[202]Arts. 14, 56(1) Qanuni-I Hakami'at Tijarati'i Afghanistan (Afghanistan Commercial Arbitration Law) (1386) (2007).

[203]See for example ibid., Arts. 35, 43.

[204]Art. 46, 2016 Afghanistan Customs Law.

[205]For ICSID member States see https://icsid.worldbank.org/apps/ICSIDWEB/icsiddocs/Pages/List-of-Member-States.aspx; for New York Convention see http://www.newyorkconvention.org/countries.

[206]Convention on the Recognition and Enforcement of Foreign Arbitral Awards (New York Convention), June 10, 1958, 330 U.N.T.S. 38. Afghanistan acceded to the New York Convention in 2005, https://treaties.un.org/Pages/showDetails.aspx?objid=080000028002a36b.

[207]Working Party on the Accession of Afghanistan (note 25), paras. 60–64.

disputes, which diminish the effectiveness of Afghanistan's commercial dispute settlement regime.

3.5   Afghanistan's Route into International Trade Integration

3.5.1   Accession to the World Trade Organization

As a strategic part of its post-Taliban foreign trade policy, Afghanistan applied for the membership in the WTO in 2003 and became an observer.[208] Following the accession request, the WTO General Council established an accession Working Party in 2004 to examine Afghanistan's accession application. In 2009, Afghanistan submitted its first comprehensive Memorandum of Understanding on its foreign trade regime (MFTR) as main part of its accession pre-requisites to the WTO.[209] The Working Party held four meetings from 2011 to 2015 to examine Afghanistan's accession package including the MFTR. The Working Party finalized the examination of Afghanistan's accession package in November 2015 and submitted it for the endorsement of the WTO Ministerial Conference held in December 2015 in Nairobi.[210]

The MoIC is the overall responsible ministry for carrying out Afghanistan's WTO commitments and obligations. Following Afghanistan accession request, the MoIC established the WTO Department which is tasked with coordination and notification of activities related to Afghanistan's foreign trade regime, WTO laws and WTO decisions concerning Afghanistan's foreign trade regime. The MoIC also established a Department for regional trade and transit agreements which is tasked with coordination and notification of activities related to Afghanistan's concluded RTAs and transit agreements.[211]

In assessing many regulatory areas of Afghanistan's foreign trade regime, the Working Party further reviewed Afghanistan's RTAs.[212] In its assessment, the

---

[208]Afghanistan Accession Proposal to the WTO, WT/ACC/AFG/1 (April 2003) & WT/ACC/AFG/2 (November 2004); see also Request for Observer Status at the Cancun Ministerial Conference, WT/L/538 (August 2003).

[209]WTO General Council Meeting, Afghanistan Accession Proposal, WT/GC/M/90 (February 2005), 5–8.

[210]Working Party on the Accession Afghanistan (note 25). The MFTR provides a "comprehensive summary of the acceding Government's foreign trade regime, including relevant statistical data". WTO Secretariat, User Guide to WTO Accession, Accessions Division Note 14-25/Rev.1, 2.

[211]See MoIC Website, https://moci.gov.af/en/directorates.

[212]Working Party on the Accession Afghanistan (note 25), paras. 293–299.

Working Party approved that RTAs concluded by Afghanistan were compatible with the WTO rules on RTAs.[213]

Afghanistan's accession package contains specific commitments concerning substantial legal and institutional reforms which make up Afghanistan's obligations under its Accession Protocol and an integral part of the WTO Agreement.[214] Since becoming a WTO member, the Afghan Government has been successful in delivering some of these legal and institutional commitments.[215] The WTO accession has been a key factor of Afghanistan's efforts to expedite the reform of its legal trade regime and institutions. The enactment of most of the laws and regulations as well as the development most polices and strategies that were discussed in previous sections of this chapter are results of the WTO accession requirements that Afghanistan was obliged to fulfil. As an LDC member, however, Afghanistan was granted some transitional periods and exemptions for carrying out its commitments to the WTO. For example, Afghanistan has received exemptions for the application of MFN principle on specific services for 5 years from the date of its accession to the WTO,[216] which will terminate in 2021.[217] As discussed earlier, Afghanistan has also committed to the WTO to remove most of those exemptions on services (e.g., the priority to Afghan suppliers in the mining sector) by January 2021.[218]

One may, however, make a subtle observation about Afghanistan's WTO commitments as an LDC member. The Afghan Government did not make use of most of the legal benefits that the WTO rules offer to acceding members, particularly to LDCs. One major example is, for instance, the exemptions on the application of the MFN principle to services as granted by the WTO General Agreement on Services (GATS). While the Annex on Article II GATS exemptions allows an acceding member to request an exemption from MFN application of some specific GATS obligations for a period of 5 years, the granted exemption can be further extended to another 5 years depending on the member's need for such extension.[219] This is, however, not possible if an acceding member undertakes a commitment to terminate the exemption at the end of the first 5 years and does not reserve itself a right for the

---

[213]The report of the Working Party however does not state anything about the review of Afghanistan's RTAs. The statement was made by Anna Varyanik of the WTO Secretariat who was a member of the Working Party on Afghanistan Accession to the WTO. Interview with Anna Varyanik, WTO Secretariat (WTO Headquarter, June 10–11, 2016).

[214]WTO, Protocol on the Accession of the Islamic Republic of Afghanistan, Part I, WT/MIN (15)/ 39. WT/L/974; see also Working Party on the Accession Afghanistan (note 25), para. 301; WTO, Afghanistan Schedule of Specific Commitment on Goods and Services, WT/ACC/AFG/36/Add.1, WT/ACC/AFG/36/Add.2.

[215]See Overview of Afghanistan's Commitments to the WTO (note 86).

[216]The WTO Agreement entered into force for Afghanistan in July 2016.

[217]For Afghanistan list of MFN exemptions on Services see WT/ACC/AFG/36/Add.2.

[218]For more details see WTO, Afghanistan's Schedule of Commitments on Services, WT/ACC/ AFG/36/Add.2.

[219]Annex on GATS Article II Exemptions, paras. 3 & 4.

extension of the exemption.[220] For almost all of its requested exemptions and transitional periods to its WTO services obligations, Afghanistan has committed to the WTO to remove some of them at the end of the 5th year from the date of the entry into force of the WTO Agreement, which would be for Afghanistan mid-2021, and for some of them even earlier than 5 years. For an LDC member like Afghanistan that is still struggling to acquire the necessary technical assistance, capacity building and other necessary supports, it would have been a better decision not to commit for concrete termination date for exemptions and transitional periods for carrying out its WTO obligations and instead, reserve its right to further renegotiations based on the review of its need for the extension of those exemptions and transitional periods.

3.5.2   Afghanistan's Regional Trade Agreements in a Nutshell

Afghanistan's history of engagement in international trade goes centuries back to those times in which the Silk Road was one of the biggest international trade route in Asia connecting Afghanistan, Central Asian countries, the Middle East, China and Europe.[221] However, legally, the history of Afghanistan's engagement in international trade agreements does not go beyond the past century.[222] Afghanistan's oldest concluded trade agreement was the 1965 Transit Trade Agreement with Pakistan, which was replaced by its successor APTTA in 2010.[223]

Since the beginning of the Post-Taliban area, Afghanistan obtained membership of some regional economic organizations and concluded a number of regional agreements in various areas, including the trade in goods and services and transit relationships. Currently, Afghanistan is party to 31 bilateral trade and investment agreements, ten economic agreements along with some memoranda of understanding with Asian countries and other economies worldwide.[224] Most of these agreements require compatibility of their provisions with WTO law and particularly give reference to the WTO MFN and national treatment provisions. WTO accession was an incentive for Afghanistan's bilateral trade agreements with other WTO members and facilitated the conclusion of several market access agreements for the trade in goods and services for Afghanistan. As part of its accession negotiations,

---

[220]Annex on GATS Article II Exemptions, para. 5.

[221]See generally Xinru (2010); see also Glassner (1967), p. 10.

[222]However, available data suggests that Afghanistan has had non-trade regional and cross regional agreements with other countries, which is not relevant to this work. *See* The Official Gazette of the Islamic Republic of Afghanistan, http://moj.gov.af/content/files/Pages/OfficialGazetteIndex_D-header.htm.

[223]The Official Gazette of the Islamic Republic of Afghanistan, Afghanistan Transit Trade Agreement (ATTA) 57, (1965) [Abolished].

[224]Working Party on the Accession of Afghanistan (note 25), 5.

Afghanistan signed nine market access bilateral preferential agreements on trade in goods with Canada, the EU, Japan, Korea, Norway, Chinese Taipei, Thailand, Turkey and the US. These bilateral preferential agreements grant Afghanistan's exports lower tariff concessions. Afghanistan also signed seven bilateral market access agreements.[225] In addition, Afghanistan has concluded a number of bilateral and plurilateral transit and cross-border transport agreements such as APTTA, the Chabahar Agreement, Cross-Border Transit Agreement and ECO Cross-border Transport Framework Agreement. Among these transit and transport agreements, APTTA has been the most challenging agreement in terms of implementation, transparency and compliance.

Since 2007, Afghanistan has been a member to the South Asian Association for Regional Cooperation (SAARC) and has ratified the relevant trade agreements. Afghanistan signed the South Asian Free Trade Agreement (SAFTA) in 2008, which was ratified in 2010.[226] SAFTA aims to enhance mutual trade and trade liberalization among SAARC member states by providing preferential market access to their products through reducing tariff and non-tariff barriers.[227] The Agreement requires its members to lower their tariff rates to 0–5% from their existing national tariff rates within 10 years after the ratification.[228] The deadline for Afghanistan to apply the 0–5% tariff rate is 2021.[229] Afghanistan also signed the SAARC Agreement on Trade in Services (SATIS) in 2010 and ratified it in 2012.[230] SATIS aims to allow free movement of services among SAARC member States territories.[231] SAFTA and SATIS provide MFN and national treatments to goods and services of all SAARC member States in accordance with WTO MFN and national treatment provisions.[232]

Apart from tariff reduction as a tool to enhance the liberalization of trade among contracting States, SAFTA further provides for free movement of goods across their territories. It states that "SAFTA shall involve free movement of goods among contracting states through elimination of tariff and non-tariff restrictions and any other equivalent measures".[233] Similarly, Article 8 SAFTA imposes a best endeavor obligation on the contracting parties to adopt trade facilitation measures for, *inter alia*, transit facilities, especially to landlocked contracting States.

---

[225]Overview of Afghanistan's Commitments to the WTO (note 86).

[226]The Official Gazette of the Islamic Republic of Afghanistan, South Asian Free Trade Area Agreement (SAFTA) 1019 (2004) [Ratification date for Afghanistan: 2010].

[227]Ibid.

[228]Ibid., Art. 7(3)(a).

[229]South Asian Association for Regional Cooperation (SAARC), Secretariat, Afghanistan Accession Protocol of SAFTA (Colombo, 2008).

[230]The Official Gazette of the Islamic Republic of Afghanistan, SAARC Agreement on Trade in Service (SATIS), 1147 (2010) [Ratification date for Afghanistan: 2012]; for Afghanistan membership to the SAARC see www.saarc-sec.org.

[231]See generally SATIS.

[232]Arts. 3(b), 5 SAFTA; Arts. 2, 11 (5), 20 SATIS; Annex I SATIS.

[233]Art. 3(2) SAFTA.

However, SAFTA has been criticized for being inconsistent with Article XXIV GATT, which addresses the issue of RTAs concluded between WTO members outside the WTO system. The critique concerns particularly the compatibility of the SAFTA list of sensitive goods[234] with the GATT understanding of such agreements, as removing "substantially all the trade barriers on commerce" between RTA constituent parties.[235] Article 7(2) (a) SAFTA allows its contracting States to include a large number of import items on a list of sensitive goods which are not subject to SAFTA bound tariff rates and the contracting States retain the autonomy to apply a higher tariff rate on them. Although, at the 17th SAARC summit, held on Maldives in November 2011, member States agreed to work on reducing the number of sensitive items on the SAFTA list, they nonetheless have not yet lowered the high tariffs on their list of sensitive goods.[236] In this context, Afghanistan, like all other SAFTA contracting States, has listed certain types of goods as being sensitive.[237] As discussed earlier in this chapter, Afghanistan applies preferential tariffs to imports from SAARC member States at its lowest tariff rates, except for some products from Pakistan as a reciprocal action as Pakistan does not apply preferential tariffs to Afghan products as its SAFTA obligations.

The Economic Cooperation Organization (ECO) is another regional organization to which Afghanistan has been a member since 1996. Founded in 1985, the ECO's fundamental goal is to develop cooperation among its member States in economy, trade, technical and cultural areas. Currently, the ECO has ten member States from South, West and Central Asia, namely Afghanistan, Pakistan, Iran, Turkey, Turkmenistan, Azerbaijan, Kazakhstan, Kyrgyz Republic, Tajikistan and Uzbekistan.[238]

The ECO has several agreements in the area of trade, transit and transport. One of these agreements is the ECO Trade Agreement (ECOTA) that was signed and ratified by ECO member States, including Afghanistan, in 2003.[239] Afghanistan, however, ratified the ECOTA in 2008.[240] ECOTA is designed to enhance trade liberalization among ECO member States through providing preferential tariff concessions and market access opportunities to their exports. It provides low tariffs on most goods, except for those that are part of the sensitive list.[241] ECOTA contains a 'best-endeavor' clause on free transit between contracting States with special

---

[234]Ibid., Art. 7(3)(a)(b).

[235]Art. XXIV (8) GATT; for literature review see Islam (2010), p. 8–1.

[236]SAARC, 17th Ministerial Council Summit (Addu, Maldives, November 2011).

[237]SAARC Secretariat, Afghanistan revised sensitive list: Phase II, http://saarcsec.org/uploads/document/01%20Afghanistan%20%20Revised%20Sensitive%20List%20(PhaseII)_20120318113525.pdf.

[238]Economic Cooperation Organization (ECO) Website, http://www.eco.int/general_content/85059-MemberStates.html?t=General-content.

[239]ECO Secretariat, ECO Trade Agreement (Islamabad. July 2003), http://www.ecosecretariat.org/ftproot/Documents/Agreements/ECOTA.htm.

[240]MoIC, Trade Agreements, http://moci.gov.af/en.

[241]ECO, http://www.ecosecretariat.org/Detail_info/About_ECO_D.htm.

reference to importance of free transit to ECO landlocked members.[242] The Agreement, however, has not been operational yet despite many progressive efforts by ECO member States to bring the Agreement into operation.[243]

Moreover, Afghanistan acceded to the Central Asian Regional Economic Cooperation (CAREC) in 2005 and subsequently signed and ratified the CAREC Cross-Border Trade Agreement.[244] CAREC was established in 1997 between Kazakhstan, Uzbekistan, Kyrgyz and China aiming to facilitate mutual trade and economic growth among these countries. Currently, the Organization has ten member states including Afghanistan and Pakistan.[245] The Membership to CAREC was an important milestone for Afghanistan's accession to the WTO since part of CAREC main objectives is to facilitate the WTO accession process for its member states by offering technical assistance and legal support to harmonize national trade legislation with the WTO rules.[246]

In addition to its reciprocal RTAs, Afghanistan concluded some non-reciprocal preferential market access agreements mainly with developed countries under the WTO Generalized System of Preference (GSP) and the 'Enabling Clause'. Countries that have granted Afghan exports zero tariff preferential market access under the GSP are the EU, the US, Canada, Japan, Korea, Norway, Turkey, Thailand, and Chinese Taipei.[247] The EU, for example, under its preference system of Everything but Arms (EBA) grants duty and quota free access to goods originating from Afghanistan, except for weapons.[248]

Afghanistan also has few bilateral preferential trade deals with some neighboring countries. For example, under the WTO 'Enabling Clause', Afghanistan had a preferential trade agreement with India between 2003 and 2012, through which both countries offered another zero and lower tariffs to several goods.[249] The Agreement was, however, superseded by SAFTA in 2012 where both countries continued the same reciprocal preferences to goods for one another. Similarly, in

---

[242]Art. 13(2) ECOTA.

[243]ECOTA Cooperation Council, 6th Meeting Report (2015).

[244]Regional Economic Cooperation Conference on Afghanistan (RECCA), Fifth Conference (RECCA V), Progress Report for November 2010–March 2012, 23; see also Central Asian Economic Cooperation (CAREC), http://www.carecprogram.org/index.php?page=carec-countries.

[245]CAREC, http://www.carecprogram.org/index.php?page=carec-countries.

[246]See CAREC Secretariat, Trade Policy Strategic Action Plan for 2013–2017 (2013), 24.

[247]See Working Party on the Accession of Afghanistan (note 25), para. 295; Overview of Afghanistan's Commitments to the WTO (note 86); see also EC, European Union Preferential Imports Schemes, http://trade.ec.europa.eu/doclib/press/index.cfm?id=840; Office of the United States of Trade Representative, Generalized System of Preferences: Country Specific Information, https://ustr.gov/issueareas/trade-development/preference-programs/generalized-system-prefer ences-gsp/gsp-use-%E2%80%93-coun.

[248]See EC, Preferential Imports Schemes (note 247).

[249]Ministry of Commerce and Industry of India, India-Afghanistan Preferential Trade Agreement (March 2003). [Entry into force: May 2003], http://commerce.nic.in/trade/international_ta_indafg. asp.

recent years, Afghanistan and China have established a joint economic and trade commission, under which China agreed to grant zero tariffs to 97% of the Afghan exports accessing the Chinese market.[250]

Afghanistan also continued to establish close cooperation with its regional counterparts by setting up joint regional economic commissions in order to maintain follow-up activities and discussions concerning implementation of existing RTAs and further regional economic collaborations. Currently, Afghanistan has joint bilateral economic commissions with China, Iran, and Pakistan and most Central Asian countries. Each of these commissions have so far held several meetings and have had some success in solving economic, trade and transit issues.[251]

Although Afghanistan's regional trade agreements have supported the country towards regional economic integration, transparency, compliance and functionality of some of these agreements remain challenging. Some South Asian and Central Asian countries including Afghanistan are members to more than one of these agreements which provide a different set of tariff provisions and therefore create an overlap of obligations and commitments.[252] For instance, SAARC, ECO and CAREC each have a trade agreement that sets out specific tariff provisions creating a different set of trade obligations and commitments among the same countries, which negatively affects the carrying out of those obligations and commitments. Similarly, for some agreements, members are not yet inclined to comply and bring their commitments and obligations into action. For instance, ECOTA, 15 years after its conclusion and CBTA, almost 8 years after its conclusion, have both not yet entered into force. In terms of compliance, looking for instance at APTTA, the contracting parties—allegedly Pakistan—reportedly violate the Agreement provisions. Therefore, conclusion of more trade agreements with the same countries has created more challenges to the effective implementation of those agreements.

3.6 Conclusion

For the past two decades Afghanistan carried out several extensive economic and legal projects to reform and develop its economic and trade systems. Modernization and liberalization measures were the central focus of the reforms carried out in relation to its foreign trade regime. The reform of the foreign legal trade regime has been relatively successful, particularly looking at areas of privatization of SOEs and promotion of the private sector, trade and investment liberalization, improvement of

---

[250]MoF, Brief Report on Three Years 2015–2017 Main Activities and Achievements of Ministry of Finance, (2018), 23; see also MoF, 3rd Joint Economic and Trade Commission between Afghanistan and China and Signing Cooperation Agreements, http://mof.gov.af/en/news/the-3rd-joint-economic-and-trade-commission-betweenafghanistan-and-china-and-signing-cooperation-agreements.

[251]MoF, Brief Report (note 250), 19–29.

[252]See generally for example SAFTA & ECOTA.

customs and other trade-oriented institutions. The privatization of SOEs, which granted the private sector the right to hold substantial share in SOEs, paved the country's path to an extensive development of the private sector.

Similarly, trade liberalization resulted in developing new tariff and non-tariff trade regimes granting low tariffs for imports and reducing non-tariff barriers. Investment climate, particularly for foreign investment, has improved through introducing liberal investment laws and policies allowing foreign investors not only to hold a 100% equity share in Afghani investments but also to transfer their shares and dividends freely. Introducing MFN and national treatment principles through various trade laws was a milestone within the process of bringing Afghan laws in line with international trade principles and presenting a non-discriminatory trade regime. Finally, institutional reforms helped the Afghan Government to upgrade its old economic institutions and establish new economic and trade agencies simplifying the ease of doing business in the country and escalating the customs procedures for imports and exports.

However, despite all the economic and legal reforms carried out, Afghanistan still faces substantial challenges on its way towards a successful and conducive trade and investment environment at national level as well as foreign trade regime at international level. At national level, the challenges are mainly caused through poor management skills, lacking legal expertise within relevant institutions, corruption, weak implementation and transparency of laws and measures, and of course, continuing security challenges. Needless to say that the uncertain security and peace environment have also affected trade and economic affairs, particularly foreign direct investment. Following the 2014 withdrawal of numerous international military forces from Afghanistan coupled with the uncertain future of current peace negotiations with the Taliban, the growth of trade and economy has experienced a downfall.[253]

At international level, although membership to the WTO and many regional economic organizations and its concluded RTAs supported Afghanistan's integration into international markets, the country still faces internal and external challenges in the effective use of its rights granted under the concluded multilateral and regional agreements. The Afghan Government faces the struggle that it does not have sufficient strategies and policies to help the country effectively negotiate and subsequently implement its concluded agreements. From an external position, transparency, compliance, implementation and overlap of some of the concluded agreements have been major challenges. The question thus remains to be answered as to how far Afghanistan's concluded RTAs have supported and facilitated Afghanistan's foreign trade regime. One can say that many of the RTAs which have the same scope of subject, contracting parties, but different set of legal obligations pose challenges to maintaining an effective cross-border trade regime. Therefore, it creates divergence and declination rather than convergence and inclination towards complying with

---

[253]See generally for example WBG, Afghanistan Development Update: Building Confidence Amid Uncertainty (July 2019); see also Akseer and Rieger (2019), p. 84.

legal obligations under RTAs. Furthermore, political hostilities among Asian countries, particularly in South Asia, negatively affected the implementation of concluded RTAs and the level of cooperation within the established regional organizations. This is particularly visible when looking at the case of SAARC. Although, some of these regional organizations and RTAs provide joint economic commissions as a platform for follow-up meetings and exchange information, the established joint commissions do not hold regular follow up meetings to discuss ongoing trade issues among contracting parties.

If functioning effectively, the joint economic commission model is a successful platform for closer cooperation and discussions of internal and external challenges existing for countries within Asia. Such a platform may encourage its members to review their commitments, internal and external policies and measures to implement their concluded agreements, and to seek cross-border regulatory cooperation. For Afghanistan, it is necessary to focus on the practical effectiveness of RTAs it decides to sign or join, instead of merely relying on the number of agreements concluded. The Afghan Government should actively participate in regional arrangements and in the meetings of joint economic commissions and address the implementation challenges of its RTAs.

References

Afghanistan Business Law Handbook, vol 1. International Business Publications, DC, 2013, pp 29–30

Akseer T, Rieger J (eds) (2019) Afghanistan in 2019: a survey of the Afghan people. 15th Annual Opinion Survey, The Asia Foundation, 2 December 2019, p 84

Aldosari A (2007) World and its politics: Middle East, Western Asia, and Northern Africa, vol 3. Marshall Cavendish Corp., p 341

Dowdy J, Erdmann A (2013) After the war economy: the role of private sector in Afghanistan future. Aspen Institute, DC, pp 261–281

Eltizam ZA (1996) Afghanistan foreign trade. Middle East J 20:95–103

Glassner MI (1967) Transit problems of three Asian land-locked countries: Afghanistan, Nepal and Laos. Reprint Ser Contemp Asian Stud 57:10

Goodhand J (2004) From war economy to peach economy? Reconstruction and state building in Afghanistan. J Int Aff 58:155–160

Hoban T et al (2002) Food biotechnology: benefits and concerns. J Nutr 132:1384–1385

Islam R (2010) Constraint of the agreement on South Asian Free Trade Area and SAARC Agreement on trade in service. Brigham Young Univ Int Law Rev 7:8–1

Maxwell FJ (1974) The Afghan economy: money, finance, and the critical constraints to economic development. Brill, ch. 3

Parto S et al (2012) Afghanistan and regional trade: more, or less, imports from Central Asia. Working Paper 3, University of Central Asia, Institute of Public Policy, p 15

Xinru L (2010) The silk road in world history, 1st edn. Oxford University Press

Chapter 4
Afghanistan's Transit Regime

Afghanistan's transit regime combines national, regional, and multilateral rules and regulations. This chapter reviews Afghanistan's national and international transit regime and provides a selective study of its international transit agreements. It particularly focuses on APTTA and the Chabahar Agreement, due to their role in facilitating Afghanistan's access to the sea. Section 1 of the chapter reviews Afghanistan's national transit and transport laws and regulations. Section 2 discusses international plurilateral transit agreements concluded between Afghanistan and neighboring countries within the framework of regional economic organizations. Section 3 provides a comparative study of APTTA and the Chabahar Agreement and compares the legal advantages of the both agreements for Afghanistan's freedom of transit and access to the sea through an assessment of their legal provisions.

4.1 National Transit Regime

The 2012 Law on Transit Duty, the 2018 Road Transport Law, transit provisions of the Customs Law (chp.10), and the Freight Forwarding Regulation set out Afghanistan's national transit and transport regime. In addition, a number of policies such as the 2018–2023 National Trade Policy set out rules and legal guidance for transit and transport matters. None of these laws defines transit but Article 75(1) of the Customs Law defines traffic in transit as "goods that have entered Afghanistan with the intent of moving through Afghanistan to another Country".

Afghanistan's transit regime is non-discriminatory and provides MFN and NT treatments to all traffic in transit through the territory of Afghanistan. Although as part of its obligations under the WTO and its regional agreements Afghanistan allows free transit of foreign goods through its territory based on MFN and NT principles, certain goods are permanently banned from transit through the territory of

S. Akbari, *The WTO Transit Regime for Landlocked Countries and its Impacts on Members' Regional Transit Agreements*, European Yearbook of International Economic Law 17, https://doi.org/10.1007/978-3-030-73464-0_4

Afghanistan. These goods are the same goods such as alcoholic drinks that are permanently banned from importation into Afghanistan. Apart from this, there are no other non-trade barriers and restrictive measures applicable to movement and transit of goods across Afghanistan.

Afghanistan does not apply customs tariffs on traffic in transit except for few duties and fees applicable to transport and infrastructural services such as use of roads. For this purpose, the 2018 Road Transport Law introduces road pass fees and transport fees and determines their applicable amount and collecting mechanism. A road pass fee is an entry permit fee that is applicable to all means of foreign transport entering into Afghanistan, whether or not they carry goods or passengers.[1] In order to enter into Afghanistan and pay a road pass fee, a foreign transport should first obtain a road pass certificate from a transport attaché of an Afghan consulate in their national country or from a country where Afghanistan has an embassy or consulate. Under emergencies where a transport does not have a road pass certificate (e.g., when a vehicle carries perishable goods), border agencies of the Ministry of Transport would issue a road pass certificate at Afghan borders.[2] The applicable amount of road pass depends on the weight of goods and cargos. For example, there is a road pass fee of 100 USD for goods and cargos weighing up to 25 tones, and a road pass fee of 200 USD for goods and cargos weighing above 25 tones. As for transport fees, they are applicable to all means of transport including motorcycles that move across Afghanistan. Vehicles that carry goods on major paved roads should pay a transport fee of 0.003 USD per ton per km and vehicles that carry goods on major unpaved roads should pay a transport fee of 0.004 USD per ton per km.[3]

Afghanistan's transit regime provides enforcement measures when persons and road vehicles fail to pay their road pass fee and transport fee. As such, a person failing to pay the applicable road fee and transport fee and other relevant duties will be obliged to pay, in addition to the payment of the actual fees, a cash fine of 300% of the actual fees.[4]

Afghanistan's transit regime also provides transit security to goods in international road transit. A transit security aims to prevent smuggling of transit goods into Afghan markets and ensure that customs duties on transit goods are paid in case they are smuggled into Afghan markets. Such a transit security does not, however, apply to transit goods via airplane, pipeline, and railway. Transit vehicles are required to deposit a one-time transit security with Afghan Customs. Traders or their representatives or freight forwarders are required to deposit a transit security of 110% of the applicable customs duties of transit goods to Afghan customs offices. Customs offices are obliged to refund the transit security payment upon the exit of transit

---

[1]Art. 3 (2) Qanuni-i Transport Jada'i Afghanistan (Afghanistan Road Transport Law) (1397) (2018).

[2]Ibid., Art. 11.

[3]Ibid., Arts. 21, 22.

[4]Ibid., Art. 27.

goods from Afghanistan.[5] However, freight forwarders or any other persons responsible for goods in transit can request Afghan customs offices for a transit security waiver. The Customs Law authorizes customs offices to waive a transit security under specific conditions (1) if the requester resides in Afghanistan, or has a registered office in Afghanistan, (2) continuously uses the internal transit process, (3) has a stable financial situation that meets his transit commitments, (4) has not violated Afghan Customs Law or fiscal laws, and (5) pledges to pay any duties and fees connected with transit in accordance with transit procedure.[6] The freight forwarders or any other persons requesting the transit security waiver receive a transit security waiver certificate which would be valid for six months with the possibility of an extension.[7]

Although the Customs Law provides for individual transit guarantee, since the reactivation of the TIR system in 2013,[8] Afghanistan applies the TIR international guarantee (TIR Carnet) for transit security. It accepts TIR international guarantee for transit of foreign goods through its territory and issues TIR Carnet for transit security of Afghan exports.[9] Currently Afghanistan's Chamber of Commerce and Industries (ACCI) as authorized by Afghan Customs authorities is the TIR international guarantor agency and issues TIR Carnets to Afghan transit road vehicles and containers.[10] However according to the Afghanistan National Trade Policy 2018–2023, the MoIC is working on launching an Exportation Bank that would provide insurance and transit security (TIR international guarantee) to Afghan traders and transport companies.[11]

Afghanistan's transit regime, currently, applies all the transit principles of the TIR Convention and provides for the compatibility of its transit and transport procedures with those principles. For example, Afghan customs procedures do not allow physical examination of secure vehicles and containers while in transit across its territory.[12] Before reactivating the TIR system, foreign traders had to submit individual transit and transport security to Afghan customs authorities, which was a cumbersome process and thus a barrier to free trade and transit. Although reactivating the TIR system has increased facilitation in road transit and transport, Afghanistan still, nonetheless, faces internal and external challenges in full implementation of TIR principles.

---

[5] Arts. 94, 95, 2016 Afghanistan Customs Law.

[6] Ibid., Art. 95.

[7] Ibid.

[8] Afghanistan initially acceded to the TIR Convention in 1976 but due to domestic wars the system was not active.

[9] See for example Art. 47 Afghanistan Road Transport Law; Arts. 41–50, 2016 Afghanistan Customs Law.

[10] *See* ACCI Website, http://www.acci.org.af/da/services/tir.html.

[11] Afghanistan National Trade Policy 2018–2023 (Ch. 3, note 9), 34.

[12] See for example Art. 47 Afghanistan Road Transport Law; Arts. 41–50, 2016 Afghanistan Customs Law.

Internal challenges include poor knowledge of customs personnel from the TIR principles and poor technical facilities that have resulted in poor enforcement of TIR customs principles. Between 2013 and 2018, the ACCI has issued only 50 TIR Carnet to Afghan exports, while Afghan customs offices have received 4000 transit trucks with TIR Carnet from foreign countries including Central Asian countries.[13] Lately, the MoIC, Ministry of Transport, the ACD and the ACCI each have been running a number of TIR training programs for their personnel in order to enable them to apply customs transit procedures in full compliance with the TIR principles. With regard to external challenges, according to authorities at the MoIC and Ministry of Transport, neglect of some neighboring countries in treating Afghan vehicles in accordance with TIR principles are one main external challenge for Afghanistan.[14] For instance, obtaining transit visa has been a major problem for Afghan transit vehicle drivers.[15] The challenges remain despite Afghanistan's conclusion of a number of agreements and memoranda of understandings with neighboring countries including Iran, Tajikistan and Turkmenistan for closer collaborations concerning appropriate implementation of TIR principles and facilitating the transit visa process for Afghan drivers.

4.2 Afghanistan's Transit Trade Agreements

Given the direct impact of free transit and trade by the sea on the cost and time of trading, Afghanistan has concluded several transit trade agreements with neighboring countries over the past nearly two decades. The ECO Transit and Transport Framework Agreement, the CAREC Agreement on Cross-Border Transport of Persons, Vehicles and Goods, the Lapis Lazuli Trade, Transit and Transport Agreement, APTTA and the Chabahar Agreement are among the major transit agreements concluded by Afghanistan. However, before jumping into reviewing these transit agreements, it is important to shed some light on a number of ongoing transit and transport projects between Afghanistan and neighboring countries to better understand the ongoing transit paradigm between Afghanistan and neighboring countries and the potential and opportunities therein for them.

---

[13]In-person Interview with authorities in ACCI (Kabul, Apr. 18 & 22, 2018). For countries that have issued TIR Carnets between 2001 and 2017 *see* ENECE, https://www.unece.org/filead min/DAM/tir/figures/TIRCarnets20012017.pdf. In this list, Afghanistan has issued only 50 TIR Carnet during 2013 and has not issued any TIR Carnet between 2014 and 2018.

[14]Various media press covered the press conference concerning Implementation of the TIR procedures by Afghanistan and neighboring countries. See for example Ministry of Transport of Afghanistan, http://mot.gov.af/Content/files/%D8%B3%DB%8C%D8%B3%D8%AA%D9%85% 20%D8%AA%DB%8C%D8%B1.pdf; ACCI, http://www.acci.org.af/da/component/content/arti cle/875-n.html.

[15]Ibid.

In recent years, neighboring countries have launched a number of transit corridors and infrastructural projects with Afghanistan transforming Afghanistan into a transit hub connecting Central and South Asian countries. In fact, these countries depend on transit through the territory of Afghanistan in order to access each other's markets. Therefore, realizing Afghanistan's strategic location as a land bridge, neighboring countries have been keen to tightening their transit connections with Afghanistan, which have resulted in running a number of transit corridors and infrastructural projects, energy power transit projects, and concluding a number of regional transit and road transport agreements.

The transit corridors, infrastructural projects and energy power transit projects have been administered and carried out within the framework of the Regional Economic Cooperation Conference on Afghanistan (RECCA). RECCA was launched in 2005 by Afghanistan, neighboring countries and the international community in order to direct regional cooperation in connection with economic integration, trade and transit between Afghanistan and other Asian countries.[16] One of the main objectives of RECCA is to locate Afghanistan as a secure transit and energy passage hub in South and Central Asia. Until now, RECCA has held eight conferences, which have focused on improving Afghan ports and transit facilities, rebuilding the Silk Road Route, and building railways that link Afghanistan with different parts of Asia and the world.[17]

The transit corridors and infrastructural projects include, but not limited to, the CAREC Corridor 5, the Five Nations Railway Project, the Lapis Lazuli Corridor and the Aata Murad–Aqina Railway.[18] The CAREC Corridor 5 is among the sixth CAREC corridors that connects Central Asia, East Asia, Middle East and South Asia through Afghanistan, Tajikistan and the Kyrgyz Republic.[19] Similarly, the Five Nations Railway Corridor with a length of 2,100 km connects China with Iran through the Kyrgyz Republic, Tajikistan and Afghanistan.[20] Accordingly, the Lapis Lazuli Corridor combines different types of transit routes and allows use of multimodal transport. It serves as a combined road, railway and sea transit route for

---

[16] See RECCA Website, http://recca.af/.

[17] Chief of Staff's Office of the President, Media Directorate, The Unity Government: Three years Achievements at a Glance (February 2018), 49, https://ocs.gov.af/uploads/documents_dr/17.pdf. For English version see http://afghanembassy.ca/dari/wp-content/uploads/2018/05/3YearsAchievements-EnglishSummary.pdf; see also MoF, RECCA VII, Towards Regional Economic Growth and Stability: The Silk Road through Afghanistan (2015).

[18] See RECCA VII Declaration, Deepening Connectivity and Expanding Trade through Investment Infrastructure and Improving Synergy, Annex II (Ashgabat, Nov. 14–15, 2017).

[19] Other CAREC corridors that connect these regions are: Corridor 1 connects East Asia and Europe, Corridor 2 connects East Asia and Mediterranean, Corridor 3 connects Russian Federation, Middle East and South Asia, Corridor 4 connects East Asia and Russian Federation, and Corridor 6 connects East Asia, South Asia and Europe. See for example CAREC Secretariat, CAREC Corridor Performance Measurement and Monitoring—Annual Report 2016 (January 2018), 2–5, 19–30; CAREC, CAREC Transport Corridors at Safely Connected: A Regional Road Safety Strategy for CAREC Countries 2017–2030 (2016), 3–4.

[20] RECCA VII Declaration (note 18).

Afghanistan and Central Asian countries to access to European markets through Turkey. The Corridor has a total length of 2200 km and begins in two land ports in Afghanistan—Aqina port in Northern Province of Faryab and Turghundi port in western province of Herat and continue through Turkmenistan, Azerbaijan, Georgia and finally Turkey to the final destination Europe.[21] The Lapis Lazuli Corridor was officially inaugurated on December 13, 2018 by sending the first Afghan products shipment by vehicles under the TIR Carnet to Europe.[22]

Reports suggest that the Lapis Lazuli Corridor provides Afghanistan with a short and less costly route to access European markets compared to other available routes.[23] The first Afghan products shipment reached Turkey within 17 days, which is the shortest period that Afghanistan has ever had for its exports to Europe.[24] Afghanistan has not even had this period for its exports to South Asian countries. For example, on average, it costs a vehicle more than 5,000 USD and a period of 14 days to carry goods between Karachi port in Pakistan and Jalalabad in eastern Afghanistan.[25] The transit period for the same vehicle from Jalalabad to Europe through Kazakhstan takes around a month and costs nearly 4000 USD. The transit distance between Afghanistan and Europe through Kazakhstan is 6200 km. In comparison, on average, it costs the same vehicle around 3500 USD and a period of 17 days to carry goods from Turghundi port in Herat to Qaars port in Turkey.[26] The Corridor has appropriate infrastructural facilities. Except for Afghanistan, other contracting parties of the Corridor have railways and roads convenient to international transit. The contracting parties have been launching more infrastructural projects to upgrade their existing railway systems and establish new railway and vehicle roads. The Launch of the Aata Murad–Aqina railway between Afghanistan and Turkmenistan is one of these projects. The railway has a length of 635 km length from which 300 km is located in Afghanistan.[27] The contracting parties including Afghanistan are also

---

[21]Ibid.; see also RECCA, Afghanistan–Centered Regional Cooperation: From Planning to Implementation (November 2018), 5–6.

[22]Ibid., see also MoF, https://www.mfa.gov.af/index.php; TOLO News, President Ghani Inaugurates Lapis Lazuli Corridor (Dec. 13, 2018), https://www.tolonews.com/index.php/. For more information about the Lapis Lazuli Corridor, see RECCA documents, http://recca.af/?page_id=2080.

[23]See for example ACCI, The Lapis Lazuli Corridors is Shortest, Cheapest and Safest Route for Afghanistan's Transit Trade (Nov. 25, 2014), http://www.acci.org.af/archive/535-the-lapis-lazuli-corridor-is-shortest-cheapest-andsafest-route-for-afghanistans-transit-trade-.html.

[24]TOLO News, Lapis Lazuli an Alternative to Pakistani Trade Routes (Dec. 30, 2018), https://www.tolonews.com/business/lapis-lazuli-alternative-pakistani-trade-routes.

[25]Ibid.

[26]Ibid.

[27]See MoF Website, https://www.mfa.gov.af/index.php; see also Temmuz News, Inauguration of Afghanistan Cross–border Railway to Increase Trade with Turkmenistan, Azerbaijan, Georgia and Turkey (Nov. 28, 2016), http://www.trt.net.tr/persian/mntqh/2016/11/28/ftth-kht-rh-ahn-brwn-mrzy-fgnstn-b-hdf-tws-h-tjrt_badhrbyjn-trkhyh-trkhmnstn-w-grjstn-618960.

planning to establish free economic zones near the Corridor in their respective territories.[28]

Similarly, the energy power transit projects include mainly the Central Asia South Asia Power Project known as CASA–1000, and the Turkmenistan Afghanistan Pakistan India Gas Pipeline known as TAPI.[29] The CASA–1000, inaugurated in May 2016 in Tajikistan between the Kyrgyz Republic and Tajikistan, provides 1300 Mega Watt electricity power per annum to Afghanistan and Pakistan. The CASA–1000 energy transmission pipeline would be built across the territory of Afghanistan to transit the energy power to Pakistan.[30] Similarly, the TAPI Gas Pipeline Project, inaugurated in February 2018 in Afghanistan by Afghanistan and Turkmenistan, transfers gas power from Turkmenistan to Afghanistan, Pakistan and India.[31] Currently, both the CASA–1000 and TAPI are under infrastructural progress.[32]

Both of these energy power projects are particularly important for transit relationship between Afghanistan and Pakistan—two countries with long history of volatile transit relationship. Since Pakistan's strong need for energy power would depend on the CASA–1000 and TAPI which would have to transit through the territory of Afghanistan gives Afghanistan a bargaining power and a leverage to demand more transit facilities from Pakistan for access to the sea and ultimately to South Asian markets.

4.2.1 Afghanistan's Plurilateral Transit Trade Agreements

4.2.1.1 ECO Transit and Transport Framework Agreement (TTFA)

Facilitation in transit and transportation is among the core goals of the ECO. This is evident by the ECO Transit and Transport Framework Agreement (TTFA)—one of the oldest agreements signed by ECO member States in 1998.[33] The TTFA aims, *inter alia,* to facilitate the movement of goods, luggage and persons via road, rail and inland waterways and ensure their safety while in transit across the territory of the contracting States.[34] Article 4 TTFA provides that "each TTFA Contracting Party shall provide necessary transit facilities to other Contracting Parties through its territory, under conditions specified in this Agreement and its Annexes." In

---

[28]RECCA VII Declaration (note 18), sec. C, para. 4.

[29]See for example RECCA, Afghanistan-Centered Regional Cooperation (note 21).

[30]Ibid.; see also CASA–1000 Website, http://www.casa-1000.org/.

[31]See Asian Development Bank [ADB], Turkmenistan–Afghanistan–Pakistan–India Natural Gas Pipeline Project, Phase 3, Completion Report, Project No. 44463-013 (March 2018).

[32]RECCA, Afghanistan-Centered Regional Cooperation (note 21), 4–6.

[33]See generally ECO Transit and Transport Framework Agreement (TTFA), (Almaty, 1998).

[34]Ibid., Arts. 2, 28.

providing so, the Agreement obliges the contracting parties to abolish all customs duties, charges and taxes except charges and fees applied to services carried out for transit purposes, and charges and fees in connection with road maintenance. It also obliges the contracting parties to provide for the safety of traffic in transit across their territories and guarantee liability for motor vehicles including the third party liability that occur during transit journey.[35]

The TTFA recognizes the contracting States right to domestic transport permits but exempts transit carriers from presenting additional customs documents including a Carnet de Passage.[36] The TTFA also provides provisions on harmonization and simplification of customs procedures such as mandatory recognition of driving licenses issued in another contracting party and periodical review of those procedures, provisions on cross-border regulatory cooperation and provisions on recognition of the TIR principles.[37] The TTFA also recognizes the right of transit service providers in the territory of one contracting State to use means of transport that is registered in another contracting State.[38]

The TTFA extends its provisions to inland waterways and maritime ports facilities. The Agreement obliges contracting States to make their inland waterways open and free for the transit use of vessels from one another.[39] It also obliges coastal contracting parties to offer to other contracting parties the same port facilities that they provide non-contracting States.[40] The TTFA sets out provisions on dispute settlement mechanisms for disputes arising under the Agreement and provides for dispute settlement institutions. The Agreement provides for consultation, mediation and arbitration as means of dispute settlement and establishes the Transit Transport Coordination Council (TTCC) as the coordinating body for activities arising under the Agreement including functioning as mediation facilitator. The Agreement provides for the compatibility of arbitration rules and procedures with rules and procedures of the United Nations Commission on International Trade Law (UNICTRAL 1976).[41] However, the Agreement does not provide any enforcement mechanisms for carrying out dispute settlement decisions.

The TTFA has a provision on visa facilitation as well. Article 12 TTFA obliges the contracting States to grant multiple entry transit visa for drivers and persons engaged in international transit operations. Such multiple entry transit visa should be valid for one year with 15 days stay per entry and five more days stay in place of loading and discharge. The 15 days are extendable under necessary circumstances.

Effective implementation of the TTFA has been among the main topics of all the ECO conferences and ministerial meetings. For its newly developed vision known as

---

[35]Ibid., Arts. 5, 10, 23.

[36]Ibid., Arts. 15, 17.

[37]Ibid., Arts. 28, 30.

[38]Ibid., Arts. 16, 20.

[39]Ibid., Art. 25.

[40]Ibid., Art. 13.

[41]Ibid., Arts. 38, 39.

"Vision 2025", the ECO sets the connectivity and cooperation as the primary principle to achieve its goals and objectives. The ECO "Vision 2025" is a decade vision designed to boost regional cooperation in areas of transport and transit, trade, energy, economic growth, and tourism among ECO member States.[42] The "Vision 2025" has an Implementation Framework that sets a timeframe for carrying out specific missions and activities including full implementation of the TTFA provisions between 2015 and 2025 in order to achieve the Vision.[43] For instance, according to the Implementation Framework, the ECO should finalize the activation of an international insurance company for transit and transport by 2017. Similarly, during the period 2017–2020, ECO member States should sign and ratify the ECO Agreement on Simplification and Harmonization of Visa for Businessmen and drivers. During this period, visa sticker scheme should be operational in compliance with the TTFA provisions on business and transit visas.[44]

However, the "Vision 2025" Implementation Framework has not been successful in carrying out its scheduled programs until now. Particularly, the effective implementation of the TTFA, which has been part of the Implementation Framework has been challenging. For instance, establishing an international insurance company for transit and transport of ECO member States which was due 2017 has not been achieved. Similarly, obtaining business and transit visas is still time consuming and costly and the visa scheme which should have been operational the latest by the beginning of 2020 is still not operational. In the case of Afghanistan, for example, Afghan authorities allegedly claim Afghan drivers have difficulty in obtaining transit visas and road pass from ECO member states, particularly Iran and Pakistan who have ratified the TTFA.[45]

A recent interview conducted *by Christine Fair* with Afghan truck drivers at a cross border point between the Afghan Zaranj border and the Iranian port of Chabahar suggests that Afghan drivers face difficulties during their transit to and from Iran. The problems raised by interviewed drivers include, but not limited to, usurious visa charges, administrative corruption and insufficient petrol quotas to make the journey.[46] Therefore, symbolic follow-up meetings of the ECO member States, the "Vision 2025" Implementation Framework and implementation of TTFA provisions remain inefficient in practice.

---

[42]See generally ECO, ECO Vision 2025 and Implementation Framework (February 2017).

[43]Ibid., 4.

[44]Ibid., 4, 9, 10.

[45]In-person Interview with Akhlaqi (Ch.1, note 29); In-person Interview with Mir Saeed Sayeedy (Ch.3, note 9), (WTO Headquarter, Oct. 3 & 5, 2018); Telephone Interview with Mir Saeed Sayeedy (Dec. 12 &14, 2018).

[46]*Christine Fair*, Iran, India, and a New Way Forward for Afghanistan, The Diplomat Magazine (Nov. 30, 2018), https://thediplomat.com/2018/11/iran-india-and-a-new-way-forward-for-afghanistan/.

4.2.1.2 CAREC Agreement on Cross-Border Transport (CBTA)

The CAREC Agreement on Cross-border Transport (CBTA) governs transit and transport activities in CAREC Corridor 5.[47] Ratified in 2013, the CBTA has three contracting parties namely Afghanistan, Tajikistan and Kyrgyzstan.[48] The Agreement has not yet entered into force and its entry into force has been conditioned on developing internal customs procedures by the contracting parties.[49]

CBTA provides an MFN and national treatment based legal regime for the movement of goods, vehicles and persons via road and railway by facilitating and improving cross-border infrastructure and equipment, simplifying and harmonizing cross-border formalities and procedures of mutual recognition of technical standards, joint cross-border control measures, vehicle insurance including third person motor vehicle insurance liability, road safety, visa facilitation, and traffic rights along CAREC Corridor 5 and recognizes the principles of the TIR Convention as a governing regime of customs transit of goods among the contracting parties.[50] The Agreement has nine annexes that set out detailed provisions on transit and transport of the goods covered in the main text of the Agreement. For example, Annex 1 provides for a number of goods such as those containing pornography or religiously hatred materials subject to prohibition from movement through the territory of the contracting parties and overweight, oversized and perishable goods subject to specific restrictive measures and customs procedures such as vehicle escort and installation of special warning signage devices.

Although the Agreement presents many features of a modern transit and transport regimes, it has not yet entered into force due to the failure of the contracting parties to develop internal customs procedures required for the entry into force of the Agreement. The contracting parties' pledge, in a number of meetings and conferences including the RECCA-VI, held in November 2017, to complete their internal customs procedures required for the entry into force of CBTA as soon as possible remain unsuccessful.[51] One reason may be that over the few years, CBTA contracting parties have been busy focusing on energy power transmission projects

---

[47]See CAREC Website, https://www.carecprogram.org/?page_id=31; see also CAREC, An Institutional Framework for Facilitation Economic Cooperation in the Central Asia Region, https://www.carecprogram.org/uploads/CARECInstitutional-Framework-1.pdf.

[48]The Agreement was signed between Tajikistan and Kyrgyz Republic in 2010. Afghanistan joined the Agreement a year later. See ADB, Afghanistan Joins Tajikistan Kyrgyz Republic Cross-Border Transport Accord (Aug. 29, 2011), https://www.adb.org/news/afghanistan-joins-tajikistan-kyrgyz-republic-cross-border-transportaccord.

[49]See CAREC, Report of the Ninth Transport Sector Coordination Committee Meeting (Manila, Oct. 11–12, 2010), https://www.carecprogram.org/uploads/9th-TSCC-Meeting-Report.pdf; CAREC Corridor Performance Measurement and Monitoring, Annual Report 2016 (note 19), 2–5, 30; see also *Asadov* (2012), pp. 20–21.

[50]See generally CAREC, Cross-Border Transport Agreement (CBTA), (Manila, Nov. 5, 2010).

[51]RECCA VII Declaration (note 18), 5.

that leave them with little interest in developing measures and procedures for implementing the CBTA.

4.2.1.3   Lapis Lazuli Trade, Transit and Transport Agreement (Lapis Lazuli Route Agreement)

Signed in November 2017 among Afghanistan, Turkmenistan, Azerbaijan, Georgia and Turkey, the Lapis Lazuli Route Agreement is one of the major regional transit agreements concluded by Afghanistan very recently that has drawn regional attention positioning Afghanistan in the spotlight of transit competition in South and Central Asia. The Agreement allows accession of other countries and Afghanistan is the depository of the Agreement. The Agreement provides free and safe passage to goods and persons along the Lapis Lazuli Corridor and obliges the contracting parties to harmonize and simplify their customs procedures for transit along the corridor.[52]

However, the Agreement has some potential gaps to be addressed. For instance, although the Agreement provides national treatment to traffic in transit of contracting parties, it limits the national treatment to facilities only in maritime ports and allows the contracting parties to maintain their national regulations to dry ports facilities.[53] This provision confines the scope of national treatment as the major parts of the Lapis Lazuli Corridor have dry ports. Similarly, the Agreement does not provide for transparency except a 'best endeavor' provision under Article 10 that encourages the contracting parties for cooperation in exchange of customs information among each other. Given that transparency of rules and information is important to demonstrate the accountability and good governance of governments, its lack in the Lapis Lazuli Route Agreement creates uncertainty and unpredictability with regard to legal actions of the contracting parties and questions the intention of the contracting parties in terms of accountability and good governance. Moreover, the Agreement provisions on transit visas are also ambiguous. While the Agreement provides for transit visas to drivers and persons who are engaged in international transport operations, it is not clear whether the transit visa extends to all passengers in transit—given that the Agreement covers transit of goods and passengers in general. Would the case be otherwise, the Agreement should have determined the scope of "passenger" in the first place.

Last but important, the Lapis Lazuli Route Agreement has inadequate provisions on dispute settlement mechanism and institutional arrangement. It provides for consultations as the only means of dispute settlement and does not recognize other means of dispute settlement such as adjudication and appeal.[54] Imagine a scenario where a consultation fails to resolve an arisen dispute, it is not clear how the

---

[52]See generally Lapis Lazuli Route Agreement.

[53]Ibid., Art. 11.

[54]Ibid., Art. 18.

contracting parties would proceed next to settle the dispute. The Agreement is silent about whether recourse to other regional or multilateral dispute settlement forums should be sought. Had the Agreement recognized such resource, it would have filled the gap to some extent. The Agreement does also not provide for enforcement measures, which make sense as due to lack of a mandatory dispute settlement and decision-making mechanism there would be no binding enforcement measures. Similarly, the Agreement has inadequate provisions on institutional arrangements. Article 16 of the Agreement establishes a Joint Consultative Groups (JCG), which is responsible to conduct follow-up meetings on implementation of the Agreement and provide consultations on disputes. Except for this abstract provision, the Agreement does not provide for any mechanism to carry out the JCG activities and decisions. With this, it would be fair to conclude that while the Lapis Lazuli Corridor has the required physical facilities to serve as a conducive international transit route, its regulatory regime has potential gaps that needs to be filled in order for the Lapis Lazuli Route Agreement to serve as an effective cross-border regulatory regime of the Lapis Lazuli Corridor.

4.2.2 Afghanistan's Transit Agreements with Coastal Neighboring States: A Comparative Study of APTTA and the Chabahar Agreement

Pakistan in the south and east and Iran in the west are the two direct coastal neighboring States with which Afghanistan has concluded APTTA[55] and the Chabahar Agreement respectively. Both agreements are important to this study. APTTA is particularly important due to, on one hand, the significant role of Pakistan as one of the primary trading partners of Afghanistan and, on the other hand, the implementation challenges of the Agreement that have raised continuous complaints. APTTA grants Afghan exports free transit to India and other South Asian markets through Pakistani sea and land ports. In exchange, it grants Pakistani exports free transit to Central Asian countries through Afghanistan's land ports and airports. Similarly, the study of the Chabahar Agreement is important as Iran is also a primary trading partner of Afghanistan and, most importantly, the Agreement has been presented as an alternative to APTTA.

Since the conclusion of APTTA, the contracting parties have alleged frequent violations of the Agreement, which has been one main reason persuading Afghanistan to conclude the Chabahar Agreement with Iran and India in 2016 to offset its dependence on Pakistan to access to India and other South Asian countries via the sea. The Chabahar Agreement opens up the respective markets for Afghan and Indian products through the Iranian seaport of Chabahar. This section provides a comparative analysis of both agreements to assess which of them offers broader legal

---

[55]See generally APTTA.

transit trade opportunities for Afghanistan and whether the Chabahar Agreement is a viable alternative to APTTA.

4.2.2.1 Afghanistan-Pakistan Transit Trade Agreement (APTTA)

Sharing 2430 km[56] borderline, Afghanistan and Pakistan are the largest trading partners for each other in the region. Since post-Taliban, bilateral trade between the two countries has significantly increased. Followed by India, both countries are the first largest exports markets to one another.[57] Afghan exports to Pakistan mainly include raw cotton, carpets, fresh fruits including grapes and dry fruits including nuts, and Pakistan's exports to Afghanistan mainly include wheat, chemical products, mineral products, metals, machinery, plastics and rubbers, live animals, non-alcoholic drinks, fruits, dairy products, vegetables and meat.[58]

For both countries, the exports to and imports from one another account for more than 30% of their total world trade.[59] The volume of bilateral trade exchanged between the two countries increased from 25 million USD during the Taliban regime to half a billion USD in 2004 and further increased to more than 1.5 billion USD during 2005–2010. Between 2011 and 2014, trade between the two countries reached approximately two billion USD with more than two-third of it belonging to Pakistani exports to Afghanistan and less than one-third belonging to Afghan exports to Pakistan.[60] Due to political and security tensions, and implementation challenges of APTTA, trade between the two countries has decreased to less than 1.5

---

[56]UN, Office on Drugs and Crime, Country Profile: Pakistan, https://www.unodc.org/pakistan/en/country-profile.html; see also Institute for the Study of War, Afghanistan and Pakistan, http://www.understandingwar.org/pakistan-and-afghanista.

[57]There are discrepancies in exports market position of both countries to one another. Some reports rank Pakistan as the first largest exports market for Afghan exports and Afghanistan as the third largest exports market for Pakistani exports. Some other reports and literature rank Pakistan as the first largest exports market for Afghan exports and Afghanistan as the second largest exports market for Pakistani products. See for example PAJCCI, Pak Afghan Trade (2018), 2, http://www.pajcci.com/PressRelease/PressReleaseImage_107.pdf; see also Government of Pakistan, Development Authority of Pakistan, Country Report on Afghanistan: Executive Summary (2018), https://www.tdap.gov.pk/word/AFGHANISTAN.pdf; *Hanif* (2018), pp. 94–97.

[58]See PAJCCI, Pak Afghan Trade (note 57), 1. According to this data by PAJCCI, Pakistani chemical export products are mainly soaps and acids. Mineral products are refined petroleum and cement. Machines are mainly refrigerators, washing machines and pumps. Foods also include sugar and chocolates.

[59]See for example Government of Pakistan, Country Report on Afghanistan (note 57), 4; WB, Analysis of Afghanistan Pakistan Transit Trade Agreement (May 2014); The Pakistan Business Council, Afghanistan's Transit Trade Patterns Pre and Post APTTA (June 2015), https://www.pbc.org.pk/wp-content/uploads/AfghanistansTransitTradePatternsPrePostAPTTA.pdf; see also https://wits.worldbank.org/CountryProfile/en/Country/AFG/Year/2016/Summary.

[60]See Government of Pakistan, Foreign Office Yearbook 2002–03 (Foreign Office of Pakistan, 2003), 11–13; Government of Pakistan, Foreign Office Yearbook 2005–06 (Foreign Office of Pakistan, 2006), 10–14; Pakistan Bureau of Statistics, www.pbs.gov.pk/sites/default/files//

USD for the past couple of years.[61] In contrast, Afghan trade with other regional potential trade markets has grown—mainly with Iran and India. In recent years, while Pakistan has remained the first exports market for Afghanistan, Iran has replaced Pakistan as Afghanistan's first imports partner and maritime transit route.[62]

Historically, Afghanistan has relied on Pakistan for access to the sea for its exports to India and South Asia. For this purpose, the two countries concluded the first Afghanistan-Pakistan transit trade agreement (ATTA) in March 1965.[63] ATTA granted Afghan exports free access to the Indian Ocean through Pakistani maritime port of Karachi.[64] To reach port of Karachi, Afghan exports were allowed to transit only via the land routes of Peshawar and Chaman and Pakistan.[65] The Agreement did not grant Afghan exports a transit through Gwadar seaport, which is the shortest maritime transit route to Afghan exports. The Agreement did also not grant Afghan exports a transit via Wagha land port, which is the shortest land transit route to Afghan exports to India. Similarly, the Agreement did not allow imports from India to Afghanistan through these ports. In exchange, the Agreement granted free transit to Pakistani exports through specified land ports of Afghanistan to reach Central Asian markets.[66] Several reports by the WB indicate that Pakistan often violated ATTA by banning and restricting transit of certain Afghan goods on the basis of a list of sensitive products.[67] Pakistan justified its ban and restriction necessary to avoid the smuggling of Afghan transit exports into Pakistani markets and damaging its domestic trade.[68]

Although ATTA was legally in force, its implementation was stalled for decades until it was replaced by the new APTTA in 2010. With the growth of bilateral trade between the two countries and given the importance of access to Central Asian markets for Pakistan and access to Indian and other South Asian markets for Afghanistan,[69] Afghanistan and Pakistan signed APTTA in 2010.[70] The Agreement entered into force in June 2011. APTTA has 52 Articles and two annexes. Annex

---

external_trade/8_digitlevel/exp/5_exp_2008-09_to_2012-2013.pdf; PAJCCI, Draft Annual Report 2014 (2014), 28; see also *Fair* (2008), p. 216; *Sultana* (Ch.1, note 14).

[61] See Government of Pakistan, Country Report on Afghanistan (note 57), Executive Summary.

[62] Again, discrepancies exist in exports market positions of both the countries. According to Afghanistan National Trade Policy 2018–2023, 60 percent of Afghan products are exported to Pakistan and India. National Trade Policy 2018–2023, supra note 117, at 52; see also Mazhar, supra note 418, at Executive Summary.

[63] See generally ATTA.

[64] Prmb ATTA; Annex, sec I, para (1)(b).

[65] Ibid.

[66] Ibid.

[67] See for example WB, Analysis of Afghanistan Pakistan Transit Trade Agreement (note 59), 3.

[68] Ibid., see also Waqar Hussain (2008), pp. 1–8; *Rizvi Shamim Ahmed*, Pak–Afghan Trade, Pakistan Economist Weekly (Sept. 9–15, 2002); *Sultana* (Ch.1, note 14), 28–29.

[69] See for example Country Profile: Pakistan, Afghanistan, 1998–1999 (London, The Economist Intelligence Unit Ltd., 1999), 5–48.

[70] Art. 54 & prmb APTTA.

1 provides for a list of transit routes in both countries and Annex 2 includes four binding protocols that provide for technical and administrative mechanism and implementation procedures for APTTA provisions. APTTA is a bilateral agreement and is silent on the accession of other countries. However, in practice, news and reports indicate that Afghanistan and Pakistan are open to the accession of other countries, particularly Tajikistan and India. Accession of Tajikistan and India would require replacing APTTA with a quadrilateral transit agreement with new terms and conditions.

As mentioned earlier, since APTTA is concluded, both countries have alleged frequent violations of the Agreement and the implementation of the Agreement has been challenging. The implementation challenges are several. One challenge derives from the substance of the Agreement. The Agreement does not allow transit of imports from India to Afghanistan through Pakistan's territory making it hard for Afghanistan to import from India as one of its main imports partners. Similarly, the Agreement sets out some rigorous provisions that make it difficult for the contracting parties to implement them. These provisions mainly include customs control mechanism and transit security means. The contracting parties, particularly Afghanistan, do not have the necessary facilities and tools to fulfill these mechanisms and means, which challenge Afghanistan in implementation of those provisions. Moreover, adoption of QRs on transit goods by contracting parties, allegedly Pakistan, under list of sensitive goods and adoption of frequent border closure measures are the two other main challenges posed to effective implementation of the Agreement. Other APTTA implementation challenges include lack of transparency in the adoption and application of cross-border measures, exchange of information, poor administrative cooperation, and corruption in customs. This section does not get into the details of all of these challenges and rather focus on assessment of APTTA substantive provisions.

4.2.2.1.1 Freedom of Transit and Exceptions

Although APTTA introduces an MFN and NT based free bilateral transit regime, due to banning transit of Afghan imports from India through Pakistan, the established regime is not fully free and non-discriminatory.

Article 3 APTTA defines freedom of transit as follows:

1. There shall be freedom of transit through the territory of each contracting party, via the pre-settled routes most convenient for international transit, for traffic in transit to or from the territory of the other contracting party. No distinction shall be made which is based on flag of the vessel, the place of origin, departure, entry, exit or destination, or any circumstances relating to the ownership of goods, vessels or other means of transport;
2. If any contracting party is of the opinion that some goods or class of goods being allowed in transit are smuggled back in its territory and are hurting the economy, industry or import revenue, it may file a complaint with the Authority, stating its

grievances along with facts and figures and damages being caused to the contracting party. On receipt of the complaint, the Authority shall convene a meeting within three months of the filing of the complaint and may agree on taking any appropriate measures to address the problem.

Article 3 provides few important provisions. One important provision, as provided by paragraph 1, is choice of transit routes as being 'most convenient for international transit'—a criterion recognized by most multilateral agreements including Article V GATT for international transit routes. Another important provision, as provided by paragraph 1, is the MFN principle that prohibits all kinds of discrimination during a transit journey.[71] Similarly, another important provision, as provided by paragraph 2, is the issue of 'smuggling trade'. APTTA is straightforward about what should be done when smuggling trade is suspected during a transit journey, which is to resolve the issue through discussion and cooperation within the framework of APTTA authorized institutions and take appropriate measures accordingly. This provision is important for the fact that, for a long time, smuggling trade has been a trade and transit challenge to both countries. However, the two countries have barely resolved the issue of smuggling trade in transit through official means and rather have sought unilateral QR measures.

To ensure freedom of transit, APTTA exempts transit goods from customs duties and charges, except charges applied to roads and to services rendered. The Agreement also prohibits the adoption and application of unnecessary restrictive measures.[72] However, APTTA contains 'best endeavor' provisions on general and security exceptions that allow the contracting parties to derogate from their obligations when their fulfilment harm societal values and endanger the territorial security of the contracting parties. Article 53 APTTA provides:

> The contracting parties agree to ensure that no measure taken under the Agreement could risk harming or destroying (i) public morals; (ii) human, animal and plant life; (iii) national treasures; (iv) security of its own territory; and (v) any other interests as mutually agreed upon.

Similarly, Article 9 Protocol 1 of APTTA provides:

> The contracting parties may restrict or prohibit traffic in transit on certain routes for the duration of repair work or for the duration of a danger to public safety, including traffic safety or public emergency. Before traffic in transit is restricted or prohibited for reasons other than emergencies, the contracting party imposing restrictions or prohibition shall notify the competent authorities of the other contracting party well in advance of taking actions.

APTTA provisions on general and security exceptions under Article 53 and Article 9 Protocol 1 reflect some ambiguities. One main ambiguity comes from the lack of definition and scope of certain important terms in those articles. APTTA does

---

[71] Ibid., Art. 33. Article 33 provides also national treatment to traffic in transit of another contracting party with respect to all rules, laws, measures, charges, fees, and any other financial obligations.

[72] Ibid., Arts. 30, 32.

not define what constitutes the 'security of its own territory' and whether it includes any emergencies as provided in Article 9 Protocol 1. Similarly, while Article 9 Protocol 1 provides for traffic safety and public emergency as examples of public safety, it does not define what constitutes a public safety and whether a public emergency as one type of public safety would fall under territorial security as provided under Article 53 APTTA. Another ambiguity arises in the extent of the exceptions listed under Article 53 APTTA. Article 53 does not provide for any conditions such as whether and to what extent it would be necessary to derogate from APTTA obligations when their fulfilment could risk the listed exceptions including the exception on the territorial security of the contracting parties. Unlike Article 53, Article 9 Protocol 1 contains two conditions for the application of a transit restriction or prohibition, which are (i) the restriction or prohibition to be applied *during* a repair work or a danger to public safety and (ii) advance *notification* of the restriction or prohibition unless there is an emergency. If one considers that public safety is one of the issues of territorial security within the meaning of Article 53 APTTA, the conditions listed for a restrictive measure protecting public safety under Article 9 Protocol 1 raise the question as to whether application of a restrictive measure for territorial security under Article 53 should also be limited to the duration of the prevailing risk or subject to advance notification to the other contracting party.

4.2.2.1.2   Pre-Settled Transit Routes

APTTA determines a number of seaports, airports and land ports in Pakistan and a number of airports and land ports in Afghanistan as applicable transit routes and obliges the contracting parties to ensure the safety and maintenance of the routes and undertake repair measures when necessary.[73] Seaports of Karache, Qasim and Gawadar and the land port of Wagah are the main transit ports in Pakistan that channel Afghan exports to India and other South Asian markets.[74] In exchange, several land ports in different parts of Afghanistan channel Pakistani exports to Central Asia, Iran and East Asia. For instance, Torghundi port in west and Aqina port in north of Afghanistan channel transit of Pakistani exports to Turkmenistan, Ai Khanum and Sherkhan ports in the northeast channel transit to Tajikistan, Hairrantan port in the north channels transit to Uzbekistan, and Zarang and Islam Qalah ports in the west channel transit of Pakistani exports to Iran.[75]

APTTA allows only transit of Afghan exports to India through Pakistan and bans transit of imports from India to Afghanistan through Pakistan.[76] Afghan transit vehicles must either return empty from Pakistani ports or carry Pakistani exports

---

[73]Ibid., Art. 4.

[74]Ibid., Arts. 7, 8. Annex 1 of the Agreement provides a list of all pre-settled entry-exit ports.

[75]Ibid., Annex 1, Art. 3.

[76]Ibid., footnote 2.

on their way to Afghanistan.[77] Afghan transit vehicles are also not allowed to carry Pakistani goods from Pakistani ports in order to discharge them back in Pakistan.[78] Due to increasing costs and length of trading, the transit ban on Indian exports through Pakistan and empty return of transit vehicles have been challenging for Afghan traders making them seek alternative routes, i.e., via Iran, to import from India. Although with the opening of the Iranian seaport of Chabahar under the Chabahar Agreement, the challenge to import from India has been, to some extent, reduced, the costs of imports through this route are relatively higher due to insufficient infrastructural and other port facilities.

4.2.2.1.3   Simplification and Harmonization of Customs Procedures and Formalities

To facilitate free transit, APTTA requires that customs procedures and transit formalities should be harmonized and simplified and their necessity should be reviewed periodically.[79] For instance, as means of harmonization, APTTA provides for mutual recognition of documents and technical requirement certificates of road transit vehicles and obliges the contracting parties to carry out periodic examination of safety standards and technical conditions of road transit vehicles registered in their territory.[80] It also obliges the contracting parties to recognize the certificate of those periodic examinations from each other. APTTA provides similar provisions on mutual recognition of driving license and vehicle registration documents such as vehicle plates and obliges the contracting parties to recognize those documents from each other. Similarly, it provides for harmonization of customs procedures through mutual administrative assistance such cooperating in customs control procedures and taking joint customs control actions at cross-border checkpoints and exchange of relevant information between customs offices of the contracting parties.[81] As such, APTTA obliges the contracting parties to recognize customs control certificates from each other and, except for seal and stamp check, refrain from physical inspection of goods inside transit vehicles and containers that comply with all technical requirements, and conformity standards. Under exceptional cases such as when customs offices suspect inconformity with customs requirements APTTA allows the contracting parties to run physical inspections of transit vehicles and containers or for a risk management purpose examine up to five percent of transit containers.[82]

---

[77] Art. 11(4) APTTA.

[78] MoIC, Asnad wa Procejar hae zarori dar Chaokat APTTA [Required Documents and Procedures under APTTA], http://moci.gov.af/fa/page/8603/8604/8605.

[79] Art. 28 APTTA.

[80] Ibid., Arts. 16, 18; Art. 4 Protocol 1.

[81] Art. 20 APTTA Protocol 3.

[82] Ibid., Art. 10; Art. 21(4) APTTA.

APTTA has a special provision on customs control of vehicles and containers that carry animals, perishable and urgently needed goods and obliges the contracting parties to facilitate and accelerate movement of those vehicles and containers by granting priority in customs clearance and avoiding SPS controls of them.[83]

4.2.2.1.4 Recognition of Relevant International Rules and Standards

APPTA recognizes rules and procedures of other international conventions and multilateral agreements and provides that its provisions do not affect the rights and obligations of the contracting parties under those international conventions and multilateral agreements.[84] APPTA particularly recognizes Article V GATT for matters related to freedom of transit, rules and procedures of the World Health Organization (WHO), Food and Agriculture Organization (FAO), and IOE for cross-border SPS control of goods, the UN Customs Layout Key as customs documentation guidelines for harmonizing customs documents and other formalities, and rules and procedures of the 1999 Revised Kyoto Convention for exceptional physical inspection of vehicles and containers.[85] Although APTTA remains silent on the TIR procedures, Afghanistan and Pakistan currently apply its procedures to their customs and transit. The reason for the absence of recognition of the TIR procedures could be that Pakistan was not a member of the TIR Convention at the time when APTTA was concluded.

4.2.2.1.5 Transport Conditions and Permits

APTTA sets out a number of rigorous technical requirements for road transit vehicles and some general and specific requirements for transport operators. The rigorous technical requirements for road transit vehicles include carrying bonded carrier license and tracking devices. A tracking device is an electronic device attached to vehicles and controlled by customs administrations and enables customs administrations to track movement and location of goods.[86] Similarly, bonded carrier license means that a reputable carriage company has insured a transport vehicle (has posted a bond) and undertaken all financial liabilities for the vehicle.[87]

As for transport operators, in order to undertake international transport operations of goods in transit, they should be licensed in the country where they have registered their transport operation business and obtain a temporary admission document from

---

[83] Arts. 21, 23, 25 APTTA Protocol 3.

[84] Arts. 27, 28, 52 APTTA.

[85] Ibid., Arts. 27, 28.

[86] Ibid., Art. 13.

[87] Ibid.

a transit contracting party.[88] A temporary admission document is an entry and exit or passage permit issued by transit contracting party, at a border entry point, for temporary admission of registered vehicles of the other contracting party.[89] Accordingly, temporary admission of vehicles are customs procedures that allow a registered vehicle of one contracting party to enter temporarily into the territory of the other contracting party without paying import taxes.[90] The temporary admission document is valid for 30 days, after its expiry, the transit vehicle should exit the territory of the contracting party.[91] Border agencies of the contracting parties issue the document free of charge but only after they inspect the vehicle and check all the required documents.[92] APTTA allows these authorities to suspend or revoke the issued temporary transit document when a transport operator violates a law or commits an illegal action while in transit through the territory of a transit contracting party.[93]

4.2.2.1.6 Visa Facilities

APTTA provides multiple entry transit visa to drivers and persons involved in international transit activities for a period of 6 months with each stay no longer than 15 days.[94] However, under emergencies, the Agreement provides for extension of the transit visa.[95]

Taking into account the poor physical infrastructural road facilities across Afghanistan and Pakistan which affect the time of movement of goods, the APTTA transit visa period per entry is not adequate. Not to mention that customs inspection and clearance of goods in both countries, despite many reforms carried out, are still lengthy and cumbersome. Therefore, often, the transit visa period per each entry expires before exports can exit the territories of the contracting parties. Although, APTTA provides for an extension of transit visa, it limits it to emergencies.

---

[88]Ibid., Arts. 10, 11.

[89]Ibid., Art. 2; Art. 3 Protocol 1.

[90]Art. 4 APTTA Protocol 2.

[91]Ibid., Art.12.

[92]Arts. 23, 24, 27 APTTA Protocol 1.

[93]Ibid., Art. 30. APTTA provides some additional criteria for road transport operators. A road transport operator must represent sufficient financial means to guarantee the start and management of the road transport operation. Similarly, he/she should not be convicted for serious breach of laws, barred from exercising road carriage profession because of violation of road carriage regulations, or declared bankrupt. In addition, he/she must prove professional competency in the field of road transport carriage through proof of general education, passing specific exams, or practical experience. Protocol 1, arts 17, 18, 19.

[94]Ibid., Art. 20.

[95]Ibid., Art. 9.

4.2.2.1.7   Transit Security and Insurance

APTTA provides a relatively strict transit security regime for transit goods and transit vehicles. APTTA defines a transit security for transit goods as "[c]ashable financial guarantee acceptable to Customs, submitted by the traders or through their authorized brokers, on transit goods, for an amount equivalent to the import levies of Contracting Parties."[96] The definition has four main particulars: (1) the transit security is a financial guarantee that is cashable in both countries, (2) traders or their authorized brokers submit the transit security means, (3) the transit security should meet the satisfaction of customs for acceptance, and (4) the amount of the transit security should be equivalent to the import customs duties value of transit goods. The two contracting parties have agreed on a 110% amount of imports customs duties value of transit goods as transit security.

Similarly, for a transit security for transit vehicles APTTA provides that "the transporter shall provide a bank guarantee or revolving bank guarantee or carnet-de-passage (when operational) as a pre-requisite for Temporary Admission Document, on his convenience, acceptable to the Host Country."[97] This definition has also four particulars: (1) the transit security for vehicles is a bank guarantee or carnet-de-passage, (2) transporters should present it to customs, (3) the transit security should meet the satisfaction of customs for acceptance, and (4) the transit security is a condition for temporary admission of vehicles or in other words, for temporary admission of transit vehicles, the APTTA requires transporters to submit a bank guarantee or carnet de passage. The guaranteeing banks or institutions who issue transit security, undertake customs transit liabilities for transit vehicles and containers. APTTA requires a bank guarantee not only to secure the payment of customs taxes and charges but also to ensure the compensation of charges and fines for irregularities and legal violations such as violation of customs laws and regulations of the transit contracting party, or failing to exit the transit territory within the period specified in the temporary admission document or transit visa.[98] Vehicle operators should carry the proof of transit security in a Customs document called Transit and Inland Customs Clearance Document.[99] This document guarantees the payment of all customs duties, charges, and fines and contains information about the place and period of departure and destination of transit vehicles. The document is valid for one transit journey and each transit vehicle or transport unit should carry one document.[100]

---

[96] Art. 3 APTTA Protocol 3.

[97] Art. 14 APTTA Protocol 2.

[98] Ibid., Art. 15.

[99] Art. 13 APTTA Protocol 3.

[100] Arts. 192, 14(2) APTTA Protocol 2.

In addition to transit security, APTTA requires that transit vehicles should be insured. The insurance should also include compulsory insurance for third party vehicle liability during the transit journey.[101]

Currently, Pakistan does not allow Afghan vehicles without presenting these guarantees and insurances. Both Afghan officials and traders report challenges in their ability to provide these guarantees and insurances. The challenge comes initially due to reluctance of banks both in Afghanistan and Pakistan to provide Afghan vehicles with a guarantee. In most cases, uninsured vehicles return to Afghanistan after long inspections at the borders. However, in 2016, for a temporary solution, the Afghan Ministry of Transport and Civil Aviation issued a guarantee letter for Afghan vehicles and requested the Government of Pakistan to recognize the issued guarantee letter for transit of Afghan transit vehicles.

APTTA provisions on transit security are strict and ambiguous. They are strict because they require separate transit security for transit goods and vehicles, which traders in both countries, particularly Afghanistan often are not able to provide. They are also ambiguous with regard to subjecting both guaranteeing banks and traders to liability for payment of customs taxes and other charges. Paragraph 1 of Article 23 Protocol 3 of APTTA provides that "the guaranteeing institution shall be separately or jointly with the person for whom the sums are directly due, liable to pay the imports and exports duties, taxes, fines and interests…" This provision does not provide for the procedure and method of carrying out the joint liability. For instance, it is not clear whether customs authorities would directly refer to traders or their authorized brokers during transit journey for liability or to guaranteeing banks.

APTTA transit security is one of the areas that should be reformed if the contracting parties renegotiate the Agreement in future. The contracting parties could use simplified and harmonized systems of transit guarantee such as the TIR Carnet for both transit goods and transit vehicles. Similarly, they could use unified regional insurance systems. For instance, as mentioned in previous sections, ECO is in the process of establishing an international insurance system for its member States and once operational, Afghanistan and Pakistan should seek to use ECO insurance system for APTTA insurance scheme.

4.2.2.1.8 Transparency

APTTA has some transparency provisions but their implementation has been challenged. Article 29 APTTA requires the contracting parties to publish their regulations, policies and advance rulings concerning their bilateral transit trade. It also requires them to notify each other in advance on adopting and applying any measures that affect implementation of APTTA provisions. APTTA particularly requires prior notification of measures concerning change in rules and procedure

---

[101] Art. 19 APTTA.

of transit visa[102] and protective actions.[103] However in practice, the contracting parties barely notify each other on the adoption of transit measures. As such, it remains uncertain because of a lack of notification that when one of the contracting parties adopt and apply a unilateral measure, i.e., close borders or adopt a new list of sensitive products.

As a means of transparency, APTTA also provides for exchange of customs information through the AUSYCUDA system between customs offices of the contracting parties and establishes enquiry offices at customs borders to provide customs and transit information to traders and other interested persons and bodies. In practice, however, due to poor knowledge of customs regulations and rules, the enquiry offices have not been successful in providing information to traders. Similarly, the AUSYCUDA system has not been efficiently operational as, on one hand, customs authorities in both countries are not well trained to use the system and, on the other hand, the regular operation of the system is affected by inadequate electricity power.

In addition, other factors such as poor customs cooperation, corruption at customs borders and the longstanding political tensions between the two countries have affected the implementation of APTTA transparency provisions. For instance, Afghan traders and drivers allege unexpected change in rules and measures at Pakistani borders.[104] They also allege that Pakistani goods enter Afghan markets without paying import taxes and Afghan customs, in exchange for bribe, issue transit documents and exempt them from import duties.[105] Border customs do not cooperate in exchange of information and the two countries rarely hold follow-up meetings on the implementation of the Agreement and addressing ongoing disputes and challenges.

4.2.2.1.9 Institutional Arrangements and Implementation of APTTA

APTTA introduces the Afghanistan Pakistan Transit Trade Coordination Authority (APTTCA), Pakistan Afghanistan Joint Economic Commission (Afghan-Pak JEC) and the Secretariat as APTTA institutions. APTTCA is tasked to implement and oversee APTTA provisions and resolve disputes in the first place. It comprises officials from ministries of commerce and industries and representatives of private sectors of the contracting parties. A deputy minister from Afghanistan's MoIC and a

---

[102]Ibid., Art. 20.

[103]Art. 9 APTTA Protocol 1.

[104]Despite attempts made, the author was not able to conduct interview with Pakistani officials for their opinion on this issue. Due to security threats, the author was also not able to conduct interview with Pakistani vehicle drivers who pass through Afghanistan.

[105]Tolo News, News (Jan. 19, 2019), https://www.youtube.com/watch?v=-g-fnUakZ28 [From min 19:10 to min 21:57].

deputy minister from Pakistan's MoIC co-chair APTTCA's meetings.[106] APTTCA holds its ordinary meetings every six months and extraordinary meetings upon request by contracting parties and adopts its final decisions by consensus of votes.[107]

Since its inception, APTTCA has not demonstrated appropriate capacity to implement and oversee APTTA provisions and resolve ongoing disputes. There are many factors affecting its capacity and decision-making including the decision-making mechanism. APTTCA's consensus based voting mechanism has stalled the authority's decision-making, as it has not always been able to receive a consensus of votes to take its final decisions.[108] Similarly, APTTCA does not have an implementation mechanism and a mutual policy to carry out its decisions and decisions often remain in papers.[109] For example, although at its fourth and fifth meetings, APTTCA decided not to require the use of bonded carrier and tracking devices for Afghan transit vehicles until the vehicles can afford them, Afghan trader allege that local customs in Pakistan still require Afghan transit vehicles to present bonded carrier license and charge them for lack of tracking devices.[110] Similarly, Afghanistan has been alleged to neglect carrying out some of its obligations under APTTCA. For example, Pakistan has claimed that despite Afghanistan having pledged to waive the road pass fee for Pakistani transit vehicles, still charges Pakistani vehicles 100 USD road pass fee.[111]

Other factors include reluctance of the contracting parties to hold meetings and the poor representation of delegations in APTTCA's meetings. Since 2011, the Authority has held only six meetings (both ordinary and extraordinary) with its last meeting held in February 2016.[112] Similarly, for meetings, the two countries do not send the relevant official delegation, which affect the process of an effective

---

[106] Arts. 34, 35 APTTA.

[107] Ibid., Arts. 36, 37.

[108] For example, at the 1st meeting of the APTTCA, Afghanistan stated that Pakistan unilaterally interpreted the requirements for transit security means for transit goods and vehicles, which was not acceptable to Afghanistan. Although both the countries discussed the issue, they did not reach an agreement. See Afghanistan Pakistan Transit Trade Coordination Authority (APTTCA), Minutes of 1st Meeting (Islamabad. Feb. 11–12, 2011), 3.

[109] For example, although, at the 2nd meeting of the APTTCA, the delegations again discussed the transit security and reached an agreement, they did not implement their decision. At the 2nd meeting, Pakistan agreed that instead of a transit security equivalent to full customs duties, it would accept from Afghanistan a transit security equivalent to 25% of customs duties. For transit goods security, both the countries agreed to accept insurance guarantee for the import duty value of transit goods and traders could submit to customs offices an insurance guarantee issued by any reputable insurance company. APTTCA, Minutes of 2nd Meeting (Kabul. May. 31–June 01, 2011), 3.

[110] See APTTCA, Minutes of 4th Meeting (Kabul. Oct 8–9, 2013), 4; APTTCA, Minutes of 5th Meeting (Islamabad. Jan. 10, 2014), 4; see also Pakistan Customs news Portal, Transit Cargos to Move through Registered Carriers Only (Feb. 7, 2017), https://customnews.pk/2017/02/07/transit-cargo-to-move-through-registered-carriers-only/.

[111] See generally APTTCA, Minutes of the 4th and the 5th Meetings (note 110).

[112] For APTTCA's minutes of meetings see PAJCCI, http://www.pajcci.com/Regulations.aspx.

decision-making in APTTCA. It is claimed that Pakistan does not usually send high officials and Afghanistan, instead of officials from relevant branches of the MoIC who are at internal level responsible for APTTA implementation, send officials from other ministries, i.e., Ministry of Finance, to APTTCA meeting.[113] All these factors accompanied by political tensions between the two countries have paralyzed the activities of APTTCA.

Another institution APTTA introduces, in a limited provision, is the Afghan-Pak JEC. APTTA provides that APTTCA should report its activities and decisions to the JEC and does not provide further provisions for the Commission's activity mechanism and decisions regarding APTTCA's activities reports. The question arises whether APTTCA could request the Commission for a final decision when lack of a consensus blocks its own decisions—particularly in the event of a critical transit issue that creates a serious threat to bilateral trade and thus needs to be resolved immediately.

4.2.2.1.10   Dispute Settlement Mechanism

With few gaps, APTTA provides a moderate dispute settlement mechanism. It provides cooperation, consultations and arbitration as means of dispute settlement.[114] As a primary step, APTTA requires that disputes including concerns and complaints about contraband should be resolved through cooperation in APTTCA. APTTA does not define cooperation but it is a non-binding administrative resolution mechanism offered by APTTCA. If APTTCA fails to resolve the dispute through cooperation, contracting parties can request consultations with one another.[115] If the consultations fail to resolve the dispute or a contracting party who has received a request for consultation fails to respond to the request within the due period, the other party can request establishing an arbitral tribunal to resolve the dispute.[116] APTTA establishes an arbitral tribunal with three arbitrators, two arbitrators from nationals of each contracting party and a third arbitrator from a third neutral State. The third arbitrator, who would be selected mutually by the contracting parties, chairs the tribunal proceedings. He/She should not have been or currently be resident in any of the contracting parties and should not have been involved in the issue under dispute at any stage prior to the arbitration.[117]

While APTTA obliges the arbitral tribunal to apply provisions of APTTA to the dispute before it, it requires the tribunal to resolve the dispute in accordance with the

---

[113]In-person Interview with Akhlaqi (Ch.1, note 29). Interview with Omid Ghafori, Director, International Department, ACCI (Kabul, Apr. 18, 2018).

[114]Arts. 39–48 APTTA.

[115]Ibid., Art.41.

[116]Ibid., Art.42.

[117]Ibid., Art.43.

WTO dispute settlement mechanism.[118] APTTA also provides that the tribunal should apply customary rules of interpretation of public international law when interpreting APTTA provisions.[119] The arbitral tribunal adopts its award by two-third of votes within 30 days from the date it has been established. The award is final and not subject to appeal.[120] APTTA allows the contracting parties to withdraw jointly their disputes at every stage of an ongoing arbitration but prior to issuing of an award.[121]

Compliance with WTO dispute settlement procedures and customary rules of interpretation of public international law gives a moderate feature to APTTA DSM and establishes a clear relationship between APTTA and these regimes when a dispute arises. However, APTTA DSM has few gaps. For instance, the provision on consultations does not provide which authorities from the contracting parties should hold the consultations and who will implement results of the consultation? What would be the difference in terms, procedures and decisions between the dispute settlement through cooperation and bilateral consultations? Similarly, APTTA does not provide for dispute settlement enforcement measures and therefore it remains unclear what should be done when a contracting party that is subject to implementation of a dispute settlement decision does not follow the decision.

In conclusion, the substantive analysis of APTTA provisions suggests that although the Agreement reflects few features of a moderate international transit regime, it has a number of strict ambiguous provisions that have challenged the implementation of the Agreement and affected negatively free and facilitated movement of goods between the two countries. The strict and ambiguous provisions include, *inter alia*, the transit ban on Indian exports to Afghanistan, different transit security means for transit goods and vehicles, broad yet unclear general and security exceptions and lack of enforcement measures for dispute settlement decisions. Notwithstanding, given the long and undeniable trade relationship between Afghanistan and Pakistan on one hand, and their strategic location to connect one another to their neighboring countries markets on the other hand, maintaining APTTA as a legal regime to govern the transit trade relationship between the two countries is a must. Pakistan is the easiest, shortest and least costly route for Afghan exports to find their market in India and subsequently in South Asia. Similarly, Pakistan does not have direct and easy access to Central Asian countries, which makes its trade with these countries time consuming and costly for which Afghanistan plays a key role to provide the easiest, shortest and least costly route. Therefore, the two countries need to maintain APTTA, bring their APTTA implementation concerns to the cooperation table and suggest necessary cooperation mechanism for the implementation of the Agreement and suggest amendments to the Agreement where necessary.

---

[118]Ibid., Art.45.

[119]Ibid., Art.39(3).

[120]Ibid., Art.43.

[121]Ibid., Art. 46(2).

4.2.2.2 Comparative Study of the Chabahar Agreement

Afghanistan, Iran and India signed and ratified the Chabahar Transit and Transport Agreement (hereinafter the Chabahar Agreement) in 2016 to allow trade between Afghanistan and India by transit through the Iranian seaport of Chabahar.[122] The Chabahar Agreement was concluded for ten years and is subject to automatic extension after this period unless one of the contracting parties denounce the extension. The Agreement would be ineffective to the denouncing party after 6 months from the receipt of the denunciation note.[123] The Agreement is open to accession for other countries.[124] The Chabahar Agreement is claimed to serve as an alternative to APPTA. Its conclusion has raised economic and legal debates as to whether and how far the Agreement can provide better opportunities for Afghanistan compared with APTTA. A comparative assessment of provisions of the Chabahar Agreement would answer this question.

4.2.2.2.1   Coverage Scope, Freedom of Transit, Duties and Charges, Transit Security, Customs Formalities and Visa Facilities

Unlike APTTA, the Chabahar Agreement covers transit of both goods and persons through the seaport of Chabahar but does not provide that such transit would enjoy full freedom.[125] The term freedom of transit has not been used in the entire Agreement. Similarly, unlike APTTA that abolishes all transit duties and charges except charges levied on services rendered, the Chabahar Agreement does not remove transit duties and charges and rather provides in best endeavor language for their reduction. Article 8(2) Chabahar Agreement provides that "the contracting parties shall seek to reduce government taxes, excise duties and other duties charges emanating from the services on goods on transit."

Unlike APTTA, and except for a best endeavor limited provision on harmonization and simplification of customs procedures,[126] the Chabahar Agreement does not provide sufficient provisions on customs procedures and other formalities. As for visas, it contains only an abstract provision, which provides that "contracting parties shall facilitate issuing visas"[127] and does not provide for type and period of visa. Similarly, the Chabahar Agreement lacks provisions on transit security and transport insurance.

---

[122]Prmb Chabahar Agreement.

[123]Ibid., Art. 15.

[124]Ibid., Art. 12.

[125]Ibid., Arts. 1(o), 2, 5(1), 3(1).

[126]Article 8(1) of the Chabahar Agreement provides that "contracting parties shall take steps to standardize, simplify and harmonize customs rules and procedures governing movement of goods and passengers along international transit and transport corridors."

[127]Ibid., Art. 5(2).

4.2.2.2.2 Transparency and Recognition of Other International Conventions

The Chabahar Agreement does not contain provisions on transparency. As for relationship with other international conventions and agreements, the Chabahar Agreement, the same as APTTA, provides for the non-effect of its provisions on rights and obligations of the contracting parties under their international conventions and agreements.[128] It further provides that in the event of a conflict between provisions of the Chabahar Agreement and other international conventions and agreements, the contracting parties would discuss a resolution of the conflict in the Coordination Council established under the Agreement.[129] The provision on conflict resolution is, however, ambiguous in the sense that it leaves the issue to be decided by the Council without providing a mechanism for conflict resolution i.e., whether the Council should resolve the conflict in accordance with the VCLT rules on treaty conflict resolution.

4.2.2.2.3 Institutional Arrangements

The Chabahar Agreement establishes the Coordination Council, Follow-up Committee and the Secretariat as the institutions responsible for the implementation of the Chabahar Agreement. The Coordination Council is the highest decision-making authority responsible to implement and monitor implementation of the Agreement, endorse proposals and amendment requests from the other two institutions and resolve disputes arising out of the Agreement.[130] The Council consists of deputy ministers or their legal representatives from the Ministry of Transport and Civil Aviation of Afghanistan, the Ministry of Road and Urban Development of Iran and the Ministry of Foreign Affairs of India. The Council holds ordinary meetings at least every year and adopts its decisions by consensus of votes, which could be criticized for the same reasons as the APTTCA decision-making mechanism under APTTA.[131]

Similarly, the Follow-up Committee is responsible to facilitate implementation of the Agreement and undertake procedural and administrative actions. It particularly undertakes tasks such as study of peculiar issues related to customs duties and charges, examining and determining transit routes, proposing necessary administrative protocols for implementing provisions of the Agreement and providing periodical progress reports to the Coordination Council on the implementation of the Agreement.[132] The Committee consists of officials from the relevant ministries at the minimum level of General Directorate or equivalent to it. The Committee holds

---

[128]Ibid., Art. 2(3).

[129]Ibid., Art. 2(3).

[130]Ibid., Art. 9.

[131]Ibid., Arts. 9(1), (3), (4).

[132]Ibid., Art. 10.

its ordinary meetings every year one month ahead of the Coordination Council annual meeting.[133]

Unlike APTTA, the Chabahar Agreement does not recognize participation of the private sector in its institutions. It does also not provide for commercial presence in the territories of the contracting parties to facilitate coordination and communication among traders and other interested groups. These are among the areas that make the Chabahar Agreement less liberal and less supportive of free trade.

4.2.2.2.4 Dispute Settlement Mechanism

The Chabahar Agreement introduces negotiation, administrative resolution and arbitration as its DSM.[134] Negotiation is the first step in resolving disputes under the Chabahar Agreement and is similar to consultation under APTTA. When negotiation fails to resolve a given dispute, the contracting parties can request the Coordination Council for administrative resolution. When the Cooperation Council fails to resolve the dispute within a year, the contracting parties can establish an arbitral tribunal to resolve the dispute. Unlike APTTA, the Chabahar Agreement is silent on whether it recognizes rules and procedures of other international DSMs such as those of the WTO. Similarly, while it provides that in the event of a conflict between provisions of the Chabahar Agreement and other international conventions and agreements the Coordination Council would discuss the normative conflict resolution, it does not provide any mechanism for the discussion of the normative conflict and does also not have recourse to use of the customary rules of interpretation of public international law, which is a common treaty conflict resolution mechanism broadly used by States.

To conclude, a comparative study of provisions of APTTA and the Chabahar Agreement suggests that the legal benefits of the two agreements cannot be weighed equally. Each Agreement presents different legal benefits and none of them would serve as a better alternative to another. Particularly, the Chabahar Agreement does not serve as a viable alternative to APTTA but, instead, could only serve as an additional regional transit regime to Afghanistan's transit with India and other South Asian countries. The Chabahar Agreement, however, is and would remain the only alternative for the transit of Indian exports to Afghanistan, if Afghanistan and Pakistan would not come to a solution over transit of Indian exports to Afghanistan through the territory of Pakistan.

---

[133]Ibid.
[134]Ibid., Art. 11.

4.3 Conclusion

Afghanistan' transit regime combines national, regional and multilateral rules and regulations. It particularly recognizes and applies the TIR customs transit procedures and the WTO rules on freedom of transit. In addition, Afghanistan has concluded a number of plurilateral and bilateral transit agreements for further facilitation of its transit relationship with neighboring countries. The recent concluded transit and transport agreement, the Lapis Lazuli Route Agreement is among the strategic plurilateral transit agreements that paves a transit path for Afghan products to reach European markets. Similarly, the Chabahar Agreement is another strategic transit and transport agreement that Afghanistan concluded in recent years to seek alternative transit routes to India and other South Asian countries and compensate for transit challenges the country face under APTTA.

Although the Chabahar Agreement has helped Afghanistan to reduce its dependence on Pakistan to access the sea, the Agreement presents substantial gaps and is not recommendable to serve as an alternative to replace APTTA. For instance, it does not provide explicit provisions on important issues including freedom of transit, transparency and MFN and NT principles, does not remove transit duties and charges, and instead only encourages the contracting parties to reduce them. Moreover, from infrastructural and political perspectives, the Chabahar port, which is the only seaport under the Chabahar Agreement, faces uncertainty as it is still in a pilot stage with the need to the development of infrastructural facilities. Likewise, the restart of the US economic sanctions against Iran has affected Iran's trade with the rest of the world including investments in the infrastructural projects of the Chabahar port. Although US president Donald Trump issued a waiver to infrastructural investment projects by India in the Chabahar port,[135] given the deadlock in negotiations between Iran and the US and the rapid downfall of Iran's economic situation, it is difficult to rely on the duration of the waiver and ultimately on the viable and facilitated operation of the port. Some perhaps still suggest that due to the tense political relations between Afghanistan and Pakistan and between Pakistan and India the Chabahar Agreement is an alternative to APTTA, but the volatilities in political changes for the implementation of the Chabahar Agreement should also not be underestimated. This would affect the Agreement as a viable alternative.

The Chabahar Agreement, however, would remain the only alternative for the transit of Indian exports to Afghanistan, if Afghanistan and Pakistan would not come to a solution over transit of Indian exports to Afghanistan through the territory of Pakistan.

---

[135]Radio Free Europe, U.S. Exempts Iran's Chabahar Port from Sanctions in Nod to Afghanistan (Nov.7, 2018), https://www.rferl.org/a/us-exempts-iran-chabahar-port-project-from-sanction-in-nod-toafghanistan-india/29586874.html; see also *Harsh V. Pant*, The Chabahar Disconnect, Commentaries (Observer Research Foundation, July 19, 2019), https://www.orfonline.org/research/the-chabahar-disconnect-52964/.

References

Asadov S (2012) Tajikistan's Transit Corridors and their Potential for Developing Regional Trade. Working Paper 6. University of Central Asia, Institute of Public Policy and Administration, pp 20–21

Fair C (2008) Pakistan's relations with Central Asia: is past prologue? J Strat Stud 31(1):216

Hanif K (2018) Pakistan Afghanistan's Economic relations after 9/11. J Punjab Univ Hist Soc 31:94–97

Waqar Hussain S (2008) The impact of Afghan transit trade on NWFP's economy. Pan-Graphics Ltd., Peshawar, pp 1–8

Chapter 5
WTO Rules on Freedom of Transit

The following chapter examines the WTO rules on freedom of transit contained in Article V GATT and Article 11 TFA and discusses the legal status of landlocked members thereunder. It specifically seeks to answer whether, and if so, how the WTO rules on freedom of transit shape the transit relationship between coastal and landlocked members inside and outside of transit agreements. Section I of the chapter assesses provisions of Article V GATT on freedom of transit, Section II the provisions on freedom of transit of Article 11 TFA, Section III the SDT provisions in the TFA and other WTO agreements, Sect. 5.3 tests the relationship of Article V GATT with Article 11 TFA and other WTO relevant rules and Sect. 5.4 concludes the chapter.

5.1 Article V GATT on Freedom of Transit

Article V GATT grants MFN based but reciprocal freedom of transit to all WTO members without any distinction between coastal or landlocked, developed or developing members. However, it does not contain any provision on special transit needs of landlocked members.

5.1.1 Article V:1 GATT—Transit and Traffic in Transit

Article V:1 governs traffic, traffic in transit and means of traffic in transit. It provides:

> Goods (including baggage), and also vessels and other means of transport, shall be deemed to be in transit across the territory of a contracting party when the passage across such territory, with or without trans-shipment, warehousing, breaking bulk, or change in the mode of transport, is only a portion of a complete journey beginning and terminating beyond the

frontier of the contracting party across whose territory the traffic passes. Traffic of this nature is termed in this article "traffic in transit".

Although Article V:1 does not define what exactly transit means, it can generally be understood as an act of passage across the territory of a WTO member that is part of a traffic journey, which is beginning in or outside of the territory of that WTO member. Similarly, the WTO case law provides a dictionary definition of transit as "the action of passing across or through; passage or journey from one place or point to another".[1]

The second sentence of Article V:1 provides for means of transport in a broad sense as reflected through the term 'other means of transport'. This not only covers goods and vessels but also any other available means of transport. However, as addressed in Article V:7, Article V does not recognize aircraft as a means of transport and only recognizes the air transit of goods including baggage as traffic in transit within the meaning of Article V:1.

Article V:1 allows both direct transit of traffic and transit with transshipment. Direct transit means that transit goods are carried through the territory of the transit country with the same means of transport as the ones used in their country of departure.[2] The unloading and reloading of means of transport in the country of transit is known as transshipment.[3] Article V:1 does not define transshipment itself, but the Revised Kyoto Convention provides a legal definition of transshipment as:

> The Customs procedures under which goods are transferred under Customs control from the importing means of transport to the exporting means of transport within the area of one Customs office which is the office of both importation and exportation.[4]

Although Article V:1 allows traffic in transit to undergo a transshipment, it does so only because of necessity and not as a condition for transit of traffic through the territory of a member. In *Colombia—Indicative Prices and Restriction on Ports of Entry (Colombia—Ports of Entry)* Panama challenged Colombian legislation requiring transshipment of transit goods from Panama into other modes of transport, when transiting through Colombia, and prohibited any direct transit of Panamanian goods.[5] Panama argued that the legislation was inconsistent with Colombia's obligation under Article V:1 and that Colombia violated Panama's right to freedom of

---

[1] Panel Report, *Colombia – Indicative Prices and Restriction on Ports of Entry,* WT/DS366/R, para. 7456 (2009) [hereinafter *Colombia – Ports of Entry*]. The *Colombia – Ports of Entry* was the first case that provided a definition for some terms under Article V including transit. See also IRU, Principles Governing International Transit – Drawn up by the International Road Transport Union based on the Opinion of a Panel Appointed by the World Trade Organization, https://www.iru.org/apps/cms-filesystemaction?file=Webnews2009/Gatt-transit.pdf; for literature review see Ibarra (2010), p. 3.

[2] IRU, Principles Governing International Transit (note 1), 3.

[3] See Council of the European Union, User's Guide to Council Common Position 2008/944/CFSP (2008), 23.

[4] The Revised Kyoto Convention, 2303 U.N.T.S 148/ [2008] ATS 2 / 37 ILM 22 (1999).

[5] Panel Report, *Colombia – Ports of Entry*, para 7. 422.

transit under Article V. In its ruling the panel decided in favor of Panama and concluded that subjecting transit goods to transshipment was "in plain contravention of the definition given to the term of 'traffic in transit' under Article V:1.[6] In light of the decision in *Colombia—Ports of Entry* it should be noted that neither Article V:1 nor WTO case law provide under which conditions a transit country may subject traffic in transit across its territory to transshipment. In addition, it is not clear, if the country of origin of the transit goods can choose to transship its traffic in transit or change the mode of transport while they are transiting through the territory of another country.

However, some relevant sources such as those from International Road Transport Union (IRU) suggest that transit operators should be the ones who decide on whether or not transit goods should be transshipped and that transit countries should only be allowed to subject transit goods to transshipment or other requirements, such as transiting in breaking bulk or entering a warehousing, for special and legitimate reasons.[7] As transshipment causes delay and increases cost and time of transit (e.g., through the change of means and modes of transport, different documents may be required and additional handling costs may occur), it should be limited to those instances in which it is necessary.[8]

5.1.2   Article V:2 GATT—Freedom of Transit and MFN Treatment

Article V:2 provides:

> There shall be freedom of transit through the territory of each contracting party, via the routes most convenient for international transit, for traffic in transit to or from the territory of other contracting parties. No distinction shall be made which is based on the flag of vessels, the place of origin, departure, entry, exit or destination, or on any circumstances relating to the ownership of goods, of vessels or of other means of transport.

Article V:2 provides freedom of transit to all WTO members but does not give a conclusive definition of it. Nevertheless, Article V:2 sets out two requirements for providing freedom of transit, which are, to grant freedom of transit via routes 'most convenient for international transit' and the obligation to offer MFN treatment to traffic in transit of all WTO members without any kind of discrimination. Therefore, any national and regional legal arrangements between WTO members that their implementation precludes freedom of transit constitutes a breach of freedom of transit within the meaning of Article V:2.[9]

---

[6]Ibid., para 7. 417.

[7]See IRU, Principles Governing International Transit (note 1), 5.

[8]See ibid.

[9]See ibid., 4.

A definition of freedom of transit can be found within the WTO case law. In the case of *Colombia—Ports of Entry,* the panel started defining 'freedom' as an "unrestricted use of something" and continued that 'freedom of transit' is the "unrestricted access via the most convenient routes for the passage of goods in international transit whether or not the goods have been transshipped, warehoused, break bulked, or have changed modes of transport."[10] The panel further provided that freedom of transit is the "protection from unnecessary restrictions, such as limitations on freedom of transit, or unreasonable charges or delays (via paragraphs 2-4), and the extension of MFN treatment to Members' goods which are traffic in transit (via paragraphs 2 and 5) or have been in transit (via paragraph 6)."[11] The panel's definitions both combine different paragraphs of Article V, which suggest that all the provisions of Article V should contribute to a comprehensive understanding of the meaning of freedom of transit within the context of Article V.

5.1.2.1 Criteria for the Routes 'Most Convenient for International Transit'

Although the first sentence of Article V:2 states that freedom of transit should be granted via the routes 'most convenient for international transit', it does not specify what constitutes a transit route as 'most convenient for international transit'. However, in *Colombia—Ports of Entry* the panel stated that 'convenient' refers to the practicality of something and that 'most convenient' in connection to transit route means how practical the use of a transit route is.[12] Nevertheless, the panel did not set out any criteria for routes 'most convenient for international transit'. Some WTO members argue that the routes should be based on criteria such as the modes of transport, charges and administrative formalities applicable along a transit route, the number and quality of available routes, length, safety and cost of using transit routes.[13]

Similarly, the *Colombia—Ports of Entry* implicitly gives the choice of route. In this dispute Panama argued that Colombia's legislation, which required Panamanian transit goods to enter into Colombia only via Barranquilla seaport and Bogota airport, violated freedom of transit within the meaning of the route 'most convenient for international transit' in the first sentence of Article V:2. The Panel concluded: "Panamanian exporters' choice of port was substantially affected by imposition of the port of Barranquilla and Bogota airport (. . .)."[14] The panel's conclusion implies

---

[10]Panel Report, *Colombia – Ports of Entry,* para. 7. 400.

[11]Ibid., para. 7. 387.

[12]For more explanation see for example IRU, Principles Governing International Transit (note 1), 6.

[13]Panel Report, *Russia – Measures Concerning Traffic in Transit,* WT/DS512/R, paras. 7. 157, 7. 164–165 (April 5, 2019) [hereinafter *Russia – Traffic in Transit*].

[14]Panel Report, *Colombia – Ports of Entry,* para. 7. 604.

that transit operators have the right to choose a route and that choice of route is onus of transit operators and not the transit State.[15]

However in the same dispute, another part of the panel's analysis implied that it is possible for the exporting country as well as the transit country to decide on the choice of routes—given that they provide sufficient proof as to why they consider a route practical and most convenient for international transit. Although Colombia argued that the Barranquilla seaport and Bogota airport were the most convenient routes for Panamanian transit goods entering into Colombia, it did not prove how these ports were the most convenient in comparison to other ports available for international transit. Therefore, the panel rejected Colombia's argument. The panel further supported its ruling by stating that Panama did not provide that other routes were impractical or impossible for transit goods.[16] Ironically, when Panama argued that its first goods shipment reached Ecuador and Venezuela successfully via a road route that directs transit goods to Colombia, the panel rejected Panama's argument. Further, the panel rejected Colombia's response to Panama's proposed road route through Ecuador and Venezuela arguing that such route was 'highly unrealistic' due to business 'impracticalities'. The panel concluded: "Panama has not sufficiently demonstrated to the Panel the possibility let alone the practicality of goods arriving in Colombia via a route through Ecuador, nor has Colombia provided any evidence to demonstrate that such a route is impossible, even if it is impractical."[17] The panel's statement implies that it is possible for an exporting country and a transit country to decide on choice of route, given that they prove the practicality of the route as to most convenient for international transit. This being said, the criterion 'the routes most convenient for international transit' establishes a legitimate restriction on the freedom of transit, as a transit State is not obliged to extend freedom of transit to all of its routes.[18]

5.1.2.2 Freedom of Transit and MFN Treatment

The second sentence of Article V:2 imposes an unconditional MFN treatment obligation on a WTO member to grant freedom of transit to traffic from another member. A member cannot grant special transit treatment to traffic in transit of another member unless it extends such treatment to all other WTO members without any distinction on the basis of the flag of a vessel, the ownership of the goods or ownership of means of transport, place of origin, departure, entry, exit or destination of traffic in transit.

---

[15]IRU, Principles Governing International Transit (note 1), 5.

[16]Panel Report, *Colombia – Ports of Entry*, para. 7. 592.

[17]Ibid., para 7. 422.

[18]Ibid., para. 7. 400; see also WTO Secretariat, Article V of The GATT 1994 – Scope and Application, Note by the Secretariat, G/C/W/408, 4.

In *Colombia—Ports of Entry*, the panel held that Colombia violated the MFN principle by restricting Panama's choice of route and requiring transshipment while allowing in the same time goods from other countries to transit via multiple routes without having to undergo transshipment.[19] The panel concluded that WTO members should not discriminate between goods, which are "traffic in transit" and should provide "identical level of access and equal condition while proceeding in international transit".[20]

However, Article V:2 raises the question whether or not freedom of transit under Article V applies to all countries engaged in a transit process in a WTO member country. In other words, the question is whether a transit State, who is a WTO member, is obliged to grant freedom of transit to traffic in transit coming from a non-WTO member. The WTO case law states that the conjunctional term 'or' has multiple grammatical functions. The two most common ones are to introduce "two or more alternatives in a phrase or sentence" and to "connect two words denoting the same thing".[21] In *Russia—Traffic in Transit*, the panel held that the conjunctional term 'or' created two separate obligations meaning that "each Member is required to guarantee freedom of transit through its own territory for traffic in transit *to* the territory of any other Member, *or from* the territory of any other Member."[22] This means that there is no condition that all countries engaged in a transit process should be WTO members but rather only the transit country and the exporting country of transit goods are enough to put an obligation on the transit country to grant freedom of transit within the meaning of Article V. This claim can be further supported by the panel's conclusion in *Colombia—Ports of Entry*. The panel argued that WTO members should grant free passage to goods from any WTO member to a third country.[23] The third country can be any country including the country of ultimate destination of transit goods and cannot be subject to disclosure at the time entry or during the transit of goods through the territory of the transit country.[24]

---

[19]Panel Report, *Colombia – Ports of Entry*, paras. 7. 430–31.

[20]Ibid., para. 7. 402.

[21]Panel Report, *European Communities – Anti-Dumping Measures on Farmed Salmon from Norway*, WT/DS337/R, para. 7.165 (Nov. 16, 2007) [hereinafter *EC – Salmon (Norway)*]; see also AB Report, *United States – Definitive Safeguard Measures on Imports of Circular Welded Carbon Quality Line Pipe from Korea*, WT/DS202/AB/R, para. 164 (2002) [hereinafter *US – Line Pipe*].

[22]Panel Report, *Russia –Traffic in Transit*, para. 7. 168.

[23]Panel Report, *Colombia – Ports of Entry*, para. 7. 401.

[24]ECOSOC, *Report of the Technical Sub-Committee* (Ch. 2, note 54), 8.

5.1.3 Article V: 3–5 GATT—Prohibition of Unnecessary Delays, Restrictions, Transit Duties and Other Charges

Except for the first part of Article V:3, which regulates temporary entry of transit goods into the customs house of transit State, Article V:3–5 address transit delays, restrictions, transit duties and other charges. Article V:3–5 should be looked at in a coherent and interconnected way in terms of transit charges. Article V:3 prohibits unnecessary delays and restrictions, transit duties and other charges in connection to traffic in transit but permits specific charges entailed by transit, such as the cost of services or administrative expenses rendered. Article V:4 provides for the reasonability of those specific permissible charges and Article V:5 obliges transit States to accord MFN treatment when applying those charges.

Article V:3 provides:

> Any contracting party may require that traffic in transit through its territory be entered at the proper customs house, but, except in cases of failure to comply with applicable customs laws and regulations, such traffic coming from or going to the territory of other contracting parties shall not be subject to any unnecessary delays or restrictions and shall be exempt from customs duties and from all transit duties or other charges imposed in respect of transit, except charges for transportation or those commensurate with administrative expenses entailed by transit or with the cost of services rendered.

Article V:4 provides:

> All charges and regulations imposed by contracting parties on traffic in transit to or from the territories of other contracting parties shall be reasonable, having regard to the conditions of the traffic.

Article V:5 provides:

> With respect to all charges, regulations and formalities in connection with transit, each contracting party shall accord to traffic in transit to or from the territory of any other contracting party treatment no less favorable than the treatment accorded to traffic in transit to or from any third country.

As mentioned, the first part of Article V:3 creates an exception to unrestricted passage of traffic in transit by allowing transit State to subject them to temporary entry at its customs warehouse. However, a temporary entry into a warehouse is only allowed when the transit State finds that the traffic in transit does not comply with its national customs regulations. In that case, the transit State should have a proper customs warehouse available for the entry of traffic in transit and the entry should be temporary and should not cause unnecessary delay or restrictions. Article V:3 does not provide what renders a delay or restriction unnecessary but the term 'unnecessary', as provided by WTO case law, can be understood as the opposite of 'necessary'. For instance, within the meaning of Article XX(d) GATT, the Appellate Body (AB) endorses a panel definition that "a measure cannot be considered necessary if an alternative which a WTO member could reasonably be expected to employ and which is not inconsistent with other GATT provisions is available to it".[25] By application of this a measure is unnecessary when a WTO law inconsistent measure is adopted when another WTO consistent measure is available.

The second part of Article V:3 prohibits the imposition of any kind of customs duties and transit charges on traffic in transit but allows to render charges on transportation, administrative expenses and services in connection to traffic in transit. As provided by Article V:4, the application of these charges should be reasonable and in accordance with conditions of traffic. Otherwise, even if a measure is reasonable but does not relate to the condition of traffic, it should be considered unreasonable within the meaning of Article V:4.[26] According to WTO case law, the term 'reasonable' in connection to charges and costs means "appropriate or suitable to the circumstances or purpose that reflect flexibility and balance"[27] or "implies a degree of flexibility that involves consideration of all circumstances of a particular case".[28] As such, the term reasonable used with a measure, charge, or cost refers to the degree of flexibility of that measure, charge or cost and consideration of circumstance rising to their application.

Moreover, another ordinary meaning of the term 'reasonable' is "not extreme or excessive, moderate, fair".[29] In addition, the reasonable application of the permissible charges, as provided by Article V:5, should be based on MFN treatment. Article V:5 further extends the application of MFN treatment to all regulations and formalities affecting traffic in transit.

Although provisions under Article V:3–5 are interrelated in terms of transit charges, the drafting history of Article V GATT shows a different perception by the GATT contracting parties with regard to the scope and relevance of these paragraphs. For instance, Australia believed that the exemption of customs transit charges and duties should not imply that no duties and charges, which are applicable to domestic products on transit, should be imposed on traffic in transit of foreign contracting parties. Similarly, India argued that Article V:3 conflicted with Article V:4, because it prohibited transit charges while Article V:4 allowed transit charges to a reasonable level. Responding to India's argument, France suggested that they should consult with the text of Article 3 of the Barcelona Statute on Freedom of Transit to clarify as to whether or not reasonable charges allowed by Article V:4 were the same as those permitted or prohibited by Article V:3.[30]

---

[25]AB Report, *European Communities – Measures Affecting Asbestos and Products Containing Asbestos*, WT/DS135/AB/R, paras. 170–171(Mar. 12, 2001) [hereinafter *EC – Asbestos*].

[26]See IRU, Principles Governing International Transit (note 1), 9.

[27]Panel Report, *Mexico – Measures Affecting Telecommunications Services*, WT/DS204/R, para. 7 (Apr. 2, 2004) [hereinafter *Mexico – Telecommunications Services*].

[28]AB Report, *United States – Measures on Certain Hot-Rolled Steel Products from Japan*, WT/DS184/AB/R, para. 84 (Aug. 23, 2001) [hereinafter *US – Hot-Rolled Steel*].

[29]See IRU, Principles Governing International Transit (note 1), 9.

[30]ECOSOC, *Report of the Technical Sub-Committee* (Ch. 2, note 54), 9–10, paras. (a), (b) (c) & (d). The Barcelona Statute on Freedom of Transit served as the primary source of consultations for Article V GATT preparatory work. Article V: 3–5 provisions (e.g., permissible charges such as

Article 3 of the Barcelona Statute on Freedom of Transit obliges contracting parties to refrain from imposing any kind of customs charges for transit except for those, which solely arose by supervision and administration of transit.[31] It further provides that such charges should be equally applicable to all contracting parties and that their rate must closely answer the expenses covered. Article 3 of the Barcelona Statute states:

> Traffic in transit shall not be subject to any special dues in respect of transit (including entry and exit). Nevertheless, on such traffic in transit there may be levied dues intended solely to defray expenses of supervision and administration entailed by such transit. The rate of any such dues must correspond as nearly as possible with the expenses which they are intended to cover, and the dues must be imposed under the conditions of equality laid down in the preceding Article, except that on certain routes such dues may be reduced or even abolished on account of differences in the cost of supervision.

The sentence "...must correspond as nearly as possible with the expenses which they are intended to cover" corresponds with the term "reasonable" under Article V:4 GATT and complements the rest of the sentence "having regard to the condition of traffic in transit". The phrase "conditions of equality", which refers to MFN treatment in connection to place of origin, ownership of vessels and transit goods...*etc.* provided in the Barcelona Statute on Freedom of Transit, corresponds with MFN provision under Article V:5 GATT. Therefore, transit charges and their requirements established through the application of Article V: 4–5 GATT is limited to those charges allowed by Article V:3 (transportation, administrative or service charges).

5.1.4 Article V: 6 GATT—Treatment by Country of Destination

While Article V: 1–5 contain obligations for transit countries to fulfill in relation to traffic in transit across their own territory, Article V:6 imposes an MFN obligation on the country of destination to goods that transited through the territory of another WTO member before they entered into the country of destination.[32]

Article V:6 provides:

> Each contracting party shall accord to products which have been in transit through the territory of any other contracting party treatment no less favourable than that which would have been accorded to such products had they been transported from their place of origin to their destination without going through the territory of such other contracting party. Any contracting party shall, however, be free to maintain its requirements of direct consignment

---

transportation charges, reasonability of charges and MFN obligation) find their roots in Article 3 of the Barcelona Statute.

[31] League of Nations, Treaty Series, VII Publication of Treaties and International Engagements Registered with the Secretariat of the League of Nations, 1921–1922, 27.

[32] For more explanation see IRU, Principles Governing International Transit (note 1), 10–11.

existing on the date of this Agreement, in respect of any goods in regard to which such direct consignment is a requisite condition of eligibility for entry of the goods at preferential rates of duty or has relation to the contracting party's prescribed method of valuation for duty purposes.

Article V:6 initiated cutovers discussion, particularly as to whether the MFN obligation addressed therein only applies to the country of destination or also extends to transit States.[33] For instance, in *Colombia—Ports of Entry*, Panama argued that Colombia's ports of entry measures violated *inter alia* Article V:6, as they restricted entry of international goods, which transited through Panama, to the ports of Barranquilla and Bogota. Colombia, however, allowed entry of international goods at other ports without any restrictions such as transshipment if they did not transit through Panama.[34] Colombia refuted that Article V:6 was only applicable to traffic in transit because all the obligations set out for transit States in Article V only applied to the freedom of transit of goods across their own territories and did not extend to the country of destination.[35]

To assess whether Article V:6 poses an MFN obligation to the country of destination or transit countries, the panel first examined whether products within the meaning of "products which have been in transit" of Article V:6 referred to goods within the scope of "traffic in transit" addressed throughout Article V:1–5 provisions. The panel stated that for two reasons "products which have been in transit" under Article V:6 did not fall within the scope of "traffic in transit" under the other paragraphs of Article V. First, Article V:6 does not mention "traffic in transit" and second, the provision in the second sentence of Article V:6 on "direct consignment", "eligibility for entry", and "method of valuation for duty purpose" does not apply to "traffic in transit" but only to goods that enter an importing country and undergo customs clearance.[36] The panel further provided that "both the first and the second sentences of Article V:6 apply to a member's territory serving as the final destination of the goods, which were in international transit".[37] The panel, therefore, concluded that the country of destination has an MFN obligation to accord the same treatment to goods that passed the territory of other WTO members as it would accord to goods that were imported directly into its territory without passing the territory of any other WTO member.[38] Supporting its conclusion, the panel consulted the preparatory work of Article V GATT and cited the report of the Technical Sub-Committee regarding the content of paragraphs 2–5 and 6 of Article 10 of the Havana Charter, which closely corresponded to the paragraphs of Article V GATT.[39] The report provides:

---

[33] See for example Panel Report, *Colombia – Ports of Entry*, para. 7. 455.

[34] Ibid., para. 7. 447.

[35] Ibid., paras. 7. 450 –51.

[36] Ibid., paras. 7. 457–59.

[37] Ibid., paras. 7. 466, 7. 475.

[38] Ibid., paras. 7. 477.

[39] Ibid., paras. 7. 470.

It is understood that paragraphs 2–5 of this Article cover the treatment to be given by a member country to products in transit through its territory between any other member country and any third country, and paragraph 6 covers the treatment to be given by a member country to products cleared from customs within its territory after transit through any other member country.[40]

Therefore, a major understanding is that Article V GATT creates two sets of MFN obligations: 1. an MFN obligation on transit states to grant freedom of transit to traffic in transit through provisions under Article V:1–5 and 2. an MFN obligation on the country of destination through Article V:6.

Although Article V provisions do not seem to be complicated in the context of rights and obligations of WTO members related to the freedom of transit, ambiguity and shortcoming nonetheless exist. For instance, the definition and scope of some terms, such as "the routes most convenient for international transit", addressed in Article V remain controversial and are seen as a restriction to freedom of transit. Similarly, and most importantly from a landlocked LDC perspective, Article V GATT reveals one important shortcoming, which is the lack of an SDT recognition for special transit needs of landlocked LDCs. Unlike the Havana Charter, which at least contains an interpretive note to paragraph 6 of Article 33 recognizing an SDT for landlocked LDCs, Article V GATT does not recognize such and governs the transit relationship between members on a general reciprocal basis without any distinction. Therefore, one may conclude that while WTO law guarantees an unconditional MFN right to freedom of transit among its members, it fails to protect the special needs of its landlocked LDC members.

5.2   Article 11 of the Trade Facilitation Agreement on Freedom of Transit

The TFA entered into force in February 2017 after 12 years of negotiations, as the most recent WTO multilateral trade agreement.[41] Although the TFA does not provide a definition and scope of the term 'trade facilitation', the WTO itself defines trade facilitation as "removing obstacles to the movement of goods across borders".[42] The TFA particularly aims at simplifying customs procedures by improving legal aspects of Article V GATT on the freedom of transit, Article VIII GATT on fees and formalities connected with importation and exportation, and Article X GATT on publication and administration of trade regulations. In doing so, the TFA recognizes the particular needs of developing and LDC members and provides SDT provisions in favor of these countries in order to enable them to implement their

---

[40]ECOSOC, *Report of the Technical Sub- Committee* (Ch. 2, note 54), 11.

[41]See WTO Website, https://www.wto.org/english/news_e/spra_e/spra157_e.htm; see also EC Website, http://trade.ec.europa.eu/doclib/press/index.cfm?id=1626.

[42]See also WTO Secretariat, *Speeding up Trade* (Ch.2, note 58), 35.

TFA commitments. However, like Article V GATT, the TFA recognizes equal rights to freedom of transit to both WTO coastal and landlocked members and does not provide a specific SDT provision for the special transit needs of landlocked LDC members.

Transit provisions of the TFA are contained in Article 11, which in addition to confirming the exiting rights and obligations under Article V GATT, enhance those rights and obligations, and establish GATT plus provisions on freedom of transit. Although not reflected in the final text of Article 11, the drafting history of Article 11 shows the WTO members' discussions on improvement and clarifications of some controversial provisions of Article V GATT, such as those on the choice of route and transit restrictions. The TFA drafters believed that choice of route should be the onus of both the transit State and the exporting State, and that they should actively cooperate with the private sector and traders within the process of decision making.[43]

Nonetheless, the questions on what constitutes a route 'most convenient for international transit' and who has the right to choose a route still remain controversial under both Article V GATT and Article 11 TFA. Even if transit operators decide which route they wish to take, transit States retain the right to endorse transit on those routes, due to the principle of territorial sovereignty.[44]

Similarly, the TFA drafters discussed that WTO members were allowed to restrict freedom of transit on the basis of Article XX GATT on general exceptions and Article XXI on security exceptions but emphasized the immediate removal or change of those restrictions when circumstances that led to their adoption end, change or could be addressed in less restrictive manner.[45] Further, the TFA drafters suggested that members should notify the WTO Committee on Trade Facilitation on the duration of those restrictions and a failure to do so should allow other concerned members to inform the Committee on Trade Facilitation on the imposed

---

[43]WTO Negotiating Group on Trade Facilitation, List of Documents, Note by the Secretariat, TN/TF/W/133/Rev.2/Corr.1 (Oct. 23, 2008). The former Republic of Macedonia, Mongolia, Switzerland and Swaziland presented a proposal for a provision on regional transit agreements that, *inter alia*, govern choice of route. The proposal stated that "[m]embers shall promote bilateral and regional transit agreements or arrangements with a view to reducing trade barriers and enhance freedom of transit. Members shall take full account of international standards and instruments when designing and applying those agreements or arrangements. In particular Members that are contracting parties to regional transit agreements or arrangements shall strive to: (i) agree on common, simplified documents, or electronic messages, that shall be aligned with international standards; (ii) allow the same set of documents or electronic messages to accompany the consignment from the country of departure to destination; (iii) mutually recognize authorized trader schemes; (iv) define common measures relating to the monitoring of transit, inter alia the appointment of national transit corridors; performance indicators (e.g. target clearance times) or public private partnership to manage and monitor the arrangement; (v) include matters which are relevant beyond customs in the context of transit, such as road and transport issues." See TN/TF/W/133/Rev.3, para. 20.

[44]See for example IRU, Principles Governing International Transit (note 1), 6.

[45]WTO Negotiating Group on Trade Facilitation, TN/TF/W/143/Rev.3.

restrictions.[46] However, the TFA drafters did not tackle the question as to what the consequences would be for a country failing to notify its restrictive regulations to the Committee on Trade Facilitation. The question remained unaddressed until to date and lack of legal provisions and guidance in this matter means that there are no consequences for a country failing to notify the WTO on its restrictive measures and regulations.

Article 11 TFA contains 17 paragraphs. Some of them are identical with Article V GATT provisions and some improve the existing provisions of Article V GATT or provide new provisions. For instance, Article 11:2 TFA on transit charges is identical with Article V:3 GATT and Article 11:4 TFA on the MFN principle is identical with Article V:3 GATT. The remaining paragraphs of Article 11 TFA introduce new provisions, such as voluntary restraints, non-application of technical barriers to trade (TBT), regulations in connection to transit goods, transit guarantees (transit security), transparency and use of transit convoys or escorts along a transit journey.

5.2.1   Restrictive Regulations and Formalities

Article 11:1 TFA addresses the issue of restrictive regulations, formalities and other restrictive measures and implicitly recognizes the application of Article XX GATT in connection to the freedom of transit. Unlike Article V GATT, which does not contain a provision on whether or not transit States can adopt rules and measures restricting freedom of transit, Article 11:1 TFA allows such rules and measures. However, it stresses that they should not be "maintained if the circumstances or objectives giving rise to their adoption no longer exist or if the changed circumstances or objectives can be addressed in a reasonably less trade restrictive manner". It provides also that the measure should not be applied "in a manner that constitute a disguised restriction on traffic in transit". These requirements are similar to requirements on the adoption and application of restrictive measures necessary to protect certain exceptions listed under Article XX GATT.

5.2.2   Voluntary Restraints

Voluntary restraints are generally understood as restrictive measures on exports—addressed as voluntary exports restraints (VERs). The Organization for Economic Cooperation and Development (OECD) defines VERs as "arrangements between exporting and importing countries in which the exporting country agrees to limit the quantity of specific exports below a certain level in order to avoid imposition of

---

[46]Ibid.; for literature review see *Melgar* (Ch.1, note 2), 182–284.

mandatory restrictions by the importing country. The arrangement maybe concluded either at the industry or government level."[47] Voluntary restraints, however, could also be understood as unilateral governmental restrictions that countries apply on trading goods, including transit goods during a specific period.[48]

WTO agreements prohibit the adoption and application of voluntary restraints on trading goods, whether imports, exports or transit goods. For example, the Agreement on Safeguards prohibits the adoption and application of all kinds of voluntary restraints on exports or imports unless those specifically allowed under other provisions of the Agreement or under provisions of WTO Annex 1A agreements including GATT.[49]

The Prohibition of voluntary restraints on transit goods is addressed under Article 11:3 TFA—a new concept on freedom of transit not covered by Article V GATT. Article 11:3 provides:

> Members shall not seek, take, or maintain any voluntary restraints or any other similar measures on traffic in transit. This is without prejudice to existing and future national regulations, bilateral or multilateral arrangements related to regulating transport, consistent with WTO rules.

Voluntary restraints seem similar to regulations and formalities allowed under Article 11:1. In that case, the question arises as to whether this creates a conflict between the provisions of Articles 11:1 and 11:3 TFA. If regulations and formalities under Article 11:1 would include QRs, they would also then include voluntary restraints because voluntary restraints mainly represent themselves in the form of QRs, the application of which is explicitly prohibited by Article 11:3 on transit goods. Uncertainty in this regard is particularly driven by lack of a definition for voluntary restraints in the context of transit goods under Article 11:3 TFA and the absence of any WTO case law on this issue.

5.2.3   Non-application of TBT Measures to Transit Goods

Article 11:8 TFA prohibits application of technical regulations and conformity assessment measures within the meaning of the WTO Agreement on Technical Barriers to Trade (TBT Agreement) on transit goods. The reason is explicit. Governments apply technical regulations and conformity assessment measures on imported goods or their own goods that are destined to exportation to ensure the quality, safety and environmental aspects of those goods. This purpose does not fit

---

[47]The Organization for Economic Cooperation and Development (OECD), Glossary of Statistical Terms, https://stats.oecd.org/glossary/detail.asp?ID=2882.

[48]WTO Negotiating Group on Trade Facilitation, Clarifying and Improving GATT Article V, TN/TF/W/176 (Nov. 7, 2011); for further explanation see *Melgar* (Ch.1, note 2), 284; see also Pogoretskyy (2017), pp. 180–185.

[49]WTO Agreement on Safeguards, 1869 U.N.T.S. 154 (June 1, 1995), Art. 11.1(b).

the essence of goods in transit and therefore Article 11:8 was added in Article 11 TFA to prohibit TBT restrictions.[50]

However, Article 24:6 TFA explicitly recognizes the supremacy of provisions of the TBT Agreement over TFA provisions, which raises the question as to whether Article 24:6 conflicts with Article 11:8. Article 24:6 provides that "nothing in this Agreement shall be construed as diminishing the rights and obligations of Members under the Agreement on Technical Barriers to Trade and the Agreement on the Application of Sanitary and Phytosanitary Measures." Normative conflict could be seen in these two provisions as well as between the TBT Agreement, given that the TBT allows application of TBT measures to transit goods. The normative conflict between Article 11:8 with Article 24:6 should be resolved in accordance with general rules of treaty interpretation. The principle of *lex specialis derogats legi generali* (a specific norm prevails over the general norm) which is one of the common principles of treaty interpretation, applies to this conflict. By making the non-application of the TBT measures specific to transit goods, Article 11:8 TFA establishes *lex specialis* over Article 24:6 TFA.

Since Article 11:8 is only explicit on the non-application of TBT measures within the meaning of the TBT Agreement, the question arises whether it allows the application of technical measures and conformity assessment within the meaning of other WTO agreements, such as the SPS Agreement and the Agreement on Trade Related Aspect of Intellectual Property Rights (TRIPS), that allow members to adopt and apply technical and conformity assessment measures to goods. To assess this question, particularly regarding the application of SPS measures, the relationship between the TFA and the SPS Agreement should first be analyzed. The relationship between the two agreements becomes explicit in Article 24:6 TFA, which provides in relevant part that "nothing in this Agreement shall be construed as diminishing the rights and obligations of Members under the Agreement on the Application of Sanitary and Phytosanitary Measures." Since Article11:8 TFA does not prohibit application of SPS measure and rather is silent about it, it does not conflict with Article 24:6 TFA and ultimately with provisions of the SPS Agreement if they provide that members are allowed to extend SPS measures to transit goods.[51]

Until to date, there has been no WTO dispute concerning application of TBT and SPS measures to transit goods. Only one dispute arose, the *EU and a Member State—Seizure of Generic Drugs in Transit (EU—Generic Drugs)*, which dealt with the application of technical and conformity assessment measures for intellectual property (IP) purposes within the meaning of the TRIPS Agreement. Although the dispute does not have a direct linkage to TBT and SPS measures, it is interesting to see whether or not technical and conformity measures for other purposes such as IP protection can be applied to transit goods.

---

[50]See for example Pogoretskyy (2017), p. 183.

[51]For literature review See for example *Serra Ayral*, TBT and TFA Agreements: Leveraging Linkage to Reduce Trade Costs, WTO, Working Paper ERSD-2016-02 (June 2016), 12–13.

The *EU—Generic Drugs* case addressed India's complaint against the Netherland's transit ban on Indian generic medicines destined for Brazil and other developing countries pursuant to the EU Customs Regulation No 1383/2003 (EC Border Measures Regulations BMR). India argued the transit ban was inconsistent with the Netherland's obligations under, *inter alia*, Article V:1–2 GATT.[52] In response, the Netherlands argued that its measures were in accordance with Article 51 TRIPS Agreement, which allows members to adopt border measures such as suspension of goods when an IP right holder or customs authority suspects counterfeit trademarks or pirated copyright of goods. Moreover, the Netherlands justified, that its measures were necessary for the protection of public health. However, it did not provide a legal basis for this, e.g., Article XX(b) GATT to justify such protection.[53] Similarly, the Netherlands seemed to overlook the main goal of Article 51 TRIPS Agreement— which is the right to suspend the release of goods that are subject to import or export, for counterfeit trademarks or pirated copyright suspect, and not goods subject to international transit. Although footnote 13 to Article 51 TRIPS Agreement still gives a discretion to members to extend Article 51 provisions to goods in transit as TRIPS plus standards,[54] these plus standards are unlikely to be applicable to developing countries such as India as per Doha development agenda.[55] For the same reasons, some scholars argue against the application of IP measures to goods in transit, while trying to answer the question whether or the freedom of transit can be restricted for IP purposes.[56]

The *EU—Generic Drugs* case was resolved by means of consultation, which resulted in an interim agreement, under which the Netherlands agreed to stop detaining generic drugs from India while in transit through its territory. In return, India agreed to refrain from requesting the WTO for establishing a dispute settlement panel.[57] If the dispute had undergone a WTO judicial settlement proceeding, the Netherlands would have had the chance to argue that the measure was based on Article XX (b) GATT, which allows WTO members to adopt restrictive measure in

---

[52]WTO, *European Union and a Member State – Seizure of Generic Drugs in Transit,* WT/DS 408/1, Request for Consultations by India, WT/DS 409/1 Request for Consultations by Brazil. (May 19, 2010) [hereinafter *EU – Generic Drugs in Transit*].

[53]WTO, *EU – Generic Drugs in Transit,* WT/DS 408/ 1.

[54]Footnote 13 to Article 52 TRIPS Agreement provides that "there shall be no obligation to apply such procedures with regard to goods in transit".

[55]See *Melgar* (Ch.1, note 2), 146; see also GATT, Protocol Amending the GATT to Introduce part IV on Trade and Development, INT (65)105 (Jan. 1, 1965); WTO, Doha Work Programme: Decisions Adopted by the General Council on 1 August 2004, WT/L/579 (Aug.1, 2004).

[56]See for example *Cherise Valles,* Article V GATT, in: Rüdiger Wolfrum, *et al.,* (eds.), WTO – Trade in Goods, vol. 5 (Max Planck Commentaries on World Trade Law, 2011), 193; Ruse-Khan and Jaeger (2009), p. 507.

[57]WTO, *EU—Generic Drugs in Transit,* WT/DS 408/ 1; The Economic Times, EU Agrees to Stop Confiscation of India Generic Drugs, The Economic Times (Jul. 29, 2011), http://articles.economictimes.indiatimes.com/2011-07-29/news/29829346_1_customs-regulations-indian-generic-drugs-international-intellectualpropertyagreement; for literature review see Baker (2012), http://digitalcommons.wcl.american.edu/cgi/viewcontent.cgi?article=1026&context=research.

order to protect public health. Moreover, it could have based its argument on Article XX(d) that allows restrictive measures to secure compliance with national laws, including customs laws (in this dispute, compliance with the EU BMR), which are not themselves inconsistent with WTO rules. However, it would not have been easy for the Netherlands to prove that Indian generic drugs, which were not intended to enter the EU's market, would harm public health in the EU and thus were necessary to be prevented from transit through the EU territory. Based on strict assessment of the "necessity" requirement by WTO adjudicators in some other disputes dealing with Article XX GATT,[58] it could have been difficult, if not impossible, to Netherlands to prove the likelihood of a threat resulting from the transit of Indian generic drugs.[59]

5.2.4 Transit Securities and Escorts

Article 11:11 TFA allows a transit State to subject traffic in transit to temporarily deposit a transit guarantee, be the guarantee in monetary or non-monetary form, single or multiple transaction guarantee(s). To ensure the transparency of these guarantees, Article 11:11–14 TFA require that information on transit guarantees have to be publicly available and that transit States discharge such guarantees promptly once the transit requirements are fulfilled, i.e., when transit goods exit the transit State's territory. In addition to the transit guarantee(s), Article 11:15 TFA allows the transit State to require that customs convoys should escort the traffic in transit through its territory. Article 11:15, however, limits the application of such measures to situations where the passage of traffic is associated with high risks or that a transit guarantee does not sufficiently ensure compliance with customs laws of the transit state.

The issue of transit security has been raised in *Colombia—Ports of Entry*. Colombia stated that although the road route through Ecuador and Venezuela was highly unrealistic and impractical to use, it allowed transit of Panamanian goods via that route if the Panamanian exporters deposited a transit security, an insurance letter and further guaranteed that their goods would exit Colombian territory.[60] The panel did not discuss whether a transit State could subject traffic in transit to security and insurance under Article V GATT. The panel did not address this issue not only because the issue did not have a legal basis under Article V GATT but also because there were already enough reasons for the panel to find Colombian measures

---

[58]For example Panel Report, *Korea – Measures Affecting Imports of Fresh, Chilled and Frozen Beef*, WT/DS169/R, paras. 657–60 (July 31, 2000) [hereinafter *Korea – Frozen Beef*]; AB Report, *Korea – Frozen Beef*, WT/DS161/AB/R, paras. 161–162 (December 2000); AB Report, *EC – Asbestos*, para. 119.

[59]*Melgar* (Ch.1, note 2), 149.

[60]Panel Report, *Colombia – Ports of Entry*, para 7. 422.

inconsistent with Article V and, therefore, there was no need to examine Colombia's statement on transit security and other guarantees. With Article 11:11 TFA now serving as a legal basis for transit security, it is explicit that transit States can subject traffic in transit to a transit security.

5.2.5   Special and Differential Treatment Provisions (SDT)

5.2.5.1   General Overview

In the WTO regime, SDT is an exception to the MFN principle and to the idea of 'single undertaking' and reciprocity. WTO law embodies a substantial set of SDT provisions in favor of developing and LDC members, which provide flexibility to these countries in carrying out their WTO obligations and commitments, depending on their economic development, administrative and institutional capabilities.[61] Precisely, WTO SDT provisions cover five main areas to strengthen the trade integration of developing country members into world markets (1) flexibility in carrying out WTO obligations, (2) transitional period for implementing WTO obligations, (3) safeguarding interests of developing country members, (4) granting more favorable treatment for LDCs, and (5) offering technical assistance and capacity building support.[62]

WTO SDT provisions find their roots in GATT 1947 and their emphasized importance in the Doha development agenda.[63] GATT 1947 contracting parties adopted a Declaration on the Trade Promotion of LDCs in 1961 and subsequently established a Committee on Trade and Development (CTD) in 1964 (the Committee functions now as the WTO CTD) to address the trading needs and concerns of developing States.[64] In 1965, the contracting parties added a new part IV in GATT 1947, which contained non-reciprocal and non-legally binding provisions on trade

---

[61]WTO Agreement: Marrakesh Agreement Establishing the World Trade Organization, Apr. 15, 1994, 1867 U.N.T.S. 154, 33 I.L.M. 1144 (1994) [hereinafter WTO Agreement], Art. XI:2; Decision on Measures in Favor of Least-developed Countries, WT/COMTD/W/196, preamble (Dec. 11, 1993); for literature review see *Melgar* (Ch.1, note 1), 23 & 40.

[62]WTO Negotiating Group on Trade Facilitation, List of Documents (note 43); TN/TF/W/43/Rev.19 (June 30, 2009); TN/TF/W/165 (Dec.14, 2009).

[63]See for example GATT, Protocol Amending the GATT to Introduce part IV (note 55); WTO, Doha Work Programme (note 55); for a summary of GATT 1947 and WTO works related to trade and development see WTO, Special and Differential Treatment for Least-developed Countries, Note by the Secretariat, WT/COMTD/W/135, paras. 3–8 (Oct.5, 2004); see also GATT Analytical Index, Part IV, 1039–51; Doha Ministerial Declaration WT/MIN 01/DEC/1 (Nov. 20, 2001); for literature review see *Melgar* (Ch.1, note 2), 23–55 and 80–104; Hoekman and Kostechi (1997), pp. 230–237; *Michael Finger* & *John Wilson*, Implementing a WTO Agreement on Trade Facilitation: What Makes Sense? World Bank Policy Research Working Paper, WP/S3971 (August 2006), 7.

[64]See GATT Analytical Index, Part IV, 1040–1047.

and development and was later incorporated into GATT 1994.[65] Similarly, continuous efforts for more SDT provisions resulted in the 1979 GATT Decision on "Differential and More Favorable Treatment – Reciprocity and Fuller Participation of Developing Countries" known as the "Enabling Clause".[66] The Enabling Clause constitutes an integral part of GATT 1994. It covers a variety of areas, from tariff and non-tariff concessions to transitional periods for implementing WTO commitments, capacity building trainings and technical assistance for LDCs.[67]

The Enabling Clause tariff concessions are unilateral non-reciprocal treatment under which developed members have agreed to reduce or eliminate import tariffs on products originating from developing members. Grantor countries decide on scope and time limit of those tariff concessions. The Generalized System of Preferences (GSP) reflects a common type of these preferential tariff concessions under the Enabling Clause.[68] Currently, Australia, Canada, the EU, Japan, Korea, New Zealand, Switzerland and the USA have their individual GSP programs for developing members. Each country's GSP program varies in tariff schemes and time schedules.[69] In addition to the Enabling Clause, many other WTO agreements contain SDT provisions. For example, Article 24 DSU requires the WTO DSB to pay special attention to an LDC member involved in a dispute settlement process.

An important question concerning the application of WTO SDT provisions is, whether or not the provisions are mandatory and non-discriminatory in their application to all developing members. Mandatory provisions are those, which contain 'shall plus verb' language while non-mandatory provisions or 'best endeavor' provisions contain language such as 'may', 'as appropriate', 'to the extent possible', 'shall endeavor', or 'should'.[70] While the general perception is that WTO SDT provisions are not legally binding and are considered 'best endeavor clauses',[71] the WTO CTD provides a list differentiating SDT provisions between mandatory and non-mandatory ones, based on the language used in the provisions,. The list contains:

---

[65]See *Kostechi* (note 63) 236; *Melgar* (Ch.1, note 2), 32–33.

[66]GATT, Differential and More Favorable Treatment – Reciprocity and Fuller Participation of Developing Countries, Decision of 28 November 1979, L/4903 (Nov. 28, 1979) [hereinafter The Enabling Clause].

[67]Ibid.; WTO Secretariat, Special and Differential Treatment for Least-developed Countries (note 61); see also *Melgar* (Ch.1, note 2), 35–48.

[68]See generally The Enabling Clause (note 66).

[69]See for example EU GSP, http://ec.europa.eu/trade/policy/countries-and-regions/development/generalised-schemeofpreferences/; for a summary of GSP programs of these countries see Sekkel (2009).

[70]See for example Cook (2015), pp. 326–329; Hamanaka (2014), p. 344.

[71]Hoekman and Kostechi (2001), pp. 390–394.

   (i) Provisions aimed at increasing the trade opportunities of developing country members;

  (ii) Provisions under which WTO members should safeguard the interest of developing country members;

 (iii) Provision on flexibility of commitments, of actions, and use of policy instruments;

 (iv) Provisions on transitional periods;

  (v) Provisions on technical assistance; and

 (vi) Provisions relating to LDCs.[72]

Provisions under categories (i), (ii), (v) and some provisions under category (vi) are both mandatory and non-mandatory provisions, while provisions under categories (iii), (iv) and some provisions under category (vi) are only non-mandatory.[73] An example of a mandatory provision under category (i), which is not applicable anymore, was contained in Article 2.18 of the Agreement on Textile and Clothing.[74] An example of a non-mandatory SDT provision from the same category is contained in paragraph 2(a) of the Enabling Clause. It states that developed country members *may* accord preferential tariff treatment to products originating in developing countries under preference scheme such as the GSP. Similarly, some mandatory SDT provisions from category (ii) are set out in Article 10.1 SPS Agreement [75] and in Article 12. 1–4 and Article 12.8–10 TBT Agreement.[76] An example of a non-mandatory SDT provision under the same category is set out in Article 12.4 TBT Agreement. It provides that WTO members "recognize" that developing countries "should" not be expected to use international standards, which are not commensurate to their level of development, financial and trade needs, as basis for their national technical regulations and standards.

Moreover, SDT provisions on safeguarding the interests of developing countries, such as those of the Anti-dumping Agreement and Safeguards Agreement are

---

[72]See WTO Secretariat, Special and Differential Treatment for Least-developed Countries (note 63), para. 1; see generally WTO, Implementation of Special and Differential Treatment Provisions in WTO Agreements and Decisions: Mandatory and Non-Mandatory Special and Differential Treatment Provisions, WT/COMTD/W/77/REV.1/Add.1 (Dec. 21, 2001); see also *Melgar* (Ch.1, note 2), 42; for more examples on each of these provisions see https://www.wto.org/english/tratop_e/devel_e/teccop_e/s_and_d_eg_e.htm.

[73]WTO, Implementation of Special and Differential Treatment Provisions in WTO Agreements and Decisions (note 72).

[74]Article 2.18 of the Agreement on Textile and Clothing provides that "a member imposing restrictions on imports *shall* provide meaningful improvement on market access of imports from developing countries and that the import restrictions on imports from developing country members *shall* account only for 1.3% or less of the total restrictions imposed by the importing country on imports." WTO Agreement on Textile and Clothing, 1868 U.N.T.S. 14 (June 1, 1995), Art. 2.18.

[75]Article 10 (1) SPS Agreement provides that WTO members "shall" take into account the special needs of developing countries, particularly the LDCs, as they adopt and apply SPS measures.

[76]Articles 11 and 12 TBT Agreement provide that WTO members "shall" provide SDT treatment to developing countries while applying TBT measures and "shall" provide technical assistance to these countries to enable them carry out their TBT obligations and commitments.

mandatory in nature. For example, Article 9.1 Safeguards Agreement embodies a legally binding SDT provision, which provides that "[s]afeguard measures shall not be applied against a product originating in a developing country Member as long as its share of imports of the product concerned in the importing Member does not exceed three percent..." Similarly, the SDT provision of Article 15 of the Anti-dumping Agreement is a mandatory provision and provides that "[p]ossibilities of constructive remedies provided for by this Agreement *shall be explored* before applying anti-dumping duties where they would affect the essential interests of developing country Members." In comparison, SDT provisions related to support and technical assistance are 'best-endeavor' or non-mandatory in their nature.[77]

WTO case law answers the questions surrounding the mandatory and non-mandatory nature of some WTO SDT provisions. For instance, in *United States—Definitive Safeguard Measures on Imports of Circular Welded Carbon Quality Line Pipe from Korea* (*US—Line Pipe*), which dealt with the US safeguard measures on exports from Korea, the AB held that the SDT provision under Article 9.1 Safeguards Agreement was legally binding. Further, the US safeguard measures violated this provision by restricting Korean exports, which did not exceed 3% of Korea's total exports to the US, and therefore were subject to exemption from the application of safeguards measures pursuant to Article 9.1 Safeguards Agreement.[78]

Similarly, in *EC—Conditions for the Granting of Tariff Preferences to Developing Countries* (*EC—Tariff Preferences*), the panel implicitly addressed the mandatory nature of some parts of the Enabling Clause as it dealt with the question surrounding non-discriminatory application of tariff preferences under the Enabling Clause. The dispute, brought by India, challenged the EU's drug arrangement measures taken pursuant to an EC Regulation of 2001 on implementation of the GSP scheme. The 2001 Regulation provided for special tariff preferences to a limited number of developing countries with whom the EU had special arrangements for combating drug production and drug trafficking (known as drug arrangement).[79] India argued that the drug arrangement measure was discriminatory, as it limited the EU tariff preferences to a specific group of developing countries. Therefore, India alleged that the EU violated its MFN obligation under Article I:1 GATT in relation to benefits accruing to India under paragraphs 2(a) and 3(a) of the Enabling Clause.[80] India argued that the term 'non-discriminatory' in footnote 3 to paragraph 2(a) of the Enabling Clause referred to the 1971 UNCTAD Agreement on the establishment of a system providing for "generalized, non-reciprocal and non-discriminatory preferences beneficial to the developing countries".[81]

---

[77] See for example Arts. 1, 13, 21 TFA; for literature review see for example Eliason (2015), p. 645.

[78] AB Report, *US – Line Pipe*, paras. 133, 263.

[79] For a comprehensive analysis of the Enabling Clause, see AB Report, *European Communities – Conditions for the Granting of Tariff Preference to Developing Countries*, WT/DS246/AB/R, paras. 106–141(April 7, 2004) [hereinafter *EC – Tariff Preferences*].

[80] WTO, *EC – Tariff Preferences*, WT/DS246/1, G/L/521, Consultation by India (Mar. 12, 2002).

[81] Ibid.

Both the panel and the AB found that by favoring a specific group of developing countries the EU violated its MFN obligation under Article I:1 GATT.[82] However, each of them provided different reasons as to the extent the measures constituted a non-discriminatory treatment. The panel held that, although the term 'non-discriminatory' addressed in footnote 3 to paragraph 2(a) of the Enabling Clause suggests that "identical tariff preference should be granted to all developing countries without differentiation", different tariff preferences are justified if made "for the implementation of a priori limitations".[83] The panel therefore rejected India's claim and concluded that as long as the higher or lesser preference granted to a developing country was commensurate with its development needs, the non-discriminatory nature of such a preference was not undermined.[84] Its conclusion was based on paragraph 3(c) of the Enabling Clause, which allows different degrees of tariff preferences to different developing countries given that they are taken to respond positively to a specific development need of that specific beneficiary developing country.[85]

The AB confirmed in its reasoning that footnote 3 to paragraph 2(a) of the Enabling Clause allows different tariff preferences, but added that such different tariff preferences should be based on an objective criterion to respond positively to specific economic or financial development needs of developing country (ies).[86] According to the AB, the EU had failed to demonstrate that its drug arrangement measure was based on an objective criterion, which if met by other developing countries could be extended to them. Therefore, the AB concluded that the measure was inconsistent with paragraph 2(a) of the Enabling Clause and ultimately with Article I:1 GATT.[87]

Since WTO case law suggests that different level of SDT treatments can be granted to developing countries based on their economic or financial development needs, the question arises, what characteristics the WTO takes into account when measuring the economic and financial needs of a developing country. WTO law does not provide an exact definition and scope of what constitutes a "developing country" and leaves the question open as a matter of "self-declaration".[88] This provides a broad opportunity to those members that are in rapid graduation from the developing status. Although the AB held that the term 'developing country' does not mean *all* developing countries and that GSP countries are allowed to grant different tariff preferences to different sub-categories of GSP beneficiaries,[89] it remains silent on

---

[82]AB Report, *EC – Tariff Preferences*, paras. 80, 81, 90.

[83]Panel Report, *EC – Tariff Preferences*, paras. 7. 161.

[84]Ibid., paras. 7. 64–65.

[85]Ibid., para. 7. 65.

[86]AB Report, *EC – Tariff Preferences*, para. 173.

[87]Ibid., paras. 188–189.

[88]WTO, Who Are Developing Countries in the WTO? https://www.wto.org/english/tratop_e/devel_e/d1who_e.htm.

[89]AB Report, *EC – Tariff Preferences*, para. 175.

what criteria developing countries could be categorized to different sub-categories of GSP beneficiaries.

Notwithstanding, most WTO SDT provisions are 'best-endeavor' commitments and a developing member cannot invoke them to force a developed member to carry out those commitments. Particularly, provisions on technical assistance to LDCs are non-mandatory and an LDC member cannot enforce a developed member to comply. Moreover, it is particularly hard for a landlocked LDC to invoke even a mandatory SDT provision, as none of the WTO SDT provisions, mandatory or non-mandatory, specifically address the special transit needs of landlocked LDCs. This being said, one can conclude that landlocked LDCs gain nothing or very little if they invoke an SDT provision in support of a special transit treatment.

5.2.5.2   SDT Provisions in TFA

Almost one-third of the TFA contains SDT provisions, which are mostly of mandatory nature.[90] The TFA reflects a detailed sub-categorization of developing countries based on the ability of these countries to implement TFA provisions. The Agreement emphasizes the need to assess a developing country member's individual capacity (self-assessment) to implement TFA provisions.[91] Based on the assessment the countries are categorized into three categories A, B and C.[92] The TFA grants different implementation periods to commitments in each category and provides developing country members with the right to suggest a time-period to implement their TFA commitments.[93] For example, under category A, the developing country commits to implement its TFA obligations upon the entry into force of the TFA for it, under category B, after a transitional period following the entry into force of the TFA for it and under category C, after a transitional period has passed and then only after it has received technical assistance and capacity building support.

The TFA category system grants a developing country member the chance to draw back from its TFA obligations for a specific period while it expects other members to fulfil their TFA obligations toward that developing member.[94] The TFA also provides additional flexibilities to developing country members by recognizing their right to (1) extension of the transitional period for implementing obligations under category B and C, (2) offering expert groups to assess the need for an extension of the transitional period for the implementation of a TFA obligation, (3) shifting transitional periods under categories B and C, and (4) benefiting from a

---

[90]Article 24:2 TFA provides that "all provisions of this Agreement are binding on all Members".

[91]Ibid., Art. 13.

[92]Ibid., Arts. 14–19.

[93]WTO, *Ministerial Declaration of 18 December 2005*, WT/MIN/05/DEC, Annex E, para. 5 (Dec. 18, 2005) [hereinafter Hong Kong Declaration].

[94]For literature review see *Nora Neofeld*, Implementing the Trade Facilitation Agreement: From Vision to Reality, Working Paper ERSD-2016-14 (WTO, September 2016).

grace period, which means that a developing country member will not be challenged before the WTO dispute settlement system for implementing its TFA obligations during a specific period starting from the date when the member begins to implement its TFA obligations.[95]

The CTD reviews, at least annually, implementation and capacity building progress of developing country members under each TFA category to evaluate their readiness to implement their TFA obligations and commitments.[96] The category system and the need to review implementation capacity of developing country members is an indication that different level of SDT provisions could be applicable to developing members based on their economic development needs.

5.3 Article V GATT Relationship with Article 11 TFA and Other WTO Provisions

The following section explores Article V GATT relationship with Article 11 TFA and other relevant WTO provisions. To this end, the relationship will be looked at from two angles: (1) the relationship between conflicting or overlapping agreements dealing with the same subject matter and (2) the relationship between agreements dealing with the same subject matter, but that are providing different provisions without necessarily conflicting with each other.

5.3.1 WTO Provisions When in Conflict with Each Other

In international law, normative conflict arises (whether between provisions of one or more treaties) when two or more legal norms impose contradictory obligations; thereby making a simultaneous compliance with all impossible.[97] A normative conflict occurs between two treaties with contradictory obligations, when the treaties in question have the same parties and deal with the same substantive subject matter.[98] This is a narrow definition of a normative conflict, limited to a conflict between obligations.[99] However, in broad sense, normative conflict can also arise between an obligation and an explicit conferred right, be it in one or different treaties.[100] Both the narrow and broad definitions of 'normative conflict' are found within WTO case law. A narrow definition of 'normative conflict' within WTO case

---

[95] A grace period for a developing country is 2 years and 8 years for an LDC.

[96] Sec II, paras. 5, 7 TFA.

[97] Bindschedler and Bernhardt (1984), p. 468; see also Wilfred (1953), p. 427.

[98] Bindschedler and Bernhardt (1984), p. 468.

[99] Wilfred (1953), p. 426; Marceau (2001), p. 1084.

[100] See for example Pauwelyn (2003), pp. 168–69; Vranes (2006), p. 395.

law means a "clashes between obligations" and its broad definition is understood as "a situation where a rule in one agreement prohibits what a rule in another agreement explicitly permits".[101] Given the nature of the WTO as a balanced system of obligations and rights, which mandates its dispute settlement bodies to "preserve the rights and obligations of Members under the covered agreements"[102] a broader definition of 'normative conflict' seems appropriate, as it allows WTO adjudicators to make a reasonable choice between an obligation and an explicit conferred right.[103]

To resolve the normative conflict between different provisions of an agreement or between overlapping agreements, treaty interpreters and dispute settlement bodies give recourse to the general rules of treaty conflict resolution contained in the Vienna Convention on the Law of Treaties (VCLT). For overlapping treaties dealing with the same subject matter, Article 30 VCLT on "Application of Successive Treaties Relating to the Same Subject-Matter" and a few general principles of international law, including the principle of *lex specialis* are applicable.

For example, Article 30(2) VCLT applies to a normative conflict when treaties of the same subject matter contain a priority clause under which one treaty recognizes the priority or supremacy of the other in the event of a conflict. It provides that "when a treaty specifies that it is subject to, or that it is not to be considered as incompatible with, an earlier or latter treaty, the provisions of that other treaty prevail." Similarly, in the absence of a priority clause applicable to a normative conflict between treaties, Article 30(3) VCLT applies which provides that provisions of the earlier treaty will only apply to the extent they are compatible with provisions of the latter treaty. Thereby it establishes a *lex posterior* (latter treaty prevails over earlier treaty) for the latter treaty.[104] However, the *lex posterior* principle does not apply to overlapping treaties that entered into force at the same time or to treaties such as the WTO agreements that contain special legal and constitutional characteristics and do not establish a hierarchy between each other regardless of when an agreement entered

---

[101]Panel Report, *European Communities – Regime for the Importation, Sale and Distribution of Bananas, WT.DS27/R*, para. 7. 159 (May 22, 1997) [hereinafter *EC – Bananas III*]; International Law Commission provides a broad definition of normative conflict as "a situation where two rules or principles suggest different ways of dealing with a problem." International Law Commission (ILC), Fragmentation of International Law: Difficulties Arising from the Diversification and Expansion of International Law, Report of the Study Group of the International Law Commission, A/CN.4/L.682 (Apr. 13, 2006), para. 25.

[102]Dispute Settlement Rules: Understanding on Rules and Procedures Governing the Settlement of Disputes, Marrakesh Agreement Establishing the World Trade Organization, Annex 2, 1869 U.N.T.S. 401, 33 I.L.M. 1226, art 3.2 (1994). Accordingly, Article 19.2 DSU provides that ". . . the panel and Appellate body cannot add or diminish the rights and obligations provided in the covered agreements."

[103]In *India – Patents*, the AB reiterated the importance of broad context of normative conflict by stating that "the legitimate expectations of the parties to a treaty are related it the language of the treaty itself." See AB Report, *India – Patent Protection for Pharmaceutical and Agricultural Chemical Products*, WT/DS 50/AB/R, para. 45 (Dec. 17, 1997) [hereinafter *India – Patents*]; see also Pauwelyn (2003), p. 175.

[104]Marceau (2001), p. 1090.

into force.[105] Treaty interpreters or adjudicators, including WTO adjudicators usually refer to the *lex specialis* principle as a useful tool of interpretation to solve a normative conflict in these kind of treaties.[106] The International Law Commission (ILC) defines the *lex specialis* principle as "a generally accepted technique of interpretation and conflict resolution in international law which suggests that whenever two or more norms deal with the same subject matter, priority should be given to the norm that is more specific".[107] One should note, however, that the *lex specialis* principle applies only when there is a conflict between provisions of treaties and does not apply to situations where one treaty is more specific than the other, but where there is no conflict between the provisions.[108]

In WTO law, only a few limited priority clauses exist.[109] One of these priority clauses is embodied in Article XIV:3 WTO Agreement. It establishes supremacy of the WTO Agreement over the agreements covered in the annexes in the event of a conflict.[110] As for the relationship between covered agreements, except for a priority clause listed in Annex 1A to the WTO Agreement, WTO law does not establish an explicit relationship between other WTO covered agreements.[111] According to the Interpretative Note to Annex 1A, when there is a normative conflict, Annex 1A covered agreements will prevail over GATT. However, the established relationship between Annex 1A covered agreements and GATT should be looked at in the absence of any priority clause in provisions of Annex 1A covered agreements as it is possible that some of these agreements contain a priority clause under which they

---

[105]For relationship between WTO agreements see for example Panel Report, *Brazil – Measures Affecting Desiccated Coconut*, WT/DS22/R, para. 227 (Oct. 17, 1996); AB Report, *Korea – Definitive Safeguard Measures on Imports of Certain Diary Products*, WT/DS98/AB/R, para. 74 (Dec. 14, 1999) [hereinafter *Korea – Desiccated Coconut*]; for literature review See for example Chase (2012), pp. 793, 796, 809.

[106]See for example Bankovic and Others v. Belgium and Others, 3 Bankovic and Others v. Belgium and Others, Admissibility, App. No 52207/99, Eur. Ct. H.R, para. 57 (Dec. 12, 2001); Borgen (2005), pp. 576–579.

[107]ILC Report, 58th Sess., GAOR, 61st. Sess. Suppl. 10 (A/61/10, at 408 (August 2006); see also *Bernhardt* (note 97), 469. This definition provided by ILC is reflected in WTO panel reports. See for example Panel Report, *Thailand – Customs and Fiscal Measures on Cigarettes from the Philippines*, WT/S371/R, para. 7.1047 (Nov. 15, 2010) [hereinafter *Thailand – Cigarettes*].

[108]See for example Panel Report, *Korea – Measures Affecting Government Procurement*, WT/DS163/R, para. 7. 96 (May 1, 2000) [hereinafter *Korea – Procurement*]; for literature review see Wilfred (1953), p. 425; see also Bindschedler and Bernhardt (1984), p. 469.

[109]For literature review see for example Cook (2015), pp. 86–92; Chase (2012), pp. 791–99.

[110]Art. XVI:3 WTO Agreement.

[111]WTO Agreement, general interpretative note to Annex 1A, https://www.wto.org/english/docs_e/legal_e/05anx1a_e.htm. The covered agreements under Annex 1A, which all concern trade in goods including GATT are: (1) Agreement on Agriculture Agreement, (2) the SPS Agreement, (3) Agreement on Textiles and Clothing, (4) the TBT Agreement, (5) the TRIMS Agreement, (6) Agreement on Implementation of Article VI of GATT, (7) Agreement on Implementation of Article VII of GATT, (8) Agreement on Pre-shipment Inspection, (9) Agreement on Rules of Origin, (10) Agreement on Import Licensing Procedures, (11) Agreement on Subsidies and Countervailing Measures, (12) Agreement on Safeguards, and (13) the TFA.

recognize the supremacy of one or more provisions of GATT over their provisions. For instance, TFA is an Annex 1A covered agreement, therefore, its provisions will prevail over those of GATT to the extent of a conflict. However, TFA contains a priority clause in Article 24:7, which recognizes application of *all* GATT exceptions and exemptions to *all* provisions of the TFA. In this case, Article 24:7 overrides the priority clause established under Interpretative Note to Annex 1A of the WTO Agreement.

As mentioned, unlike the precedence established for Annex 1A covered agreements over GATT, no such normative relationship exists to resolve conflict between GATT and other agreements listed in Annex 1B[112] and Annex 1C.[113] The lack of such a relationship may lie in the fact that the WTO Agreement treats all of the agreements covered in its annexes equally.[114] However, review of WTO case law suggests that a normative conflict between WTO covered agreements is inevitable, which needs to be resolved and through a system of norm hierarchy, when faced with the question which provisions of which agreement prevail. Therefore, WTO adjudicators have, to some extent, filled the vacuum by exercising margins of appreciation when interpreting and applying overlapping provisions of different agreements on a case-by-case basis by giving recourse to treaty conflict resolution principles of international law such as the *lex specialis* principle and other rules of treaty interpretation contained in Articles 31 and 32 VCLT.[115]

Particularly, extensive recourse has been given to the *lex specialis* principle for conflict resolution between different obligations or between an obligation and a right under one or more WTO covered agreements.[116] For instance, in *European Communities—Regime for the Importation, Sale and Distribution of Bananas (EC–Bananas III)*, the AB referred to the *lex specialis* principle to assess whether Article X:3(a) GATT or Article 3.1 of the Licensing Agreement would apply. The AB held that the Licensing Agreement dealt specifically and in detail with the administration of import licensing procedures and therefore the consistency of the measures should be first assessed in light of Article 3.1 of the Licensing Agreement.[117] The AB's

---

[112] Annex 1B covers General Agreement on Trade in Services (GATS).

[113] Annex 1C covers the TRIPS Agreement.

[114] For example, in *Korea – Diary*, the AB confirmed the panel's statement that "it is now well established that WTO Agreement is a Single Undertaking" and therefore all WTO obligations are generally cumulative and members must comply with all of them simultaneously". AB Report, *Korea – Definitive Safeguard Measures on Certain Diary Products*, WT/DS98/AB/R, para. 74 (Dec. 14, 1999) [hereinafter *Korea – Dairy*]; see also Chase (2012), p. 796, footnote 7.

[115] Vienna Convention on the Law of Treaties (VCLT), 1155 U.N.T.S. 331 (entered into force Jan. 27, 1980). Article 31 VCLT on general rules of interpretation provides, *inter alia*, that: 1) "[a] treaty shall be interpreted in good faith in accordance with the ordinary meaning to be given to the terms of the treaty in their context and in the light of its object and purpose." Similarly, Article 32 VCLT on supplementary means of treaty interpretation provides that in interpreting a treaty, recourse to supplementary instruments of the treaty in question including its negotiating documents maybe given; for literature review see Cook (2015), pp. 86–92; Chase (2012), pp. 792–93.

[116] For a series of these disputes, Cook (2015), pp. 86–92.

[117] AB Report, *EC – Bananas III*, para. 204.

approach in this dispute has been cited in several later disputes by panels to support application of the *lex specialis* principle to interpretation and conflict resolution of WTO provisions.[118] Nevertheless, WTO adjudicators have applied the *lex specialis* principle with caution. Meaning that in parallel to having recourse to the *lex specialis* principle, they have also given meaning and effect to the terms and context of each overlapping provision in question on a case-by-case basis.[119]

Taking into account the terms and context of each provision is a method of effective treaty interpretation embodied within Article 31 VCLT. Article 31 contains provisions on general rules of treaty interpretation and provides, *inter alia*, that "a treaty shall be interpreted in good faith in accordance with the ordinary meaning to be given to the terms of the treaty in their context and in the light of its object and purpose." It is possible that conflicting provisions will allow a *lex specialis* interpretation on the surface, but a deeper examining of terms and context of those provisions will maybe lead to a withdrawal of the application of the *lex specialis* principle or maybe result in finding that no normative conflict exists. This scenario can be seen, for example, in *European Union – Anti-dumping Measures on Certain Footwear from China* (*EU—Footwear*). Assessing whether Article 6.2 of the Anti-dumping Agreement was in conflict with Article 6.4 of the same agreement, the panel held that Article 6.2 does not add any specific obligation to Article 6.4. By relying on terms and context of both provisions, the panel did not find a normative conflict and therefore held that Article 6.4 applied to the situation at hand and its compliance was not in normative conflict with Article 6.2.[120]

A more convoluted, but yet a relevant example of a normative conflict where, in parallel to the *lex especialis* principle, meaning and effect was given to the terms and context of each provision is *EU–Generic Drugs*. In this dispute, the relationship between Article V GATT and footnote 13 to Article 51 TRIPS Agreement was assessed. As mentioned earlier, this dispute was resolved by consultations. However,

---

[118]For example, in *US – Shrimp*, by referring to the AB's approach in *EC – bananas III*, the panel held that between Articles III:4 and VI GATT, Article VI including its Ad Note dealt with the measure at issue directly and specifically and therefore constituted a *lex specialis* that would prevail over Article III:4. Panel Report, *United States – Import Prohibition of Certain Shrimp and Shrimp Products*, WT/DS58/R, para. 7. 159–162 (May 15, 1998) [hereinafter *US – Shrimp*]; *see also* Panel Report, *United States – Anti-dumping Act of 1916*, para. 6. 269 (Mar. 31, 2000) [hereinafter *US – 1916 Act*].

[119]WTO adjudicators have stressed on the importance of effective treaty interpretation. For example, in *China – Rare Earths*, the AB held that any possible conflict between different WTO provisions should be resolved on a case-by-case basis by giving recourse to terms and conditions of each different provisions. AB Report, *China – Measures related to the Exportation of Rare Earths, Tungsten and Molybdenum*, WT/DS431/AB/R, para. 5. 56 (Aug. 4, 2014) [hereinafter *China – Rare Earths*]; *see also* Panel Report, *Indonesia – Certain Measures Affecting the Automobile Industry*, WT/DS54/R, para. 14. 28 (July 2, 1998) [hereinafter *Indonesia – Autos*].

[120]Panel Report, *European Union – Anti-dumping Measures on Certain Footwear from China*, WT/DS405/R, para. 7. 598 & footnote 1210 (Oct. 28, 2011) [hereinafter *EU – Footwear*]. Similarly, in *Indonesia – Autos*, the panel dealt with a similar situation and found out, through effective methods of treaty interpretation, that there was no conflict between provisions of the GATT and the SCM Agreement in question. Panel Report, *Indonesia – Autos*, para. 14. 28.

if a panel would have been established to review the dispute, it would have been relevant for the panel to have recourse to the *lex specialis* principle and to the methods of effective treaty interpretation to assess whether the right to suspend release of transit goods in accordance with footnote 13 to Article 51 TRIPS Agreement would prevail over the obligation to grant freedom of transit under Article V GATT.[121] Although it seems on the surface that by allowing members to suspend release of transit goods in a specific situation (piracy or counterfeit) footnote 13 is more specific than Article V GATT, which should prevail over the obligation to grant free and unrestricted transit, if a closer look is taken at the terms and context of both provisions in accordance with effective methods of treaty interpretation the conclusion will change. To this end, first, it is important to interpret whether the phrase "there shall be no obligation" in footnote 13 is an explicitly conferred right in order to be treated equally versus the substantial obligation to grant freedom of transit. The wording of the "there shall be no obligation" does not present an explicit conferred right. Furthermore, there was no panel proceeding for *EU—Generic Drugs* and one cannot certainly imagine whether a panel would have interpreted the term "no obligation" as a right or as a situation of discretion. Since it would not confer in both cases an explicit right, but rather an implied or discretionary right, it should be treated as lower in hierarchy compared to Article V GATT, which imposes a straightforward mandatory obligation on members to grant free and unrestricted transit.

The difference in the degree of legal force between both provisions requires that Article V GATT, which carries a mandatory obligation, to prevail over footnote 13 that carries a discretionary right and not an obligation or an explicit conferred right. As such, the *lex specialis* principle is unlikely to be relevant in determining the relationship between the two provisions. This conclusion is only possible when in parallel to assessing whether footnote 13 would constitute a *lex specialis*, meaning and effect should be given to terms language and context of both provisions.

5.3.2   The Relationship Between Different but Non-conflicting WTO Provisions

A normative conflict does not arise when legal norms impose different obligations or different obligations and rights compliance with which would not necessarily contradict each other.[601] In this case, it is possible that provisions of both treaties complement each other and apply cumulatively to the matter in question.[122]

WTO case law presents a broad application of the cumulative approach to this kind of WTO provisions, particularly, the provisions of Annex 1 covered agreements, including GATT. For instance, when case law provides that provisions of

---

[121]For literature review see for example *Melgar* (Ch.1, note 2), 146.

[122]Ibid.; see also Panel Report, *EC – Bananas III*, para. 7.160.

other Annex 1 covered agreements do not contradict provisions of GATT but rather add to GATT obligations, both GATT and other Annex 1 agreements could co-exist without the need to assess whether a member is required, or capable of fulfilling all the sets of obligations.[123] In *European Communities—Protection of Trademark and Geographical Indications for Agricultural Products and Foodstuffs (EC—Trademarks and Geographical Indications)*, the panel established a cumulative relationship between GATT and the TRIPS Agreement. It held that the obligations under both agreements co-exist and that none of them overrides the other.[124] The panel further held that the WTO "covered agreements apply cumulatively and that consistency with one does not necessarily imply consistency with them all."[125]

However, WTO adjudicators have not applied a cumulative approach to every dispute involving provisions of different covered agreements of Annex 1.[126] For example, departing from its ruling in *EC—Trademarks and Geographical Indications*, the panel in *India—Patent Protection for Pharmaceutical and Agricultural Chemical Products (India—Patents)* held that the TRIPS Agreement "occupies a relatively self-contained *sui generis* status in the WTO Agreement".[127] The self-contained status of the TRIPS Agreement means that its provisions provide minimum IP standards and that WTO members are allowed to adopt higher national IP standards given that those higher national IP standards are to be considered as TRIPS plus standards and do not contravene provisions of the TRIPS Agreement. The panel also held that "when interpreting the text of the TRIPS Agreement, the legitimate expectations of WTO Members concerning the TRIPS Agreement must be taken into account, as well as standards of interpretation developed in past panel reports in the GATT framework".[128] Protection of WTO members' legitimate expectations, as addressed by Article 3.2 DSU, means that WTO panels are obliged to preserve members' rights and obligations. One might argue that the panel interpretation of the TRIPS Agreement in *India—Patents* brings controversy to the interpretation and the relationship between Article V GATT and footnote 13 to Article 51 TRIPS Agreement provided earlier. As discussed above, Article V GATT prevails over footnote 13 to Article 51 TRIPS Agreement when recourse is made to effective methods of treaty interpretation. This conclusion is, however, different from the panel's decision on the protection of legitimate expectations of members under the TRIPS

---

[123]Panel Report, *EC – Bananas III*, para. 7. 160.

[124]Panel Report, *European Communities – Protection of Trademark and Geographical Indications for Agricultural Products and Foodstuffs*, WT/DS174/R, paras. 7. 208, 7. 227 & footnote 239 (Mar. 15, 2005) [hereinafter *EC – Trademarks and Geographical Indications*].

[125]Ibid.; see also AB Report, *Argentina – Safeguard Measures on Import of Footwear*, W/DS121/AB/R, para. 81 (Dec. 14, 1999) [*Argentina – Footwear (EC)*]; *Korea – Dairy*, para. 74; Panel Report, *EC – Bananas III*, para. 7. 160.

[126]See for example Chase (2012), pp. 817–819.

[127]Panel Report, *India – Patent Protection for Pharmaceutical and Agricultural Chemical Products*, WT/DS50/R, para. 7. 19 (Sept.5, 1997) [hereinafter *India – Patent*]; see also See for example Chase (2012), p. 818.

[128]Panel Report, *India – Patents*, para. 7. 22.

Agreement, but given WTO adjudicators' lack of a single interpretation approach for interpreting WTO agreements in similar disputes, it does not necessarily indicate that it would be an inapplicable approach. This rather suggests that WTO adjudicators should clarify WTO provisions on a case-by-case basis by taking into account terms and conditions of each provision and each case.

5.3.3 How WTO Adjudicators Interpret WTO Provisions

According to Article 3.2 DSU, WTO adjudicators refer to customary rules of interpretation of public international law contained in Articles 31 and 32 VCLT to determine whether or not a conflict exists between WTO provisions. These rules contain, *inter alia*, methods of effective treaty interpretation. Effective treaty interpretation suggests that in addition to the ordinary meaning of a treaty, effect and meaning should be given to the terms and context of the treaty in light of its object and purpose[129] as well as recourse to supplementary means of interpretation, such as negotiating instruments of the treaty in question.[130] For example, according to Article 31(2)(a) VCLT an effective treaty interpretation requires that meaning and effect given to the context of a treaty also include, in addition to the text of the treaty itself, "any agreement relating to the treaty which was made between all the parties in connection with the conclusion of the treaty". Similarly, effective treaty interpretation under Articles 31(3)(a) and 31(3)(c) VCLT respectively, further requires that consideration is given to "any subsequent agreement between the parties regarding the interpretation of the treaty or the application of its provisions" and "any relevant rules of international law applicable in the relations between the parties".

WTO case law frequently relies on all these rules when interpreting WTO provisions. For example, in *Brazil—Desiccated Coconut*, the panel had recourse to Article 31(3)(a) VCLT in order to assess whether the 1979 Tokyo Round Subsidies and Countervailing Code Measure (SCM) could be a subsequent agreement for interpreting Article VI GATT on subsidies and countervailing measures. The panel held that in accordance with Article 31(3)(a) VCLT, the Tokyo Round SCM Code could only serve as a subsequent agreement to GATT 1947 and not to the GATT 1994. Therefore, Article VI GATT cannot be interpreted in light of the Tokyo Round SCM Code.[131] Similarly, WTO adjudicators often referred to 'any relevant rules of international law applicable in the relations between the parties' pursuant to Article 31(3)(c) VCLT to interpret WTO provisions.

---

[129]Art. 31 VCLT.

[130]Art. 32 VCLT.

[131]Panel Report, *Brazil – Desiccated Coconut*, para. 255; for more discussion *see* Cook (2015), *supra* note 566, at
    294–299.

Article 31(3)(a) VCLT and the reflections made by the panel in *Brazil—Desiccated Coconut* can be directly applied to the relationship between Article V GATT and Article 11 TFA. As explicitly addressed in its preamble, the main purpose of the TFA is to improve certain GATT provisions, including those on freedom of transit. The TFA as a WTO covered agreement, dealing with the same subject matter as GATT, entered into force 20 years after the GATT 1994 and therefore serves as a subsequent agreement. Hence, Article V GATT should be interpreted in light of Article 11 TFA and Article 11 should refer to Article V GATT if necessary for interpretation.[132] If the provisions of Article V GATT and the TFA are in conflict, the TFA provisions will prevail over GATT, since the TFA is listed in Annex 1A of the WTO Agreement. If there is no conflict, WTO case law suggests a cumulative compliance with both GATT and other covered agreements, including the TFA.

5.4 Conclusion

Article V GATT and Article 11 TFA create an unconditional obligation for a WTO member to grant freedom of transit across its territory to traffic in transit coming from or going to another WTO member without discriminating traffic based on its place of origin, departure, entry or exit, flag or similar. They also impose an MFN obligation on the country of destination to treat international goods that transited through the territory of other WTO members no less favorable than goods that were directly imported.

Although Article V GATT and Article 11 TFA provisions do not seem to be complicated in the context of rights and obligations of WTO members related to freedom of transit, ambiguity and shortcoming nonetheless exist. For instance, the definition and scope of some terms such as 'the routes most convenient for international transit' remain highly controversial and are believed to act as restriction to the freedom of transit.

Similarly, and most importantly from a landlocked LDC's perspective, these articles reveal one more important shortcoming, which is lack of an SDT provision on recognition of special transit needs of landlocked LDCs. Unlike the Havana Charter, which at least contains an interpretive note to paragraph 6 of Article 33 that recognizes an SDT for landlocked LDCs, Article V GATT and Article 11 TFA do not recognize such SDT and govern the transit relationship between WTO members on a general reciprocal basis without any distinction between coastal and landlocked, developed or developing members. This suggests that the WTO fails to protect the special needs of its landlocked LDC members. In particular shortcoming of the TFA in that fails to recognize the serious transit needs of landlocked LDC members, despite the fact that one-third of the Agreement includes SDT provisions to enhance trade facilitation for developing countries. Although LDCs including landlocked

---

[132]See for example *Melgar* (Ch.1, note 2), 286, 297; Merkouris et al. (2010), pp. 136–140.

LDCs generally benefit from the TFA, the high costs of trading due to lack of easy access to the sea remain main challenge for landlocked LDC members.[133] The drafting history of the TFA shows that landlocked members actively participated in drafting of the Agreement (e.g., landlocked LDC members proposed the inclusion of the provision on non-application of TBT measures on transit goods).[134] Therefore, it is even more surprising that the landlocked LDC members, which are 25 in total, making up nearly two-thirds of all landlocked countries, did not propose a specific mandatory SDT provision on the special transit needs of landlocked LDCs.

References

Baker BK (2012) Settlement of India/EU WTO dispute and seizures of in transit medicines: why the proposed EU border regulation isn't good enough, PIJIP Research Paper, 4. American University of Washington, Washington, http://digitalcommons.wcl.american.edu/cgi/viewcontent.cgi?article=1026&context=research

Bindschedler, Bernhardt R (eds) (1984) Encyclopedia of public international law, vol 7. North Holland, Amsterdam, p 468

Borgen CJ (2005) Resolving treaty conflicts. George Washington Int Law Rev 37:576–579

Chase C (2012) Norm conflict between WTO covered agreements – real, apparent or avoided? Int Law Q 61:791

Cook G (2015) A digest of WTO jurisprudence on public international law concepts and principles, 1st edn. Cambridge University Press, Cambridge, pp 326–329

Eliason A (2015) The trade facilitation agreement – a new hope for the World Trade Organization. World Trade Rev 14:645

Hamanaka S (2014) WTO agreement on trade facilitation: assessing the level of ambition and likely impacts. Global Trade Customs J 9:344

Hoekman B, Kostechi M (1997) The political economy of the world trading system: from GATT to WTO. Oxford University Press, Oxford

Hoekman B, Kostechi M (2001) The political economy of the world trading system: WTO and beyond. Oxford University Press, Oxford, pp 390–394

Ibarra PG (2010) The challenge of implementing the domestic trade policy measures: the Colombia ports of entry case. International Center for Trade and Sustainable Development, Geneva, p 3

Marceau GZ (2001) Conflict of norms and conflict of jurisprudence: the relationship between the WTO agreement and the MEAS and other treaties. J World Trade 35:1084

Merkouris P, Fitzmaurice M, Elias O (eds) (2010) Treaty interpretation and the Vienna Convention on the law of the treaties. Nijhoff, Leiden, pp 136–140

OECD (2015) Reducing trade costs for least developed countries. In: OECD (ed) Aid for trade at a glance 2015: reducing trade costs for inclusive, sustainable growth. OECD, Paris, p 133

Pauwelyn J (2003) Conflict of norms in public international law: how WTO law relates to other rules of international law. Cambridge University Press, Cambridge, pp 168–169

Pogoretskyy V (2017) Freedom of transit and access to gas pipeline networks under WTO law. Cambridge University Press, Cambridge, pp 180–185

---

[133] According to the OECD, cost of trading for landlocked LDCs is two times higher than that for their coastal neighboring countries. See OECD (2015), pp. 133 & 140.

[134] See WTO, Fifth Meeting of Trade Ministers of Landlocked Developing Countries (2016).9.

Ruse-Khan G, Jaeger TH (2009) Policing patents worldwide? EC border measures against transiting generic drugs under EC – and WTO intellectual property regimes. IIC 40:502

Sekkel JV (2009) Summary of major trade preference program. Center for Global Development, Washington, D.C.

Vranes E (2006) The definition of norm conflict in international law and legal theory. Eur J Int Law 17:395

Wilfred J (1953) The conflict of law-making treaties. Br Yearb Int Law 30:427

Chapter 6
WTO Law and Public International Law: Focus on UNCLOS Rules on Freedom of Transit of Landlocked States

This chapter explores the relationship between WTO law and other sources of public international law with specific focus on the interaction between WTO rules on the freedom of transit and the UNCLOS rules on freedom of transit. In doing so, it particularly provides a comparative study of the UNCLOS rules on freedom of transit of landlocked State parties and assesses the possibility of WTO landlocked members to invoke their right in WTO dispute settlement proceedings.

This chapter contains three sections. Section 6.1 discusses the relationship between WTO law and public international law and its role within WTO dispute settlement proceedings in general. Section 6.2 analyzes the WTO interaction with UNCLOS, reviews UNCLOS rules on freedom of transit with the focus on transit rights of landlocked State parties and assesses the possibility to invoke those rules in WTO dispute settlement proceedings in general. Section 6.3 concludes the chapter. This chapter is especially important for the understanding as to whether WTO landlocked LDC members, such as Afghanistan, can invoke different multilateral transit rules, such as those of UNCLOS, before the WTO dispute settlement body. It further answers the question on the extent such invocation can support their legal bargaining in the WTO.

6.1 Relationship Between WTO Law and Other Sources of Public International Law

Widespread consensus is that WTO law is part of public international law and it therefore shall not to be read in 'clinical isolation' from other rules of public international law.[1] Although the WTO Agreement, as the mother law of the

---

[1] See for example AB Report, *United States – Standards for Reformulated and Conventional Gasoline*, WT/DS2/AB/R, 17 (May 20, 1996) [hereinafter *US – Gasoline*]; see also *Jackson*

multilateral trading system, does not establish any explicit relationship between WTO law and other sources of public international law, and despite the fact that the DSU provisions specify WTO covered agreements as the primary applicable law in the WTO,[2] the WTO regime still embodies several legal principles and rules of international law.[3] For instance, Article 3.2 DSU provides that WTO panels clarify provisions of WTO agreements in accordance with customary rules of interpretation of public international law as is contained in Articles 31 and 32 VCLT.

This recourse can be extensively found in WTO case law, which confirms that WTO law is not a self-contained regime and WTO adjudicators do not read WTO provisions in 'clinical isolation' from other rules of international law.[4] For instance, in *Korea – Procurement*, the panel held that Article 3.2 DSU does not exclude the application of other rules of international law and that those rules of international law generally apply to the economic relations between WTO members, unless WTO provisions explicitly provide otherwise or parties mutually exclude them.[5] Similarly, in *EC – Approval and Marketing of Biotech Products* (*EC – Biotech*), the panel held that rules of international law must include all sources of public international law.[6] In *Peru – Additional Duty on Imports of Certain Agricultural Products* (*Peru – Agricultural Products*) the panel held, that it was "only authorized to rule on the

---

(1998), pp. 25–30; *Marceau* (Ch. 5, note 99), 1081; *Pauwelyn*, Conflicts of Norms in Public International Law (Ch. 5, note 100), 26–30; *Pauwelyn* (2001), pp. 538–540; *Pauwelyn* (2005), pp. 1406–1423.

[2]Articles 1.1, 3.4 & 7.1 DSU mandate panels to apply provisions of the WTO covered agreements to disputes before them.

[3]See for example Article 3.2 DSU provides that WTO panels clarify WTO provisions in accordance with customary rules of interpretation of public international law. Articles 3.10 and 4.3 DSU provide that all WTO members should engage in WTO dispute settlement procedures in good faith and in effort to resolve their disputes. For WTO disputes reflecting principles and rules of international law see for example AB Report, *US – Shrimp*, para. 114 and Panel Report, *Korea – Procurement*, para. 7. 93 for the principle of 'good faith'; Panel Report, *Turkey—Restrictions on Imports of Textile and Clothing Products*, WT/DS34/R, paras. 33–43(Nov. 19, 1999) [hereinafter *Turkey—Textiles*] for the principle of 'State responsibility'; Panel Report, *Korea—Procurement*, paras. 7. 123–24 for the principle of 'error in treaty formation'; Panel Report, *EC—Approval and Marketing of Biotech Products*, WT/DS291/R, para. 7. 67 (Sep. 29, 2006) [hereinafter *EC— Biotech*] for the principle of 'precautionary'; for literature review see *Mitchell* (2008), pp. 15–23; *Howse* (2002), pp. 498–500.

[4]See for example, AB Report, *US—Gasoline*, at 17; AB Report, *US—Shrimp*, para. 158; Panel Report, *EC–Biotech*, para. 67.

[5]Panel Report, *Korea – Procurement*, para. 7. 96.

[6]Panel Report, *EC – Biotech*, para. 67. Article 38 (1) of the Statute of International Court of Justice lists public international law sources as (a) international conventions whether general or particular, (b) international custom, as evidence of a general practice accepted as law, (c) the general principles of law recognized by civilized nations; and (d) judicial decisions and the teachings of the most highly qualified publicists as subsidiary source of law. [621] Panel Report, *Peru – Additional Duty on Imports of Certain Agricultural Products*, WT/DS457/R, para. 7. 69 (Nov. 27, 2014) [hereinafter *Peru – Agricultural Products*].

invocation of any rule of public international law applicable to the relations between the parties to the extent that the invocation of that rule of international law is based on a relevant provision of the covered agreements that has been invoked by one of the parties to the dispute."[7]

Literature argues that the absence of an express prohibition of non-WTO sources of international law is an implication for the application of those sources within the WTO regime.[8] Even the confirmation of certain rules of international law does not exclude the use of other rules of international law as long as they are relevant and compatible. In fact, a right that has its foundation in international law cannot merely be excluded from a treaty because the treaty is silent about the application of that right. Therefore it can be said that WTO silence on the explicit prohibition of other rules of international law allows their application in relevant cases before the WTO dispute settlement bodies.[9] One can fairly contend that the DSU recognition of customary rules of interpretation of public international law opens the door to all sources of public interpretational law for interpretation and clarification of WTO provisions where relevant and compatible. For example, Article 31(3)(c) VCLT, which contains the customary rules of treaty interpretation, mandates that a treaty interpreter has to have recourse to "any relevant rules of international law applicable in relations between the parties" when interpreting a treaty in order to make a reasonable choice when provisions are different or conflicting.

Article 31(3)(c) VCLT is one of the most controversially discussed rules of treaty interpretation within the WTO dispute settlement regime. WTO case law shows that WTO adjudicators have made reference to all sources of public international law listed in Article 38 (1) of the ICJ Statute.[10] They did so as a mandatory task and not as a matter of discretion.[11] Moreover, WTO case law provides that 'any relevant rules of international law applicable to relations between the parties' means that the rule first of all has to be relevant to the subject matter of a given dispute and that all the parties to that dispute need to have given prior consent to that rule (e.g., if it is an international agreement or convention, all the disputing parties should be parties to that convention).[12] In that case, it is mandatory for WTO adjudicators and not just a matter of discretion to have recourse to such relevant rule of international law when

---

[7]Panel Report, *Peru – Additional Duty on Imports of Certain Agricultural Products*, WT/DS457/R, para. 7. 69 (Nov. 27, 2014) [hereinafter *Peru – Agricultural Products*].

[8]See for example *Pauwelyn* (2001), p. 541; *Pauwelyn* (2005), pp. 1406–1423; *Bartels* (2001), pp. 503–509.

[9]See ibid.; see also ICJ, Advisory Opinion, Legal Consequences for States of the Continued Presence of South Africa in Namibia (South West Africa) notwithstanding Security Council Resolution 276 (1970), REP. 16, para. 96 (1971).

[10]See for example AB Report, *US – Anti-Dumping and Countervailing Duties*, paras. 308–309; AB Report, *US – Shrimp*, para. 158 & footnote 157; Panel Report, *EC – Biotech*, para. 7. 67.

[11]Panel Report, *EC – Biotech*, paras. 7. 69–70.

[12]See AB Report, *US – Anti-Dumping and Countervailing Duties*, paras. 308–9; AB Report, *US/Canada – Continued Suspension of Obligations in the US – Hormones Dispute*, WT/DS321/AB/R, para. 382 (Oct. 16, 2008) [hereinafter *Canada – Continued Suspension*].

interpreting a WTO provision. In *EC – Biotech*, the panel stated: "Article 31(3)
(c) should be interpreted to mandate consideration of rules of international law which
are applicable in the relations between *all* parties to the *treaty* which is being
interpreted."[13] The panel further stated: "we are not required to take into account
other rules of international law which are not applicable to one of the parties to this
dispute."[14] However, WTO adjudicators have not always taken the same approach.
In some disputes, they rejected some rules of international law even if they would
qualify under Article 31(3)(c). Such approach is particularly conceivable with regard
to the WTO treatment of members' regional agreements in WTO disputes.[15] In some
cases on the other hand, adjudicators had recourse to a rule of international law even
if it would not qualify under Article 31(3)(c) VCLT.[16]

The controversy of approach WTO adjudicators have taken mostly arose from the
question of whether they should have recourse to other rules of international law as
informative sources for clarification and interpretation of WTO provisions or
whether they could also consider those rules as legal provisions to be directly applied
to WTO disputes because, in principle, Article 1.1 DSU[17] mandates WTO adjudicators to apply WTO covered agreements in disputes before them and refer to other
sources of public international law only to interpret and clarify the meaning of those
covered agreements.[18] Nonetheless, WTO adjudicators have exercised discretional
power to the application of other rules of international law if relevant for disputes at
hand.[19] Additionally, they not only have opted to apply other rules of international
law where relevant for WTO disputes, but also considered reviewing disputes arising
outside the WTO agreements. WTO adjudicators do so because on one hand, WTO
law does not establish any explicit relationship to other rules of international law,
including multilateral agreements, and on the other hand, mandated terms of reference of WTO panels under Article 1.1 DSU is not an exclusive clause and does not

---

[13]Panel Report, *EC – Biotech*, paras. 7. 68, 7. 71. In *Argentina – Poultry,* the panel stated that "it is
not clear to us that a rule applicable between only several WTO members would constitute a
relevant rule of international law."

[14]Panel Report, *EC – Biotech,* para. 7. 71.

[15]For example, in *EC – Poultry*, the AB refused to apply other laws except WTO covered
agreements as applicable law in the dispute and reversed the panel's application of the Oilseed
Bilateral Agreement in force between Brazil and the EC.

[16]See for example Panel Report, *EC – Biotech*, para. 7. 67.

[17]See also Arts. 3.2, 7. DSU. Moreover, Article 2.1 DSU provides only for the application of WTO
plurilateral agreements to a dispute where relevant.

[18]For example, in *US – Anti-Dumping and Countervailing Duties,* the AB stated that the applicable
law was the WTO SCM agreement and taking account of the ILC provisions as relevant rules of
international law was to interpret meaning of terms of the SCM agreement and not to apply ILC
provisions in the dispute. AB Report, *US – Anti-Dumping and Countervailing Duties*, para. 316.

[19]See *Cook* (Ch. 5, note 70), 65; *Pauwelyn* (2001), p. 554.

prohibit applying other rules of international law to a WTO dispute when appropriate and necessary.[20]

Exercise of such discretional power by WTO adjudicators is called 'implied or incidental jurisdiction'.[21] In support of implied or incidental jurisdiction of WTO adjudicators, the AB has widely referred to the accepted international rule that "an international tribunal is entitled to consider the issue of its own jurisdiction on its own initiative, and to satisfy itself that it has jurisdiction in any case that comes before it."[22] As such, in the absence of an explicit prohibition by the DSU or unless WTO provisions are expressly excluded, WTO adjudicators apply certain rules of international law, especially provisions of non-WTO multilateral agreements, to disputes before them, and are likely to continue doing so in the future. Such application becomes relevant and legitimate when WTO agreements incorporate or recognize provisions of certain multilateral agreements, i.e., the TRIPS Agreement incorporates provisions of the Rome Convention for the Protection of Performers, Producers of Phonograms and Broadcasting Organizations.[23]

The subsections below provide a selective case study of different approaches taken by WTO adjudicators with regard to the recourse made to other sources of public international law.

6.1.1 International Conventions

6.1.1.1 Multilateral Agreements

WTO case law shows that non-WTO multilateral agreements are used to inform adjudicators about the interpretation of WTO provisions or serve as factual evidence in WTO disputes when their application was considered in certain WTO disputes. An example of a multilateral agreement that served as an informative source to interpret WTO provisions is the Biosafety Protocol, which is an annexed Protocol to the Biological Diversity Convention and consists of all of the parties of the Biological Diversity Convention. In *EC – Biotech,* the panel referred to this Protocol as the relevant 'rule of international law applicable to the relations between the parties' pursuant to Article 31(3)(c) VCLT to interpret provisions of the SPS Agreement.[24] Another example is the UNCLOS. In *United States – Import Prohibition of Certain Shrimp and Shrimp Products (US – Shrimp),* the AB referred to the UNCLOS definition for 'exhaustible natural resources' in order to define the same term for

---

[20]*Pauwelyn* (2001), pp. 560–563.

[21]Ibid., 557.

[22]AB Report, *US – Anti-Dumping Act of 1916*, para. 54 & footnote 30.

[23]*Pauwelyn* (2001), p. 555.

[24]Panel Report, *Peru – Additional Duty on Imports of Certain Agricultural Products*, WT/DS457/R, para. 7. 69 (Nov. 27, 2014) [hereinafter *Peru – Agricultural Products*].

Article XX(g) GATT.[25] Article XX(g) GATT allows members to adopt measures necessary for the protection of environmental values, which includes those for the conservation of exhaustible natural resources. As a result, the AB stated that the term 'exhaustible natural resources' was generic and that its conceptual definition under the UNCLOS covered both living and non-living resources.[26] WTO adjudicators have also made recourse to non-WTO multilateral agreements as relevant rule of international law, even if they would not qualify under Article 31(3)(c) VCLT requirement of 'applicable to relations between the parties'.[27]

For example, in *US – Shrimp*, the AB provided, although the US was not a party to the UNCLOS, a revolutionary meaning of 'exhaustible natural resources' by having recourse to the UNCLOS definition.[28] Citing the AB recourse to UNCLOS in *US – Shrimp*, the panel in *EC – Biotech*, stated that "the mere fact that one or more disputing parties are not parties to a convention does not necessarily mean that a convention cannot shed light on the meaning and scope of a treaty term to be interpreted."[29]

Similarly, WTO adjudicators have referred to non-WTO multilateral agreements as factual evidence to support facts in WTO disputes. For example, in *United States – Tax Treatment for Foreign Sales Corporations (Article 21.5 – EC)[US – FSC (Article 21.5 – EC)]*, the panel and the AB referred to a number of international conventions including the Model Taxation Convention of the Organization on Economic Cooperation Development (OECD) as factual evidence to review a WTO members' taxation practice.[30] In *US – Shrimp*, the AB referred to the Inter-American Convention as a piece of factual evidence to hold that "consensual and multilateral procedures were available and feasible to conserve sea turtles"[31] and "a significant number of other international instruments and declarations" and further recognized that concerted and cooperative efforts were important for protection and conservation of highly migratory species of sea turtles.[32] In *EC – Tariff Preferences*,

---

[25]AB Report *US – Shrimp*, paras. 130–131. In the same dispute, the AB made reference to the Appendix 1 of the Convention on International Trade in Endangered Species of Wild Fauna and Flora (CITES) in support of its argument that sea turtles were exhaustible natural resource (para. 132).

[26]Ibid.; see also Aegean Sea Continental Shelf (Greece. v. Turkey), 1978 I.C.J., pg. 3 (December 19); for literature review of evolutionary interpretation see *Pogoreskky* (Ch.5, 48), 140–41; *Howse* (2002), pp. 8–10.

[27]In *EC – Biotech,* the panel stated that recourse to multilateral agreements to interpret WTO provisions in accordance with Article 31(1) VCLT was still possible even if those multilateral agreements maybe not applicable to relations between all parties of a given dispute. Panel Report, *EC – Biotech*, para. 7. 92.

[28]AB Report, *US – Shrimp*, para. 130.

[29]Panel Report, *EC –Biotech*, para. 7. 94.

[30]Panel Report, *United States – Tax Treatment for Foreign Sales Corporations (Article 21.5 – EC)*, WT/DS108/R, footnote 195 (Oct. 8, 1999) [hereinafter *US – FSC (Article 21.5 – EC)*].

[31]AB Report, *US – Shrimp*, para. 170.

[32]Ibid., para. 168.

the AB agreed with the EC's reference to "several international conventions and resolutions" as factual evidence for recognizing "drug production and drug trafficking as entailing particular problems for developing countries".[33] As a result, the AB concluded that the EC's tariff preferences to some developing countries were consistent with the EC MFN obligation under the WTO Enabling Clause as they contained an agreement to combat drug production and drug trafficking.[34]

An example for the possibility to apply provisions of non-WTO multilateral agreements is the AB's conclusion in *Argentina – Measures Affecting Imports of Footwear, Textile and other Items (Argentina – Textile and Apparel)*. The implicit finding of the AB in this dispute shows that it is possible for a member's obligation under another multilateral agreement to prevail over that member's GATT obligations. In *Argentina – Textile and Apparel* it was held, that a measure requiring importers to pay a three percent statistical services tax on imports was inconsistent with Article VIII GATT on import-export fees and formalities. Argentina argued that it took the measure as part of its obligation to the International Monetary Fund (IMF). According to a Memorandum of Understanding (MoU) between Argentina and the IMF, Argentina was allowed to introduce an import surcharge temporary tax of up to three percent. In response to Argentina's argument, the AB agreed with the panel's conclusion that Argentina failed to provide that it had a legally binding agreement with the IMF and also failed to identify any irreconcilable conflict between its obligation under the MoU with the IMF and its obligation under Article VIII GATT. According to the panel and the AB, the three percent statistical services tax was different from the non-obligatory temporary three percent surcharge tax on imports and it did also not result out of an agreement with the IMF.[35] The AB, therefore, opined that the temporary three percent surcharge tax was a non-binding commitment under the Argentina-IMF MoU and did not constitute an IMF obligation for Argentina that would supersede Argentina's obligation under Article VIII GATT.[36]

---

[33]AB Report, *EC – Tariff Preferences*, para. 163 & footnote 335.

[34]Ibid.

[35]The relationship between IMF agreements and GATT is addressed under Article VII:4(c) GATT that provides: "the CONTRACTING PARTIES, in agreement with the International Monetary Fund, shall formulate rules governing the conversion by contracting parties of any foreign currency in respect of which multiple rates of exchange are maintained consistently with the Articles of Agreement of the International Monetary Fund."

[36]AB Report, *Argentina – Measures Affecting Imports of Footwear, Textile and other Items*, WT/DS56/AB/R, para. 69 (Mar. 27, 1998) [hereinafter *Argentina – Textile and Apparel*]. In a similar situation in *Argentina – Hide and Leathers*, Argentina argued that its financial measures were necessary to meet its commitment under an agreement with the IMF. The panel held that there was no requirement in Argentina's agreement with the IMF to prevent compensating discrimination and damages inferred to importers as a result of Argentina's measures nor Argentina proved that it was impossible for it to meet its deficit target it compensated importers. Panel Report, *Argentina – Measures Affecting the Export of Bovine Hide and the Import of Finished Leather*, WT/DS155/R, para. 11. 328 (Dec. 19, 2000) [hereinafter *Argentina – Hide and Leather*].

Therefore, despite lacking substantive jurisdiction over disputes arising out of non-WTO multilateral agreements, it lays within the discretionary power of WTO adjudicators whether and when they would opt to apply a non-WTO multilateral agreement to a given dispute.

6.1.1.2   Regional Agreements[37]

The relationship between regional agreements and WTO law and recourse to them as 'relevant rule of international law applicable in relations between the parties' to interpret WTO provisions is a controversial matter. Although, in rare occasions, WTO adjudicators considered provisions of a regional agreement when interpreting a WTO provision and even applied them to a WTO dispute where relevant and compatible, the common practice is reluctant to interpret WTO provisions in light of provisions of a regional agreement or consider the application of its provisions in a dispute before them. Nevertheless, WTO adjudicators refer to regional agreements as factual evidence to support their conclusions. For example, in *European Communities – Measures Affecting Trade in Commercial Vessels* (*EC – Commercial Vessels*), the panel referred to a bilateral agreement in force between EC and Korea as factual evidence in order to assess Korea's argument that EC' measure as a 'specific action against subsidy of another member' violated Article 32.1 SCM Agreement. In doing so, the panel explicitly stated that the bilateral agreement "only serves the purpose of enabling the panel to decide a factual issue' and that the panel was "not interpreting the bilateral agreement in order to determine the rights and obligations of the parties under that bilateral agreement."[38]

A central controversy is seen in the question whether or not WTO adjudicators can apply provisions of regional agreements in WTO disputes. As mentioned before, WTO adjudicators have in principle only substantive jurisdiction to hear disputes that were brought to them because a party violated WTO provisions. The DSU mandates WTO panels to apply provisions of covered agreements in those disputes[39] and only provides for the application of WTO plurilateral agreements to a dispute where relevant.[40] However, WTO case law and GATT 1947 case law show that in some instances WTO and GATT 1947 adjudicators have not only considered applying provisions of regional agreements in force between members but have also exercised jurisdiction over disputes arising out of regional agreements. In order to do so, the adjudicators relied on the argument that the provisions of the concerned

---

[37]This study prefers to use the term 'regional agreements' instead of 'regional trade agreements' (RTAs) as in WTO law, RTAs are limited to those falling under Article XXIV GATT and not all types of regional agreements that affect trade between WTO members, be it a trade agreement, an investment agreement, environmental agreement or a transit agreement.

[38]Panel Report, *European Communities – Measures Affecting Trade in Commercial Vessels*, WT/DS301/R, para. 7. 131 & footnote 275 (Apr. 22, 2005) [hereinafter *EC – Commercial Vessels*].

[39]Arts. 1.1, 3.2 DSU; for literature review see *Pauwelyn* (2001), p. 554.

[40]Art. 2.1 DSU.

regional agreement had close relationship with the relevant GATT/WTO provisions that required them to examine the provisions of that regional agreement. For example, in *Canada – EC Wheat*, the GATT arbitrator applied provisions of a bilateral agreement in force between the disputing parties after examining the regulatory connection between that bilateral agreement and GATT provisions in questions. The GATT Arbitrator stated:

> In principle a claim based on a bilateral agreement cannot be brought under the multilateral dispute settlement procedures of the GATT. An exception is warranted in this case given the close connection of this particular bilateral agreement with the GATT, given the fact that the Agreement is consistent with the objectives of the GATT, and that both parties joined in requesting recourse to the GATT Arbitration procedures.[41]

WTO adjudicators have taken a similar approach in a few disputes to examine whether they should apply and interpret provisions of a regional agreement in a dispute before them. In *European Communities – Regime for the Importation, Sale and Distribution of Bananas (EC – Bananas III)* WTO adjudicators faced the question whether it should examine and apply provisions of the Lomé Convention. Both the panel and the AB agreed to examine and apply the Lomé Convention to the dispute.[42] The Lomé Convention contained a waiver that granted the EC's preferential treatment for bananas originating in African, Caribbean and Pacific (ACP) developing countries without extending it to other WTO members.[43] The waiver was originally granted by the GATT contracting parties in December 1994 to the EC and the ACP and was added to the Lomé Convention.[44] In 1997, the US, Mexico, Ecuador, Guatemala and Honduras challenged the waiver before the WTO panel based on Article I GATT on MFN treatment and Article XXIII GATT on nullification and impairment.[45] To examine the compatibility of the waiver with WTO rules, the panel referred to the Lomé waiver of the Lomé Convention and stated that it had no alternative but to examine the Lomé waiver in the context of WTO law because the GATT contracting parties incorporated a reference to the Lomé Convention for the Lomé waiver and therefore the Lomé Convention becomes a GATT issue.[46] The Lomé waiver explicitly provided that the preferential treatment was an exception to Article I GATT.[47] The AB upheld the panel's decision.[48]

---

[41] Award by the Arbitrator, Canada/European Communities, Article XXVIII, B.I.S.D 37S/80, para. 84 (Oct. 16, 1990).

[42] Panel Report, *European Communities – Regime for the Importation, Sale and Distribution of Bananas,* WT/DS27/R/GTM, paras. 3. 33–35 (May 22, 1997) *[EC – Bananas III]*; AB Report, *EC – Bananas III,* WT/DS27/AB/R, paras. 175–78 (Sept. 9, 1997).

[43] Panel Report, *EC – Bananas III,* para. 4. 44.

[44] Ibid., paras. 3. 33–35.

[45] Ibid., para. 4. 1.

[46] Ibid., paras. 7. 96, 7. 98, 7. 107.

[47] Ibid., para. 4. 44.

[48] AB Report, *EC – Bananas III,* paras. 167 & 178.

Similarly, in *European Communities – Measures Affecting Importation of Certain Poultry Products* (*EC – Poultry Products*), Brazil challenged the consistency of EC tariff quotas with the Oilseed Agreement and argued that the Agreement was applicable to the WTO dispute since Brazil and the EC negotiated and concluded the Oilseed Agreement in accordance with Article XXVIII GATT.[49] The panel first addressed the question whether it had jurisdiction to apply provisions of the Oilseed Agreement because it was not a 'covered agreement' within the meaning of Article 1.1 DSU.[50] In answering this the panel referred to previous disputes where GATT and WTO adjudicators examined concerned regional agreements to determine whether their provisions should be applied to disputes before them. The panel particularly made reference to *Canada – EC Wheat* of GATT 1947 and *EC – Bananas III* of the WTO and decided to apply provisions of the Oilseed Agreement to the dispute at hand. The panel reasoned that the Oilseed Agreement was compatible with Article XXIV GATT on the formation of RTAs and had a close relationship with GATT provisions as it was negotiated in accordance with Article XXVIII GATT.[51] Surprisingly, the AB refused, in the same dispute, to apply other laws except for WTO covered agreements as applicable law. This shows that WTO adjudicators do not always take the same approach, which makes it difficult to answer the question whether provisions of a regional agreement can be invoked in WTO dispute settlement proceedings.

Another controversial question concerning WTO law and regional agreements is whether a WTO member can simultaneously file the same dispute before the WTO and a regional agreement dispute settlement forum. WTO case law suggests that the possibility of such undertaking should first be seen in the context of a given regional agreement. For instance, in *Argentina – Poultry Anti-Dumping Duties*, the panel concluded that: "a MERCOSUR dispute settlement proceeding could be followed by a WTO dispute settlement proceeding of the same measure."[52] The panel reached this conclusion after it found out that the Brasilia Protocol, which is governing the dispute settlement of the MERCOSUR Agreement, was silent on whether a MERCOSUR party could bring the same dispute that it brought to the MERCOSUR dispute settlement forum, to the WTO DSB.[53] Similarly, in *Mexico – Tax Measures on Soft Drinks and other Beverages* (*Mexico – Soft Drinks*), the panel and the AB rejected Mexico's request that a WTO panel should decline exercising its

---

[49]Ibid., para. 196.

[50]Ibid.

[51]Panel Report, *EC – Poultry Products*, paras. 206, 207, 209; for literature review see *Melgar* (Ch.1, note 2), 11.

[52]Panel Report, *Argentina –Poultry*, para. 7. 38.

[53]Ibid., para. 7. 38. In this dispute, the question at issue was based on Article 1 of the newly adopted MERCOSUR protocol of Olivos, which provides that once a MERCOSUR party decides to file a dispute with either MERCOSUR or WTO, it cannot file the same dispute with the other dispute settlement proceeding. Since the Protocol had not entered into force at that point of time, the Panel drew its conclusion based on the Brasilia protocol. For more discussion, see WTO Analytical Index, GATT 1994-Article XXIV, 21.

jurisdiction over the dispute in favor of an arbitration under the North American Free Trade Agreement (NAFTA). The panel concluded that "[u]nder the DSU, it had no discretion to decide whether or not to exercise its jurisdiction in a case properly before it."[54] However, the term 'properly' remains ambiguous as to what constitutes a dispute 'properly before the WTO panels'. If it means that the case should be registered with the WTO DSB according to DSU procedures, it follows that the complaining party should submit a case *prima facie* violation in writing. The written complaint should contain factual reasons to the dispute, the measures at issue, and provisions of the WTO Agreement concerned as the legal basis for the complaint.[55]

Both of these disputes suggest that a dispute arising out of a regional agreement can be filed with the WTO DSB given that the dispute is 'properly' registered, and that the regional agreement does not explicitly prevent a proceeding at the WTO. This is the case when the dispute involves a parallel breach of WTO provisions. However, none of the discussed disputes can answer the question whether WTO adjudicators apply provisions of regional agreements all the time or generally hear disputes arising out of regional agreements. While the possibility to do so exists, the common practice of WTO adjudicators does not suggest a broad inclination toward regional disputes.

Notwithstanding, trade agreements are rapidly proliferating and their consideration by WTO adjudicators seems inevitable. Due to rapid proliferation of regional trade agreements and the inclination of WTO members to apply provisions of regional agreements in their trade relations, it seems possible that WTO adjudicators will be inclined not only to consider provisions of regional agreements in interpreting WTO provisions but also opt to apply provisions of those agreements to WTO disputes or hear disputes arising out of them. In both instances, the question then arises how WTO adjudicators will resolve a possible normative conflict arising as a result of applying provisions of a regional agreement or hearing a dispute arising under a regional agreement.

6.1.1.3 Normative Conflict Resolution Between WTO Rules and Regional Agreements

If one accepts that WTO adjudicators can and should consider applying provisions of regional agreements to WTO disputes where relevant and compatible, the question on how to address conflicting obligations and rights stemming from WTO agreements and those regional agreements needs to be answered.

---

[54] Panel Report, *Mexico – Tax Measures on Soft Drinks and other Beverages*, WT/DS308/R, para. 7. 1 (Oct. 7, 2005) [hereinafter *Mexico – Soft Drinks*]. The AB upheld the panel's conclusion and ruled that "we express no view as to whether there may be circumstances in which legal impediments could exist that would preclude a panel from ruling on the merits of the claims on dispute before it". AB Report, *Mexico – Soft Drinks*, para. 54 (Mar. 24, 2006).

[55] Art. 4.4 DSU.

Recalling the discussion on treaty interpretation in the previous chapter, the primary approach is to look whether WTO rules and the regional agreement in question have established any explicit relationship according to Article 30 (2) VCLT.[56] If the regional agreement provides that it is subject to WTO rules or it is not to be considered incompatible with them, WTO rules will prevail over provisions of that regional agreement. In such scenario the relationship between them is similar to the relationship of a constitutional law with an ordinary law of a nation, that when in conflict is subordinate to the prevailing constitutional provision.[57]

However, it is problematic to rely on Article 30 VCLT when a regional agreement contains a priority clause providing for supremacy of its provisions over WTO rules or does not establish a relationship at all. Although Article 30 generally applies to all types of international treaties regardless of their form e.g., multilateral or regional, it is controversial whether it is still applicable when a regional agreement is explicit about the preference of its provisions over provisions of some multilateral treaties that have their unique design and rulemaking such as the WTO.[58] In the case of WTO rules and regional agreements, there is no consensus for the same effect as to when a regional agreement contains a provision on the preference of its rules over those of the WTO. The problem becomes significant, as the WTO Agreement itself does not establish any explicit relationship with other international agreements. In particular, whether its provisions prevail when in conflict with other international agreements or regional agreements. An answer can be found in some WTO supplementary documents such as the WTO 1996 Singapore Ministerial Declaration. It provides for the supremacy of WTO provisions over RTAs that are concluded in accordance with Article XXIV GATT. The Singapore Ministerial Declaration states the following:

> We reaffirm the primacy of the multilateral trading system, which includes a framework for the development of regional trade agreements, and we renew our commitment to ensure that regional trade agreements are complementary to it and consistent with its rules.[59]

Therefore, it is argued that Article 30 VCLT does not fit the relationship between WTO law and regional agreements.[60] WTO law has its own conditions and deviations of non-discriminatory rights and obligations in connection to regional agree-

---

[56]*Borgen* (Ch.5, note 106), 585–87.

[57]See ibid.; *Kearney and Dalton* (1970), p. 495, 517.

[58]*Cottier and Foltea* (2006), pp. 53–55; *Borgen* (Ch.5, note 106), 585–587.

[59]WTO, Ministerial Declaration of 18 December 1996, WT/MIN/(96)DEC (Dec. 18, 1996) [hereinafter Singapore Declaration]; for literature review see for example *Cottier and Foltea* (2006), pp. 56–57.

[60]*Cottier and Foltea* (2006), pp. 57; *Pauwelyn*, Conflicts of Norms in Public International Law (note 1), 321.

ments that raises the question of treaty hierarchy. That would mean supremacy of WTO law over regional agreements and would fall under other provisions of the VCLT and not Article 30.[61]

In the absence of an explicit normative relationship between WTO law and regional agreements, Article 41 VCLT entitled "agreements to modify multilateral treaties between certain of the parties only" would be most relevant to assess the relationship between WTO law and regional agreements particularly RTAs concluded under Article XXIV GATT.[62] Article 41(1) VCLT allows parties to a multilateral treaty to conclude an agreement that would modify their multilateral treaty rights and obligations only between them—provided that the multilateral treaty allows such a modification or does not prohibit it. However, the modification shall not affect the rights and obligations of other parties to the multilateral treaty or include a provision or a derogation that is incompatible with the purpose and objective of the multilateral treaty. Applying this to the relationship between WTO law and regional agreements, WTO provisions prevail over a regional agreement that contains a provision or a waiver that is incompatible with the purpose and objective of the WTO agreements.[63]

WTO law supremacy can also be assessed based on Article XXIV GATT that lays the foundation for RTAs concluded between WTO members and presents a limited exception to other GATT provisions. Since an RTA concluded between two or more WTO members gets its legitimacy from Article XXIV GATT, its relationship with WTO law depends upon Article XXIV, and since Article XXIV is an exception to the MFN principle, it should not be treated on an equal legal footing with other GATT or WTO substantive rules nor should be its constituted RTAs.[64] WTO members can also invoke WTO rules before their regional dispute settlement forums when provisions of regional agreements contradict with their WTO substantial rights and obligations.[65]

However, one should bear in mind that reliance on Article XXIV GATT to discuss the supremacy of WTO provisions is limited to those regional agreements governing the direct trade relationship between WTO members. Article XXIV does not apply to regional agreements that do not feature a direct trade relationship between the parties e.g., transit agreements. The relationship between Article XXIV GATT and RTAs can also be seen based on the relationship between an international norm establishing an institution and that established institution, which creates a supremacy of the international norm in relation to its established

---

[61]Ibid.

[62]See *Cottier and Foltea* (2006), pp. 53–55.

[63]See *Pauwelyn*, Conflicts of Norms in Public International Law (note 1), 321.

[64]See Singapore Ministerial Declaration, Section on Regional Trade Agreements; see also *Cottier and Foltea* (2006), pp. 56–57.

[65]See for example NAFTA, Panel Decision on Remand, Certain Softwood Lumber Products from Canada (Countervailing Duty), USA-CDA-1992-1904-01 (Dec. 17, 1993). The NAFTA panel held that "it is no matter for legal or economic surprise, then, that an independent GATT panel found no theoretical obstacle to a stumpage program, like that conducted in Canada, being a subsidy".

institution.[66] Therefore, when in conflict WTO provisions prevail over provisions of regional agreements, particularly in relation to RTAs established pursuant to Article XXIV GATT.

6.1.2   Judicial Decisions and General Principles of International Law

WTO adjudicators have on frequent occasions had recourse to general principles of international law and, in some instances, to judicial decisions to interpret WTO provisions and resolve normative conflicts between them. Unlike the possibility for international conventions and agreements to be applied in WTO disputes, recourse to general principles of law and judicial decisions is only to give guidance on meaning and interpretation of WTO provisions. For instance, in *Argentina – Poultry*, the panel stated that any recourse to judicial decisions is a mere matter of discretion and that Article 3.2 DSU did not bind WTO panels to follow panel reports, even if they are adopted. The panel statement was in response to Argentina's claim that the previous MERCOSUR tribunal ruling on the same dispute constituted a relevant normative conflict pursuant to Article 31(3)(c) VCLT and therefore had to be applied by the panel in the given dispute.[67]

Hence, WTO adjudicators only refer to judicial decisions of other international tribunals to support their interpretation of WTO provisions. For example, in *Korea – Definitive Safeguard Measures on Imports of Certain Dairy Products* (*Korea – Dairy*), the AB referred to some international legal doctrines and judicial decisions including the ICJ judgment in the *Ambatielos Case* (1953) to clarify what it means to provide an effective interpretation for a treaty in its terms and context as a whole. As a result, the AB held that interpreting a treaty as a whole means to "read all applicable provisions of a treaty in a way that gives meaning to all of them, harmoniously".[68] Similarly, in *United States – Standards for Reformulated and Conventional Gasoline* (*US – Gasoline*), the AB referred to some judgments of the ICJ, including the judgment in *Chad v. Libya*, to supplement its interpretation of Article XX(g) GATT that the general rules of treaty interpretation contained in Article 31 VCLT require to give effect and meaning to all terms of a treaty.[69]

In *China – Measures Affecting Trading Rights and Distribution Services for Certain Publications and Audiovisual Entertainment Products* (*China – Publications and Audiovisual Products*), the AB rejected China's argument that the terms

---

[66]*Schreuer* (1995), p. 477; *Kelsen* (1946), p. 373.

[67]Panel Report, *Argentina – Poultry,* para. 7. 41.

[68]AB Report, *Korea – Diary,* para. 81 & footnote 44.

[69]AB Report, *US – Gasoline,* para. 23 & footnote 45.

'sound recording' and 'distribution' should be given the meaning they had in 2001, when China acceded to the WTO, and not what they meant in the present time. In support of the statement that the terms were generic, the AB cited the ICJ judgment of *Costa Rica v. Nicaragua.*[70] In the case the ICJ found the term 'commercio' (commerce) in an agreement between Costa Rica and Nicaragua to mean both commerce in goods as well as commerce in services, even if the term only referred to commerce in goods at the time the two countries concluded the agreement.[71]

As for general principles of international law, the principles of 'error in treaty formation', 'good faith', 'evolutionary interpretation', 'proportionality', 'precautionary' and 'State sovereignty' are among the general principles that are often reflected in WTO case law.[72] For example, in *Korea – Procurement,* under which the US brought a non-violation complaint pursuant to Article XXIII:2 GATT against Korea alleging that its measures were inconsistent with the WTO Agreement on Government Procurement (GPA), the panel referred to 'error in treaty formation' the principle to assess whether the US assumption, that a project was covered by the GPA schedules as a result of Korea's accession to the GPA, constituted an 'error in treaty formation' with regard to GAP schedules between the US and Korea.[73] The 'error in treaty formation' is a principle under the customary rules of interpretation of public international law, which is reflected in Article 48(1) VCLT. Article 48 (1) provides:

> A State may invoke an error in a treaty as invalidating its consent to be bound by the treaty if the error related to a fact or situation which was assumed by that State to exist at the time when the treaty was concluded and formed an essential basis of its consent to be bound by the treaty.

In the same dispute, the panel also took the principle of 'good faith' into account to determine the extent a member could initiate a case of non-violation pursuant to its nullification or impairment right under Article XXIII:2 GATT.[74]

In *US – Shrimp*, based on the 'evolutionary interpretation' principle as a method of effective treaty interpretation[75] and in light of the definition provided by the UNCLOS for 'exhaustible natural resources', the AB found that the term exhaustible natural resources contained in Article XX(g) GATT was a generic term and that its meaning evolved to include both living and non-living natural resources.[76] The panel also assessed the balance between the measures at issue and the necessity of

---

[70]Navigational and Related Rights (Costa Rica. v. Nicar), 2009 I.C.J (July 13).

[71]AB Report, *China – Measures Affecting Trading Rights and Distribution Services for Certain Publications and Audiovisual Entertainment Products,* WT/DS363/AB/R, para. 396 & footnote 705 (Dec. 21, 2009) [hereinafter *China – Publications and Audiovisual Products*].

[72]See for example (note 1).

[73]Panel Report, *Korea –Procurement*, paras. 7. 122–123.

[74]Ibid., paras. 7. 93–95.

[75]*Howse* (2002), p. 499.

[76]AB Report, *US – Shrimp*, para.130; see also AB Report, *China – Publications and Audiovisual Products*, footnote 705.

those to protect exhaustible natural resources, based on the 'proportionality' princi-ple.[77] The meaning and scope of application of the 'proportionality' principle alters in different fields of international law.[78] In the context of WTO law, it is mostly used to ensure a balance between costs and benefits of a measure and establishes a reasonable connection between the measure and its goals.[79]

In *EC – Biotech*, the panel took account of the 'precautionary' principle as a 'relevant rule of international law' pursuant to Article 31(3)(c) VCLT when interpreting the provisions of the SPS Agreement.[80] It is worth noting that the SPS Agreement itself implicitly reflects the 'precautionary' principle in Articles 3.3 and 5.7. According to the definition provided by the WTO glossary of terms, the 'precautionary' principle is "a kind of safety-first approach to deal with scientific uncertainty".[81] Articles 3.3 and 5.7 provide that WTO members have an autonomous right to introduce WTO SPS-plus standards (or international standards such as Codex Alimentarius) under an appropriate system of risk management when there is sufficient scientific evidence for the introduction of those SPS plus standards. This means that members may apply the 'precautionary' principle to examine scientific information for the adoption of SPS plus standards.[82]

Similarly, in *China – Measures Related to the Exportation of Various Raw Materials* (*China – Raw Materials*), the panel referred to the principle of 'State sovereignty' to interpret the extent of WTO members' sovereignty over natural resources in accordance with Article XX(g) GATT. In doing so, the panel defined the 'State sovereignty' as a fundamental principle of international law that denotes "equality of all states in competence and independence over their own territories and encompassing the right to make laws applicable within their own territories without intrusion from other sovereign states."[83] Accordingly, in *US – Shrimp*, the AB held that a WTO member, as a sovereign State, is allowed to adopt unilateral measures to condition access of imports to its markets to domestic policies and regulations.[84]

---

[77]The AB thus held that the US measures were "not disproportionately wide in its scope and reach in relation to the policy objective of protection and conservation of sea turtle species." AB Report, *US – Shrimp*, para. 141.

[78]*Franck* (2010), p. 230.

[79]See generally Ibid.

[80]Panel Report, *EC – Biotech,* para. 7. 67; AB Report, *US – Shrimp*, para. 158 & footnote 157.

[81]WTO, Glossary of Terms.

[82]See for example AB Report, *EC – Hormones*, paras. 173, 175; AB Report, *Japan – Agricultural Products II*, para. 79; WTO Analytical Index, SPS Agreement – Article 3 (Jurisprudence), 12–13.

[83]Panel Report, *China – Measures Related to the Exportation of Various Raw Materials*, WT/DS394/R, para. 7. 377–378 (July 5, 2011) [hereinafter *China – Raw Materials*].

[84]AB Report, *US – Shrimp,* para. 121.

6.2   The Possibility to Invoke UNCLOS Rules on Freedom of Transit in WTO Dispute Settlement Proceedings

6.2.1   General Overview

As discussed earlier, WTO adjudicators opted to consider non-WTO multilateral agreements not only to clarify and interpret WTO provisions but also to apply their provisions to disputes before them where relevant and compatible with WTO provisions. With this said, while recourse to UNCLOS provisions to clarify and interpret WTO provisions cannot be denied, their application where compatible and relevant to a given dispute could also be possible—keeping in mind that consideration of such application should be based on circumstances of each dispute and lies in the discretional power of WTO adjudicators.

The interaction between WTO law and UNCLOS is mostly understood in an environmental context as many disputes brought to the WTO DSB mainly dealt with free trade and the environment in which WTO adjudicators referred to UNCLOS provisions for interpretational purposes. Although the environmental interaction between WTO law and UNCLOS is not directly relevant to the freedom of transit, particularly freedom of transit of landlocked States under the two regimes, its discussion may still be enlightening in assessing whether an analogy can be drawn for the WTO law interaction with other regulatory areas of the UNCLOS, i.e., freedom of transit.

The *US – Shrimp* and *Chile – Swordfish* [hereinafter the Swordfish case] are among the most popular WTO disputes involving a clash of trade and environmental rules. In *US – Shrimp*, Malaysia challenged US measures, which banned the import of shrimp and shrimp products that were caught with Turtle Excluding Devices (TED).[85] The AB assessed the US measures under Article XX(g) GATT and found that they were inconsistent with Article XX GATT chapeau due to their arbitrary and discriminatory application.[86] As part of its ruling, the AB had to answer the question whether the term 'exhaustible natural resources' under Article XX(g) GATT included both living and non-living natural resources. The AB did so by referring to the UNCLOS definition of exhaustible natural resources.[87]

Similarly, the Swordfish case is another WTO dispute involving trade and environment. The case was brought simultaneously and separately to WTO DSB and the International Tribunal on the Law of the Sea (ITLOS) by the EC and Chile, respectively. It tackles questions on both choice of applicable law and choice of dispute settlement forum under WTO law and UNCLOS. The dispute dealt with the EC's challenge of the Chilean Fishery Law that banned the unloading of vessels at Chilean ports for reasons of overfishing of swordfish across the South-eastern Pacific

---

[85]Panel Report, *US – Shrimp*, paras. 1. 1–5.

[86]AB Report, *US –Shrimp*, paras. 121, 177.

[87]Ibid., para .130; see also Aegean Sea Continental Shelf (Greece. V. Turkey) 1978 I.C.J., 3 (December 19); for literature review see *Pogoretskyy* (Ch.5, note 48),140–141; *Howse* (2002).

Ocean.[88] Chile argued that its law was consistent with UNCLOS as it aimed at conserving swordfish.[89] The EC, however, claimed that the ban constituted a restraint of the freedom of transit and a restriction on market competitiveness of EC's swordfish. Therefore, the EC argued that Chile violated its obligations under Articles V:1–3 and XI:1 GATT and initiated a dispute settlement proceeding at the WTO.[90] In return, Chile, instead of defending its measure under available WTO provisions, particularly XX(g) GATT, initiated a parallel dispute settlement proceeding at the ITLOS arguing that the EC violated its obligations to protect and preserve the maritime environment under UNCLOS provisions.[91]

However later, Chile agreed to enter into an arrangement with the EC allowing the EC to fish in the Chilean economic exclusive zone (EEZ) based on the condition that the EC withdraws its complaint in the WTO.[92] Although it did not withdraw, both States still suspended their disputes at the WTO DSB and ITLOS and reached a mutual agreement outside of these fora.[93] Since the dispute was never resolved by any of the two dispute settlement fora, the question of what would have happened if each forum would have issued a different decision is limited to hypothetical assessment and arguments by relevant literature.

The swordfish case is analyzed in different ways. Using *US – Shrimp* as a supporting example, an opinion supporting free trade suggests that if the swordfish dispute had undergone a dispute settlement proceeding at the WTO, the panel would have ruled in favor of the EC.[94] It is also argued that the WTO is a trade-oriented

---

[88]WTO, *Chile – Measures Affecting the Transit and Importation of Swordfish,* Request for Consultations by the European Communities, WT/DS193/1. (Apr. 26, 2000) [hereinafter *Chile – Swordfish*].

[89]WTO, *Chile – Swordfish,* Communication from Chile, WT/DS193/3/Add.1 (Apr.9, 2001).

[90]WTO, *Chile – Swordfish,* Request for the Establishment of a Panel by the EC, WT/DS193/2 (Nov. 7, 2000).

[91]International Tribunal for the Law of the Sea [ITLOS], Case Concerning the Conservation and Sustainable Exploitation of Swordfish Stocks in the South-Eastern Pacific Ocean (Chile/European Community), Case No 7, Order 2007/3, (Nov. 30, 2007).

[92]WTO, *Chile – Swordfish – Arrangement between the EC and Chile,* Communication from the EC, WT/DS193/3, (Apr. 6, 2001).

[93]Ibid.; see also ITLOS, *Request for Provisional Measures* (Order), ITLOS No. 10 (2001).

[94]See for example *Karaman Igor* (2012), p. 266 & footnote 59. Igor also cites the report of the GATT panel in *Tuna – Dolphin I* to support its argument. In *Tuna – Dolphin I*, the GATT panel stated that non-discriminating national environmental measures that impose barriers to free trade were not allowed to contradict the GATT provisions even if they were adopted in good faith. The panel further stated that a contracting party cannot adopt trade measures to implement its environmental regulation outside its territory. In *Tuna – Dolphin I*, the US import embargo of tuna and tuna products that were not fished according to standards set out under the US Marine Mammal Protection Act was challenged, *inter alia*, for its extra-territorial application. See GATT, *Tuna–Dolphin I*, DS21/R, 55 (Sep. 3, 1991). [Not adopted], https://www.wto.org/english/tratop_e/envir_e/edis04_e.htm.

regime and the applicable law in the WTO is international trade agreements, not other laws, i.e., environmental law or law of the sea.[95]

However, this view is outdated, as the WTO is no longer a mere trade forum bound by specific multilateral trade agreements. For example, Article XX GATT on 'general exceptions' is a substantive provision that considers the protection of societal values such as life and health of plants and the environment pivotal to the WTO regime.[96] This opens up the window for WTO adjudicators to look at and also use other international agreements such as UNCLOS when compatible with Article XX exceptions.[97] Similarly, the preamble of the WTO Agreement imposes a best endeavor obligation on members for collective cooperation in the area of 'sustainable development' and stresses the importance of environmental protection. Furthermore, the WTO Doha Mandate on Multilateral Environmental Agreements aims to negotiate environmental issues with other multilateral environmental agreements (MEAs) for effective cooperation, especially in areas in which those MEAs impose trade obligations.[98] Among environmental issues, the maritime environment has been part of the Doha development agenda, which sets a specific focus on adopting and strengthening WTO rules related to fishery subsidies to avoid overcapacity and overfishing through the prohibition of certain forms of fishery subsidies.[99] The WTO has a Committee on Environment and Trade, which is tasked to exchange information with other MEAs secretariats on trade and environmental policy commitments of WTO members to ensure that they are in line with international environmental standards.[100] This goal does not only include the trade aspect of the issue but also covers environmental objectives.

In the case of *US – Shrimp*, although the AB ruled against the US measures, the subtlety of the AB's decision has not been looked at carefully. The AB's decision does not indicate trade rules overriding environmental protection rules. It regards the discriminatory and arbitrary nature of environmental protection measures by the US, which failed the chapeau test of Article XX GATT and was considered as an abuse

---

[95]*Karaman Igor* (2012); see also *McLaughlin* (1997), p. 72.

[96]Other WTO agreements also address these values. For example, the SPS Agreement allows WTO members to adopt regulatory measures concerning the life and health of animal, plant and environment. Similarly, the TRIPS Agreement allows WTO members to adopt regulatory measures and policies on promoting green technology and reducing the functioning of other technologies that harm the environment. For WTO disputes involving environmental issues see for example AB Report, *US – Shrimp*; AB Report, *EC – Asbestos*; AB Report, *US – Gasoline*; see also WTO Secretariat, Harnessing Trade for Sustainable Development and a Green Economy (2011).

[97]*Stoll and Veoneky* (2002), pp. 33–34.

[98]See generally Doha Ministerial Declaration; see also Hong Kong Ministerial Declaration, paras. 9–11.

[99]See Hong Kong Declaration, Annex D, para. 9; WTO, WTO members hold discussions aimed at deepening talks on fisheries subsidies (Apr. 6 &11, 2017), https://www.wto.org/english/news_e/news17_e/fish_06apr17_e.htm.

[100]See WTO Committee on Trade and Development, The Doha Mandate on Multilateral Environmental Agreements (MEAs), https://www.wto.org/english/tratop_e/envir_e/envir_neg_mea_e.htm.

of environmental protection exception under Article XX(g).[101] The panel and the AB, both took into account the importance of environmental protection objective of the US measures as they referred to the WTO preamble reiterating the role of sustainable development goals in growth of trade.[102] The AB additionally referred to the 1994 WTO Ministerial Decision on Trade and the Environment and also to the Rio Declaration to stress the importance of environmental protection within the WTO regime.[103] The preamble to the 1994 WTO Ministerial Decision provides that "considering that there should not be, nor need be for, any policy contradiction between upholding and safeguarding an open, nondiscriminatory and equitable multilateral trading system on the one hand, and acting for the protection of the environment, and the promotion of sustainable development on the other".[104]

Last but an important note, when the US brought its measures in line with the Article XX requirements as recommended by the panel and the AB, the next AB decision, which dealt with the same complaint, was issued this time in favor of the US.[105] As such, the US measures were justified as environmental protection even though they were trade restrictive and had extra-territorial application.

This conclusion has strong normative implications for the Swordfish dispute. Had the dispute undergone a judicial proceeding before a WTO panel and had Chile invoked Article XX(g), the panel would have had the discretion to turn to other relevant international multilateral rules, particularly the UNCLOS environmental protection provisions.[106] This can be further supported by WTO case law (e.g., panel conclusions in *EC – Biotech* and *Korea – Procurement*) that recognizes the application of all sources of international law where compatible with WTO rules, regardless of whether or not those sources are explicitly addressed in the WTO covered agreements. With regard to a possible transit dispute before the WTO DSB, WTO adjudicators would have the discretional power to consider UNLCOS transit rules to clarify WTO transit rules or to apply them in the dispute. However, they are only authorized to do so when those rules are relevant to the dispute and compatible with WTO provisions on freedom of transit. To this end, the following subsection reviews UNCLOS rules on freedom of transit.

---

[101] AB Report, *US – Shrimp,* at paras. 147 & 159.

[102] *Id.,* for literature review *see, e.g., Broude* (2008), pp. 173, 202–203.

[103] AB Report, *US – Shrimp,* at 154. Paragraph 4 of the Rio Declaration provides that "[i]n order to achieve sustainable development, environmental protection shall constitute an integral part of the development process and cannot be considered in isolation from it." U.N. CONF. ENVT. & DEV, Annex I, Rio Declaration on Environment and Development, UN Doc A/CONF.151/26 (Vol I), 31 I.L.M 874 (1992).

[104] WTO, *Ministerial Decision on Trade and the Environment,* adopted by Ministers at the Meeting of the Trade Negotiations Committee at Marrakesh, April 14, 1994.

[105] AB Report, *US – Shrimp, Recourse to Article 21.5 of the DSU by Malaysia,* WT/DS58/AB/R, paras. 140, 141, 153, 154 (Oct. 22, 2001).

[106] *Stoll and Veoneky* (2002), pp. 33–35.

6.2.2   UNCLOS Rules on Freedom of Transit

UNCLOS was signed in 1982 at the third United Nations Conference on the Law of the Sea and entered into force on 16 November 1994. As of June 2016 with the accession of the landlocked State of Azerbaijan, UNCLOS has 168 members, including 27 landlocked State parties.[107] The landlocked LDC Afghanistan signed the Convention on 18 March 1983 but has not ratified it yet.[108] UNCLOS governs four fundamental activities related to freedom of high seas. These activities are navigation, resource exploitation, scientific research, and environmental protection.[109] Among them, freedom of navigation, which is defined by the UNCLOS as freedom of passage and includes freedom of transit,[110] is the oldest activity recognized by customary international law.[111]

Unlike the WTO provisions on freedom of transit, which are articulated in a general reciprocal MFN context without recognizing the special transit needs of landlocked members, particularly landlocked LDCs, the UNCLOS rules on the freedom of passage recognize the special needs of landlocked parties to free access to the sea on non-reciprocal and non-MFN basis. Moreover, the rules require coastal state parties to refrain from imposing unnecessary delays or difficulties on transit of landlocked states.[112] However, the UNCLOS subjects terms and modalities of freedom of transit of landlocked states to be decided by regional agreements between them and transit states, which limits in practice the non-reciprocity of the right of freedom of transit for landlocked states. Similarly, the UNCLOS provisions on the special recognition of freedom of transit of landlocked states does not preclude transit states from taking necessary measures to protect their security and other legitimate interests. With these limitations, landlocked states do not recap much of the so-called special, non-MFN and nonreciprocal right of freedom of transit and access to the sea granted by the UNCLOS compared to the general recognition of their MFN right of freedom of transit under the WTO.

---

[107]See UNCLOS, Chronological lists of ratification of, accession and succession to the Convention and related Agreements, https://www.un.org/Depts/los/reference_files/chronolog ical_lists_of_ ratifications.htm; see also UNOHRLLS, UNCLOS and Landlocked Developing Countries: Practical Implications: Summary Report (2012), 2.

[108]UNTC, https://treaties.un.org/Pages/ViewDetailsIII.aspx?src=TREATY&mtdsg_no=XXI6& chapter=21&Temp=mtdsg3&clang=_en#4.

[109]Art. 87 UNCLOS.

[110]Art. 18(1) UNCLOS.

[111]*Melgar* (Ch.1, note 2), 171.

[112]Prmb, part X & Art. 148 UNCLOS; for literature review see *Liu* (2009), pp. 28–34.

6.2.2.1   UNCLOS Rules on Freedom of Passage

UNCLOS recognizes two different types of free passages to the high seas to its State parties, irrelevant of whether the State is landlocked or coastal (1) right of innocent passage, and (2) right of transit passage.[113] Article 19 UNCLOS defines an innocent passage as a passage that takes place in the territorial sea or internal waters of coastal states without being prejudicial to peace, good order or security of coastal States. Similarly, Article 38(2) UNCLOS defines transit passage as "[t]he exercise [. . .] of the freedom of navigation and overflight solely for the purpose of continuous and expeditious transit of the strait between one part of the high seas or an exclusive economic zone and another part of the high seas or an exclusive economic zone." As such innocent passage takes place in territorial sea and internal waters of coastal states, while transit passage takes place through straits by both ships and aircrafts.[114] Notwithstanding the type of passage, whether innocent or transit, it should always be expeditious and continuous unless under a force major.[115]

The terms laid down in the definitions provided above need to be defined before continuing the discussion on transit passage. First, it needs to be defined what constitutes high seas and how it is different from straits and territorial seas. Article 86 UNCLOS defines high seas as "all parts of the sea that are not included in the exclusive economic zone, in the territorial sea or in the internal waters of a State, or in the archipelagic waters of an archipelagic State." According to this definition the territorial sea and internal waters belong to the sovereignty of coastal States and do not constitute parts of the high seas. It should also be clarified what constitutes territorial sea and internal waters. UNCLOS defines the territorial sea as an adjacent sea belt covering twelve nautical miles of the sea from the baseline coast of a coastal State subject to full sovereignty of that State.[116] Similarly, UNCLOS defines internal waters of a coastal State as "waters on the landward side of the baseline of the territorial sea form part of the internal waters of the State."[117]

Next, freedom of the high seas should be defined. Article 87 UNCLOS provides:

> The high seas are open to all states, whether coastal or landlocked" for the freedom of "[the four activities]" as mentioned earlier. Moreover, a literature definition of the high seas means "any use compatible with the status of the high seas – that is, a use which involves no claim to appropriation of part of the high seas and which involves no unreasonable interference with the rights of others – should be admitted as a freedom unless it is excluded by some specific rule of law.[118]

---

[113]Arts. 17, 24, 37(1) UNCLOS; for literature review See for example *Ngantcha* (1990).

[114]Art. 39 UNCLOS. It should be noted that although UNCLOS recognizes overflight passage as transit passage and recognizes aircraft as means of traffic in transit, it provides that rules of the 1994 International Civil Aviation Organization Convention should govern overflight passage by aircraft. Art. 39 (3) UNCLOS.

[115]Art. 18(2) UNCLOS.

[116]Ibid., Arts. 2, 3.

[117]Ibid., Art. 8(1).

[118]*Churchil and Lowe* (1988).

Another term that needs to be defined is the 'exclusive economic zones' (EEZ). UNCLOS defines the EEZ as "an area beyond and adjacent to the territorial sea, subject to the specific legal regime. . ."[119] which "shall not extend beyond 200 nautical miles from the baselines from which the breadth of the territorial sea is measured".[120] Unlike full sovereignty over its territorial sea, a coastal State does not have territorial sovereignty over EEZs and only enjoys some jurisdiction over specific activities, such as such as fishing, mining, oil exploration, protection and preservation of natural resources and marine environment and conducting marine research across the EEZ.[121] Therefore, the EEZs remain open to the free use of all States, whether landlocked or coastal, for exercising activities related to the freedom of high seas.[122]

Moreover, the term 'international strait' which is subject to the freedom of transit needs to be defined. According to Article 37 UNCLOS a strait or an international strait is a body of water that is located "between one part of the high seas or an [EEZ] and another part of the high seas or an [EEZ]" and is "used for international navigation".[123] A strait is part of the territorial sea of coastal States, but the qualifying factor making it an open international route to transit passage is its geographical location connecting two parts of the high seas or EEZs. While the geographical location is the primary characteristic of a strait to serve as an international transit passage route to the high seas, it actually needs to have been used for international transit. As such, a strait qualifies as 'international' route for sea passage when (1) it connects two parts of the high seas, and (2) it is been used for international transit.[124]

Just like innocent passage, a transit passage should also not be prejudicial to the peace, good order or security of coastal States.[125] In that case, UNCLOS recognizes the right of coastal States to implement necessary security measures and temporary suspension of transit passage.[126] Adoption of such measures also contains restrictive

---

[119] Art. 55 UNCLOS.

[120] Ibid., Art. 57.

[121] Ibid., Art. 56.

[122] Ibid., Art. 58(1).

[123] According to literature a strait is "a narrow natural passage or arm of water connecting two larger bodies of water." *Churchill and Lowe* (1988), p. 87.

[124] Art. 37 UNCLOS; for literature review see *Churchill and Lowe* (1988), p. 3. The criteria for a strait to serve as an international transit route can be further elaborated in the Corfu Channel Case. In 1949, the UK deployed a naval team to the Corfu Channel without notifying the Albania which the Corfu Channel was laid in its territory. Albania challenged the UK in the ICJ for the UK violation of its territorial sovereignty over the Channel. Albania alleged that the Channel was not a strait for international navigation. The ICJ rejected Albania's argument and held that "the decisive criterion is rather its geographical situation as connecting two parts of the high seas and the fact of its being used for international navigation. Corfu Channel (U.K. v. Albania), 1949 I.C.J., 28 (April 9).

[125] Arts. 19(2), 39(1)(c), 40, 45 UNCLOS; see also ICJ, *United Kingdom v Albania,* pg. 28; For literature review see *Melgar* (Ch.1, note 2), 176.

[126] Art. 25(1) UNCLOS.

port access measures including border closure measures for legitimate reasons as a result of State sovereignty of coastal States over their ports.[127] However, the coastal States are allowed by UNCLOS to consider the imposition of a port restriction when necessary to protect their security, as long as it is applied on a transparent and non-discriminatory basis, even if the passage is innocent. Article 25(2) UNCLOS provides that "the coastal State may, without discrimination in form or in fact among foreign ships, suspend temporarily in specified areas of its territorial sea the innocent passage of foreign ships if such suspension is essential for the protection of its security, including weapons exercises. Such suspension shall take effect only after having been duly published." Although innocent passage is not the same as transit passage, it is nevertheless essential for the exercise of freedom of the high seas, which includes freedom of transit, particularly for landlocked States.[128] For instance, if landlocked State A needs to access to the high seas and therefore needs to transit through the territory of coastal State B including its territorial sea, it can do so only if its passage is innocent.

Furthermore, Article 38(2) UNCLOS recognizes the free use of other routes such as air, rivers, and land (roads and railways) in the territory of coastal States to facilitate the free transit passage to the sea through international straits. It provides "however, the requirement of continuous and expeditious transit does not preclude passage through the strait for the purpose of entering, leaving or returning from a State bordering the strait, subject to the conditions of entry to that State."[129] It should be pointed out that by subjecting the entry into the territory of coastal states to its conditions of entry, UNCLOS gives the authority to coastal States to apply their national customs regulations. For instance, UNCLOS allows them to adopt laws and regulations in accordance with applicable rules of international law when necessary to prevent, reduce and control oil, fishing by fishing vessels and loading or unloading of any commodity or persons while in transit which does not comply with their national laws.[130]

Moreover, in the course of exercise of free transit passage, both coastal States and States whose traffic is in transit through the coastal States [hereinafter flag States] have some further rights and obligations. While coastal States are obliged not to cause any unnecessary delay to the passage of traffic in transit, flag States have to make sure that their traffic in transit (a) proceeds without any delays and without engaging it in any activities different to what normal passage has to undergo, except for special circumstances such as force major or distress, (b) refrain from the use of threat or force against the sovereignty, territorial integrity or political independence

---

[127]Ibid. In Nicaragua case, the ICJ held also that "by virtue of its sovereignty that a coastal State may regulate access to its ports." Military and Paramilitary Activities (Nicar. V. U.S), 1986 I.C.J. 14, 213 (June 27).

[128]*Tabibi* (1958).

[129]Similarly, besides ships and aircrafts, UNCLSO recognizes railway rolling stock, lake and river craft; road vehicles and where local conditions require, porters and pack animals as traffic in transit. Art. 124(1)(d) UNCLOS.

[130]Art. 42 UNCLOS.

of coastal States or violation of generally accepted norms of international law embodied in the United Nations Charter, and (c) comply with generally accepted international regulations.[131] Likewise, UNCLOS prohibits coastal States from subjecting traffic in transit to any customs charges, fees and other duties except those as a result of transit service or administrative expenses rendered.[132]

In addition to generally recognizing the right of transit passage to all State parties through straits available for international navigation, UNCLOS introduces a special regime of freedom of transit to landlocked State parties. UNCLOS further grants SDT treatment to landlocked LDCs in relation to free access to the sea for the purpose of exercise of all legitimate activities including freedom of transit.

6.2.2.2 UNCLOS Rules on Freedom of Transit of Landlocked States

UNCLOS provisions regarding freedom of transit of landlocked States are articulated in Part X (Articles 124–132).[133] Part X excludes the principle of reciprocity and the application of the MFN principle for transit and grants vessels of landlocked States equal MFN treatment in accessing maritime ports.[134] However, UNCLOS provides that terms and modalities of exercise of freedom of transit of landlocked States are to be decided under regional agreements between landlocked States and transit States, which limits in practice the nonreciprocity of the right of freedom of transit for landlocked States. Similarly, although recognizing the special need of freedom of transit of landlocked States, UNCLOS does not preclude the right of transit States taking measures necessary to protect their security and other legitimate interests.

Article 124 UNCLOS defines freedom of transit of landlocked States and sets out the scope of traffic in transit including means of transport. Article 124 addresses only freedom of transit from and to landlocked States but does not specify any criteria for transit routes such as that under Article V GATT as being 'most convenient for international transit'. Article 124(1)(c) provides:

> Traffic in transit means transit of persons, baggage, goods and means of transport across the territory of one or more transit States, when the passage across such territory, with or without trans-shipment, warehousing, breaking bulk or change in the mode of transport, is only a portion of a complete journey which begins or terminates within the territory of the landlocked State.

---

[131] Ibid., Arts. 39, 40.

[132] Ibid., Art. 127.

[133] For literature review see *Melgar* (Ch.1, note 2), 189–226; *Liu* (2009), pp. 119–123; *Proelss* (2017), pp. 89–935.

[134] Arts. 124, 125, 126, 131 UNCLOS. The equal treatment to vessels flying the flag of landlocked States put an end to the traditional understanding of nationality of vessels through their port of registration. See *Rothwell and Stephens* (2016), p. 214.

Similarly, Article 124(2) provides for means of transport to include: "(i) railway rolling stock, sea, lake and river craft and road vehicles; (ii) where local conditions so require, porters and pack animals." Although, unlike Article V GATT, Article 124 (2) UNCLOS provides a specific list of means of transport, it is not incompatible with Article V GATT. Article V mentions of vessels as means of transport that by definition is a means of transport through sea, lake and river. Article V also mentions of the term 'other means of transport' that could include any means of transport used for the carriage of traffic in transit.

The exclusion of the MFN principle in relation to freedom of transit and access to the sea of landlocked States is articulated in Article 126, that provides:

> The provisions of this Convention, as well as special agreements relating to the exercise of the right of access to and from the sea, establishing rights and facilities on account of the special geographical position of land-locked States, are excluded from the application of most-favoured-nation clause.

Similarly, Article 127 UNCLOS exempts traffic in transit from "any customs duties, taxes or other charges except charges levied for specific service rendered in connection with such traffic" and therefore obliges transit States to provide national treatment to means of transport of traffic in transit. The exemption of transit charges and taxes except for those carried out for transit services under Article 127 is comparable and compatible with Article V:3 GATT. However, the non-discriminatory basis for the permissible charges or duties under Article 127 UNCLOS is different from GATT, as it requires national treatment when levying those charges and taxes, while Article V:4 GATT grants MFN treatment when levying permissible transit charges and taxes.[135]

One should then see whether existence of a national treatment provision under Article 127 UNCLOS and its absence in Article V:4 GATT constitutes incompatibility or normative conflict. For the sake of discussion, a hypothetical example will illustrate whether there is any incompatibility or normative conflict between Article 127 UNCLOS and Article V:4 GATT. Assume, State A, who is a WTO member and an UNCLOS party, brings a claim to the WTO dispute settlement against an alleged discriminatory treatment by State B, who is also a WTO member and an UNCLOS party. State A claims that transit charges are levied on its traffic in transit by State B and that State B's treatment is less favorable than that it has or does provide to its own traffic in transit and therefore is violating its Article V GATT obligation to provide non-discriminatory treatment to traffic in transit from other WTO members. During the proceeding State A fails to cite an exact provision of Article V GATT or Article 11 TFA that provides for national treatment with regard to transit charges, except for MFN treatment under Article V:4 GATT, but invokes Article 127 UNCLOS to support its argument and argues that Article 127 UNCLOS should be considered as "a relevant rule of international law applicable to relations between the parties."

---

[135]*Tanaka* (2015), p. 409.

Recalling the discussion on treaty conflict resolution in the previous sections Article 127 UNCLOS does not seem to be incompatible with Article V GATT as conflict or incompatibility only arises when one legal provision allows what another legal provision prohibits. While Article V GATT is explicit on the application of MFN treatment to transit charges, it is silent about whether transit States shall also apply transit charges based on national treatment. As such, the UNCLOS national treatment of transit charges can rather be seen as Article V GATT plus obligation and not as an incompatible provision. The question now arises whether this could be a valid invocation to support State A's argument and whether a WTO adjudicator would consider the application of a GATT plus obligation, which is outside of WTO rules. The silence in WTO agreements needs to be interpreted and for this recourse to Article 31(3)(c) VCLT is most relevant to answer this question. For States A and B, who are both UNCLOS parties, recourse to Article 127 UNCLOS will serve as a 'relevant rule of international law applicable to relations between the parties to the dispute' and its application lies within the discretional power of WTO adjudicators.

The next UNCLOS provision on freedom of transit of landlocked States is Article 125. It sets out the foundational provision for non-reciprocal freedom of transit of landlocked States and provides:

1. Land-locked States shall have access to and from the sea for the purpose of exercising the rights provided for in this the right of Convention including those relating to the freedom of the high seas and the common heritage of mankind. To this end, land-locked States shall enjoy freedom of transit through the territory of transit States by all means of transport.
2. The terms and modalities for exercising freedom of transit shall be agreed between the land-locked States and transit States concerned through bilateral, subregional or regional agreements.
3. Transit States, in the exercise of their full sovereignty over their territory, shall have the right to take all measures necessary to ensure that the rights and facilities provided for in this Part for land-locked States shall in no way infringe their legitimate interests.

Article 125 raises some legal controversies. It does so not only regarding its compatibility with Article V GATT and Article 11 TFA, but also in relation to the extent of non-reciprocal freedom of transit that UNCLOS actually grants to land-locked States in practice. For instance, while Article 125(1) lies down the provision on freedom of transit of landlocked States on non-reciprocal basis by specifying that "land-locked States shall enjoy freedom of transit through the territory of transit States" (without specifying that transit States shall enjoy the same freedom through the territory of landlocked States), it subjects the terms and modalities of exercise of that freedom of transit to regional agreements between landlocked States and transit States. While regional agreements can be reciprocal and non-reciprocal, in practice they have been mostly reciprocal—thus a reciprocal regional agreement limits the non-reciprocity nature of freedom of transit granted to landlocked States under

Article 125(1).[136] Furthermore, Article 125(2) paves the way for restrictive terms and modalities forced by transit States and puts landlocked States in a weaker position, which ultimately restricts the effective exercise of freedom of transit by landlocked States.[137] This being said, Article 125(2) raises the risk of the misuse of power by transit States by imposing restrictive terms and modalities of their own preference on landlocked States.[138] Although UNCLOS contains a good faith provision obliging State parties to carry out their UNCLOS rights and obligations in good faith,[139] given the subjectivity nature of good faith and lack of any further provision or a procedure to examine UNCLOS parties' veracity in carrying these out, it is difficult to rely on the mere principle of good faith to prevent a misuse of Article 125(2) UNCLOS.[140]

Furthermore, and especially when a regional agreement is reciprocal, a landlocked State cannot legally claim against a condition or rule that it has explicitly agreed under a binding agreement. It would also be consistent with Article 41 VCLT, which its application UNCLOS recognizes.[141] However, one may argue that since Article 41 VCLT provides that such modification shall not be incompatible with the multilateral agreement or with its overall object and purpose, terms and modalities that restrict freedom of transit of landlocked States are incompatible with the UNCLOS objective and purpose reflected in its preamble, and with Article 125 (1) that imposes a mandatory obligation on transit States to respect freedom of transit of landlocked States. Although throughout its text, UNCLOS does not provide what constitutes 'freedom', a literature definition of 'freedom' from the previous chapter as an 'unrestricted access' suggests that regional agreements imposing restrictive terms and modalities for the exercise of freedom of transit of landlocked States are incompatible with the essence of freedom of transit.

Finally, but yet importantly, Article 125(2) UNCLOS raises the question as to how landlocked States can exercise their right to freedom of transit and free access to the sea when there is no regional agreement between them and transit States or both sides are not able to come to an agreement at all. UNCLOS does not envisage the stance and remains silent about it. Although freedom of transit as a principle of international law cannot be suspended, in practice, without any clear terms and modalities the effective exercise of freedom of transit is impeded and a transit State will then consider imposition of terms and modalities of their own preference as part

---

[136]See for example *Melgar* (Ch.1, note 2), 195–197; *Proelss* (2017), p. 91; *Tanaka* (2015); *Uprety* (2005), p. 113.

[137]See *Melgar* (Ch.1, note 2), 195–197; *Proelss* (2017), p. 91; *Rothwell and Stephens* (2016), p. 210.

[138]See *Rothwell and Stephens* (2016), pp. 211–212.

[139]Art. 300 UNCLOS.

[140]See *Rothwell and Stephens* (2016), p. 212.

[141]Article 311(3) UNCLOS provides that Article 41 VCLT is applicable to conflict between UNCLOS provisions and other international agreements concluded by UNCLOS State parties.

of their legal sovereignty or their territorial sovereignty.[142] An example of bilateral agreement demonstrating strict terms and modalities of exercise of freedom of transit between a coastal State and a landlocked State is the 1965 transit agreement (ATTA) between Afghanistan and Pakistan. As mentioned in earlier chapters, the conclusion of ATTA was influenced by the UNCLOS drafting negotiations but ATTA, due to its limited provisions on freedom of transit and strict terms of modalities of exercise of freedom of transit, could not resolve the transit challenges Afghanistan faced in terms of freedom of transit and access to the sea through Pakistan's territory. This is probably a reason why Afghanistan, for nearly three decades since signing UNCLOS, has yet not ratified the Convention.

Another legal controversy arises from Article 125(3) regarding the right of transit States to adopt all types of measures necessary to protect their legitimate interests when those are affected by the exercise of freedom of transit of landlocked States. This provision serves both as a general as well as a security exception. Similarities can be drawn to those of GATT, but they differ in the way that Article 125(3) is ambiguous and has unlimited scope. First, although protection of 'legitimate interests' can be compared with the list of legitimate interests laid down in Article XX GATT, it is still not clear what constitutes 'legitimate interests' of parties and whether those legitimate interest are subject to review by UNCLOS dispute settlement bodies.[143] The undetermined extent of the 'legitimate interests' in Article 127 (3) UNCLOS, on one hand, and the lack of requirements as to whether or not transit states are obliged to prove the necessity of their measures to protect those interests, on the other hand, increase the risk of abuse of Article 125(3).

The Article 125(3) provision on 'legitimate interests' as a ground for adopting restrictive measures is also broader compared with XXI GATT on security exceptions. Article XXI allows members to adopt any kind of measures they consider necessary for the protection of their 'essential' security interests. This means that not all legitimate interests are 'essential'. Moreover, Article XXI limits the adoption and application of measures necessary to protect essential security interests to specific circumstances, which are circumstances of war and other emergencies in international relations.

So far, the right to freedom of transit of landlocked States were discussed in a general context for all landlocked States whether developed, developing or LDC as set out under Part X UNCLOS. While Part X does not provide for a particular recognition of the special needs of landlocked LDCs to freedom of transit and free

---

[142]See *Tanaka* (2015), p. 409; *Uprety* (2005), p. 86.

[143]WTO case law provides a relatively broad definition for 'legitimate interests'. In *Canada – Pharmaceutical Patents*, the panel defined 'legitimate interests' as "justifiable interests in the sense that they are supported by relevant public policies or other social norms. Panel report, *Canada – Patent Protection of Pharmaceutical Products*, WT/DS114/R, para. 7. 69 (Mar. 17, 2000) [hereinafter *Canada – Pharmaceutical Patent*]. Similarly, in *US – COOL*, the panel provided an ordinary meaning to the term 'legitimate' as, *inter alia*, 'justifiable', 'lawful' and 'proper' and cited the panel definition of 'legitimate interests'. Panel report, *United States – Certain Country of Labelling (COOL) Requirements*, WT/DS384, paras. 7. 630–32 (Nov. 18, 2011) [hereinafter *US – COOL*].

access to the sea, Article 48 UNCLOS gives special consideration to the interests and needs of landlocked developing States in relation to their activities in the regime of high seas, which includes their free access to and from the sea. However, Article 125 (2) UNCLOS still governs the exercise of freedom of transit of landlocked LDCs and thus there is no special consideration for them different from those addressed under Part X.

To conclude, the condition for the exercise of the non-reciprocal freedom of transit of landlocked States as granted by Part X UNCLOS still depends on regional arrangements between landlocked States, including landlocked LDCs and transit States. Moreover, by respecting full sovereignty of transit States and allowing them to subject freedom of passage including transit passage to domestic laws and regulations, UNCLOS makes its provisions on freedom of transit more convenient to transit States than to landlocked States. Therefore, in practice, UNCLOS does not grant transit privileges that are higher or broader than those granted by Article V GATT and Article 11 TFA. Lastly, the question as to whether WTO landlocked members can invoke UNCLOS provisions on freedom of transit in WTO dispute settlement proceedings, the answer is yes, given that those provisions do not conflict with WTO rules on freedom of transit.

6.3   Conclusion

WTO law establishes a harmonious relationship with other sources of public international law and recognizes their application as clarification instruments for the interpretation of WTO provisions. Although in principle, the applicable law in WTO dispute settlement proceedings is only the WTO covered agreements and any recourse to other sources of public international law is limited to clarification and interpretation of provisions of the covered agreements, WTO adjudicators have opted to consider non-WTO multilateral agreements not only to clarify and interpret WTO provisions but also to apply their provisions where compatible and relevant to a given dispute.

The relationship between WTO law and UNCLOS can be established for both interpretation and application purposes. While recourse to UNCLOS provisions by WTO adjudicators to clarify and interpret WTO provisions cannot be denied, the application of UNCLOS provisions is also possible—keeping in mind that recognition of such application is based on circumstances of each dispute and only lies within the autonomous power of WTO adjudicators. Looking at the relationship between WTO law and UNCLOS provisions in the context of freedom of transit of landlocked States, it is possible that WTO adjudicators would have recourse to the application of UNCLOS provisions on freedom of transit of landlocked States but only to the extent that those provisions do not conflict with those of the WTO. However, the assessment carried out under the UNCLOS provisions on freedom of transit of landlocked States suggests that landlocked States, including landlocked LDCs, do not reap so much out of the UNCLOS provisions that it makes a significant difference in rights and privileges compared to those in a WTO dispute settlement proceeding. One may conclude that WTO provisions on freedom of transit, even though they are not specific on the transit needs of landlocked States, guarantee freedom of transit across the territory of all members in a stronger and broader way compared with those of the UNCLOS as they first of all do not directly give full sovereignty to transit States and secondly they do not subject exercise of freedom of transit of members to terms and modalities to be decided by regional agreements.

References

Bartels L (2001) Applicable law in WTO dispute settlement proceedings. J World Trade 35:503–509

Broude T (2008) Principles of normative integration and the allocation of international authority: the WTO, the Vienna Convention on the law of treaties, and the Rio declaration. Loyalo Univ Chicago Int Law Rev 6(173):202–203

Churchil RR, Lowe AV (1988) The law of the sea 167. Manchester University Press

Cottier T, Foltea M (2006) Constitutional functions of the WTO and RTAs. In: Bartels L, Ortino F (eds) Regional Trade Agreements and the WTO Legal System: economic analysis of Regional Trade Agreements, pp 53–55

Franck TM (2010) Proportionality in international law. Law Ethics Human Rights 4:230

Howse R (2002) The appellate body rulings in the Shrimps/Turtles Case: a new legal baseline for the trade and environment debate. Columbia J Environ Law 27:498–500

Jackson JH (1998) World Trading System: law and policy of international economic relations, 2nd edn. MIT Press, Cambridge, pp 25–30

Karaman Igor V (2012) Disputes in the law of the sea. BRILL, p 266

Kearney RD, Dalton RE (1970) The treaty on treaties. Am J Int Law 64:495, 517

Kelsen H (1946) General theory of law and states, 2nd edn. Harvard University Press, p 373

Liu C (2009) Maritime transport services in the law of the sea and the World Trade Organization, vol. 14. Peter Lang Publishers, pp 28–34

McLaughlin RJ (1997) Settling trade-related disputes over the protection of marine living resources: UNCLOS or the WTO? Georgetown Int Econ Law Rev 10:72

Mitchell AD (2008) Legal principles in WTO disputes. Cambridge University Press:15–23

Ngantcha F (1990) The right of innocent passage and the evolution of the international law of the sea 52. Pinter Publishers, London

Pauwelyn J (2001) The role of public international law in the WTO: how far can we go? Am J Int Law 95:538–540

Pauwelyn J (2005) The application of Non–WTO rules of international law in WTO dispute settlement. In: Pauwelyn J (ed) World Trade Organization: legal, economic and political analysis. Springer, pp 1406–1423

Proelss A (ed) (2017) United Nations Convention on the law of the sea: a contemporary. C.H. Beck, pp 89–935

Rothwell DR, Stephens T (2016) The international law of the sea, 2nd edn. Hart, p 214

Schreuer C (1995) Regionalism v. Universalism. Eur J Int Law 6:477

Stoll P-T, Veoneky S (2002) The Swordfish case: law of the sea v. Trade. Heidelberg J Int 62:33–34

Tabibi AH (1958) Free access to the sea for countries without sea-coast: position of Afghanistan on this question. Publisher Unknown

Tanaka Y (2015) The international law of the sea, 2nd edn. Cambridge University Press, p 409

Uprety K (2005) The transit regime for landlocked states, law, justice and development series. WB, p 113

Chapter 7
The Relationship Between Freedom of Transit and General and Security Exceptions Under WTO Rules

Chapter 5 on WTO rules on the freedom of transit concluded that Article V GATT and Article 11 TFA impose an MFN obligation on WTO members to grant freedom of transit throughout their territories to traffic in transit. They further provide that any unnecessary restriction on the freedom of transit constitutes a violation of those provisions. However, the GATT embodies some general and security exceptions that allow members, if their conditions are fulfilled, to deviate from their GATT obligations including an obligation to grant free and unrestricted transit passage. These exceptions, set out in Articles XX and XXI GATT, support national trade policies and trade restrictive measures designed by members to protect, *inter alia,* life or health of humans, animals, plants; preserve the environment; secure compliance with national laws and safeguard their essential national security interests. Since the inception of the WTO, members frequently invoked these exceptions in order to justify their GATT inconsistent trade restrictive measures.[1] There were 1118 QRs notified by members to the WTO as of May 2019, which 705 QRs or 75.1% notified QRs invoked Article XX GATT on general exceptions and 16.7% of them invoked Article XXI GATT on security exceptions.[2] Similarly, members frequently invoked these exceptions before the WTO dispute settlement as a defense for *prima facie* violations of their GATT obligations.

This chapter reviews the relationship between WTO rules on freedom of transit and the GATT general and security exceptions. The chapter contains two main sections. Section 7.1 discusses Article XX GATT on general exceptions and assesses its relationship with WTO rules on freedom of transit and contains a case study of its implications for the transit relationship between Afghanistan and Pakistan. Section 7.2 discusses Article XXI GATT on security exceptions and assesses its

---

[1] Not only for the violation of their obligations under GATT but also their obligations under other WTO agreements.

[2] WTO, Report by the Secretariat, Quantitative Restrictions: Factual Information Notification Received, G/MA/W/114/Rev. 2 (May 20, 2019).

© The Author(s), under exclusive license to Springer Nature Switzerland AG 2021
S. Akbari, *The WTO Transit Regime for Landlocked Countries and its Impacts on Members' Regional Transit Agreements*, European Yearbook of International Economic Law 17, https://doi.org/10.1007/978-3-030-73464-0_7

relationship with WTO rules on freedom of transit. In doing so, it analyses the WTO case law and particularly assesses the recent WTO panel conclusion in *Russia— Traffic in Transit*.

7.1 Article XX GATT on General Exceptions: Scope of Application and Requirements

Article XX GATT on general exceptions contains ten paragraphs—of which members have frequently invoked a few in the WTO dispute settlement to justify violation of a GATT obligation.[3] Article XX allows members to design national trade policies, adopt and apply trade restrictive measures that are (a) necessary to protect public morals, (b) necessary to protect life or health of humans, animals or plants, (c) relating to the importation or exportation of gold or silver, (d) necessary to secure compliance with members' WTO consistent national laws and regulations, including regulations governing customs enforcement, protection of intellectual property and prevention of deceptive practices, (e) relating to the products of prison labor, (f) imposed for the protection of national treasures of artistic, historic or archaeological value, (g) relating to the conservation of exhaustible natural resources, (h) taken in pursuance of obligations under any WTO compatible inter-governmental commodity agreement, (i) involving non-discriminatory restrictions on exports of domestic materials to ensure essential quantities of such materials to a domestic processing industry during periods when the domestic price of such materials is below the world price as part of a governmental stabilization plan, and (j) essential to the acquisition or distribution of products in general or in local short supply.

In order to justify a GATT inconsistent measure as one of the listed exceptions of Article XX, members need to fulfill two main requirements known as 'two-tier test'.[4] The 'two-tier test' requires that a member's GATT inconsistent measure not only is necessary and falls within one of the listed exceptions of Article XX, but also meets the requirements set out in the chapeau of Article XX. A member invoking Article XX has to prove, to the satisfaction of WTO panels, that the measures at stake were 'necessary' to protect one of the listed exceptions and that no other alternatives were 'reasonably available' to address the issue in a less-trade restrictive manner.[5]

---

[3]For literature review see for example Van Den Bossche and Zaouc (2018), pp. 544–613, Lester et al. (2011), pp. 373–443; Wolfrum (2010), pp. 455–478; see also WTO Analytical Index, GATT 1994—Article XX (Jurisprudence).

[4]The AB first introduced the concept of 'two-tier test' under Article XX GATT in *US—Gasoline*.

[5]See for example AB Report, *Korea—Measures Affecting Imports of Fresh, Chilled and Frozen Beef*, WT/DS161/AB/R, paras. 659, 674 (Jan. 10, 2001) [hereinafter *Korea—Beef*]; AB Report, *EC—Asbestos*, para. 119; AB Report, *United States—Measures Affecting the Cross-Border Supply of Gambling and Betting Services*, WT/DS285/AB/R (Apr. 5, 2005) [hereinafter *US—Gambling*]; for literature review see Regan (2007), pp. 347–369.

Moreover, a measure needs to be 'provisionally justified', meaning that a member applying such measure is required to end or modify its measure as soon as circumstances giving rise to the adoption and application of that measure ended or changed in such a way that they can be addressed in a less-trade restrictive manner.[6] The responding party carries the burden of proof on the necessity of measures, whereas the complaining party caries the burden of proof whether there were other alternatives available to the responding party. Moreover, it is onus of the responding party to prove that such alternatives were not available to it.[7]

However, these requirements alone are not enough to justify a GATT inconsistent measure under Article XX. The measure further needs to fulfill the requirements set out in the chapeau of Article XX. The chapeau only allows adoption and application of an otherwise GATT inconsistent measure that falls under one of the listed exceptions, when its application does not constitute "a means of arbitrary or unjustifiable discrimination between countries where the same conditions prevail" or a "disguised restriction on international trade".[8] The primary aim of the chapeau test, as stressed by the AB[9] and reflected in drafting history of Article XX,[10] is to safeguard the listed exceptions of Article XX from abuse by members.

Fulfilling all of these requirements is not an easy task for an invoking member, nor is it for WTO adjudicators to assess all of the factors involved in a given dispute and to establish a substantive legal connection between a given measure, the invoked exception of Article XX and the GATT violated provision.[11] Notwithstanding, WTO members have and will continue adopting restrictive measures, such as QRs, and will maintain justifying them by invoking Article XX GATT.

7.1.1   The Necessity Test

The necessity degree of measures justified under Article XX has been a matter of controversy to WTO adjudicators. The core of the issue is the question as to what extent a measure is necessary and whether it demonstrates an 'inevitable necessity' to be qualified under the Article XX exceptions. WTO case law presents stringent but yet different degrees of necessity for a measure to be qualified under Article XX. In *Korea—Beef*, the AB applied an ordinary dictionary meaning of 'necessary' and stated that the term conveyed various meanings, which can extend to useful, convenient, proper, suitable or conducive; and is not limited to an inevitable

---

[6]AB Report, *US—Gasoline*, part. IV, 22.

[7]AB Report, *Brazil—Retreaded Tyres*, para. 156; AB Report, *US – Gambling,* para. 309.

[8]See AB Report, *US—Gasoline*, part. IV, 22–28.

[9]For example ibid., AB Report, *Brazil—Retreaded Tyres*, para. 215; AB Report, *US—Gambling*, para. 339.

[10]UNESC, E/PC/T/C.11/50 (Nov 13, 1946), 7.

[11]AB Report, *US—Shrimps*, paras. 158, 159.

necessity.[12] Nevertheless, the AB asserted that in the given dispute and in the context of Article XX(d) the meaning of 'necessary' was closer to 'inevitable or indispensable necessity', and upheld the definition and scope provided for the necessity by the panel in the same dispute.[13]

The dispute challenged Korea's 'dual retail system', which imposed import quantitative restrictions on fresh, chilled and frozen beef. In response to the US complaint that Korea was violating its obligation under Article III:4 GATT, requiring national treatment of like products. In response Korea invoked Article XX (d) GATT to justify that the measure was necessary to secure compliance with Korea's "Unfair Competition Act". According to Korea, imported beef was being sold in its retail markets as domestic beef without clarifying its source of origin, which created an unfair competition in Korean markets and was prohibited by the "Unfair Competition Act".[14] While the panel stated that it was possible for Korea to invoke Article XX(d), it concluded that Korea did not fulfill the necessity requirements of Article XX as it failed to prove that its 'dual retail system' was indeed 'necessary' to secure compliance with the 'Unfair Competition Act'. Moreover, it also failed to prove that no other less-trade restrictive measures were available or sufficient to address the problem and to secure compliance with its national regulations.[15] The panel further stated that there were indeed other Article XX GATT consistent less-trade restrictive measures available to Korea, which Korea used in the past to tackle similar situations.[16]

WTO adjudicators have applied the 'proportionality' approach to assess the necessity of a measure under Article XX. The principle of 'proportionality', as mentioned in the previous chapter, is a general principle of international law that assesses the balance between cost and benefits of a measure to examine how sufficient the positive impacts of a measure is to protect certain values in relation to its costs (e.g., the impact of measures on protection of exceptions listed under Article XX against trade costs resulted from the application of those measures).[17] Some WTO agreements provide for proportionality of trade measures. For instance, Article 22.4 DSU provides for the proportionality of suspension of concessions by stating that "suspension of concessions must be equivalent to the level of nullification and impairment". In US—Shrimp, the AB concluded that the US measures

---

[12]AB Report, *Korea—Beef,* paras. 161–162 (Jan. 10, 2001); for literature review see Condon (2006), pp. 94–96.

[13]AB Report, *Korea—Beef,* paras. 161–162.

[14]Ibid., para. 145; Panel Report, *Korea—Beef,* paras. 620–675.

[15]Panel Report, *Korea—Beef,* paras. 659, 674–676.

[16]For example, there was a situation of deceptive practice where Korean dairy beef was misrepresented with Hanwoo beef. Korea adopted measures other than that of a 'dual retail system' to offset the negative effects of the unfair competition, which according to the panel was less-trade restrictive. Panel Report, *Korea—Beef*, para. 649.

[17]For example Panel Report, *US – Shrimp*; Panel Report, *US – Gasoline*; *Australia – Salmon,* (Article 2.2 SPS Agreement; for literature review see *Howse* (Ch. 6, note 3), 8; *Mitchell* (Ch. 6, note 3), 177–235; Andenas and Zleptnig (2006), pp. 54–64.

applied under Article XX(g) GATT were "not disproportionately wide in its scope and reach in relation to the policy objective of protection and conservation of sea turtle species."[18] In *Brazil—Measures Affecting Imports of Retreaded Tyres (Brazil—Retreaded Tyres)*, the AB stated that "in order to determine whether a measure is 'necessary' within the meaning of Article XX(b) of the GATT 1994, a panel must assess all the relevant factors, particularly the extent of the contribution to the achievement of a measure's objective and its trade restrictiveness, in light of the importance of the interests or values at stake."[19]

Taking account of all relevant factors is a heavy task not only for the invoking member, who has to provide and prove all of them, but also for WTO panels who are tasked to review the consistency of those factors with each and every element of the necessity test. Even if a measure falls in one of the listed exceptions, is proportionate, and passes the necessity test it still not be justified by Article XX, if it does not pass the chapeau test.

7.1.2   Chapeau Test: 'Arbitrary or Unjustifiable Discrimination' and 'Disguised Restriction'

The chapeau of Article XX ensures that WTO members do not circumvent the listed exceptions of Article XX. To this end, if a measure passes the necessity test but fails the chapeau test, it does not qualify under Article XX. The chapeau test is failed if WTO adjudicators find that the measure was applied in a manner that constitutes an 'arbitrary' or 'unjustifiable' discrimination 'between countries where the same conditions prevail', or constitutes a 'disguised restriction on international trade'.[20] The chapeau test thus complements the necessity test and only becomes relevant when the necessity test is fulfilled. For example, in *Colombia—Textiles,* the panel and the AB did not consider it necessary to examine Colombia's 'compound tariff' measure under the chapeau test of Article XX after Colombia failed to prove that its measure was necessary under Article XX(a) or Article XX(d).[21]

To assess the extent a measure passes or fails the chapeau test, it is necessary to provide a definition and application of the scope of terms set out in the chapeau.

---

[18]AB Report, *US—Shrimp,* para.141; see also AB Report, *US—Gasoline,* para. 18.

[19]AB Report, *Brazil—Retreaded Tyres,* para. 156.

[20]For example, in *Brazil—Retreaded Tyres,* although the measure on import ban on emoulded tyres was provisionally justified under Article XX(b) GATT, the measure was found not justified under Article XX as according to the AB it constituted unjustifiable discrimination. (AB Report, *Brazil—Retreaded Tyres,* para. 228). Similarly, in *US—Gasoline,* the measure at issue, which was provisionally justified under Article XX and passed the necessity test, failed to fulfil the chapeau requirements and thus did not justify under Article XX. (AB Report, *US—Gasoline,* part. IV).

[21]Panel Report, *Colombia—Measures Relating to the Importation of Textiles,* Apparel and Footwear, WT/DS461/R, para. 7. 550, (Apr. 21, 2016) [hereinafter *Colombia – Textiles*]; AB Report, *Colombia—Textiles,* paras. 5. 152–153.

WTO case law provides strict definitions and structure for the chapeau terms that makes it difficult for an invoking member to pass it. In *US—Gasoline*, the AB requested a close relationship between terms of the chapeau and stated that they are coherent, and impart meaning to another.[22] According to the AB, a 'disguised restriction' includes a 'disguised discrimination' and extends to any restrictions that constitutes arbitrary or unjustifiable discrimination and cannot be limited to concealed or unannounced restriction or discrimination.[23] However, according to the panel in *China—Rare Earths*, an 'unjustifiable' discrimination may constitute a disguised restriction on trade but a 'disguised' restriction can even exist in the absence of a discrimination.[24]

Moreover, in *US—Gasoline*, the AB also analyzed the relationship between each term in the clause 'arbitrary or unjustifiable discrimination between countries where the same conditions prevail'. It drew a distinct line between the 'discrimination' requirement of the chapeau of Article XX and discrimination requirement of other GATT provisions including Article I GATT on MFN treatment and Article III:4 GATT on national treatment of like products. The distinct line is the 'arbitrary' or 'unjustifiable' nature of discrimination which is only addressed in Article XX chapeau, which means that unlike Articles I and III that prohibit any kind of discrimination in trade relationships between members, the chapeau of Article XX allows discrimination but prohibits it in instances where 'arbitrary or unjustifiable'.[25] These requirements alone are however not sufficient to qualify by themselves as discrimination requirements of the chapeau. The 'arbitrary or unjustifiable discrimination' follows the next phrase 'between countries where the same conditions prevail'. In *EC—Seals*, to measure the degree of 'the same conditions', the AB concluded that it assumes them being the same if a responding party fails to prove that the 'conditions' giving rise to are not 'relevantly different' from 'conditions' in another member.[26]

WTO adjudicators have applied different approaches to test whether a justified measure constitutes an 'arbitrary or unjustifiable discrimination' or 'disguised restriction'. For example, in *Brazil—Retreaded Tyres*,[27] the panel applied an *effect* approach to assess the discrimination resulting from Brazil's measure by examining the volume (*quantity*) of retreaded tyres imports from MERCOSUR countries, which were exempt from the Brazilian import ban. The panel concluded that since the volume of retreaded tyre imports from MERCOSUR had not been significant to the extent that it undermined the objective pursued by the import ban, the application of the import ban did not constitute 'arbitrary or unjustifiable' discrimination between

---

[22]AB Report, *US – Gasoline*, part. IV, 25.

[23]Ibid.; for literature review *see* Lo (2013), p. 120.

[24]Panel Report, *China—Rare Earths*, paras. 7. 826 & 7. 925.

[25]AB Report, *US—Gasoline*, part. IV, at 23; *see also* AB Report, *US—Shrimp*, para. 150.

[26]AB Report, *European Communities—Measures Prohibiting the Importation and Marketing of Seal Products*, WT/DS401/AB/R, para. 5. 317 (May 22, 2014) [hereinafter *EC—Seal Products*].

[27]See also AB Report, *US—Gasoline*, part. IV.

retreaded tyres from non-MERCOSUR countries and retreaded tyres from MERCOSUR countries.[28] The AB, on the contrary, applied a *rationale* approach in the same dispute to examine the cause or the rationale of the discrimination; thereby focusing on the objective link between a justified measure and its contribution to the objective it seeks to achieve.[29] Based on this approach, the AB reversed the panel's conclusion[30] and held that there has been no rational connection between the discrimination and the objective the measure sought to achieve under Article XX (b) and that the Brazilian import ban constituted 'arbitrary or unjustifiable' discrimination.[31] The AB applied the same approach to assess whether the application of the import ban constituted a 'disguised restriction on international trade' of other countries and for the same reasons ruled that the Brazilian import ban of retreaded tyres also constituted a 'disguised restriction on international trade' of non-MERCOSUR countries as the ban exemption had caused benefits to retreaded tyres from MERCOSUR countries.[32]

Interpretations and approaches taken by WTO adjudicators in assessing the extent a trade restrictive measures can be justified under Article XX GATT present a convoluted legal scenario that depending on the particular circumstances of each case, requires rigid and in-depth examination of all factors of a given dispute and establishment of an equilibrium between the measure, the objective the measure seeks to achieve, the extent the measure contributes to its given objective, and finally the systematic satisfaction of all the requirements set out under Article XX.

7.1.3 Substantive Scope of Article XX

Two critical questions surround the scope of Article XX GATT (1) substantive scope, and (2) territorial application. The question surrounding Article XX substantive scope is whether Article XX justifies a member's violation of other GATT provisions or also extends to the provisions of other WTO agreements.[33] The implication of this question is particularly relevant for the relationship between Article XX and Article 11 TFA. The question surrounding the territorial application is whether Article XX justifies a measure that seeks to protect a listed exception beyond a member's national territory.

GATT 1947 and WTO case law provide both narrow and broad substantive scopes for Article XX. Article XX narrow substantive scope relies on the

---

[28]Panel Report, *Brazil—Retreaded Tyres*, paras. 7. 287–289.

[29]AB Report, *Brazil –Retreaded Tyres,* paras. 227.

[30]Ibid., paras. 233.

[31]Ibid., paras. 225, 227, 229.

[32]Ibid., para. 239.

[33]Panel Report, *China—Publications and Audiovisual Products,* para. 7. 743; for literature review see for example Van Den Bossche and Zaouc (2018), pp. 548–554.

introductory clause "nothing in this agreement..." of the chapeau of Article XX, which is limiting its scope to only other GATT provisions. A narrow substantive scope of Article XX can be found in GATT panel's conclusion in *US—Section 337 Tariff Act.* Relying on the phrase "nothing in this Agreement..." the GATT panel concluded that the phrase 'this agreement' only refers to provisions of GATT and therefore Article XX applies "only to measures inconsistent with another provision of the General Agreement..."[34]

A broad substantive scope of Article XX extends also to obligations under other WTO agreements. Two legal scenarios can be taken into account here. One is when other WTO agreements give reference to the GATT general exceptions or contain their own general exceptions. In this scenario, it is straightforward that for the first part Article XX GATT applies to those agreements. The TFA and the Agreement on Trade Related Investment Measures (TRIMs), for instance, do not contain any general exceptions but give explicit reference to the application of all GATT exceptions and exemptions to their provisions.[35] In contrast, Article XX GATT does not apply to a WTO agreement that has its own general exceptions. For instance, the TBT Agreement, particularly Article 2 on adoption and application of technical measures, is similar to Article XX GATT and a violation of a TBT provision qualifies a justification under TBT exceptions, i.e., Article 2, but not under Article XX GATT. In *US—Clove Cigarettes*, the AB concluded that "Article XX GATT was not available to justify a breach of technical barrier to trade agreement".[36] The AB reaffirmed the same conclusion in *China—Rare Earths*.[37]

The other legal scenario is that the other WTO agreement neither contains a general exception clause nor makes a reference to GATT general exceptions. WTO case law presents a case-by-case evaluation and application of Article XX that is taking into account the circumstances of each case (e.g., the relationship of given measures with provisions of WTO agreements in question).[38] In *China—Publications and Audiovisual Products,* the AB ruled that Article XX can also be invoked as a defense against the violation of other WTO agreements given that the measure fulfills the Article XX requirements and establishes an objective link between the protecting exception and the violated WTO obligation.[39] As for this particular dispute, the central question whether China could invoke Article XX to justify its measures that were found by the panel to be inconsistent with China's trading rights

---

[34]Report of the Panel, *United States Section 337 of the Tariff Act of 1930*, L/6439—36S/345, para. 5. 9 (Nov. 7, 1989) [hereinafter GATT, *US—Section 337 Act*].

[35]Art. 24:7 TFA; TRIMS Agreement: Agreement on Trade-Related Investment Measures, Apr. 15, 1994, Marrakesh Agreement Establishing the World Trade Organization, Annex 1A, 1868 U.N.T.S. 186, Art. 3 [hereinafter TRIMS Agreement]; see also AB Report, *China—Rare Earths*, para. 5. 56.

[36]AB Report, *United States—Measures Affecting the Production and Sale of Clove Cigarettes*, WT/DS406/AB/R, paras. 96 & 101 (April 4, 2012) [hereinafter *US—Clove Cigarettes*].

[37]AB Report, *China—Rare Earths*, para. 5. 56.

[38]See for example ibid., para. 5. 74.

[39]AB Report, *China—Publications and Audiovisual Products,* paras. 223, 228, 229.

commitments under its Accession Protocol. China adopted and applied measures that granted a full trading right of audiovisual entertainment products to Chinese SOEs while limiting the import and distribution of these products for foreign enterprises and foreign traders. The panel held that these measures, constituted a breach of China's trading rights commitments under, *inter alia,* paragraphs 1.2, 5.1 and 5.2 of its Accession Protocol.[40]

China invoked Article XX(a) GATT on protection of public morals to justify that its measures were consistent with the introductory clause of paragraph 5.1 of China's Accession Protocol, which provides that "without prejudice to China's right to regulate trade in a manner consistent with the WTO Agreement". China argued that this clause allowed China to apply trade measures that are inconsistent with China's trading rights commitments but "consistent with the WTO Agreement". The AB examined the phrase "consistent with the WTO Agreement. . ." and stated that the phrase could cover any WTO obligation and discipline including its general exceptions set out under Article XX and its annexed agreements including China's Accession Protocol.[41] Thus, it held that China's measures were "consistent with the WTO Agreement" and that China could invoke Article XX(a) to justify its measures inconsistent with its trading rights commitments under its Accession Protocol.[42] The AB supported its conclusion by defining the term 'rights' in the introductory clause of paragraph 5.1 of China's Accession Protocol to include "both entitlements or powers, and immunities or protected interests".[43]

However, in two later similar disputes, which again concerned China's invocation of Article XX as a defense for the violation of provisions of its Accession Protocol, the panel and the AB concluded that Article XX was not available to China to justify its measures.[44] The concise reasoning of both the panel and the AB were that there was no clause such as the introductory clause of paragraph 5.1 of China's Accession Protocol available for the given disputes to establish an objective relationship between the measures and the provisions of the Accession Protocol in question.[45]

Regarding question of the territorial application of Article XX, WTO case law presents controversial findings. Although it would be fair to say that Article XX should not justify measures that have extraterritorial application, which would otherwise "undermine the WTO multilateral trading system",[46] WTO case law and available literature present varying approaches and findings. It may be possible, given the circumstances of a given dispute, that some extraterritorial applicatory

---

[40]Ibid., paras. 1 & 2.

[41]Ibid., para. 222.

[42]Ibid., para. 221.

[43]Ibid., paras. 223, 228, 229.

[44]AB Report, *China—Raw Materials*, paras. 303, 304.

[45]See for example ibid., para. 304; AB Report, *China—Rare Earths*, para. 5. 74.

[46]Panel Report, *US—Shrimp*, paras. 7. 44–45.

measures can be justified under some exceptions of Article XX,[47] provided that they sufficiently pass a 'two-tier test'.

Extraterritorial application of Article XX(a) on 'public morals', XX(b) on 'life or health of human, animals or plants' and XX(g) on 'conservation of exhaustible natural resources' have been particularly assessed to test their implications for contemporary evolving values such as human rights and environmental issues beyond national territories.[48]

The *US—Shrimp* case presents an interesting perspective on how the territorial scope of different exceptions of Article XX can be read in a broad and controversial manner. *US—Shrimp* dealt with the question whether the US could invoke Article XX(g) to justify its measures, which limited market access for shrimps from certain countries that did not fulfill the US shrimps harvesting requirements. US law provided that only those shrimps could access the US markets whose harvesting methods complied with or were comparable to the US shrimps harvesting methods. The US claimed that its measures were to protect the conservation of sea turtles that were in danger as a result of detrimental harvesting methods of some countries.[49] The panel held that members' markets access conditions for domestic policies requirements "would undermine the multilateral trading system".[50] The AB, on the contrary, provided an 'evolutionary meaning' to 'exhaustible natural resources' that extends to sea turtles and thus ruled that the US could invoke Article XX(g) to justify the extraterritorial application of its measures.[51] However, the ultimate conclusion of the AB nevertheless disagreed to justify the US measures under Article XX as the AB found that the measures were applied in a manner that constituted 'arbitrary and unjustifiable discrimination' and a 'disguised restriction on international trade'.[52]

In summary, it has often been difficult for members to establish to the satisfaction of WTO panels and the AB on the one hand a sufficient objective link between their challenged measures and the objective aimed to be protected extraterritorially or broadly, and, on the other hand, to fulfill the chapeau requirements of Article XX. WTO adjudicators assess the matter on a case-by-case basis taking into account the particular circumstances of each case. Provided that there is no explicit substantive rule prohibiting a broad substantive and territorial application of Article XX, it lies within the invoking member's justification approach—as WTO law allows members to choose their own level of protection.

---

[47]See for example AB Report, *US—Shrimp*, para. 121.

[48]See for example Ibid., para. 130; AB Report, *China—Audiovisual,* para. 7. 759; for literature review see Van Den Bossche and Zaouc (2018), pp. 552–554; Joseph (2013), pp. 101–107.

[49]Thailand, Malaysia, India and Pakistan.

[50]Panel Report, *US—Shrimp*, para. 7. 45.

[51]AB Report, *US—Shrimp,* paras. 121, 133.

[52]Ibid., paras. 172, 177; see also Panel Report, *EC—Seal Products*, para. 7. 448.

7.1.4   The Relationship Between Freedom of Transit and General Exceptions Under WTO Rules

The applicability of Article XX GATT to Article V GATT on freedom of transit is simply understandable from the phrase "nothing in this Agreement. . ." clause of the chapeau of Article XX. The focus, therefore, should be given to the applicability of Article XX to Article 11 TFA, particularly Article 11:8 on non-application of TBT measures to transit goods.

As mentioned earlier, WTO law establishes a precedence for other Annex 1A covered agreements over GATT to the extent of a conflict.[53] All the WTO agreements on trade in goods including the TFA, TBT and SPS are listed under Annex 1A.[54] As such, TFA provisions generally prevail over GATT provisions to the extent of conflict. However, the TFA relationship with GATT is the opposite with regards to Article XX GATT. Article 24:7 TFA explicitly recognizes the application of *all* GATT exceptions and exemptions to *all* provisions of the TFA, which of course applies to the Article 11 TFA provisions on freedom of transit including Article 11:8 on non-application of TBT measures to goods in transit.

Therefore, and particularly in the instance of Article XX GATT overriding Article 11:8 TFA, the question arises as to whether Article XX can justify the application of technical measures and conformity assessments to transit goods not only within the meaning of the TBT Agreement but also within the meaning of other WTO agreements, such as the SPS Agreement. Article 11:8 TFA is only explicit on non-application of technical measures within the meaning of the TBT Agreement and is silent on non-application of such measures within the meaning of the SPS Agreement. However, Article 24:6 TFA establishes a clear relationship with the SPS Agreement, which allows WTO members to apply SPS conformity assessment measures to goods in transit. Since the TFA itself recognizes the application of SPS conformity assessment measures, such measures therefore can be adopted under both Article 24:6 TFA and Article XX GATT.

The relationship between all the mentioned agreements with each other and with Article XX GATT is in line with VCLT rules of treaty interpretation. Articles 30 and 41 VCLT are particularly relevant for this discussion. Discussed in the previous chapter, Article 30 VCLT governs normative conflicts in successive treaties with the same subject matter.[55] According to Article 30(2) VCLT, the provisions of the earlier treaty will prevail and govern the conflict if a latter treaty provides that it is subordinate to the earlier treaty or it is considered to be compatible with it. In such a scenario, the relationship is similar to compatibility of national ordinary laws with

---

[53]General Interpretative Note to Annex 1A, https://www.wto.org/english/docs_e/legal_e/05-anx1a_e.htm.

[54]See WTO, https://www.wto.org/english/docs_e/legal_e/legal_e.htm.

[55]UN Vienna Convention on the Law of Treaties (VCLT), 1155 U.N.T.S. 331 (entered into force Jan. 27, 1980); for more discussions See *Foltea* (Ch. 6, 58); *Borgen* (Ch.5, note 104), 576–579.

constitutional law.[56] However, according to Article 30(3) VCLT if a latter treaty does not contain a provision as foreseen in Article 30(2), the provision of the earlier treaty will only be applicable to the extent that it is compatible with the provisions of the later treaty and provided that all parties to the earlier treaty are also parties to the latter treaty. This VCLT provision only had an implication for the relationship between Article XX GATT and Article 11:8 TFA if the TFA did not contain Article 24:7 provision.

The TFA is a recent WTO Agreement and there is still no case law concerning the relationship between Article XX GATT and Article 11 TFA. However, *EU—Generic Drugs in Transit* is relevant, and the only dispute so far, to assess how Article XX could interact with other WTO agreements (e.g., the TRIPS Agreement) to restrict the freedom of transit. The dispute was brought up by India and Brazil, individually, against the Netherlands that seized generic drugs while transiting through its territory. India and Brazil challenged the measure for its inconsistency with the Netherland's obligations under Article V:1–2, Article V:4–5 and Article V:7 GATT and requested consultations with the EU and the Netherlands.[57] The measure was implementing the EU's Customs Regulation No 1383/2003 on Protection of Intellectual Property Rights, which required band and seizure of generic drug imports into the EU markets unless they conform to the EU's rules on IP rights.[58]

The Netherlands argued that its measure was necessary for the protection of public health but instead of invoking the Article XX relevant exceptions [Article XX(b) or Article XX(d)] it invoked Article 51 TRIPS Agreement.[59] Article 51 TRIPS Agreement on the suspension of release by customs authorities allows WTO members to adopt border measures, such as those to suspend the release of imported goods for valid suspect of counterfeit trademarks or pirated copyrights of those goods. An important part of Article 51 that the Netherlands may have ignored or overlooked is, that while Article 51 allows suspension of the release of counterfeit goods, which are subject to import or export to or from the territory of members, it does not expressly extend its application to goods in transit; except for footnote 13 to Article 51 that provides "there shall be no obligation to apply such procedures with regard to goods in transit." Footnote 13 gives legitimacy to WTO members to apply Article 51 TRIPS Agreement to goods in transit as TRIPS-plus requirements but does not impose an obligation to do so.[60]

---

[56]For more discussion see for example Kearney and Dalton (1970), p. 517; *Borgen* (Ch.5, note 104).

[57]WTO, European Union and a Member State—Seizure of Generic Drugs in Transit, WT/DS 408/1, Request for Consultations by India; WT/DS 409/1, Request for Consultations by Brazil (May 19, 2010); for literature review see *Melgar* (Ch.1, note 2), 140–150.

[58]Ibid.

[59]Ibid.

[60]See *Melgar* (Ch.1, note 2), 146.

Although this dispute was resolved through consultations,[61] the application of TRIPS plus standards to transit goods of a developing country member raised controversial debates among WTO members and at academia. The debate focused on the question whether WTO members could restrict the freedom of transit under their national IP laws, which was highlighted by India's concern of the EU reinforcing its measures on restricting transit of Indian generic drugs.[62] Although the Netherlands justified its measure based on the provisions of the TRIPS Agreement, the assessment of the measure should also be seen in the context of Article XX GATT as to whether Article XX could justify IP restrictive measures within the meaning of the TRIPS Agreement. This assessment is particularly relevant for Article XX(b) on the protection of public health as the Netherlands claimed that its measure was necessary for the protection of public health. The assessment is also relevant with regard to Article XX(d) as the measure was also taken to secure compliance with the EU IP regulations under Article XX(d). Article XX(d) GATT allows members to adopt and apply measures that are 'necessary' to secure compliance with national laws and regulations including, *inter alia*, patent, trademark and copyright laws, provided that the law itself is consistent with WTO law.

The TRIPS Agreement is listed under Annex B of the WTO Agreement and therefore does not have precedence over the GATT.[63] WTO case law establishes equality among WTO agreements outside Annex 1A. In *EC—Trademarks and Geographical Indications*, the panel held that GATT and the TRIPS Agreement apply 'cumulatively' and that obligations under both could co-exist with none of them overriding the other.[64] The panel further held that WTO "covered agreements apply cumulatively and that consistency with one does not necessarily imply consistency with them all."[65] In this dispute the measure of concern was a provision on equivalence and reciprocity conditions in Article 12(1) of the EC Council Regulation on Trademarks and Geographical Indications of 14 July 2004, which conditioned non-EC countries geographical indications requirements to be equivalent to EC's regulations. The US and Australia respectively challenged the regulation for its inconsistency with the TRIPS Agreement and Articles I and III:3 GATT.[66] The EC did not invoke Article XX(d), which according to the panel's statement it could have if its regulation itself was consistent with the GATT.[67] Although this dispute does not directly apply to the freedom of transit, it nonetheless established a

---

[61] See *Baker* (Ch.5, note 55), 4.

[62] Ibid., 4; see also *Asit Ranjan Mishra*, India Opposes Proposed European Trademark Rules, Live Mint (Oct. 14, 2015), http://www.livemint.com/Politics/lvjQMWQbhCtEsTOLyCy0RM/India-opposes-proposed EuropeanTrademark-rules.html.

[63] See WTO Website, https://www.wto.org/english/docs_e/legal_e/legal_e.htm.

[64] Panel Report, *EC—Trademarks and Geographical Indications,* paras. 7. 208, 7. 227 & footnote 239.

[65] Ibid.; *see also, e.g.,* AB Report, *Argentina—Footwear (EC),* para. 81; AB Report, *Korea—Dairy,* para. 74; Panel Report, *EC – Bananas III*, para. 7. 160.

[66] Panel Report, *EC—Trademarks and Geographical Indications,* para. 1. 1.

[67] Ibid., paras. 7. 239 & 7. 448.

relationship between Article XX GATT and the TRIPS Agreement giving the possibility to a member to justify an IP measure under Article XX GATT.

However, taking into account the 'cumulative' nature of obligations under both agreements, the question of an overlap of obligations arises. According to the AB in *China—Rare Earths*, any possible conflict caused by overlapping provisions should be resolved on a case-by-case basis by having recourse to each term and condition of the different provisions of each agreement. In case such recourse fails to establish a relationship, recourse should be made to interpretative elements of each agreement.[68]

The relationship between Article V GATT and footnote 13 to Article 51 TRIPS Agreement should be assessed based on all terms and conditions of each provision of them. In other words, the degree of legal force of an obligation to grant freedom of transit under Article V versus a right to impose a transit restriction pursuant to footnote 13 to Article 51 TRIPS Agreement should be assessed. The difference in degree of legal force between both provisions requires that Article V GATT, carrying a mandatory obligation, to prevail over footnote 13 to Article 51 TRIPS Agreement that carries only a discretionary right and not an obligation or an explicitly conferred right. Therefore, instead of relying on Article 51 TRIPS Agreement including its footnote, a member (e.g., the Netherlands in *EC—Seizure of Generic Drugs in Transit*) can invoke the Article XX GATT relevant exceptions [e.g., XX(b) or XX (d)] to justify IP restrictions on transit goods.

Some scholars support the non-application of TRIPS measures to goods in transit from a development angle. According to them, under customary norms of international law, WTO members should not use the provisions of the TRIPS Agreement to apply their national IP laws to goods in transit. Further they conceive that the application of TRIPS-plus standards to goods in transit, particularly to transit goods from developing countries contradicts the development purpose of the WTO Doha goals.[69]

The application of TRIPS to transit goods is arguable from another perceptive as well. The main purpose of national IP protective measures, as allowed by the TRIPS Agreement, is to protect the rights of IP holders and consumer interests in the importing country.[70] This purpose does not seem to be achieved through IP restrictions on transit goods, since transit goods do not enter into domestic markets of the transit country to affect these rights and interests. Therefore, the likelihood for the transit country to find a plausible justification for the application of national IP laws to goods in transit is weak.

---

[68] AB Report, *China—Rare Earths*, para. 5. 56.

[69] *Melgar* (Ch.1, note 2), 147–149; *Cherise Valles*, Article V GATT on Freedom of Transit, in: WTO—Trade in Goods (note 3), 193.

[70] See EU Bureau, EU Agrees to Stop Confiscation of Indian Generic Drugs, The Economic Times (Jul. 29, 2011), http://economictimes.indiatimes.com/industry/healthcare/biotech/pharmaceuticals/eu-agrees-tostopconf.iscation_of-indian-generic-drugs/articleshow/9403107.cms.

Some other scholars look, however, at this matter from an illicit trade perspective and argue that freedom of transit is a conditional right and its restriction or ban in case IP rules are infringed is compatible with the provisions of the TRIPS Agreement and Article XX GATT.[71] This view can be supported from the perspective of trading of IP-infringing goods considered as illicit trading.[72] Due to its limited space, this dissertation does not seek to offer a detailed discussion of the relationship between WTO rules and illicit trade. But precisely, Article XX GATT could be invoked to justify restrictive measures adopted and applied to combat against a whole process of an illicit trade including its transit. For example, public moral in Islamic countries would suggest not only a ban on imports of pork and alcoholic drinks but also their transit through the territory of Islamic countries. While a member may challenge a WTO Islamic member State's measure or regulation banning transit of pork based on its inconsistency with Article 11:8 TFA, that Islamic State could invoke Article XX (a) or XX(d) GATT as a defense.

In conclusion, Article XX GATT provides broad opportunity to members to deviate from their obligations not only under GATT but also under other WTO agreements by invoking one or more of the exceptions listed therein. Nevertheless, Article XX does not stand independent of the rigid requirements that an invoking member needs to fulfill. It largely depends on how an invoking member justifies the necessity of its measures under Article XX exceptions as well as how sufficiently fulfils the requirements of the chapeau of Article XX GATT.

7.1.5 The Relationship Between Article XX and Regional Agreements: Case of APTTA

It was discussed in above sections that a WTO inconsistent trade restrictive measure needs to fulfill all the requirements of the two-tier test to qualify under one or more of the exceptions listed under Article XX. Although in *Brazil—Retreaded Tyres* the measure of concern was found not to fall into the scope of Article XX as it did not pass the chapeau test, the dispute itself still raises an interesting question, namely, whether an otherwise WTO inconsistent trade restrictive measure can bypass the chapeau test in favor of a dispute settlement decision under a regional agreement.[73] This question leads to the broader question as to how to address conflicting obligations stemming from WTO law and regional agreements that effect rights and obligations of members under both regimes.[74] According to Article 41 VCLT,

---

[71]Vrins (2011), p. 781.

[72]See World Intellectual Property Organization (WIPO), *Coordinating Intellectual Property Enforcement*, WIPO /ACE/14/5 REV (Aug.22, 2019), 1–8; European Union Intellectual Property Office (EUIPO), 2019 Status Report on IPR Infringement (2019), 8–12.

[73]AB Report, *Brazil—Retreaded Tyres*, paras. 214–220, 226, 231, 234, 253–257.

[74]See *Foltea* (Ch.6, note 58).

which governs compatibility of regional agreements concluded to modify a multi-lateral treaty, if a regional agreement affecting rights and obligations of other WTO members contains a provision or a waiver that is incompatible with the purpose and objective of the WTO, it would be in violation of WTO provisions.[75] For example, the APTTA provision banning transit of Indian exports to Afghanistan through Pakistan's territory would be a violation of WTO rules on freedom of transit as the transit ban not only affects India's right of freedom of transit as a WTO member but is also incompatible with the purpose and objective of Article V GATT. However, looking at the transit ban from GATT general or security exceptions, the scenario will change.

First of all, APTTA was concluded in a time in which Afghanistan was not a WTO member. Second, the APTTA provision on the transit ban of Indian exports to Afghanistan through Pakistan's territory is one of the many consequences of a long-lasting territorial conflict and security issue, which arose by the separation of the two countries. Therefore, the transit ban provision of APTTA finds its root in a security matter, which existed for decades between Pakistan and India. Since the transit ban involves a security matter, Article XX would not be relevant for its justification and it should instead be assessed under Article XXI GATT. The next section carries out this assessment. However, Article XX is relevant to assess QRs that Pakistan imposes on certain transit goods i.e., fresh fruits, wheat and sugar from Afghanistan. Pakistan imposes QRs on certain Afghan goods, characterized as goods of a sensitive character by Pakistan. Pakistani authorities consider these QRs necessary to protect their internal markets from the smuggling of goods, which are of sensitive character in terms of market competitiveness to Pakistani markets.

APTTA contains provisions on general and security exceptions,[76] which are articulated in an abstract and absolute form and are of 'best endeavor' nature. Article 53 APTTA on general exceptions provides that "contracting parties agree to ensure that no measure taken under the agreement could risk harming or destroying (i) public morals, (ii) human, animal and plant life, (iii) national treasures, (iv) security of its own territory, and (v) any other interests as mutually agreed upon." The general exceptions do not have a chapeau that is comparable to the one of Article XX GATT.

The problem with the QRs between the two countries is that no general exception has ever been invoked to justify their adoption. However, even in that case, it would be difficult to justify the QRs under one of the general exceptions, as the QRs either must protect public moral, public life or health. The two-tier test would still apply to both instances in order to ensure their justification under either Article XX GATT or the APTTA provisions on general exceptions. First, the objective to protect Pakistan's domestic market from the leak of certain competitive transit goods seems difficult to qualify under the Article XX exceptions or the APTTA general exceptions as it would be difficult to establish an objective link between QRs and the

---

[75]See for example *Pauwelyn*, Conflict of Norms in Public International Law (Ch.6, note 1), 321.
[76]Art. 53 APTTA.

objective sought to achieve and to further prove that the QRs were the only measures available to Pakistan. APTTA contains a rigid transit security regime that, *inter alia*, provides for the deposit of customs duty value of transit goods as a transit guarantee. Moreover, it requires that transit vehicles should be equipped with tracking devices so that customs authorities in both countries can track the movements of transit vehicles and make sure that they actually exit borders. Transit security particularly presents an alternative to transit countries to offset any possible damages incurred to their internal markets in the event of smuggling of transit goods that are not cleared in customs as imported goods.

The question may arise as to whether transit guarantees can be enough to compensate damage inflicted on the internal market of those sensitive goods when monetary corruption prevails in customs. This issue is another different legal scenario, for which Article 11 TFA provides a solution. That is the adoption of an appropriate system of transparency to combat corruption in customs. Accordingly, the AUSYCUDA systems are now functioning in a majority of developing countries including Afghanistan and Pakistan. The system particularly aims to reduce monetary corruption in customs including those arising from monetary transit guarantees. The international transit guarantee of TIR system, which is now functioning in both Afghanistan and Pakistan, supports the fight against monetary corruption in customs in relation to transit goods. Therefore, the QRs do not seem to be necessary and the only available measure to safeguard internal markets against the smuggling of transit goods. Even if APTTCA issues a ruling in favor of those QRs, in the case that the affected party brings the case to the WTO, by invoking Article XX or a general exception under APTTA, the measure will undergo a two-tier test.

The *Brazil—Retreaded Tyres* case presents practical implications for this assessment. In this dispute, Brazil argued that its retreaded tyres import ban exemption derived from its obligation under MERCOSUR Agreement, which prohibits any new restriction on trade among MERCOSUR countries. The import ban exemption of retreaded tyres from MERCOSUR countries was particularly in response to a MERCOSUR arbitral tribunal ruling, which disapproved of Brazil extending its import prohibition to retreaded tyres from MERCOSUR countries.[77] Based on its *rationale* approach, the AB concluded that the MERCOSUR arbitral tribunal's ruling should not be followed because the ruling did not constitute any relationship with the legitimate objective that the import ban sought to achieve under Articles XX (b) and XX(g) GATT.[78] As such, the AB held that Brazil's measure constituted an 'arbitrary' and 'unjustifiable' discrimination between countries where the same conditions prevailed and further embodied a 'disguised restriction to international trade'.[79] In the same dispute, although the panel accepted the invocation of an arbitral ruling under the MERCOSUR,[80] it held that "the invocation of any

---

[77] AB Report, *Brazil—Retreaded Tyres*, para. 226.

[78] Ibid., para. 228.

[79] Ibid., paras. 227, 228, 239.

[80] Panel Report, *Brazil—Retreaded Tyres*, para. 7. 276.

international agreement would not be sufficient under any circumstances, in order to justify the existence of discrimination in the application of a measure under the chapeau to Article XX".[81]

In *Brazil—Retreaded Tyres,* Brazil could actually invoke either Article XX GATT or the general exceptions provision of the Montevideo Treaty in force between MERCOSUR parties to justify its import ban before the MERCOSUR arbitral tribunal.[82] In either case however, Brazil still needed to pass a two-tier test to ensure that its measure was necessary and that it was not applied in a manner inconsistent with the chapeau to Article XX.[83] For Afghanistan and Pakistan, while both Article XX GATT and the APTTA general exceptions are available to justify, for example, the QRs on transit goods, they will have to undergo a major process to provide the proof that the QRs qualify a two-tier test.

It can be concluded that, although Article XX GATT allows WTO members to deviate from their substantial GATT and other WTO obligations, it nevertheless sets strict requirements that members have to fulfill in order to benefit from that deviation. WTO case law shows that even if some members successfully justified their measures under one or more of the listed exceptions of Article XX, they still could not pass a chapeau test and therefore did not qualify for the invocation of Article XX. Looking at the justification of the existing Afghanistan-Pakistan transit challenges, while the transit ban and border closure measures do not qualify under the general exceptions of either APTTA or Article XX GATT, the transit QRs are possible to qualify both of them. However, any justification of those transit QRs under general exceptions of either of the two legal regimes is still subject to a two-tier test. For the reasons provided and given the rigidity of a two-tier test, the chance for transit QRs to successfully pass all the requirements of the test is very low. For instance, if Pakistan or Afghanistan opt to invoke e.g., Article XX(d) to justify its QRs, it would not only need to determine how it sought to secure compliance with its exact law in question (e.g., the customs law or regulation its compliance has been sought to secure) and whether that law itself is a WTO consistent law, but it would also need to prove that the measure of concern was not applied in a manner constituting 'arbitrary' or 'unjustifiable discrimination between countries where the same conditions prevail' or a 'disguised restriction' to international trade.

---

[81] Ibid., para. 7. 283.

[82] AB Report, *Brazil—Retreaded Tyres*, para. 234 & footnote 445.

[83] This conclusion is implicitly reflected in the AB's statement in footnote 445 of the AB's report in *Brazil—Retreaded Tyres.*

7.2   The Relationship Between Freedom of Transit and Security Exceptions Under WTO Rules

It is a well-known realist theory in international relations that "law cannot win in conflict with national security" and that security is the overriding goal for states.[84] International trade, among other fields of international law, has taken account of states' security[85] and multilateral and regional trade agreements embody exception provisions related to national security interests. GATT is one of these multilateral trade agreements containing security exception provisions in Article XXI. An ultimate finding of the assessment carried out on almost all GATT 1947 and WTO disputes with an invocation of Article XXI GATT confirms that "law cannot win in conflict with national security". However, it was not until recently, compared with Article XX GATT, that the debate intensified on the key role that Article XXI may play in the trade relationship between WTO members. Few instances in international trade have been the main triggers of the debates on Article XXI recently, mainly the tariffs war between the US and China and the *Russia—Traffic in Transit* case.[86]

Russia—Traffic in Transit is the only WTO dispute under which a panel provided a detailed discussion on the application and interpretation of different provisions of Article XXI. This answered long lasting controversial questions surrounding the relationship between national security exceptions and WTO rules.[87] The following section provides a case study of *Russia—Traffic in Transit* but confines the discussion in most parts to the relationship between Article XXI(b) GATT and WTO provisions on freedom of transit. It then tests the implications of the assessment in *Russia—Traffic in Transit* for the existing transit challenges between Afghanistan and Pakistan.

---

[84]*Holger P Hestermeyer*, Article XXI GATT on Security Exceptions, in: WTO—Trade in Goods (note 3), 581; for the realist concept of law and security see Abbott (1999), pp. 364–65; Koskeniemi (2002), p. 481; Wolfers (1952), pp. 481–502.

[85]Bhala (1998), pp. 265 & 317.

[86]See generally Voon (2019), pp. 45–50; Panel Report, *Russia—Traffic in Transit*; see also generally WTO, *United Arab Emirates—Measures Relating to Trade in Goods and Services, and Trade-Related Aspects of Intellectual Property Rights*, Request for the Establishment of a Panel by Qatar, WT/DS526/1 (Aug. 4, 2017) [hereinafter *UAE—Goods, Services and IP Rights*]. In this dispute, Qatar challenges the UAE's measures taken for the protection of essential security interests. A panel was composed in September 2019 to hear the dispute and the panel's final report is expected to be issued in the second half of 2020. WTO, *UAE—Goods, Services and IP Rights*, Communication from Panel, WT/DS526/4 (Oct. 2, 2019).

[87]See for example Ibid., 317; Van Den Bossche and Zaouc (2018), pp. 618–622; Hestermeyer (84), pp. 571–590.

7.2.1 Provisions of Article XXI GATT

Article XXI contains three main paragraphs, which allow members to take or prevent an action that is necessary not only for their 'essential security interests' but also for international peace and security. Article XX(a) provides for non-disclosure of information that a member considers contrary to its essential security interests. Article XX(b) grants three exceptions under which a WTO member is allowed to take any action, which it considers necessary for the protection of its essential security interests. The listed exceptions under Article XXI(b) allow actions:

(i)   relating to fissionable materials or the materials from which they are derived;
(ii) relating to the traffic in arms, ammunition, and implements of war and to such traffic in other goods and materials as is carried on directly or indirectly for the purpose of supplying a military establishment;
(iii) taken in time of war or other emergency in international relations.

Similarly, Article XXI(c) allows a member to take action as part of its obligations under the United Nations Charter for the maintenance of international peace and security. Among Article XXI provisions, Article XXI(b) is the most often invoked and controversial paragraph of Article XXI, especially with regard to whether it is a justiciable clause.[88]

There was no common understanding of Article XXI(b) both among GATT 1947 contracting parties at the time and WTO members.[89] However, under GATT 1947, the understanding was that Article XXI(b) is a non-justiciable clause allowing its contracting parties to take otherwise GATT inconsistent actions, individually or collectively, for any non-economic purposes (e.g., for political motivations or protection of strategically important national industries) and that it further was not limited to essential security reasons.[90] In 1985, for instance, the US invoked Article XXI(b)(iii) to justify its import embargo on Nicaraguan goods, which was a politically motivated act and not taken in time of war or other emergencies of international relations as provided by Article XXI(b)(iii).[91] Likewise, in 1982, the collective import restrictions on Argentina, which were jointly imposed by some countries including the European Economic Community (EEC), Canada and Australia, were motivated by the political situation between the UK and Argentina.[92]

---

[88]Bhala (1998), p. 267.

[89]Panel Report, *Russia—Traffic in Transit*, para. 7. 80.

[90]For example, Sweden's invocation of Article XXI to defend its global imports quota system for certain footwear in relation to the protection of its national footwear industry was based on the protection of an industry of strategic importance to Sweden. WTO, Analytical Index of the GATT—Article XXI, 603.

[91]Report of the Report, *United States—Trade Measures Affecting Nicaragua*, L/6053, paras. 4. 9, 5. 10 (Oct. 13, 1986) [Unadopted] [hereinafter GATT, *US—Nicaragua*].

[92]GATT, Trade Restrictions Affecting Argentina Applied for Non-Economic Reasons, C/M/159, L/5317 (Apr. 30, 1982).

The 1982 GATT Ministerial Declaration, which states that "the contracting parties undertake, individually and jointly... to abstain from taking restrictive trade measures, for reasons of a non-economic character, not consistent with the General Agreement" provided the legal ground for such collective action.[93] However now, it is not explicitly clear, except for measures under Article XXI(c), whether WTO members can take collective actions under Article XXI(b) by relying on the 1982 GATT Ministerial Declaration.

Similarly, GATT contracting parties did not need to prove the validation of their measures taken under Article XXI as they considered the Article to be an absolute self-judging or non-justiciable exception. According to the US, the contracting parties "had no power to question that judgment",[94] or, according to the EEC, a measure taken under Article XXI(b) "required neither notification, justification, nor approval."[95] In *US—Nicaragua*, the GATT panel refrained from examining the US embargo of Nicaragua's goods under Article XXI as it found it to be contrary to its terms of reference to do so.[96] Although the panel did not examine whether Article XXI precluded the panel from examining a measure taken pursuant to Article XXI (b), its refrainment based on its mandate indicates that GATT 1947 panels considered that Article XXI(b) is a non-justiciable clause. However, the panel noted that if contracting parties would not weigh their security needs against the need to maintain stable trade relations, fundamental aims of the GATT would be endangered.[97] This statement signifies the consideration of the principle of good faith when invoking Article XXI. The principle of good faith, embodied in Articles 26 and 31(1) VCLT, requires contracting parties to a treaty to perform their treaty rights and obligation with sincere veracity and interpret their treaty provisions in good faith.[98] Moreover, according to Article 31(1) VCLT on common rules of treaty interpretation, a provision of a treaty should be interpreted based on the ordinary meaning of its words and in light the object and purpose of the treaty.[99] Therefore, a treaty provision characterized as an 'exception' does not justify a 'stricter' or 'narrower' interpretation of that exception.[100]

The significance of the application of the principle of good faith particularly in legal matters such as those addressed in Article XXI cannot be denied.[101] The negotiating history of Article XXI(b) presents that the drafters sought to articulate Article XXI(b) in a way that a balance between the exception of 'security interest'

---

[93]GATT, Ministerial Declaration, L/5424, para. 7(iii) (Nov. 29, 1982).

[94]Analytical Index of the GATT—Article XXI, 601.

[95]Ibid., 600.

[96]GATT, *US—Nicaragua*, para. 5. 3; see also Analytical Index of the GATT—Article XXI, 601, 603.

[97]Ibid., para. 5.16; see also Analytical Index of the GATT—Article XXI, 603.

[98]Arts. 26, 31(1) VCLT.

[99]AB Report, *EC—Hormones*, para. 104.

[100]Ibid.; see also *Hestermeyer* (note 84), 582.

[101]Panel Report, *Russia—Traffic in Transit*, para. 7. 133; Schloemann and Ohlhoff (1999), p. 448.

and the extent a measure could be taken to prevent an abuse of Article XXI(b) would be maintained. The term 'essential' prefixed to the phrase 'security interests' in the chapeau of Article XXI(b) is the result of those balancing efforts. Although the inclusion of the term 'essential' limited the broad scope of application to any kind of security interests, the drafters nonetheless stated that the veracity of contracting parties in interpreting Article XXI(b) would be the ultimate guarantor of Article XXI from abuse.[102]

WTO and GATT 1947 adjudicators have frequently referred to the principle of good faith in complex legal matters such as national security exceptions to test a member's veracity in adopting and applying an otherwise GATT or WTO inconsistent measure. For instance, based on the principle of good faith, the GATT Council examined Sweden's veracity in introducing a global quota system for certain footwear in 1975 designed to protect its footwear industry, which Sweden considered being a strategically important industry having crucial impact on maintaining Sweden's economic security. The Council found that the essential security interests that Sweden alleged to exist did not contain a minimum degree of plausibility and that the measure was purely motivated by commercial reasoning. The Council thus concluded that Sweden circumvented Article XXI(b) to deviate from its GATT obligations.[103] Similarly, in *US—Nicaragua*, the panel rejected the US argument that Nicaragua was not authorized to bring a case of nullification or impairment when a dispute involves a security issue.[104] The panel examined the effect that the US import embargo had on Nicaragua's trade.[105] The panel did so pursuant to the 1982 GATT Decision Concerning Article XXI of General Agreement, which provides that "when action is taken under Article XXI, all contracting parties affected by such action retain their full rights under the General Agreement."[106] The decision also provides for the transparency of measures taken under all provisions of Article XXI except for Article XXI(a) on non-disclosure of information. It provides that "contracting parties should be informed *to the fullest extent possible* of trade measures taken under Article XXI."[107]

---

[102]ECOSOC Council, EPCT/A/PV/33 (July 24, 1947), 20–21; see also Analytical Index of the GATT – Article XXI, 600.

[103]GATT Council, Minutes of Meeting, C/M/109 (Nov. 10, 1975), 8–9; see also Analytical Index of the GATT – Article XXI, 603; *Hestermeyer* (note 84), 581–82.

[104]See for example GATT, *US – Nicaragua*, paras. 4. 1, 4. 9, 5. 2.

[105]Based on its examination, the panel held that the embargo caused a standstill for the trade between the two countries and "had a severe impact on the economy of a less-developed contracting party". GATT, *US – Nicaragua*, para. 5. 16; for literature review see Dunoff (2002), p. 319; Bhala (1998), p. 278. Bhala states that a WTO panel or the AB is not likely to adjudicate a complaining party's claim against invocation of Article XXI.

[106]GATT, Decision Concerning Article XXI of the General Agreement, L/5426, para. 2 (Dec. 2, 1982) [hereinafter the 1982 Decision Concerning GATT Article XXI]; see also Analytical Index of the GATT – Article XXI, 607.

[107]The 1982 Decision Concerning GATT Article XXI, para.1; Bhala (1998), p. 270.

WTO disputes involving Article XXI(b) demonstrate similar controversies. For instance, in *United States—The Cuban Liberty and Democratic Solidarity Act (US— Helms Burton Act)* that was brought up by the EC against an action by the US that penalized US-based international companies trading in Cuba,[108] the US refused to participate in the dispute by asserting that the WTO did not have jurisdiction over issues, which are a matter of national security. The US further stated that if it opted to participate in the dispute it would invoke Article XXI(b) as a defense. The US argued that invocation of Article XXI would bar a panel from examining its measures under Article XXI.[109] Although there was no panel proceeding for this dispute, the panel in *US—Hormones* in the following year held that the panel was obliged to apply provisions of the DSU to a case of *prima facie* violation brought to it even if the dispute invoked Article XXI.[110] Article 1 DSU requires a complaining party to establish a case of *prima facie* violation before the WTO DSB for inconsistency of a measure before the other party who has taken the measure (responding party) is required to rebut and invoke a GATT exception to justify the measure of concern. When the responding party refrains from refuting the dispute, the *prima facie* case will require a WTO panel to rule in favor of the complaining party.[111]

The negotiating history of Article XXI supports that WTO panels should review a case of nullification or impairment that involves invocation of Article XXI. During drafting of the Havana Charter, the provisions of Article XXI were placed among the general exceptions contained in Article 99 of the Charter. Later, the GATT drafters incorporated the same security exceptions provisions in Article XXI and placed Article XXI after Article XX and before Articles XXII and XXIII.[112] It is broadly argued that this placement was not made without a purpose and the fact that the Article was placed before Articles XXII and XXIII means that it is subject to a review by the latter Articles.[113]

Similarly, the established relationship between Article XXI and a case of *prima facie* violation pursuant to Articles XXII and XXIII is in line with Article 31 (1) VCLT that takes account of the object and purpose of the treaty as a whole when interpreting its provisions. In the case of the WTO, its objective and purpose are to maintain the security and predictability of the multilateral trading system by securing a positive settlement of disputes brought to WTO panels. The objective and purpose would be undermined if panels did not review a case of *prima facie*

---

[108]WTO, *Untied States – The Cuban Liberty and Democratic Solidarity Act*, Request for the Establishment of a Panel, WT/ DS38/2 (1996) [hereinafter *US – Helms Burton Act*].

[109]Spanogle Jr (1997), p. 1314; *Ohlhoff* (101), 441–442; Browne (1997), p. 410.

[110]Art.1 DSU; WTO Analytical Index (3d edn. 2011), 609–10; Bhala (1998), p. 279.

[111]Panel Report, *EC – Hormones,* para. 104; AB Report, *United States – Shirt and Blouses,* at 14; see also *Ohlhoff* (note 101), 441.

[112]Analytical Index of the GATT – Article XXI, 608; see also Lester et al. (2011), pp. 574–75.

[113]Analytical Index of the GATT – Article XXI, 608; see also *Ohlhoff* (note 101), 440 & footnote 92.

violation brought to them pursuant to Articles XXII and XXIII GATT and Article 1 DSU.

Nonetheless, the controversies have continued among WTO members until recently on whether Article XXI(b) is a GATT self-judging and an all-embracing exception.[114] Unlike Article XX that is justiciable and subject to a two-tier test, Article XXI(b) gives members a considerable degree of discretion in taking any action they consider necessary for the protection of their essential security interests, and limits the authority of WTO adjudicators to examine the necessity of those actions or the extent of those essential security interests. In the WTO regime, no dispute has so far provided a better illustration of Article XXI, particularly Article XXI(b), than *Russia—Traffic in Transit*. Although probably not everyone will agree with each detail of the panel's interpretation of Article XXI (b) in this case, the panel report at large was welcomed as a progressive report in the sense that it challenged the many continuing controversies over the extent and application of Article XXI.

7.2.2 *How* Russia: Traffic in Transit *Interprets Article XXI GATT*

7.2.2.1 Background of the Dispute and Arguments of the Parties

Russia—Traffic in Transit is the latest WTO dispute dealing with the freedom of transit and national security. On 14 September 2016, the Ukraine brought a case of *prima facie* violation to the WTO under which it challenged the consistency and transparency of Russia's several restrictive transit measures with Article V:2 GATT and Article X GATT on publication and administration of trade regulations. In response, Russia invoked Article XXI(b) and refrained from any further rebuttal of Ukraine's arguments. Following the unsuccessful consultations, Ukraine requested in February 2017 establishment of a panel. The DSB established a panel in March 2017 and the panel issued its final report in April 2019.[115] The panel ruled in favor of Russia's measures and Ukraine did not appeal the panel's decision.

Russia's measures banned and imposed other restrictions on two types of transit goods (a) Ukrainian goods, and (b) international goods arriving from Ukraine and destined for Kazakhstan, the Kyrgyz Republic and other Central Asian countries.[116] The measures included:

---

[114]Browne (1997); Bhala (1998), p. 267; *Hestermeyer* (note 84), 578–79.

[115]WTO, *Russia – Traffic in Transit*, Request for the Establishment of a Panel by Ukraine, WT/DS512/3 (Feb. 9, 2017) [Request for the Establishment of a Panel by Ukraine]; Action by the Dispute Settlement Body, WT/DS512/7 (Apr. 28, 2019).

[116]WTO, *Russia – Traffic in Transit*, Request for Consultation by Ukraine, WT/DS512/1/corr.1 (Sept. 21, 2016) [Request for Consultations by Ukraine].

1) *The 2014 Russia-Belarus border bans*: these measures banned the transit of Ukrainian goods and international goods destined for Kazakhstan and third countries subject to veterinary and phytosanitary surveillance as well as those international goods that were subject to an import embargo pursuant to Russian Resolution No. 778. These measures, however, allowed the transit of Ukrainian goods subject to veterinary and phytosanitary surveillance through designated checkpoints on the Russian side of the external customs border of the Eurasian Economic Union (EAEU) border upon a derogation request from Kazakhstan. In that case additional requirements had to be fulfilled by those goods, including the requirement to present veterinary and phytosanitary surveillance permits from both Kazakhstan and Russian relevant authorities, as provided by the 2016 Belarus Transit Requirements.[117]

2) *The 2016 Belarus transit requirements*: goods coming from Ukraine destined for Kazakhstan or the Kyrgyz Republic were exceptionally allowed to enter Russia via Belarus when they fulfilled its additional customs requirements. The requirements, *inter alia*, included activation of a Global Navigation Satellite System in transit trucks while carrying goods on roads or rail and submission of special registration cards by drivers both at entry and exit customs points.

3) *The 2016 transit ban on non-zero duty and Resolution No.778*: imposed a transit ban on Ukrainian products of non-zero-tariff as required by the EAEU customs tariffs schedule and products from countries (the EU and Norway) that were subject to a Russian embargo as per Russian Regulation No. 778. The transit ban on Ukrainian products of non-zero-tariff, as alleged by Ukraine, was in response to Ukraine's rejection to join the Treaty on Establishment of the EAEU and the provisional entry into force of the economic part of the newly concluded agreement between the EU and Ukraine (EU-Ukraine Association Agreement).[118] In 2014, Russia and other members of the Common Wealth of Independent States (CIS), including Belarus, Kazakhstan, Armenia and Kyrgyz, agreed on establishing the EAEU. Before that, and since 2012, these countries had a free trade area (CIS-FTA) along with Ukraine and Tajikistan.[119] Although Ukraine participated in the initial negotiations of the EAEU treaty, it later refused to become a party and instead concluded the EU-Ukraine Association Agreement with the EU, which aims at fostering the political and economic integration with the EU.[120] Following this, Russia suspended the application of the CIS-FTA with Ukraine arguing that Ukraine's treaty with the EU changed the circumstances substantially, which were essential for Russia during the CIS-FTA conclusion.[121]

---

[117]Panel Report, *Russia – Traffic in Transit*, para. 7. 1(d).

[118]Request for Consultations by Ukraine (note 116), 3; see also Panel Report, *Russia – Traffic in Transit*, paras. 7. 12, 7. 13.

[119]Panel Report, *Russia – Traffic in Transit*, para. 7. 6.

[120]Ibid., para. 7. 7.

[121]Ibid., para 7. 13.

4) *The 2016 Presidential Decree No. 1*: ensured the economic and national interest of the Russian Federation in international cargo transiting from Ukraine to Kazakhstan through the territory of the Russian Federation. The transit restriction under the 2016 Presidential Decree No.1 and the 2016 Regulation were effective from 1 January 2016 for goods entering Russia via Belarus and destined for Kazakhstan and effective from 1 July 2016 for goods destined to Kyrgyz. However, Ukrainian goods of non-zero tariffs and goods subject to an import embargo under Regulation No. 778 were not allowed to enter Russia via Belarus at all.[122] The application of the measures later extended to goods destined for Tajikistan, Turkmenistan, and Uzbekistan.[123]

Russia invoked Article XXI(b)(iii) as a defense for the adoption and enforcement of all these measures. According to Russia the measures were necessary for the protection of its essential security interests and were taken "in response to the emergency in international relations that occurred in 2014 and posed a threat to the Russian Federation's essential security interests which continued to exist."[124] Russia refrained from any other clarification on its measures arguing that it was not obliged to disclose information contrary to its essential security interests under Article XXI.[125] Likewise, Russia argued that the panel did not have jurisdiction to further address "serious national security matters that members acknowledged should be kept out of the WTO, an organization which is not designed or equipped to handle such matters".[126] According to Russia, the wording of Article XXI (b) supports the sole discretion of an invoking member in determining "the necessity, form, design and structure of the measures taken pursuant to Article XXI".[127] In Russia's view, Article XXI(b)(iii) therefore safeguards an invoking member's right to take actions in times of war or other emergencies in international relations in a way that the member itself considers necessary.[128]

The occurrence of the 2014 'emergency in international relations' as stated by Russia involved Russia's military deployment to Crimea, a territory recognized by a UN Resolution as autonomous,[129] to annex it to the Russian territory. Following this event, certain countries such as the EU, Canada, and Norway imposed economic sanctions on Russian persons, entities and goods including an import embargo of Russia's goods.[130] In December 2016, the UN adopted another Resolution, which

---

[122]Ibid., para. 7. 1(a)(b).

[123]Ibid., para 7. 1(c).

[124]Ibid., para. 7.4.

[125]Ibid., paras. 7. 4, 7.23.

[126]Ibid., paras. 7. 22, 7. 28.

[127]Ibid., paras. 7. 27, 7. 28, 7. 57.

[128]Ibid., para. 7. 29.

[129]GAOR. No. 68/262, Exhibit UKR 89 (Mar. 27, 2014).

[130]Panel Report, *Russia – Traffic in Transit*, paras. 7. 9 & 7.10.

denounced Russia's military effort in Crimea and reaffirmed the non-recognition of Crimea's annexation.[131]

Ukraine, however, looked at Article XXI as an affirmative defense, which requires Russia to provide evidence for the justification of its measures.[132] Generally, in law, a claim or defense is affirmative if the party initiating the claim or invoking the defense is required to present evidence to support its claim or to justify its defense.[133] In WTO law, an affirmative defense means that a party invoking an exception under a WTO agreement as a defense against the violation of a WTO provision must prove the consistency of its otherwise WTO inconsistent action or legal measure with the exception it aims to invoke.[134] For example, Article XX GATT is an affirmative defense and a member invoking it to defend its measures must qualify the requirements set out by Article XX.[135] However, not all WTO exceptions are treated as affirmative defenses. It is rather a case-by-case matter and, given the nature and language of an exception, varies from exception to exception. In the case of Article XXI, no normative rule exists to justify whether or not it is an affirmative defense. However, a majority of previous disputes under both GATT 1947 and the WTO agreements show that Article XXI is not an affirmative defense, as it imposes no burden of proof on the invoking member. Ukraine, to the contrary, suggests that the affirmative nature of Article XXI gives the panel jurisdiction to review Russia's reasons for invoking Article XXI. The following subsection assesses the panel's approach to the arguments of the parties.

7.2.2.2 Whether Article XXI(b) Is a Non-affirmative Defense and Non-justiciable

The panel first defined and interpreted each term and clause under Article XXI(b) in accordance with the customary rules of interpretation of public international law, particularly those embodied in Articles 26, 31 and 32 VCLT.[136] The panel started its assessment with the chapeau of Article XXI(b). The chapeau of Article XXI (b) provides that no provision in GATT shall be construed "to prevent any contracting party from taking any action which it considers necessary for the protection of its essential security interests." Article XXI(b) then lists conditions under which a member is allowed to take any action it considers necessary to protect its essential security interests. The conditions are, *inter alia*, (iii) in time of war or other emergencies in international relations.

---

[131]GAOR. No. 71/205, *Situation of Human Rights in the Autonomous Republic of Crimea and the City of Sevastopol (Ukraine)*, GAOR. A/71/PV.65 (Dec. 19, 2016).

[132]Panel Report, *Russia – Traffic in Transit*, para. 7. 31.

[133]See Howard et al. (1990), p. 47.

[134]See for example AB Report, *US – Shirts and Blouses from India*, pg. 14.

[135]Ibid., pg. 16.

[136]Panel Report, *Russia – Traffic in Transit*, paras. 7. 59, 7. 132.

While the protection of 'essential security interests' sets out the ultimate objective for taking actions, the clause 'which in considers' gives a broad discretion to an invoking member to decide what constitutes an 'essential security interest' and what action it considers necessary to take for the protection of those interests. The term 'security' is an evolutionary subjective concept and its meaning has expanded beyond the military context. A dictionary definition of security as "the condition of being protected from or not exposed to danger" covers a broad range of non-military matters with an effect on safety such as human rights violations.[137] The 'essential security interests' is a conditional objective under Article XXI(b) with the term 'essential' serving as the qualification to 'security interests'. This means that a member cannot take an action to protect any kind of security interests but can only for those that are "absolutely indispensable or necessary".[138] Therefore, while the discretion of an invoking member to determine which of its security interests it deems 'essential' to it cannot be underestimated, such discretion is conditional and gives the WTO panels the authority to review risks and possibilities of the measure concerned.[139] Therefore, the chapeau of Article XXI(b) is partially justiciable.

The panel takes all these points into account. In defining the 'essential security interests', the panel states that it is a narrower concept than 'security interest' and generally refers to those interests "relating to the quintessential functions of the state, namely, the protection of its territory and its population from external threats, and the maintenance of law and public order internally".[140] Although the panel clarifies that threats can be external and internal, its scope within the definition of 'essential security interests' pursuant to Article XXI(b) covers external threats affecting an invoking member's territory, population, maintenance of law and public order interests inside its borders. The external nature of threats qualifying as a situation of rising essential security interests can be further confirmed by the panel definition of 'international relations' as "global political interactions".[141] According to the panel, essential security interests, depending on particular circumstances surrounding a State and a State's perception, can vary from State to State and with changing situations. The panel, therefore, looks at essential security interests as a subjective and self-interpretational matter, which is confirmed by the adjective clause 'which it considers'.[142]

The panel, however, emphasizes the invoking member's veracity when determining the extent and nature of its essential security interests and its protective actions to prevent an abuse of Article XXI.[143] It states that the subjectivity of Article

---

[137]*Holger P. Hestermeyer*, Human Rights and the WTO: The Case of Patents and Access to Medicines (2007), 289.

[138]*Ohlhoff* (101), 445.

[139]Ibid., 440, 443; see also *Hestermeyer* (note 84), 580–581 & 584; Bhala (1998), p. 271.

[140]Panel Report, *Russia – Traffic in Transit,* para. 7. 130.

[141]Ibid., para. 7. 73.

[142]Ibid., para. 7.131.

[143]Ibid., para. 7. 133.

XXI(b) "does not mean that a Member is free to elevate any concern to that of an 'essential security interests'. Rather the discretion. . . is limited by its obligation to interpret and apply Article XXI(b)(iii) in good faith. . ."[144] The panel further provides that the obligation of good faith applies not only to the chapeau of Article XXI (b) but "also and most importantly, to their connection with the measures at issue. . . this obligation is crystallized in demanding that the measure at issue meets a minimum requirement of plausibility in relation to the proffered essential security interests. . ."[145] The panel continues to interpret whether the adjectival clause "which it considers" of the chapeau extends to subparagraphs of Article XXI(b) subjecting them to self-interpretation by the invoking member. The panel states that the term "relating to" in the last sentence of the chapeau, which links actions in the chapeau to the exceptions set out in the subparagraphs, constitutes an objective relationship between those subparagraphs and the chapeau. The subparagraphs refer to objective facts and limit the adoption of protective actions in the chapeau to specific conditions, which qualify for a consistency review by WTO panels.[146] The subparagraphs thus do not fall within the adjectival clause "which it considers" and the clause qualifies only for actions in the chapeau.[147]

Following the chapeau terms, the panel continues to define the terms 'war' and 'emergency in international relations' in Article XXI(b)(iii). The term 'war' is a complicated term in international relations and, given different circumstances, the determination of what constitutes 'war' can be justiciable.[148] However, the panel definition of 'war' is a rather explicit one. The panel interprets 'war' as an armed conflict, which is a larger category of an "emergency in international relations". Similarly, the panel interprets the term 'in time' of war as 'during' war.[149]

Also, the term 'emergency in international relations' can give rise to the complicated and controversial question of whether its determination is subjective or can be subject to judicial review.[150] Although the panel confirms that the term 'emergency' does not carry such a clear meaning as 'war' does, it defines emergency as "a situation, esp. of danger or conflict that arises unexpectedly and requires urgent action" or "a pressing need. . .a condition or danger or disaster throughout a region."[151] The panel further clarifies the meaning of an emergency in international relation through testing its relationship with Article XXI(b)(i) on fissionable materials and Article XXI(b)(ii) on traffic in arms or other materials for military purposes. Based on the relationship between these paragraphs, the panel held that emergency in international relations involves similar interests such as military interests,

---

[144]Ibid., paras. 7. 132–134.

[145]Ibid., para. 7. 138.

[146]Ibid., paras. 7. 69, 7. 82, 7.101.

[147]Ibid., para. 7. 146.

[148]*Ohlhoff* (101), 445.

[149]Panel Report, *Russia – Traffic in Transit,* para. 7. 70.

[150]*Ohlhoff* (101), 446.

[151]Panel Report, *Russia – Traffic in Transit,* para 7. 72.

maintenance of law or public order interests seen in subparagraphs (i) and (ii) and demonstrates an objective state of affairs which is subject to objective review.[152] The panel then concludes that an emergency in international relations "appears to refer generally to a situation of armed conflict, or of latent armed conflict, or of heightened tension or crisis, or general instability engulfing or surrounding a State."[153] Situations such as political and economic differences between members, even if they are considered urgent or serious, are not sufficient to constitute "emergency in international relations" under Article XXI(b)(iii) because they do not give rise to military interests, maintenance of law and public order interests.[154]

However, the panel states that unlike measures under Article XX, actions fulfilling the requirement of Article XXI(b)(iii) do not need to be predetermined as WTO inconsistent measures, if they were taken during normal times and not in war or other emergencies in international relations.[155] This means that WTO panels do not evaluate whether other alternative measures exist to address the essential security interest in a less WTO inconsistent manner.[156] The evaluation of the measures of concern is limited to their qualification with the exceptions of subparagraph (iii) and once found that the measure qualifies for one of those exceptions, the panel does not consider it necessary to examine the WTO consistency of those measures in other legal contexts.[157]

An understanding from the panel interpretation of Article XXI(b) is that it is neither an affirmative defense nor a totally self-judging or non-justiciable clause.[158] The Article rather has both, a subjective and an objective nature. The chapeau of Article XXI(b) has a subjective nature conferring relatively broad discretion to an invoking member in determining its essential security interests and the nature, type and extent of its actions, which it considers necessary for the protection of those interests.[159] In comparison, Article XXI(b) subparagraphs have an objective nature confining the autonomy of an invoking member in taking actions to specific exceptions and giving WTO panels the power to examine whether the action or measure qualifies at least for one of those exceptions.[160]

Based on the objective nature of Article XXI(b)(iii) the panel ultimately concludes that it bears jurisdiction to review whether Russia's measures were taken *during* war or other emergencies in international relations,[161] and that a case of *prima facie* violation brought in accordance with Articles XXII and XXIII GATT is

[152]Ibid., paras. 7. 74, 7. 77.

[153]Ibid., para. 7. 74.

[154]Ibid., para. 7. 75.

[155]Ibid., para. 7. 108.

[156]Ibid.

[157]Ibid., para. 7. 153.

[158]Ibid., paras. 7. 102, 7.104.

[159]Ibid., para. 7. 101.

[160]Ibid.

[161]Ibid., paras. 7.102, 7.104.

subject to WTO dispute settlement even if Article XXI is invoked.[162] The panel supports its conclusion on non-justiciability of Article XXI by recourse to the object and purpose of GATT 1994 and the WTO agreements. It provides that while GATT and other WTO agreements grant members a derogation from WTO obligations under specific circumstances in favor of their non-trade legitimate objectives, it would be "entirely contrary to the security and predictability of the multilateral trading system (. . .) to interpret Article XXI as an outright potestative condition, subjecting the existence of a Member's GATT and WTO obligations to a mere expression of the unilateral will of that Member."[163] The panel also consults the drafting history of Article XXI(b) to provide what the GATT contracting parties meant by 'security interests' being as 'essential'.[164]

7.2.2.3   Whether Russia's Measures Qualify Under Article XXI(b)(iii)

To examine whether Russia's measures qualify under Article XXI(b)(iii), the panel relies on Russia's veracity as an ultimate means to review whether the essential security interests articulated by Russia have arisen from an emergency in international relations that is considered "sufficiently enough".[165] According to the panel, the level of emergency in international relations determines whether the articulation of the essential security interests by an invoking member is sufficient. As such the panel states:

> The less characterized is the 'emergency in international relations'. . .the less obvious are the defense or military interests, or maintenance of law and public order. . .in such cases a Member would need to articulate its essential security interests with greater specificity than would be required when the emergency in international relations involved, for example, armed conflict.[166]

According to the Panel, the 2014 event, that gave rise to the adoption and enforcement of Russia's measures at issue, was an 'emergency in international relations'.[167] In support of its findings, the panel gave reference to the 2016 UN Resolution concerning the 2014 event between Russia and Ukraine and the sanctions imposed on Russia by a number of countries following the event.[168] The 2016 UN General Assembly Resolution recognized the situation between Russia and Ukraine as an armed conflict and made explicit reference to the 1949 Geneva Convention,

---

[162]Ibid., paras. 7. 94, 7. 98(c).

[163]Ibid., para. 7. 79.

[164]See for example Ibid., para. 7. 92.

[165]Ibid., para. 7. 134.

[166]Ibid., para. 7. 135.

[167]Ibid., paras. 7. 126, 7.137.

[168]Ibid., para. 7. 122.

which applies in cases of declared war or other armed conflict between countries.[169] According to the panel, the period, during which the 2016 transit measures were applied, involved armed conflict, as recognized by the UN General Assembly resolutions, and at least as of March 2014 to at least end of 2016 the situation between Russia and Ukraine deteriorated to the extent that it was a matter of concern to the international community.[170] Based on these supporting evidences, the panel concluded that Russia's measures were taken during an emergency in international relations and qualified under Article XXI(b)(iii).[171] This overturned Ukraine's claim that Russia took the 2016 transit measures only in response to the entry into force of the economic part of the EU-Ukraine Association Agreement.[172] The panel, however, stated that Ukraine's economic integration with the EU and its non-participation in the EAEU was not unrelated to what happened in 2014 and consequently created an emergency in international relations.[173] Therefore the panel looked at the measures in the context of Article XXI(b)(iii) as to whether their adoption and enforcement took place during an emergency in international relations.[174] This conclusion shows how the WTO panel is exercising careful restraints when evaluating measures that are justified under Article XXI.

The exercise of careful restraints by the panel could be further seen in its statement regarding the question whether the international responsibility for creating an emergency in international relations could be subject to assessment before the panel or would affect the panel's assessment. The panel stated that determining whether a measure is enforced during an emergency in international relations, it is relevant to assess which factor or factors bear the international responsibility for the existence of an emergency in international relations and it is not necessary for the panel to characterize the situation between Russia and Ukraine under international law.[175] However, an ambiguity that remains in the panel's ruling regarding the international responsibility for an emergency in international relations is whether the ruling also means that the panel does not assess whether the responding party is involved in the emergency in international relations of a given dispute. This does not seem to be true, at least in the case of Ukraine-Russia relationship. One of the explanations Russia offered in support of the 2014 event as an event constituting 'emergency in international relations' was that the 2014 event involved Ukraine. The panel took the account of this explanation as part of the explanation for the 2014 event when reaching to the conclusion that the event was an 'emergency in international relations'. However, the UN resolutions were the main evidence for the

---

[169]Ibid., para. 7. 122; UNGAR, Situation of Human Rights in the Autonomous Republic of Crimea (note 131), 2.

[170]Panel Report, *Russia – Traffic in Transit,* para. 7. 122.

[171]Ibid., paras. 7. 124–126.

[172]Ibid., para. 7. 141.

[173]Ibid., para. 7. 142.

[174]Ibid., paras. 7. 124–125.

[175]Ibid., para. 7. 121.

panel's conclusion that the 2014 event between Russia and Ukraine constituted an emergency in international relations, which is not surprising given that the WTO does not tackle issues of security nature.

7.2.2.4 Transparency of Actions Taken Pursuant to Article XXI

As discussed earlier, one of the controversies surrounding Article XXI was whether a measure taken pursuant to Article XXI was subject to an advance notification. The 1982 Decision imposed a best-endeavor obligation on contracting parties to notify to *fullest extent possible* their actions justified by Article XXI to GATT contracting parties. The panel in *Russia—Traffic in Transit* seems to have overlooked this question despite the fact that Ukraine criticized the lack of transparency of Russia's measures at issue. Although Russia pointed out that the situation was publicly known,[176] this nonetheless does not present a clear implication for notification requirement under Article XXI. The panel's silence on notification of measures taken pursuant to Article XXI, especially Article XXI(b)(iii) makes sense because war or an emergency, as stated by the panel, often has an urgent nature that requires immediate response. An advance notification of immediate responses is difficult if not impossible. Maybe that was also one of the reasons that the 1982 GATT Decision did not provide a straight obligation on member's notification of their Article XXI actions and instead imposed only a best-endeavor obligation on GATT contracting parties to notify Article XXI actions.

7.3 Conclusion

GATT embodies some general and security exceptions. If members meet their conditions, they are allowed to deviate from all their substantial GATT and WTO obligations including the obligation to grant freedom of transit by adopting inconsistent WTO national trade policies and trade restrictive measures.

Article XX GATT is the most often invoked exception within WTO law. While Article XX allows WTO members to deviate from their GATT and some other WTO obligations, it sets out strict requirements that members need to fulfill. The WTO dispute settlement records show that despite the fact that some members successfully justified their otherwise GATT/WTO inconsistent measures under one or more listed exceptions of Article XX, most of the challenged measures could not pass the chapeau test and therefore were not justified under Article XX.

In comparison, Article XXI is a unique GATT exception, which is not invoked as frequently as Article XX. Article XXI gives WTO members a broad opportunity to deviate from their substantial GATT obligations in favor of their self-defined

---

[176]Ibid., para. 7. 119.

essential security interests and, also ties the hands of the WTO adjudicators while assessing whether a member's measure was taken to protect its essential security interests. The panel's interpretation of Article XXI(b) in *Russia—Traffic in Transit* confirms the strong restraints in WTO panels' assessment of Article XXI. However, the panel report is an innovative report as it responds to most of the substantial questions surrounding the nature and scope of Article XXI. It especially focuses on Article XXI(b) by stating that it is not totally non-justiciable and that WTO adjudicators bear jurisdiction to review a case of *prima facie* violation brought to them, even if it involves invocation of Article XXI. While a WTO member has the discretion to declare a trade restrictive measure under Article XXI(b) to justify protection of a self-determined essential security interest without being obliged to prove the relationship between its measure and the protection of an essential security interest, it still needs to prove that it took the measure during war or other emergencies in international relations. Similarly, WTO adjudicators do exercise the power to review the measures under the exceptions of Article XXI(b) and further test the invoking member's veracity to ensure that it has not circumvented Article XXI(b).

As for the Afghanistan-Pakistan existing transit challenges, the QRs seem to be invokable by each of the two countries under Article XX GATT and the APTTA general exception. But the transit ban on Indian exports and border closure measures could possibly be justified under Article XXI GATT due to the security motive behind their adoption, which will be assessed in the next chapter. In the case of QRs, any justification under Article XX GATT or the APTTA general exception to be invoked in WTO dispute settlement, is subject to a two-tier test. For the reasons provided and given the rigidity of the two-tier test, the chance is low that the transit QRs could successfully pass all the requirements of the test. For instance, if Pakistan or Afghanistan opt to invoke e.g., Article XX(d) to justify their QRs, they would need not only to determine how they have sought to secure compliance with their exact law in question (e.g., the customs law or regulation its compliance has been sought to secure) and whether that law itself is a WTO consistent law, but they would also need to prove that the measure of concern was not applied in a manner constituting an 'arbitrary' or 'unjustifiable' discrimination between countries in which the same condition prevailed or a 'disguised restriction' to international trade.

References

Abbott KW (1999) International relations theory, international law, and the regime governing atrocities in internal conflicts. Am J Int Law 93:364–365

Andenas M, Zleptnig S (2006) Proportionality and balancing in WTO law: a comparative perspective, EAIEL Policy Paper No. 2. University of Hong Kong, Pok Fu Lam, pp 54–64

Bhala R (1998) National Security and International Trade Law: what the GATT says, and what the United States does symposium on linkage as phenomenon: an interdisciplinary approach. Univ Pa J Int Law 19:265

Browne RE (1997) Revisiting "National Security" in an interdependent world: the GATT Article XXI defense after Helms-Burton. George Town Law J 86:410

Condon B (2006) Environmental sovereignty and the WTO: trade sanctions and WTO law. Transnational Publishers, Ardsley, pp 94–96

Dunoff JL (2002) The WTO's legitimacy crisis: reflections on the law and politics of WTO dispute resolution. Am Rev Int Arbitr 12:319

Howard MN, Crane P, Hochberg DA (1990) Phipson on evidence, vol 47, 14th edn. Sweet & Maxwell, London

Joseph S (2013) Blame it on the WTO? A human rights critique. Oxford University Press, Oxford, pp 101–107

Kearney RD, Dalton RE (1970) The treaty on treaties. Am J Int Law 64:517

Koskeniemi M (2002) The gentle civilizer of Nations: the rise and fall of international law 1870–1960. Cambridge University Press, Cambridge, p 481

Lester S et al (2011) World Trade Law: texts, materials and complementary, 3d edn. Bloomberg, New York, pp 373–443

Lo C-F (2013) The proper interpretation of 'Disguised Restriction on International Trade' under the WTO: the need to look at the protective effect. J Int Dispute Settlement 4:111

Regan DH (2007) The meaning of 'Necessary' in GATT Article XX and GATS Article XIV: the myth of cost-benefit balancing. World Trade Rev 6:347–369

Schloemann HL, Ohlhoff S (1999) "Constitutionalization" and dispute settlement in the WTO: national security as an issue of competence. Am J Int Law 93:448

Spanogle JA Jr (1997) Can Helms-Burton be challenged under WTO? Steston Law Rev 27:1314

Van Den Bossche P, Zaouc W (2018) The law and policy of the World Trade Organization, 4th edn. Cambridge University Press, Cambridge, pp 544–613

Voon T (2019) The security exception in WTO law: entering a new era. Am J Int Law Unbound 113:45–50

Vrins O (2011) The European Commission's proposal for a regulation concerning customs protocol on transit. J Intellect Property Law Practice 6:781

Wolfers A (1952) National security as an ambiguous symbol. Political Sci Q 67:481–502

Wolfrum R (2010) Article XX GATT on general exceptions. In: Wolfrum R et al (eds) WTO – trade in goods. Max Planck commentaries on World Trade Law. Nijhoff, Leiden, pp 455–478

Chapter 8
Implications of WTO Rules on Freedom of Transit and Security Exceptions for Afghanistan–Pakistan Transit Trade

When Afghanistan obtained WTO membership, the main expectation was that the membership would help Afghanistan overcome its transit challenges with Pakistan, perhaps by challenging Pakistan in the WTO.[1] This chapter assesses the implications of a WTO challenge against Pakistan's transit ban and border closure measures. In doing so, it seeks to answer whether or not these measures can be justified under the GATT security exceptions and tries to set out the role APTTA security exceptions could play in the process. For this purpose, the chapter relies on the assessment carried out on in *Russia – Traffic in Transit*, a case presenting some similarities to the transit situation between Afghanistan and Pakistan. The chapter also tests the relationship of APTTA security exceptions with the GATT security exceptions and other regional trade agreements in force between Afghanistan and Pakistan, to examine how a dispute involving the mentioned transit challenges could be resolved when regional agreements provide conflicting provisions on these measures. For example, what happens if a fictitious Afghanistan-Pakistan regional agreement A contains a transit ban provision and another Afghanistan-Pakistan regional agreement B prohibits transit restrictions and further does not contain a general or security exception to certain measures otherwise inconsistent with that Agreement.

8.1 Background to the Transit Ban on Indian Exports to Afghanistan Through Pakistan's Territory

The transit ban on Indian exports to Afghanistan through Pakistan's territory was not caused by APTTA. It is rooted in the tense political and security situation between Pakistan and India, which was initially created by the territorial conflict over the

---

[1] Pakistan@100 Regional Connectivity (Ch.1, note 30).

© The Author(s), under exclusive license to Springer Nature Switzerland AG 2021
S. Akbari, *The WTO Transit Regime for Landlocked Countries and its Impacts on Members' Regional Transit Agreements*, European Yearbook of International Economic Law 17, https://doi.org/10.1007/978-3-030-73464-0_8

Kashmir region during the partition of India and Pakistan into two independent sovereign States in 1947.[2] When the two countries were divided Hindu Maharaja governed the Kashmir region, which is located between the two countries' borders. The territorial conflict arose on the question to which country the region should belong to after the death of the Maharaja. None of the two countries has ever accepted its annexation to another and thus the region has remained disputed territory until to date. The ownership claim of India and Pakistan over Kashmir is the contour of all the conflicts between the two countries, which brings them often to the UN and bilateral negotiations in order to reach a peaceful resolution. The UN Security Council recognized Kashmir as a "disputed territory"[3] and the UNSC Resolutions No. 38 of January 17, 1948, calls the state of affair between India and Pakistan in relation to Kashmir a matter of urgency involving armed conflict, which "might endanger the maintenance of international peace and security". Further, it calls on India and Pakistan to use their "best endeavors" to settle their dispute over Kashmir via peaceful means of dispute settlement.[4] Since then, the UNSC has denounced, through all its resolutions, any unilateral accession attempt by India or Pakistan and recognized the free will of the Kashmiri people with regard to any decision on "the future shape and affiliation of Kashmir" or the final accession of Kashmir through a free and impartial referendum supervised by the UN.[5]

Despite of several UNSC resolutions, the two countries experienced wars, including the two direct wars of 1965 and 1971, conflicts of different kinds, including limited and latent conflicts, border clashes and frequent confrontations over the region.[6] Continuous conflicts finally brought the two countries to a table to negotiate peace and address their conflict through peaceful means of dispute settlement. Following the 1965 war, the two countries announced ceasefire in 1967 and subsequently signed the Tashkent Peace Agreement under UN supervision, which aims at restoring peace in Kashmir. Similarly, following the 1971 war, the two countries concluded the Simla peace Agreement in 1972 by which they agreed to resolve their conflict bilaterally through peaceful means of dispute settlement.[7] Still in force, the Simla Agreement provides for peaceful settlement of the dispute over Kashmir and prohibits the use of any threat or force in Kashmir, against the territorial

---

[2] See for example *Lamb* (1992), pp. 160–170; *Hoskote* (2018), pp. 74–80.

[3] See for example UNSC. RES. 38, UN Doc. S/RES/38 (Jan.17, 1948); UNSC. RES. 39, UN Doc. S/RES/39 (Jan. 20, 1948) UNSC. RES. 47, UN Doc. S/RES/47 (Apr. 21, 1948); UNSC. RES. 51, U.N. Doc. S/RES/51(June 3, 1948).

[4] UNSC. RES. 38 & UNSC. RES. 39.

[5] UNSC. RES. 41, UN Doc. S/RES/41 (Feb. 6, 1948), UNSC. RES. 47; UNSC. RES. 51; UNSC. RES. 90, UN Doc. S/RES/90 (Jan. 31, 1951), 2; UNSC. RES. 123, U.N. Doc. S/RES/123 (Jan.16, 1957); for literature review, see *Sakoor* (1998), pp. 53–63; *Sajjad Malik* (2019).

[6] *Dixit* (2002), p. 10; *Jaffrelot* (2008), p. 112.

[7] Agreement between the Government of India and the Islamic Republic of Pakistan on Bilateral Relations, Ministry of External Affairs, Government of India, (July 2, 1972) [hereinafter Simla Agreement]. For the text of the Agreement see https://mea.gov.in/in-focus-article.htm?19005/Simla +Agreement+July+2+1972.

integrity or political independence of the contracting parties in accordance with provisions of the UN Charter.[8]

Despite the bilateral peace efforts, the border conflicts continued to exist and have particularly increased in recent years.[9] Since August 2019 tensions over Kashmir rose, following the Indian Government's move to revoke the special status granted to Kashmir by Article 370 of the Indian Constitution[10] and the subsequent deployment of more military force to Kashmir, aiming to make Kashmir an integral part of India.[11] A few days after Kashmir's special status revocation, Pakistan requested the UNSC to meet them urgently on the issue.[12] However, the UNCS has not yet conducted an urgent meeting. The Indian revocation of the special status of Kashmir was criticized for its breach of the UNSC resolutions, which recognize the right of Kashmiri people to self-determination through plebiscite and moreover prevent India and Pakistan from taking any unilateral actions against the exercise of this right. In addition, the revocation is condemned for its breach of the Simla peace Agreement, which is still legally in force between the two countries and provides that any dispute between the two countries, including their conflict over Kashmir, should be bilaterally settled through peaceful means of dispute settlement.[13]

The long-lasting Kashmir territorial conflict has affected nearly all areas of regional cooperation between the two countries. One of these severely affected areas is the bilateral and regional trade and transit relationship. The two countries have had the lowest trade volume since the partition, while prior to that, more than half of their world trade took place between one another.[14] For example, since 2006, with minor exceptions, the Pakistani trade volume with India has not exceeded three percent of its total world trade.[15] The current total trade volume between the two countries accounts for two billion USD, which makes up two percent of Pakistan's world exports to India and 0.5% of Indian world imports.[16] The Indian exports to Pakistan do not exceed 0.31% of its world exports.[17] Following every war or

---

[8] Arts. I, VI Simla Agreement.

[9] See generally *Jaffrelot* (2018).

[10] Article 370 of the Indian Constitution recognizes the right of Kashmiri people to self-determination for governance system, legal system including citizenship law, property and fundamental rights.

[11] Jeffrey Gettleman *et al.*, India Revokes Kashmir's Special Status, Raising Fears of Unrest, The New York Times (Aug. 5, 2019), https://www.nytimes.com/2019/08/05/world/asia/india-pakistan-kashmir-jammu.html; DWAN, Govt resolves to take up 'annexation' of Kashmir on international forums, fight BJP's 'racist ideology' (Aug. 6, 2019), https://www.dawn.com/news/1498411/pm-imran-addresses-joint-session-of-parliament-on-in dianactions-in-occupied-kashmir.

[12] UNSC, Letter dated 1 August 2019 from the Chargé affairs a.i. of the Permanent Mission of Pakistan to the United Nations addressed to the Secretary-General, S/2019/623 (Aug. 1, 2019).

[13] Arts. I, VI Simla Agreement.

[14] Pakistan@100 Regional Connectivity (Ch. 1, note 30), 11; see also *Mirza* (1988), pp. 515–517.

[15] Pakistan@100 Regional Connectivity (Ch.1, note 30), 11.

[16] Ibid.

[17] Ibid., 11 & 17.

conflict, the primary response by each side has been the suspension of trade ties. In its first response to the Indian revocation of Article 370 in August 2019, Pakistan suspended its bilateral trade relation with India. In doing so, it closed the Wagha border, which is the most used trade and transit route between the two countries and the only land route for Afghan transit goods to India.[18]

The situation has not only affected the trade and transit between the two countries but also severely hampered their trade and transit relationship with other neighboring countries. It has particularly affected Afghanistan's transit relationship with Pakistan, the two countries who entertained the most transit trade ties with one another,[19] Afghanistan's access to the Indian Ocean, and ultimately Afghan trade with India and other South Asian countries. The transit ban on Indian exports to Afghanistan through Pakistan's territory is another major example of this effect. In addition to the permanent transit ban on Indian exports to Afghanistan, Pakistan often closes its borders to Afghan exports, transit goods and passengers. In the wake of the recent Kashmir's revocation status, the Wagha border has remained closed for Afghan's transit goods and persons.[20] However, the closing of Pakistan's borders is not only directly linked to the India-Pakistan conflict over Kashmir but has other reasons as well. Experience shows that often when regional cooperation between Afghanistan and India grows, Pakistan creates a security situation between its borders with Afghanistan and subsequently closes its borders to Afghan trade and passengers.[21] This action has been repeated for decades despite the fact that a binding bilateral transit trade agreement is in force between Afghanistan and Pakistan.

Afghanistan and Pakistan concluded, for the first time in history, a transit trade agreement in 1965 (ATTA) to address their transit problems through a legally binding agreement. ATTA resolved the transit challenges between the two countries to some extent, including the unexpectedly applied border closure measures by Pakistan. However, it still recognized the transit ban on Indian exports to Afghanistan through the territory of Pakistan, which was imposed since the partition of Pakistan and India and only allowed Afghan exports to India via limited transit routes. It can be concluded that the Agreement failed to provide an effective transit regime between the two countries, not only due to its transit ban provision, but also because of its limited provisions on transit routes available for the international transit and its transparency problems. After their trade relationship rapidly changed with the fall of the Taliban regime and the deployment of NATO forces to

---

[18]*Jessie Yeung & Sophia Saifi*, Pakistan downgrades Diplomatic ties, Suspends Trade with India over Kashmir, CNN (Aug. 7, 2019), https://edition.cnn.com/2019/08/07/asia/kashmir-pakistan-response-intl-hnk/index.html; *Mukesh Rawat*, Pakistan suspends Trade with India. Who Gains, Who Loses from Imran KHAN'S Move, India Today (Aug. 9, 2019), https://www.indiatoday.in/news-analysis/story/pakistan-suspends-trade-with-india-imrankhan-article-370-jammu-kashmir-1578817-2019-08-09.

[19]Pakistan@100 Regional Connectivity (Ch.1, note 30), 22.

[20]Telephone Interview with Akhlaqi (Ch.1, note 29), (Sept. 2, 2019).

[21]See for example *Wang* (2017), pp. 119–120; *Paliwal* (2016), pp. 468–488.

Afghanistan at the end of 2011,[22] Afghanistan and Pakistan replaced ATTA with a new transit agreement (APTTA) to improve the legal regime governing their transit relationship. Although APTTA recognizes free and unrestricted transit of goods between the two countries via a large number of transit routes available to international transit in both countries, it explicitly recognizes the transit ban on Indian exports to Afghanistan through Pakistan's territory. Like ATTA, APPTA fails to effectively address the continued transit challenges between Afghanistan and Pakistan including the frequent border closures, allegedly by Pakistan.[23]

Looking at the shortcomings of APTTA discussed above, the hope of many people was that accession to the WTO and recourse to the WTO dispute settlement mechanism would resolve the existing transit problems between Afghanistan and Pakistan. Unfortunately, the accession to the WTO was unable to fulfil these aspirations. The reason for this is the fact that Pakistan's transit ban and border closure measures, which are in regular circumstances inconsistent with Article V GATT and Article 11 TFA, are implemented because of security motives, which give Pakistan the possibility to invoke the GATT security exceptions to defend those measures.

8.2 Transit Ban and Border Closure Measures Under Article XXI GATT

A strong contribution the panel report in *Russia – Traffic in Transit* made in relation to the interpretation of Article XXI is that WTO members are unlikely to ask a WTO panel to dismiss a case of nullification or impairment by invoking a security exception. They will also not refrain from engaging in a panel proceeding of such case for security reasons.

In the case of Afghanistan's and Pakistan's transit challenges, Afghanistan could register a dispute in accordance with Articles XXII and XXIII GATT to allege that the transit ban and border closure measures imposed by Pakistan impair or nullify its benefits under Article V GATT and Article 11 TFA. One can assume that Pakistan will invoke GATT Article XXI(b) to justify its measures but, unlike the traditional approach by previous WTO invoking members, it is unlikely to ask the WTO to dismiss Afghanistan's request to establish a panel to review its claim. Once a case of *prima facie* violation of Article V GATT or Article 11 TFA is brought by Afghanistan and a security exception is invoked by Pakistan, a WTO panel will not look at Article V GATT or Article 11 TFA to assess the extent of Pakistan's violation of

---

[22]A dynamic shift in transit relationship between Afghanistan and Pakistan owed to transit of military supply of NATO forces through Pakistan's territory to Afghanistan. See Pakistan @100 Regional Connectivity (Ch.1, note 30), 11.

[23]As retaliatory action, Afghan borders have also been reported closed at few instances to Pakistan's exports.

these provisions but will instead look at Pakistan's invocation of security exception under Article XXI(b) GATT.

With this scenario in mind the state of play for the transit ban and border closure measures under Article XXI(b) needs to be assessed. Recalling the panel's strict interpretation of the chapeau of Article XXI(b) in *Russia – Traffic in Transit*, it is unlikely for the panel to review Pakistan' justification of its measures. Moreover, it would not ask Pakistan to prove the extent of its essential security interests, but would instead examine the measures under Article XXI(b)(iii) to ensure Pakistan took them *during* war or other emergencies in international relations and further test Pakistan's veracity invoking Article XXI(b).

Of the border closure measures and the transit ban, the latter would not be difficult to justify under Article XXI(b)(iii). The background of the transit ban is the highly tense political relationship involving the long-lasting armed conflict, which qualifies for the definition of both war and other emergencies in international relations as provided by the panel. The existence of such tense political relationship between India and Pakistan, as mentioned earlier was addressed in several UNSC resolutions, including the Resolution No. 38 of January 1948, which represents the state of affairs between the two countries as a matter of urgency involving armed conflict. Similarly, the increasing tension between the two countries created by the revocation of the special status of Kashmir indicates that the territorial and political relationship between India and Pakistan have often experienced armed conflict or latent armed conflict. For both countries, the claim over Kashmir creates the peak of their essential public and national security interests.

Given that the situation between India and Pakistan over Kashmir has been a matter of international and publicly known conflict, a test of good faith would also not seem difficult to pass. Recalling the approach taken by the panel in *Russia – Traffic in Transit*, an invoking member's good faith is connected to a "sufficiently enough" articulation of its essential security interest in question, which is determined on the level of war, conflict or emergency in international relations.[24] Although the Simla Agreement is still in force between the two countries, it would not bar India or Pakistan from taking actions, they consider necessary for the protection of their essential national security interests arising out of cross-border clashes. Furthermore, it is not likely for the panel to look at which of these countries initiated the border conflict or bears the responsibility for it. The transit ban is thus a practical example of how an otherwise WTO inconsistent trade measure can be adopted when it aims at protecting essential national security interests.

With some differences, the same assessment applies to border closure measures. Although compared to the transit ban, the application of border closure measures between Afghanistan and Pakistan needs a relatively deeper assessment under Article XXI(b)(iii), the measures are still likely to be justified under Article XXI (b)(iii). Even though Afghanistan and Pakistan have had a close trade relationship representing the primary exporting and importing markets for the products from one

---

[24]Panel Report, *Russia – Traffic in Transit*, paras 7. 132–135.

another, their shared borders have experienced and seem to continue experiencing armed conflict or at least latent armed conflict. During times of conflict, both countries, allegedly Pakistan, opt to close their borders to passage of trading goods and passengers from one another. Records show several instances of such border closings caused by armed conflicts or border tensions, which hurt trade and transit in both countries. For instance, following a border conflict in 2016 at the Afghanistan-Pakistan southeast cross border, Pakistan closed its borders for Afghan products, in particular to exports and transit goods of fresh fruits including grapes.[25] The border closing caused a huge trade loss for farmers in Afghanistan because tons of fresh fruits perished.[26] The same instance took place a few times between 2017 and 2018 with the same effect on Afghan trade and transit.[27]

Just like the approach taken for the assessment of a transit ban, a panel will not consider whether Afghanistan or Pakistan created the border security tensions leading to border closure measures. The nature of the conflict itself serves from the point of view of the panel as legitimate grounds for the adoption of border closure measures under Article XXI GATT. A panel would not examine whether the border closure measures contributed to the protection of Pakistan's[28] essential security interests. Moreover, it would not ask Pakistan to prove that its border closure measures were necessary for the protection of its essential security interests. Instead, the panel would limit its examination to an objective assessment of whether or not the border closure measures were taken during war or other emergencies in international relations as provided by Article XXI(b)(iii) GATT. In that case, Pakistan would need to provide the panel with factual evidence of a state of war, or other types of emergency in international relations during the time in which the measures were taken. Given the panel's definition of emergency in international relations, the border clashes leading to the adoption and application of border closure measures can be described as an emergency in international relations, if not even war, since they involve armed conflict or latent armed conflict representing "a situation, esp. of danger or conflict that arises unexpectedly and requires urgent action".

However, it is difficult to state whether the border closure measures would be justified under Article XXI(b)(iii) for the condition '*during*'. Records show, that while security interests affected by border conflicts have been the primary reason for border closure measures, the measures were often still applied for several months after the border conflict ended. In *Russia – Traffic in Transit*, the panel took account of the application of Russia's transit ban and transit restrictions in parallel to the *duration* of the emergency in international relations. It found that between 2014 and

---

[25]See Ch.1. notes 25 & 26.

[26]See Ch.1. note 26.

[27]See Ch.1. note 29.

[28]It should be noted that both Pakistan and Afghanistan have closed their borders to trade and transit from one another. This assessment picks Pakistan as an example for imposing those measures but the same assessment applies to Afghanistan's border closure measures as well.

2016, during which Russia's transit ban and transit restrictions were applied, an emergency in international relations prevailed and therefore the period was characterized as a period of emergency in international relations. As a result, the panel concluded that Russia applied its measures *during* that emergency.[29]

The border closure measures do not seem to meet this condition as the measures exceeded the emergency period. However, it may still be possible that a panel identifies all the periods during which border measures were applied as periods of emergency in international relations, given that Pakistan articulates sufficiently enough the continuance of the situation and the need to protect its essential security interests over a longer period of time. It would therefore depend upon the panel's assessment of Pakistan's good faith in connection to continuance of those measures. Given the subjectivity of good faith, it seems difficult to test Pakistan's veracity, and it lies within the panel's approach as to how it would assess that Pakistan has sufficiently enough articulated a prevailing and continuing emergency in international relations during the period in which it applied its border closure measures.

The transparency of border closure measures is another issue that will likely be and should be considered when assessing the consistency of the border closure measures with Article XXI(b)(iii). Unlike the transit ban, which does not seem to pose a transparency question because of its publicly and internationally known nature and constant application, the border closure measures will probably require a certain degree of transparency. This remains, however, a controversial question as no clear implication regarding transparency of measures taken pursuant to Article XXI(b) can be drawn from the panel report in *Russia–Traffic in Transit* nor from previous panels' decisions. The only legal WTO document that supports a transparency requirement under Article XXI GATT is the *1982 GATT Decision concerning Article XXI* that imposes a best endeavor obligation on members for a prompt notification of their measures taken pursuant to Article XXI. However, any reliance on the 1982 Decision would be for interpretation purpose and would mostly serve as a secondary supportive instrument. The Decision cannot serve as a WTO binding provision and therefore cannot mandate a panel to decide based on it.

8.3 The Relationship of the APTTA Security Exception with Article XXI GATT and Other Regional Agreements

At the outset, it should be noted that since APTTA explicitly recognizes the transit ban for Indian exports to Afghanistan through Pakistan's territory, it is not necessary to further discuss the transit ban relationship with the APTTA security exception. At this stage, the discussion is limited to the invocation of the APTTA security exception for border closure measures and the compatibility of that exception with

---

[29]Panel Report, *Russia – Traffic in Transit*, paras. 7. 102, 7. 124–126.

Article XXI GATT. The relationship of both transit ban and border closure measures, however, will be assessed with other regional agreements concluded and in force between Afghanistan and Pakistan.

APTTA sets out some general and security exceptions that allow departure from APTTA obligations in case the exceptions are met. Like its general exceptions, the APTTA security exception is best endeavor and is placed in a short and abstract form next to general exceptions under Article 53. The Article provides, in relevant part, that "contracting parties agree to ensure that no measure taken under the agreement could risk harming or destroying... (iv) security of its own territory". The security exception does not contain any condition or other elements as Article XXI GATT. Putting aside the relationship between APTTA and WTO law for a moment, including the extent of its security exception, the question arises whether the way the APTTA security exception is articulated would bar the APTTA dispute settlement body from reviewing a dispute involving a security interest.

The answer to the question simply is "no" and the APPTA dispute settlement body is likely going to review a dispute involving a security interest. The reason for this is, that the APTTA security exception lacks a provision to give discretion to its contracting parties regarding the self-determination of their essential security interests or the extent and type of actions a contracting party considers necessary to take for the protection of its essential security interests.

The APTTA security exception resembles an affirmative defense and its consistency and necessity is subject to review by an adjudicatory body. The fact that the APTTA security exception is placed in the same article next to the general exceptions also supports this claim. Moreover, the security exception is articulated in best endeavor language, which gives it a lower degree of legal force compared to other APTTA mandatory provisions including those on providing free and unrestricted transit. Hence, it is unlikely that the APTTA dispute settlement body would grant total discretion in determining the nature and type of an invoking party's actions for the protection of its essential security interests or would possibly dismiss a dispute involving an essential security interest pursuant to the APTTA security exception. On the contrary, the APTTA dispute settlement body should review a dispute involving a security interest. It would be even possible for the APTTA dispute settlement body to rule in favor of freedom of transit and against a security interest because APTTA provides mandatory provisions for freedom of transit and best endeavor provision for security exception and hence, a provision carrying a binding legal force overrides a provision carrying non-binding legal force.

However, assuming that the APTTA dispute settlement body decides not to review such a dispute, the question would be whether the complaining party could refer to Articles XXII and XXIII GATT as relevant rules of international law applicable in relations between the contracting parties pursuant to Article 31(3) (c) VCLT to argue that its right for freedom of transit granted under APTTA was nullified or impaired by the other contracting party. And that the APTTA dispute settlement body was obliged to offer a positive settlement for the *prima facie* violation brought to it. The next question would be whether the APTTA dispute settlement body would consider WTO law and the relevant case law, in particular that on the application of the GATT security exceptions. To answer this question, the relationship between WTO law and APTTA needs to be established.

APTTA provides for a clear relationship with WTO law. In addition to providing that its provisions do not diminish rights and obligations of the contracting parties under multilateral agreements, APTTA specifically imposes a mandatory obligation on APTTA arbitral tribunals to "interpret and apply the provisions of APTTA in accordance with customary rules of interpretation of public international law"[30] and in conformity to WTO rules including its dispute settlement rules and procedures in its judicial proceedings.[31] These provisions particularly give a direct applicability to WTO dispute settlement rules (e.g., Articles XXII and XXIII GATT and Article 3.7 DSU that provide for positive settlement of disputes) in arbitral decision-making in APTTA adjudicatory dispute settlement proceedings. This relationship is also in line with the common rules of treaty interpretation contained in Article 31(3)(c) VCLT on the recognition of relevant rules of international law. Therefore, APTTA dispute settlement provisions give an APTTA arbitral tribunal not only the legitimacy to review a dispute involving an essential security interest under the APTTA security exception by having recourse to WTO dispute settlement rules but also the power to consult all other relevant WTO rules and case law concerning a security exception.

In case the contracting parties are not satisfied with an APTTA arbitral award and decide to take their dispute to WTO dispute settlement, it goes without saying that a WTO panel would review their dispute applying an objective assessment under the Article XXI(b) GATT exceptions.

The discussion now shifts to assessing how a relationship between the transit ban and border closure measures and other regional agreements Afghanistan and Pakistan are parties to can be established. As discussed in previous chapters, besides APTTA, Afghanistan and Pakistan are parties to some broader regional agreements including SAFTA, ECOTA, and ECO-TTFA. Most of these agreements contain at least a clause on free movement of goods across the territory of the contracting parties; be those clauses mandatory or 'best-endeavor' obligations.[32] At the same time, some of these agreements set out general exceptions and, some of them also contain security exceptions, thereby allowing contracting parties to deviate from their substantial obligations under those agreements.[33] This section picks SAFTA as an example.

SAFTA contains a mandatory provision on free movement of goods that provides "SAFTA shall involve free movement of goods among contracting States through elimination of tariff and non-tariff restrictions and any other equivalent measures".[34] SAFTA also imposes a best endeavor obligation on its contracting parties to adopt trade facilitation measures including transit facilities, especially for landlocked

---

[30] Art. 39 APTTA.

[31] Ibid., Art. 45.

[32] See for example Art. 3(2) SAFTA; Art. 13(2) ECOTA.

[33] See for example Art. 14 SAFTA; Art. 15 ECOTA.

[34] Art. 3(2) SAFTA.

contracting parties.[35] In the meantime, SAFTA contains general exceptions, which are comparable to Article XX GATT including its chapeau, that allow departure from SAFTA obligations to protect certain societal values.[36] However, surprisingly, SAFTA does not contain any security exception. One can possibly see SAFTA's lack of a security exception from two different angles. One is that South Asian countries have often had volatile political relationships and a SAFTA security exception would have given these countries a long arm to deviate from their SAFTA obligations in favor of any undesired political and security situations, even if those situations would have not been of heightened tensions to have given rise to any essential security interest. SAFTA signatories probably envisaged a possible abuse of a security exception and therefore, opted to protect SAFTA from such abuse by not adding a security exception. Another reason might be that SAFTA has rather left the issue to be governed by other regional or multilateral regimes and, therefore, refrained from engaging in the security matters of the contracting parties.

In both scenarios, however, in the event of a trade dispute that is giving rise to the invocation of a security exception against an otherwise SAFTA inconsistent measure (e.g., a dispute challenging a border closure measure), a SAFTA dispute settlement body would encounter a critical controversy as to whether they have the jurisdiction to review such dispute and if so, what its legal basis for a review could be. While it would not be controversial if the SAFTA dispute settlement body decided to review the dispute for its inconsistency with SAFTA provisions on granting free movement of goods, provided that a responding party does not invoke a security exception, the case would be different, if the responding party chose to invoke a security exception by referring to WTO provisions and other regional agreements to which both contending parties are parties to. The question then would arise as to what happens, if the SAFTA dispute settlement body decided to conduct a full review of the dispute for its inconsistency with SAFTA provisions but the responding party argued that the matter should be seen in accordance with WTO security exceptions, which does not allow a full examination of a case involving a security exception. Another question is then, what happened to the right of the complaining party for a fair and positive settlement of the risen dispute, if the SAFTA dispute settlement body decided to dismiss the dispute due to the involved security matters not covered by SAFTA?

In either instance, it needs to be asked first, whether SAFTA establishes any relationship with WTO law. Otherwise, the legal conflict between SAFTA and WTO law will be resolved in accordance with the VCLT rules of treaty interpretation. SAFTA recognizes rights and obligations of its contracting parties under the WTO Agreement and provides that its provisions shall not diminish those rights and obligations.[37] These provisions qualify Article 30(2) VCLT. However, even if

---

[35]Ibid., Art. 8.

[36]Ibid., Art. 14.

[37]Article 3 SAFTA provides that "contracting parties affirm their existing rights and obligations with respect to each other under Marrakesh Agreement Establishing the World Trade Organization."

SAFTA does not establish an explicit relationship with WTO law, recourse to WTO rules including GATT exceptions such as Article XXI is still possible before the SAFTA dispute settlement body pursuant to Article 31(3)(c) VCLT for the same reasons explained for APTTA and also based on Article 41 VCLT on the supremacy of multilateral treaties over regional treaties consisting of the same contracting parties.[38] The applicability of WTO provisions before SAFTA dispute settlement bodies can also be assessed based on Article XXIV GATT on RTAs, which was discussed in the context of the supremacy of WTO law over RTAs in Chap. 6. Therefore, a SAFTA dispute settlement body could review a dispute involving a security matter by having recourse to Article XXI GATT and the relevant case law or other relevant supplementary WTO sources. The same assessment will also apply to other regional agreements in force between Afghanistan and Pakistan.

As for APTTA and other regional agreements e.g., SAFTA, their relationship should be established based on VCLT rules. Since neither APTTA nor SAFTA establish any relationship with other regional agreements, Article 30(2) and Article 30(3)(c) VCLT apply to the relationship between them. In this case, first the APTTA transit ban provision, as a provision of a successive treaty, prevails over SAFTA to the extent of a conflict and second serves as a relevant rule to be applicable in relations between APTTA contracting parties in SAFTA dispute settlement proceedings. Since the APTTA security exception, under which transit ban and border closure measures can be justified, is not in conflict with SAFTA as no provision under SAFTA allows or prohibits a security exception, it can be considered as a relevant rule by the SAFTA dispute settlement body to a dispute involving a security matter brought by APTTA contracting parties.

8.4   Conclusion

Based on the assessment of the provisions of Article XXI GATT and the panel report on *Russia – Traffic in Transit* this chapter concludes for the transit trade challenges of Afghanistan and Pakistan caused by national security factors that bringing a dispute in the WTO concerning the mentioned transit challenges is not the best option for Afghanistan as a WTO panel would exercise due restraints in examining the dispute due to the security matters involved. This conclusion however does not extend to seeking a positive solution for the imposition of the transit QRs by Pakistan (or by Afghanistan), since they are not based on security reasons and recourse to

---

[38]The supremacy of WTO rules over RTAs is addressed under few WTO supplementary documents and in the literature. The RTA section of the Singapore Ministerial Declaration provides that "[we] reaffirm the primacy of the multilateral trading system, which includes a framework for the development of regional trade agreements, and we renew our commitment to ensure that regional trade agreements are complementary to it and consistent with its rules". See WTO, Ministerial Declaration of 13 December 1996, WT/MIN/(96)/DEC (Dec. 18, 1996) [hereinafter Singapore Ministerial Declaration]; for literature review see for example *Foltea* (Ch. 7, 58), 56–57.

WTO dispute settlement proceedings might help to provide a positive solution for those measures.

References

Dixit JN (2002) India–Pakistan in War and peace. Routledge, London, p 10

Hoskote A (2018) Review of published literature on conflict in Kashmir, asymmetry in war, conflict resolution, & armed forces in transition. Int J Res Eng IT Soc Sci 8:74–80

Jaffrelot C (ed) (2008) A history of Pakistan and its origins. ANTHEM Press, p 112

Jaffrelot C (2018) Ceasefire violations in Kashmir: a war by other means. Carnegie Endowment for International Peace

Lamb A (1992) Kashmir: a disputed legacy 1846–1990. Oxford University Press, pp 160–170

Mirza PS (1988) Indo-Pak Trade: possibilities of expansion. Econ Polit Wkly 23:515–517

Paliwal A (2016) Afghanistan's India–Pakistan Dilemma: advocacy coalitions in Weak States. Camb Rev Int Aff 29:468–488

Sajjad Malik M (2019) Pakistan–India relations: an analytical perspective of peach efforts. Institute of Strategic Studies, Islamabad

Sakoor F (1998) UN and Kashmir. Pakistan Horizon 51:53–63

Wang J (2017) India's policy toward Afghanistan: implications to the regional security governance. Asian J Middle East Israel Stud 11:119–120

Chapter 9
Final Conclusions

9.1 Final Conclusions

Throughout history landlocked States struggled to secure their rights to freedom of transit and free access to the sea by means of recognition through international conventions and multilateral agreements. This dissertation examined the WTO transit for landlocked countries, taking the landlocked LDC Afghanistan as a particular case study. In doing so, it discussed the recognition of the special transit needs of landlocked States by the WTO legal regime and provided a comparative study of the UNCLOS provisions on freedom of transit for landlocked countries.

The study generally shows that, although landlocked States, especially landlocked LDCs, were to some degree successful in receiving international recognition of their transit needs—including a special recognition—the granted SDT nevertheless does not sufficiently address their particular need of access to the sea. Particularly looking at WTO law and UNCLOS, which both grant SDT to developing and LDC States, it becomes clear that their SDT provisions are inefficient as they are articulated in a rather general context and do not directly relate to the special needs of landlocked LDCs. Therefore, with little on their plate, landlocked LDCs continue to struggle for a special recognition of their needs for freedom of transit and access to the sea.

In the case of Afghanistan problems not only arise because of the absence of a WTO mandatory WTO SDT provision recognizing its special transit right through the territory of WTO coastal neighboring members to access to the sea. They also arise since other WTO provisions allow members to violate the right of freedom of transit in exceptional cases. When Afghanistan became a WTO member, the main perception was that the membership would help Afghanistan overcome its transit challenges with Pakistan, perhaps by challenging Pakistan in the WTO.[1] This expectation emanated mainly from the deadlock of the bilateral approach to resolve Afghanistan's transit problems with coastal neighboring countries, particularly Pakistan, which surfaced the need of a multilateral approach to overcome Afghanistan's transit challenges. Given the WTO's ability to enforce its rules through a rigorous dispute settlement system[2] the general expectation was that the WTO would provide a useful platform for this purpose.

In normal times, this perception is true, since any restrictions on transit whether under or outside of APTTA constitute a violation of WTO provisions on freedom of transit and are therefore challengeable at the WTO. However, the WTO offers members exceptional legal tools such as Articles XX and XXI GATT to justify violation of a WTO substantive rule, for example, a restriction or ban on transit, if specific requirements are fulfilled. In the case of Afghanistan and Pakistan, the ongoing transit challenges, as discussed throughout this dissertation, can be justified under those exceptions. Particularly the transit ban on Indian exports and the border closure measures are justifiable under Article XXI and therefore a challenge of those measures before the WTO is unlikely to succeed.

Notwithstanding this conclusion, it can still be possible that the measures do not fulfil one or more requirements of the exceptions under Articles XX and XXI. In that case room for modification of the measures exist so they could be brought in line with those justifiable exceptions. Any justification of measures, particularly transit QRs, under the GATT or APTTA general exceptions are subject to a two-tier test, which is difficult to pass for the reasons previously provided. For instance, if a country opts to invoke Article XX(d) to justify its QRs, it is required not only to show how this restriction seeks to secure compliance with the exact law in question (e.g., the customs law or regulation) and whether that law itself is a WTO consistent law, but also needs to prove that the measure was not applied in a manner constituting 'arbitrary' or 'unjustifiable discrimination between countries where the same conditions prevail' or a 'disguised restriction' on international trade.

Reaching all these conclusions, this study provided a detailed assessment of Article V GATT on freedom of transit, Article 11 TFA on freedom of transit, Article XX GATT on general exceptions, Article XXI GATT on security exceptions and relevant WTO disputes. Article V GATT and Article 11 TFA create an unconditional obligation for a WTO member to grant freedom of transit across its territory to traffic in transit coming from or going to another WTO member without discriminating between them based on their place of origin, departure, entry or exit, flag of means of transport as well as any other criteria related to the ownership of traffic in transit. They also impose an MFN obligation on the country of destination to grant treatment to international goods that transited through the territory of other WTO members in no less favorable manner than it would be if they were imported without undergoing international transit. Although Article V and TFA provisions do not seem to be

---

[1]Pakistan@100 Regional Connectivity (Ch.1, note 30).

[2]*Davis* (Ch.1, note 31), 179–180.

complicated in the context of rights and obligations of WTO members related to freedom of transit, ambiguity and shortcomings nonetheless exist. For instance, the definition and scope of some terms such as "the routes most convenient for international transit" remain controversial and are believed to act as a restriction to the freedom of transit.

Most importantly from a landlocked LDC's perspective, these articles reveal one important shortcoming, which is the lack of an SDT provision on recognition of the special transit needs of landlocked LDCs. Article V GATT and Article 11 TFA do not recognize such SDT and govern the transit relationship between WTO members on general reciprocal basis without any distinction between coastal and landlocked, developed or developing members. This suggests that while WTO law guarantees an unconditional MFN right to freedom of transit among members, it fails to protect the special needs of landlocked LDC members. Notwithstanding the fact that one-third of the TFA includes SDT provisions to enhance trade facilitation for developing country members, it fails in particular to recognize an explicit SDT provision on serious transit needs of landlocked LDC members. Therefore, landlocked LDCs reap no more out of the agreement than all of the developing and LDC members and the high cost of trading created by the lack of access to the sea remains a main challenge for landlocked LDC members.[3] The TFA drafting history shows that landlocked members actively participated in drafting of the agreement, e.g., landlocked LDC members proposed and backed the inclusion of a provision on non-application of TBT measures on transit goods.[4] It is surprising that these members, who make up 25 members in total, and represent two-thirds of all landlocked countries worldwide, did not push more for a specific mandatory SDT provision on special transit needs of landlocked LDCs.

Even in the case of other WTO SDT provisions, most WTO SDT provisions are 'best-endeavor' commitments and therefore a developing country member cannot invoke them to force a developed country member to carry out those commitments. Even mandatory SDT provisions are difficult for a landlocked LDC to invoke, as none of them specifically address their special transit needs.

Similarly, the assessment of WTO disputes involving a claim of the freedom of transit shows that not only landlocked members have not invoked transit disputes before the WTO dispute settlement body but also that most of the transit disputes were lost for exceptional reasons such as national security reasons. This study suggests that one reason for the missing initiative of landlocked members to proceed to the WTO dispute settlement regime lies in the lack of sufficient and specific legal guarantees for their transit needs.

After discussing the lack of an explicit recognition of a landlocked member's special right to freedom of transit and access to the sea within the WTO regime, the

---

[3] According to the OECD, cost of trading for landlocked LDCs are two times higher than that for their coastal neighboring countries. OECD & WTO (2015), pp. 139–140.

[4] See WTO Negotiating Group on Trade Facilitation, TN/TF/W/143/Rev.3; see also WTO, Trade Ministers of Landlocked Developing Countries, 5th Meeting (2016).

study assessed by examining the normative interaction between WTO law and other rules of public international law, whether or not landlocked members can invoke the provisions on freedom of transit and SDT of the UNCLOS and regional agreements to further support their transit needs before the WTO dispute settlement body. The conclusion shows that WTO law establishes a harmonious relationship with other sources of public international law and recognizes their application as clarification instruments for the interpretation of WTO provisions. In principle, the applicable laws in the WTO dispute settlement proceedings are the WTO covered agreements and WTO adjudicators are obliged to refrain from applying other rules of international law in a way that add or diminish WTO rights and obligations of members under the WTO covered agreements. Nevertheless, WTO adjudicators have opted to consider non-WTO law, especially other relevant multilateral agreements, and applied their provisions where compatible with WTO provisions and relevant to a given dispute.

As for the interaction between WTO law and UNCLOS, their relationship can be established for both interpretation and application purposes. While it goes without saying that provisions of the UNCLOS can be invoked in WTO dispute settlement proceedings as source of interpretation and clarification, recourse to the application of the UNCLOS provisions in accordance with Article 31(3)(c) VCLT in cases where compatible and relevant to a given dispute is also possible. This being said, one should still bear in mind that recognition of such application lies within the autonomous power of WTO adjudicators and is based on the circumstances of each dispute. However, the assessment carried out on the UNCLOS provisions on freedom of transit of landlocked States suggests that landlocked States including landlocked LDCs do not reap much out of the UNCLOS provisions that would make a significant difference to a WTO dispute. Although Part X UNCLOS recognizes non-reciprocal transit rights to landlocked States coupled with a specific SDT for freedom of transit of landlocked LDCs, the condition for the exercise of the granted freedom of transit including the SDT still depends on regional arrangements between landlocked and transit States. Similarly, by respecting full sovereignty of transit States and allowing them to subject freedom of passage including transit passage to domestic laws and regulations, UNCLOS makes its provisions on freedom of transit more convenient to transit States than to landlocked States.

Therefore, UNCLOS does not grant higher and broader privileges for transit needs of landlocked States, particularly for landlocked LDCs, than those of Article V GATT and Article 11 TFA. It would even be fair to conclude that WTO provisions on freedom of transit, even though not specific with regard to transit needs of landlocked States, guarantee freedom of transit across the territory of all members in a stronger and broader way compared to UNCLOS, since they first of all do not directly give full sovereignty to transit States and secondly do not subject the exercise of freedom of transit to terms and modalities to be decided by regional agreements.

However, beside the fact that it lacks an SDT for transit of landlocked States, what actually makes the WTO regime of freedom of transit restrictive and limited is the existence of the broad set of general and security exceptions available for members to justify deviations from WTO obligations including those on freedom of transit. But it should be noted that Article XX GATT on general exceptions, which is the most frequently invoked exception in the WTO, sets out strict requirements that members should fulfil while opting to benefit from exceptions provided therein. WTO case law shows that while some members successfully justified their otherwise GATT/WTO inconsistent measures under one or more of the listed exceptions of Article XX, most of the disputes did not pass a 'two tier test' and therefore did not justify under Article XX in the end. In comparison, Article XXI GATT, which is not invoked as frequently as Article XX, is a unique exception giving WTO members a broad opportunity to deviate from their GATT/WTO obligations in favor of their self-defined essential security interests. Article XXI ties the hands of WTO adjudicators when assessing whether the measure was taken to protect an invoking member's essential security interests. The panel's interpretation of Article XXI (b) on protection of essential security interests in *Russia – Traffic in Transit* confirms the strong restraints in WTO panels' assessment of Article XXI. However, the panel's interpretation in that case is an innovative interpretation of Article XXI in the sense that it responds to most of the substantive questions surrounding the nature and scope of Article XXI. Especially when stating that Article XXI(b) is not totally non-justiciable and that WTO adjudicators bear jurisdiction to review a case of *prima facie* violation brought to them even if it involves invocation of Article XXI GATT. While a WTO member has the discretion to declare a trade restrictive measure under Article XXI(b) to justify protection of a self-determined essential security interest without being obliged to prove the relationship between the measure and the protection of an essential security interest, it still has to prove that it took the measure *during* war or other emergencies in international relations. Similarly, WTO adjudicators exercise their power when reviewing measures under the exceptions of Article XXI(b) and test the invoking member's veracity to ensure it has not circumvented Article XXI(b). Notwithstanding everything said, due to State sovereignty, as evident in *Russia – Traffic in Transit*, the Article XXI security exceptions remain the most challenging exceptions for the exercise of freedom of transit among WTO members.

Therefore, it cannot be recommended to Afghanistan to seek a dispute settlement through establishment of a panel at the WTO for its transit challenges with Pakistan as a WTO panel would be restrained in examining the dispute in the likely event that Pakistan would invoke a security exception. However, Afghanistan can try a dispute settlement through consultations at the WTO.

This conclusion, however, does not extend to the imposition of transit QRs by Pakistan (or Afghanistan) as they do not involve security reasons and recourse to WTO dispute settlement might help to provide a positive dispute settlement after the prevailing deadlock of bilateral solutions. This being said, this study closes up by providing some recommendations to positively modify the transit trade relationship between the two countries.

9.2 Recommendations

9.2.1 Maintaining Bilateral Trade and Transit Relationship

Both Afghanistan and Pakistan understand that their trade relations are inextricably linked, and this cannot easily be ignored. Although the two countries mutually benefit from the WTO legal regime for the protection of their trade and transit rights, taking into account the interdependence of the two countries for trade and transit of one another, a bilateral trade and transit relationship will always be necessary. People in both countries not only rely on products of the other but also their neighboring countries rely on transit trade through the territory of the two countries. Pakistan provides short transit routes for Afghan exports to and imports from India and other South Asian countries via the sea. Similarly, Afghanistan provides the shortest transit route to Pakistani exports to and imports to and from Central Asian countries. Access to these countries is vitally important to Pakistan not only for trade in goods but also for the transfer of electricity and natural gases. The TAPI gas project signed between Turkmenistan, Afghanistan, Pakistan and India and the CASA–1000 energy power project signed between Afghanistan, Tajikistan, Kyrgyz, Pakistan, and India require a transit through Afghanistan in order to arrive in Pakistan and subsequently India. In fact, each step taken in their bilateral trade and transit relationship is either a win-win or lose-lose situation for both countries. Therefore, looking at their economic prosperity one can only recommend a more comprehensive trade and transit convergence instead of divergence. This is particularly important for Pakistan, since it would otherwise be an isolated neighbor in South Asia if its trade ties with Afghanistan deteriorate, as they already did with India.

The same is true for Afghanistan. Although the Chabahar Agreement did help Afghanistan to reduce its dependence on Pakistan to access the sea, the Agreement presents substantial gaps, as most of its provisions are best endeavor obligations only, and it is thus not recommendable to serve as a sole replacement for APTTA. For instance, it does not provide explicit provisions on important issues, such as freedom of transit, transparency, MFN and national treatment principles and does not remove transit duties and charges. Instead, it only encourages the contracting parties to reduce them. Moreover, from infrastructural and political perspectives, the Chabahar port, which is the only seaport in the Chabahar Agreement, faces unpredictability in terms of viable operation, as it is still in a pilot stage and needs further infrastructural facilities. Moreover, the restart of economic sanctions by the US against Iran affected Iran's trade with the rest of the world, which includes investments in Chabahar infrastructural projects. Although US president Donald Trump issued a waiver for infrastructural investment projects by India at the Chabahar port,[5] it is difficult to rely on the duration of the waiver and ultimately

---

[5]Radio Free Europe, US Exempts Iran's Chabahar Port from Sanctions in Nod to Afghanistan (Nov 7, 2018), https://www.rferl.org/a/us-exempts-iran-chabahar-port-project-from-sanction-in-nod-

on the viable operation of the port, given the deadlock in Iran and US negotiations and the rapid downfall of Iran's economic situations. Therefore, although the Agreement could reduce Afghanistan's dependence on Pakistan in terms of access to the sea, it cannot serve as a viable alternative to APTTA. Both APTTA and the Chabahar Agreement have their own particulars and none of them should replace the other. Instead, the Chabahar Agreement should serve as a separate and additional transit agreement providing Afghanistan with a greater variety of options to access the sea.

9.2.2   Proper Implementation of APTTA, Follow Up of the Implementation and Seeking Further Approaches Within Regional Legal Frameworks

It is rightly stated that legal frameworks are nothing but pieces of paper if they are not properly implemented.[6] While framing and concluding laws and agreements are the initial steps for setting a legal context for carrying out cross-border activities, the implementation of those agreements and laws is the part that creates an efficient operation of those activities. Therefore, it would be in the best interests of Afghanistan and Pakistan to revisit APTTA's implementation and take the APTTCA out of isolation by conducting usual meetings and discussing APTTA's implementation issues therein on a regular basis. While doing so, the two countries need to keep their political tensions separate from their mutual trade and transit interests. The negotiations should be based on the good faith to resolve the ongoing trade and transit challenges by seeking effective legal measures within the APTTA legal framework as well as within a broader set of regional and international legal frameworks available to them such as the TIR legal regime for transit procedures.

TIR contains a substantial package of customs procedures and rules followed by a large number of countries including landlocked countries because of its comprehensive package of transit and transport procedures and tools to implement those procedures. Particularly the international guarantee system of the TIR, as presented in TIR Carnet, is a practical tool to mitigate the risk of harm inflicted on the domestic markets of the two countries caused by smuggling trade. Recognizing the TIR procedures on transit from one another would therefore ensure transit securities for both Pakistan and Afghanistan. Moreover, the benefits of the TIR procedures are not only created by their application by the two countries but also by their extensive

---

toafghanistan-india/29586874.html; *see also* Pant (2019), https://www.orfonline.org/research/the-chabahar-disconnect-52964/.

[6]UNOHRLLS, Harnessing the Trade Potential of the Landlocked Developing Countries to Implement the Vienna Programme of Action and 2030 Agenda for Sustainable Development, Compilation of Statements and Presentation delivered at the Fifth Meeting of Trade Ministers of Landlocked Developing Countries (2016), 55.

application by the neighboring countries. For example, Central Asian countries are extensive users of TIR Carnets,[7] which makes the task easy for the transit procedures of goods coming from these countries destined to Afghanistan or Pakistan by a transit through Afghanistan.

9.2.3 Renegotiation of APTTA for a Quadrilateral Transit Agreement to Include Tajikistan and India

For the reasons discussed in this study, it maybe look unrealistic and impossible for Afghanistan and Pakistan to negotiate the accession of India to APTTA but separating political hostilities from trade ties, for a comprehensive trade and transit convergence, negotiation on replacing APTTA with a quadrilateral transit agreement that includes India and Tajikistan, who both play key roles in trading with Afghanistan and Pakistan, seems in the best mutual interest for both Afghanistan and Pakistan. In recent years, Afghanistan has been demanding inclusion of India in APTTA and has been using this demand as a condition to negotiate APTTA.[8] Unconfirmed reports show that Afghanistan's growing trade and transit ties with other neighboring countries have motivated Pakistan to rethink its transit and trade relation with Afghanistan, and to consider allowing Afghan imports from India under APTTA.[9] Some other reports show that Pakistan is not ready to allow India's trade with Afghanistan through its territory.[10] A quadrilateral agreement would be a better alternative for transit relationship between the two countries and should be considered in future APTTA modifications and reforms.

9.2.4 Future Collective Efforts for a Specific Mandatory SDT Provision on Freedom of Transit in WTO Law

Finally, a more general recommendation to all WTO landlocked members to join efforts towards a mandatory SDT clause on particular recognition of transit needs of these countries within future WTO trade facilitation reforms. The special SDT clause

---

[7]UNECE, TIR Handbook, ECE/TRANS/TIR/6/REV.11 (2018), 19.

[8]Interview with Akhlaqi (Ch.1, note 29); see also First Meeting of the Working Group on Trade, Commerce and Investment between India and Afghanistan (Kabul, Jan. 28, 2014); Second Meeting of the Working Group on Trade, Commerce and Investment between India and Afghanistan (New Delhi, Mar. 29–30, 2017), 1 & 3, http://commerce.gov.in/writereaddata/UploadedFile/MOC_ 636268215123005686_IndiaAfghanistan_2nd_JWG%20_minutes_29-30th_2017.pdf.

[9]Iqbal (2018), https://www.dawn.com/news/1433197.

[10]Afghanistan Times, Pakistan Refuses Afghan Trade with India through Land Routes (Sept. 17, 2018), http://www.afghanistantimes.af/pakistan-refuses-afghan-trade-with-india-throughland-routes/.

would particularly be a major example of Aid for Trade for landlocked LDCs, as Aid for Trade does not have to come with technical and financial support but also with guarantees within legal frameworks. Aid for Trade is designed as an engine of trade development for developing countries, *inter alia*, in the WTO developmental goals, reiterated in the Nairobi Ministerial Conference, and the Vienna Programme of Action and 2030 Agenda for Sustainable Development. The WTO and OECD joint database provides trade related policy and regulations in its list of categories that count as Aid for Trade.[11] Although in the context of trade related policies and regulations the database identifies, *inter alia*, training of trade officials; institutional and technical support to facilitate implementation of trade agreements and analysis of proposals by members and their impacts,[12] the proposals could include reforms of the WTO SDT rules to accommodate special transit needs of landlocked LDCs.

References

Iqbal A (2018) Pakistan willing to open allow Afghan land route to India: US Envoy. DAWN
OECD (2007) Aid for trade: making it effective in OECD. Dev Coop Rep 8(1):44
OECD & WTO (2015) Aid for trade: reducing trade costs for inclusive, sustainable growth. OECD Publishing, Paris, pp 139–140
Pant HV (2019) The Chabahar disconnect, commentaries. Observer Research Foundation, July 19, 2019

---

[11]OECD (2007), p. 44; see also OECD & WTO (2015), pp. 133–158.
[12]Ibid.

Legal Documents

Afghanistan Laws and Regulations

Qanuni Assassi Jumhuri'i Isla'mai Afghanistan (The Constitution of the Islamic Republic of Afghanistan) 1382 (2004)

Jaridai'i Rasmi Jumhuri'i Isla'mai Afghanistan (The Official Gazette of the Islamic Republic of Afghanistan), Law of the Independent Commission for Overseeing the Implementation of the Constitution, 2010, 986

Qanuni-i Jaza'i Afghanistan (Afghanistan's Penal Code) 1396 (2017)

Qanuni-i Tijarat'i Afghanistan (Afghanistan's Commercial Code)1334 (1955)

Qanuni-i Sarmayaguzari Khososi'i Afghanistan (Afghanistan's Private Investment Law) 1384 (2005)

Qanuni-i Sarmayaguzari Khososi'i Afghanistan (Afghanistan's Private Investment Law) 1395 (2016)

Qanuni-i Gumrukat'i Afghanistan (Afghanistan's Customs Law) 1321(19820

Qanuni-i Gumrukat'i Afghanistan (Afghanistan's Customs Law) 1384 (2005)

Qanuni-i Maliat bar Aáidat'i Afghanistan (Afghanistan Income Tax Lawl) 1388 (2009)

Qanuni-i Maliat bar Arzush-i Afzooda'i Afghanistan (Law on Value Added Tax of Afghanistan) 1395 (2016)

Qanuni-iStandard wa Muqararat'i Takhnik'i (Law on Standards and Technical Regulations of Afghanistan) 1396 (2017)

Qanuni-i Mili'i Standard'i Afghanistan (Afghanistan National Standard Law) 1392 (2013)

Qanuni-i Amni'a t'i Ghazai'i of Afghanistan (Law on Food Safety of Afghanistan) 1395 (2016)

Qanuni-i Hefazat'i Nabatat wa Qaranti'i Afghanistan (Law on Plant Protection and Quarantine of Afghanistan) 1395 (2016)

© The Author(s), under exclusive license to Springer Nature Switzerland AG 2021
S. Akbari, *The WTO Transit Regime for Landlocked Countries and its Impacts on Members' Regional Transit Agreements*, European Yearbook of International Economic Law 17, https://doi.org/10.1007/978-3-030-73464-0

Qanuni-i Hemayat az Mostahlik'i Afghanistan (Law on Consumer Protection) 1395 (2016)

Qanuni-i Tijarat'i Khariji'i Kala'i Afghanistan (Law on Foreign Trade in Goods of Afghanistan) 1395 (2016)

Qanuni-i Hemayat az Sana'ai Dakhli'i Afghanistan (Law on Safeguards Measures on Domestic Production of Afghanistan) 1396 (2017)

Qanuni-i Ma'adin'i Afghanistan (Afghanistan Mining and Hydrocarbon Law) 1393 (2014)

Qanuni-i Tadarikat'i Afghanistan (Afghanistan Procurement Law) 1395 (2016)

Qanuni-i Istikhda'mi Atba'i Khariji Afghansitan (Law on Foreigners Employment of Afghanistan) 1394 (2005)

Qanuni-i Hemayat az Riqabat'i Afghanistan (Law on Supporting Competition of Afghanistan) 1389 (2010)

Qanuni-i Sherkat ha'i Dawlati'i Afghanistan (Afghanistan State-Owned Enterprises Law) 1334 (1955) (amended: 2005)

Qanuni-i Hakami'at Tijarati'i Afghanistan (Commercial Arbitration Law of Afghanistan) 1386 (2007)

Qanuni-i Transport Jada'i Afghanistan (Afghanistan Road Transport Law) 1397 (2018)

Regulation of Production and Importation of Medicine and Medical Equipment of 2017 of Afghanistan

Regulation on Determining Price of Goods in Customs of 2009 of Afghanistan

Ministry of Finance, Afghan Customs Department, Schedule of Tariffs (2014)

List of International Conventions and Agreements

Agreement between the Government of India and the Islamic Republic of Pakistan on Bilateral Relations, Ministry of External Affairs, Government of India, (July 2, 1972) [Simla Agreement]

Barcelona Convention and Statute on Freedom of Transit, 7 L.N.T.S. No.171 (Signed: April 1921) (Entry into force: October 1922)

CAREC, Cross-Border Transport Agreement (November 5, 2010), Manila

ECO Transit and Transport Framework Agreement (Almaty,1998) (Ratified: 2006)

South Asian Association for Regional Cooperation [SAARC], Secretariat, Afghanistan Accession Protocol of SAFTA (2008), Colombo

Transit and Transport Cooperation Agreement, Ashgabat. Nov. 28, 2017, Türkiye Büyük Millet Meclisi Baskanligina [Grand National Assembly of Turkey], No. 2/1195 (Oct. 30, 2018) [Lapis Lazuli Route Agreement]

Revised Kyoto Convention, 2303 U.N.T.S 148/ [2008] ATS 2 / 37 ILM 22 (1999)

The Official Gazette of the Islamic Republic of Afghanistan, Mo'afiqatna'mi Tejarati Transit Bain Jumhuri'i Isla'mai Afghanistan wa Jumhuri'i Isla'mai

Pakistan [Afghanistan Pakistan Transit Trade Agreement], 10 Aqrab 1390 (Nov. 1, 2011), 1063

The Official Gazette of the Islamic Republic of Afghanistan, South Asian Free Trade Area Agreement, 1019, 2004 [Ratification date for Afghanistan: 2010]

The Official Gazette of the Islamic Republic of Afghanistan, SAARC Agreement on Trade in Service, 1147, 2010 [Ratification date for Afghanistan: 2012]

The Official Gazette of the Islamic Republic of Afghanistan, Mo'afiqatna'mi Ejadi Dahliz Haml wa Naql wa Transit Bain-ul-milali Miani Jumhuri'i Isla'mai Afghanistan, Jumhuri'i Hind, wa Jumhuri'i Isla'mai Iran [International Transport and Transit Agreement between the Islamic Repulblic of Afghanistan, Republic India and Islamic Repoublic of Iran], 25 Hoot 1395 (March 5, 2017), 1250

United Nations Convention on the Recognition and Enforcement of Foreign Arbitral Awards, 330 U.N.T.S. 38 (1968)

United Nations Convention on the Law of the Sea, Dec. 10, 1982, 1833 U.N.T.S. 397

United Nations Vienna Convention on the Law of Treaties, 1155 U.N.T.S. 331 (entered into force: Jan. 27, 1980)

United Nations Convention on Transit Trade of Land-locked States, 597 U.N.T. S.42, 44 (July 1965) (Entry into force: 8 June 1967)

United Nations Convention on the International Transport of Goods under the Cover of TIR Carnet (Signed: November 14, 1975)

List of Cases

Aegean Sea Continental Shelf (Greece. v. Turkey), 1978 I.C.J (December 19)

Appellate Body Report, *United States – Standards for Reformulated and Conventional Gasoline*, WT/DS2/AB/R, (May 20, 1996)

Appellate Body Report, *Argentina – Measures Affecting Imports of Footwear, Textile and other Items*, WT/DS56/AB/R (March 27, 1998)

Appellate Body Report, *Argentina – Safeguard Measures on Import of Footwear*, W/DS121/AB/R (December 14, 1999)

Appellate Body Report, *Korea – Definitive Safeguard Measures on Imports of Certain Diary Products*, WT/DS98/AB/R (December 14, 1999)

Appellate Body Report, *Korea – Measures Affecting Imports of Fresh, Chilled and Frozen Beef*, WT/DS161/AB/R (January 10, 2001)

Appellate Body Report, *European Communities – Measures Affecting Asbestos and Products Containing Asbestos*, WT/DS135/AB/R (March 12, 2001)

Appellate Body Report, *United States – Measures on Certain Hot-Rolled Steel Products from Japan*, WT/DS184/AB/R (August 23, 2001)

Appellate Body Report, *US – Shrimp, Recourse to Article 21.5 of the DSU by Malaysia*, WT/DS58/AB/ (October 22, 2001)

Appellate Body Report, *United States – Definitive Safeguard Measures on Imports of Circular Welded Carbon Quality Line Pipe from Korea*, WT/DS202/AB/R (August 22, 2002)

Appellate Body Report, *European Communities – Conditions for the Granting of Tariff Preference to Developing Countries*, WT/DS246/AB/R (April 7, 2004)

Appellate Body Report, *EC – Asbestos,* at para. 119; Appellate Body Report, *United States – Measures Affecting the Cross-Border Supply of Gambling and Betting Services*, WT/DS285/AB/R (April 5, 2005)

Appellate Body Report, *China – Measures Affecting Trading Rights and Distribution Services for Certain Publications and Audiovisual Entertainment Products*, WT/DS363/AB/R (December 21, 2009)

© The Author(s), under exclusive license to Springer Nature Switzerland AG 2021   231
S. Akbari, *The WTO Transit Regime for Landlocked Countries and its Impacts on Members' Regional Transit Agreements*, European Yearbook of International Economic Law 17, https://doi.org/10.1007/978-3-030-73464-0

Appellate Body Report, *United States – Measures Affecting the Production and Sale of Clove Cigarettes*, WT/DS406/AB/R (April 4, 2012)

Appellate Body Report, *European Communities – Measures Prohibiting the Importation and Marketing of Seal Products*, WT/DS401/AB/R (May 22, 2014)

Appellate Body Report, *China – Measures related to the Exportation of Rare Earths, Tungsten and Molybdenum*, WT/DS431/AB/R (August 4, 2014)

Bankovic and Others v. Belgium and Others, Admissibility, App. No 52207/99, European Court of Human Rights, at para. 57 (December12, 2001)

Corfu Channel (U.K. v. Albania), 1949 I.C.J., 28 (April 9)

GATT, *Trade Restrictions Affecting Argentina Applied for Non-Economic Reasons*, C/M/159, L/5317 (April 30, 1982)

International Tribunal for the Law of the Sea, *Request for Provisional Measures* (Order), ITLOS No. 10 (2001)

International Tribunal for the Law of the Sea, *Case Concerning the Conservation and Sustainable Exploitation of Swordfish Stocks in the South-Eastern Pacific Ocean (Chile/European Community)*, Case No 7, Order 2007/3, (November 30, 2007)

Military and Paramilitary Activities (Nicar v. U.S), 1986 I.C.J. 14, 213 (June 27)

NAFTA, Panel Decision on Remand, *Certain Softwood Lumber Products from Canada (Countervailing Duty)*, USA-CDA-1992-1904-01 (December 17, 1993)

Report of the Panel, *United States – Trade Measures Affecting Nicaragua*, L/6053 (October 13, 1986) [Unadopted]

Report of the Panel, *United States – Section 337 of the Tariff Act of 1930*, L/6439 - 36S/345 (November 7, 1989)

Report of the Panel, *Tuna – Dolphin I*, DS21/R (September 3, 1991) [Not adopted]

Panel Report, *Brazil – Measures Affecting Desiccated Coconut*, WT/DS22/R (October 17, 1996)

Panel Report, *European Communities – Regime for the Importation, Sale and Distribution of Bananas*, WT.DS27/R (May 22, 1997)

Panel Report, *India – Patent Protection for Pharmaceutical and Agricultural Chemical Products*, WT/DS50/R (September 5, 1997)

Panel Report, *United States – Import Prohibition of Certain Shrimp and Shrimp Products*, WT/DS58/R (May 15, 1998)

Panel Report, *Indonesia – Certain Measures Affecting the Automobile Industry*, WT/DS54/R (July 2, 1998)

Panel Report, *United States – Tax Treatment for Foreign Sales Corporations (Article 21.5 – EC)*, WT/DS108/R (October 8, 1999)

Panel Report, *Turkey – Restrictions on Imports of Textile and Clothing Products*, WT/DS34/R, paras. 33–43 (November 19, 1999)

Panel Report, *United States – Anti-dumping Act of 1916* (March 31, 2000)

Panel Report, *Korea – Measures Affecting Government Procurement*, WT/DS163/R (May 1, 2000)

Definition of Some Frequently Used Terms in This Dissertation (The Definitions Are Generally Extracted from the WTO Glossary of Terms)[1]

Accession Becoming a member of an international organization or party to an agreement (e.g., the WTO, TIR Convention).

Accession working party Group of WTO members negotiating multilaterally with a country applying to join the WTO.

Anti-dumping measures A countervailing action against a dumping action.[2]

Applied tariffs Tariffs applied by WTO members on imported products. These could be equal to or lower than but cannot be more than bound tariffs.

Bound tariffs Tariffs specified by WTO members in their schedule of concessions as the maximum level of tariffs that they can apply to imported products.

Countervailing measures Action taken by an importing country, usually in the form of increased duties, to offset subsidies given to producers or exporters in the exporting country or to combat dumping actions.

Domestic subsidy A domestic subsidy is a benefit not directly linked to exports.

Domestic support (sometimes "internal support") In agriculture, any domestic subsidies or other measures which act to maintain producer prices at levels above those prevailing in international trade; direct payments to producers, including deficiency payments, and input and marketing cost reduction measures available only for agricultural production.

Developed country A country with high economic condition. High-income country.[3]

---

[1]WTO, Glossary of Terms, https://www.wto.org/english/thewto_e/glossary_e/glossary_e.htm.

[2]Ibid.; see also WTO, Understanding the WTO, https://www.wto.org/english/thewto_e/whatis_e/tif_e/tif_e.htm.

[3]WTO, Glossary of Terms; see also UN, World Economic Situation and Prospects: Country Classification (2014), 144. The UNDP Human Development Index (HDI) classifies countries based on the degree of their development in areas of, *inter alia*, health care, childcare, mortality, education, per capita income, GDP, poverty, unemployment, technology, and industrialization. A country with high degree of development in these areas, except zero or low degree for poverty and

S. Akbari, *The WTO Transit Regime for Landlocked Countries and its Impacts on Members' Regional Transit Agreements*, European Yearbook of International Economic Law 17, https://doi.org/10.1007/978-3-030-73464-0

Developing country A country with middle economic condition. Middle-income country.[4]

Dumping A product is considered dumped if it is exported to another country under a lower price less than its normal value price and lower than the comparable price for like products in the exporting country.[5]

Export subsidy A benefit conferred on a firm by the government that is contingent on exports.

Foreign direct investment (FDI) An investment made to acquire lasting interest in enterprises operating outside of the economy of the investor. Direct investment enterprise is an enterprise in which a single foreign investor owns either ten percent or more of the ordinary shares or voting power of the enterprise.

Free trade A trading regime in which tariffs are zero and there are no non-tariff barriers or technical barriers to trade.

Frontier traffic Imports and exports carried out by frontier zone inhabitants between two adjacent frontier zones.

Generalized System of Preferences (GSP) Programs by developed countries granting preferential tariffs to imports from developing countries.

Harmonized System (HS) An international nomenclature developed by the World Customs Organization in six-digit codes allowing all participating States to classify trading goods on a common basis.

Landlocked State A country without a seacoast. A country is landlocked if it does not have direct access to the sea and if it has to transit through the territory of its neighboring countries in order to access maritime ports.

Least-developed country (LDC) A country with poor economic condition. Low-income country.

Most Favored Nation (MFN) principle (Article I GATT 1994) Requiring countries not to discriminate between goods based on their origin or destination.

National treatment (NT)principle (Article III GATT 1994) The principle of treating goods and services of other countries the same as national goods and services.

Quantitative restrictions (QRs) Specific limits on the quantity or value of goods that can be imported or exported during a specific period.

Regional trade agreements (RTAs) Reciprocal trade agreements between two or more partners to liberalize tariffs and services.

---

unemployment, is a developed country. A country with an average degree of development in the mentioned areas is a developing country and a country with low degree of development in the mentioned areas is an LDC. See generally UNDP, Human Development Indices and Indicators, Statistical Update (2018).

[4]WTO, Glossary of Terms; UN, World Economic Situation and Prospects (note 3).

[5]WTO, Glossary of Terms; see also Art. 2(1) WTO Agreement on the Implementation of Article VI of GATT 1994 (Anti-Dumping Agreement).

Transit Movement of goods and persons. It is passage of persons and goods including baggage and means of transport with the beginning and terminating point beyond the territory of a contracting party through whose territory the traffic passes.[6]

Traffic in transit Traffic in transit is subject of the transit and includes transit of persons, goods, baggage, and means of transport.[7]

Waiver Permission granted by WTO members allowing a WTO member not to comply with normal commitments.

---

[6]WTO, Glossary of Terms (note 3); see also Art. V:1 General Agreement on Tariffs and Trade (GATT 1947), Oct. 30, 1947, 61 Stat. A-11, 55 U.N.T.S. 194; General Agreement on Tariffs and Trade (GATT 1994 or GATT), Jan. 1, 1995, 1867 U.N.T.S 190, 33 I.L.M. 1153 (1994). Similarly, Black's Law Dictionary defines transit in general concept as "a stop-over privilege on a continuous journey granted by carrier by which a break de facto in continuity of carriage of goods is disregarded and two legs of a journey are treated as though covered without interruption." Black Law Dictionary (4th edn. 1968), 1667.

[7]Art. V:2 GATT; see also Art. 124 UN Convention on the Law of the Sea (UNCLOS), Dec. 10, 1982, 1833 U.N.T.S. 397. Black's Law Dictionary defines traffic as "the subject of transportations on a route, as persons, goods, animals, vehicles, or vessels." Black's Law Dictionary (note 6), 1670.

References

Books and Journal Articles

Abbott KW (1999) International relations theory, international law, and the regime governing atrocities in internal conflicts. Am J Int Law 93:364–365

Afghanistan Business Law Handbook, vol. 1 (International Business Publications, DC., 2013)

Aldosari A (2007) World and its politics: Middle East, Western Asia, and Northern Africa, Vol. 3. Marshall Cavendish Corp., p 341

Andenas M, Zleptnig S (2006) Proportionality and balancing in WTO law: a comparative perspective, EAIEL Policy Paper No. 2, 54–64. University of Hong Kong

Arvis JF (2005) Transit and the special case of landlocked countries. In: De Wulf L, Sokol Jose B (eds) Customs modernization handbook. World Bank, pp 243–264

Asadov S (2012) Tajikistan's Transit Corridors and their Potential for Developing Regional Trade, Working Paper 6. University of Central Asia, Institute of Public Policy and Administration

Ayral S (2016) TBT and TFA Agreements: Leveraging Linkage to Reduce Trade Costs, WTO, Working Paper ERSD-2016-02 (June 2016)

Baker BK (2012) Settlement of India/EU WTO dispute and seizures of in transit medicines: why the proposed EU border regulation isn't good enough, PIJIP Research Paper. American University of Washington, p 4

Bartels L (2001) Applicable law in WTO dispute settlement proceedings. J World Trade 35:503–509

Bayeh E (2015) The rights of Land-locked States under the international law: the role of bilateral/ multilateral agreements. Soc Sci 4(2)

Bhala R (1998) National security and international trade law: what the GATT says, and what the United States does symposium on linkage as phenomenon: an interdisciplinary approach. Univ Pennsylvania J Int Law 19

Bindschedler, Bernhardt R (eds) (1984) Encyclopedia of public international law, vol. 7. North Holland, p 468

Black's Law Dictionary (4th edn, 1968)

Borgen CJ (2005) Resolving treaty conflicts. George Washington Int Law Rev 37:576–579

Broude T (2008) Principles of normative integration and the allocation of international authority: the WTO, the Vienna Convention on the law of treaties, and the Rio declaration. Loyola Univ Chicago Int Law Rev 6:202–203

Browne RE (1997) Revisiting "National Security" in an interdependent world: the GATT Article XXI defense after Helms-Burton. George Town Law J 86:410

© The Author(s), under exclusive license to Springer Nature Switzerland AG 2021   239
S. Akbari, *The WTO Transit Regime for Landlocked Countries and its Impacts on*
Members' Regional Transit Agreements, European Yearbook of International
Economic Law 17, https://doi.org/10.1007/978-3-030-73464-0

Burdic WL (2007) The principles of roman law and their relation to modern law, 3rd edn. The Lawyers Co-operative Publishing Co., pp 360–364

Castellino J, Allen S (2003) Title to territory in international law: a temporal analysis. Ashgate

Chase C (2012) Norm conflict between WTO covered agreements – real, apparent or avoided? Int Law Q 61

Churchill RR, Lowe AV (1988) The law of the sea. Manchester University Press, p 167

Cook G (2015) A digest of WTO Jurisprudence on public international law concepts and principles, 1st edn. Cambridge University Press

Cottier T, Foltea M (2006) Constitutional functions of the WTO and RTAs. In: Bartels L, Ortino F (eds) Regional Trade Agreements and the WTO legal system: economic analysis of regional trade agreements

Depoorter BWF, Parisi F (2003) Fragmentation of property rights: a functional interpretation of the law of servitudes. Policy Research Working Paper 284. John M. Olin Center

Dixit JN (2002) India–Pakistan in War and Peace. Routledge, London, p 10

Donald R, Stephen T (2016) The international law of the sea, 2nd edn. Hart

Dowdy J, Erdmann A (2013) After the war economy: the role of private sector in Afghanistan future. Aspen Institute, pp 261–281

Dunoff JL (2002) The WTO's legitimacy crisis: reflections on the law and politics of WTO dispute resolution. Am Rev Int Arbitr 12:319

Eliason A (2015) The trade facilitation agreement – a new hope for the World Trade Organization. World Trade Rev 14 (May 1, 2015)

Eltizam ZA (1996) Afghanistan Foreign Trade. Middle East J 20:95–103

Fair C (2008) Pakistan's relations with Central Asia: is past Prologue? J Strategic Stud 1:216

Faye ML et al (2004) The challenges facing landlocked developing countries. J Humanit Dev Capabilit 5

Finger M, Wilson J (August 2006) Implementing a WTO Agreement on trade facilitation: what makes sense? World Bank Policy Research Working Paper, WP/S3971

Gabriel Ibarra P (2010) The challenge of implementing the domestic trade policy measures: the Colombia Ports of entry case. International Center for Trade and Sustainable Development

Gabriel M et al (2010) Free movement of goods. In: Gabriel M, Trone J (eds) Commercial law of the European Union. Springer, pp 39–73

Glassner MI (1967) Transit problems of three Asian land-locked countries: Afghanistan, Nepal and Laos, Reprint Series in Contemporary Asian Studies 57

Glassner MI (ed) (2001) Biography on land-locked states, 5th enlarged & revised edn. M.E. Sharpe

Goodhand J (2004) From War economy to peach economy? Reconstruction and state building in Afghanistan. J Int Aff 58:155–160

Grotius H (1916) The freedom of the seas. Oxford University Press, Oxford, pp 9–10

Hamanaka S (2014) WTO Agreement on trade facilitation: assessing the level of ambition and likely impacts. Global Trade Customs J 9

Hanif K (2018) Pakistan Afghanistan's economic relations after 9/11. J Punjab Univ Hist Soc 31:94–97

Herrmann C et al (eds) (2015) Trade policy between law, diplomacy, and scholarship, European Yearbook of International Economic Law. Springer

Hestermeyer HP (2007) Human rights and the WTO: the case of patents and access to medicines. Oxford University Press, p 289

Hoban T et al (2002) Food biotechnology: benefits and concerns. J Nutr 132:1384–1385

Hoekman B, Kostechi M (1997) The political economy of the world trading system: from GATT to WTO. Oxford University Press, pp 230–237

Hoekman B, Kostechi M (2001) The political economy of the world trading system: WTO and beyond. Oxford University Press, pp 390–394

Hoskote A (2018) Review of published literature on conflict in Kashmir, Asymmetry in war, conflict resolution, & armed forces in transition. Int J Res Eng IT Soc Sci 8:74–80

Howse R (2002) The Appellate Body Rulings in the Shrimps/Turtles Case: a new legal baseline for the trade and environment debate. Columbia J Environ Law 27

Huarte Melgar B (2015) The Transit of goods in public international law. Brill

Hussain I, Elahi A (2015) The future of Afghanistan-Pakistan Trade relations. Institute of Business Administration, Karachi

Hussain SW (2008) The impact of Afghan transit trade on NWFP's economy. Pan-Graphics Ltd., Peshawar pp 1–8

Islam R (2010) Constraint of the Agreement on South Asian Free Trade area and SAARC Agreement on Trade in Service. Brigham Young Univ Int Law Rev 7:8–1

Jackson JH (1998) World Trading System: law and policy of international economic relations, 2nd edn. MIT Press, pp 25–30

Jackson JH, Hudec RE, Davis D (2000) The role and effectiveness of the WTO dispute settlement mechanism. Brookings Institute

Jaffrelot C (ed) (2008) A history of Pakistan and its origins. Anthem Press, p 112

Jaffrelot C (2018) Ceasefire violations in Kashmir: a war by other means. Carnegie Endowment for International Peace (Oct. 24, 2018)

Jayanta R (2005) Key issues in trade facilitation, Policy Research Working Paper 3703. World Bank

Jose B (ed) (2005) Customs modernization handbook. World Bank, pp 243–264

Joseph S (2013) Blame it on the WTO? A human rights critique. Oxford University Press, pp 101–107

Kearney RD, Dalton RE (1970) The treaty on treaties. Am J Int Law 64

Kelsen H (1946) General theory of law and states, 2nd edn. Harvard University Press, p 373

Koskeniemi M (2002) The gentle civilizer of nations: the rise and fall of international law 1870–1960. Cambridge University Press, p 481

Lamb A (1992) Kashmir: a disputed legacy 1846–1990. Oxford University Press, pp 160–170

Lauterpacht H (1927) Private Law Sources and Analogies of International Law

Lesaffer R (2005) Argument from Roman law in current international law: occupation and acquisitive prescription. Eur J Int Law 16

Lester S et al (2011) World trade law: texts, materials and complementary, 3rd edn. Hart, Bloomberg, pp 373–443

Liu C (2009) Maritime transport services in the law of the sea and the World Trade Organization, Vol 14. Peter Lang Publishers, pp 28–34

Lo C-F (2013) The proper interpretation of 'disguised restriction on international trade' under the WTO: the need to look at the protective effect. J Int Disp Settlement 4

Makil R (1970) Transit rights of land-locked countries: an appraisal of international conventions. J World Trade Law 4

Malik MS (2019) Pakistan–India relations: an analytical perspective of peach efforts. Institute of Strategic Studies, Islamabad

Marceau GZ (2001) Conflict of norms and conflict of jurisprudence: the relationship between the WTO agreement and the MEAS and other treaties. J World Trade 35

Maxwell FJ (1974) The Afghan economy: money, finance, and the critical constraints to economic development. Brill, ch. 3

McLaughlin RJ (1997) Settling trade-related disputes over the protection of marine living resources: UNCLOS or the WTO? Georgetown Int Econ Law Rev 10:72

Merkouris P, Fitzmaurice M, Elias O (eds) (2010) Treaty interpretation and the Vienna Convention on the law of the treaties. Nijhoff, pp 136–140

Mitchell AD (2008) Legal principles in WTO disputes. Cambridge University Press, pp 15–23

Neofeld N (2014) The long and widening road: how WTO Members finally reached a trade facilitation agreement. WTO, Working Paper ERSD-2014-06

Neofeld N (2016) Implementing the Trade Facilitation Agreement: From Vision to Reality. Working Paper ERSD-2016-14 (WTO, September)

Neumann P (1970) The relationship between GATT and the United Nations. Cornell Int Law J 3

Ngantcha F (1990) The right of innocent passage and the evolution of the international law of the sea. Pinter Publishers, London, p 52

Paliwal A (2016) Afghanistan's India–Pakistan Dilemma: advocacy coalitions in weak states. Cambridge Rev Int Aff 29:468–488

Pant HV (2019) The Chabahar disconnect, commentaries. Observer Research Foundation, July 19, 2019

Parto S et al (2012) Afghanistan and regional trade: more, or less, imports from Central Asia, Working Paper 3. University of Central Asia, Institute of Public Policy

Pauwelyn J (2001) The role of public international law in the WTO: how far can we go? Am J Int Law 95

Pauwelyn J (2003) Conflict of norms in public international law: how WTO law relates to other rules of international law. Cambridge University Press

Pauwelyn J (2005) The application of non–WTO rules of international law in WTO dispute settlement. In: Pauwelyn J (ed) World Trade Organization: legal, economic and political analysis. Springer, pp 1406–1423

Pogoretskyy V (2017) Freedom of transit and access to gas pipeline networks under WTO law. Cambridge University Press

Pounds NJ (1959) A free and secure access to the sea. Oxford University Press, Oxford

Proelss A (ed) (2017) United Nations Convention on the law of the sea: a commentary. C.H. Beck, pp 89–935

Rana RK (2010) Right of access of land-locked states to the sea by the example of bilateral agreement between land-locked state Nepal and Port State India. Published Master's Thesis, University of Troms

Regan DH (2007) The meaning of 'necessary' in GATT Article XX and GATS Article XIV: the myth of cost-benefit balancing. World Trade Rev 6:347–369

Ruse-Khan G, Henning Jaeger T (2009) Policing patents worldwide? EC border measures against transiting generic drugs under EC – and WTO intellectual property regimes. IIC 40:502, 507

Sarup A (1972) Transit trade of land-locked Nepal. Int Comp Law Q 21

Schloemann HL, Ohlhoff S (1999) "Constitutionalization" and dispute settlement in the WTO: national security as an issue of competence. Am J Int Law 93

Schreuer C (1995) Regionalism v. Universalism. Eur J Int Law 6:477

Spanogle JA Jr (1997) Can Helms-Burton be challenged under WTO? Steston Law Rev 27:1314

Stoll P-T, Veoneky S (2002) The Swordfish case: law of the sea v. Trade. Heidelberg J Int 62

Sultana R (2011) Pakistan – Afghan economic relations: issues and prospects. Pakistan Horizon 64:21–28

Tabibi AH 1958) Free access to the sea for countries without sea-coast: position of Afghanistan on this question. Publisher unknown

Tanaka Y (2015) The international law of the sea, 2nd edn. Cambridge University Press, p 409

Tuek H (2015) Landlocked and geographically disadvantaged states. In: Rothwell DR et al (eds) The Oxford handbook of the law of the sea. Oxford University Press

Uprety K (1994) Landlocked states and access to the sea: an evolutionary study of a contested right. Penn State Int Law Rev 12

Uprety K (2003) From Barcelona to Montego Bay and thereafter: a search for landlocked states' rights to trade through access to the sea – a retrospective review. Singapore J Int Comparative Law

Valles C (2011) Article V GATT. In: Wolfrum R et al (eds) WTO – trade in goods, vol. 5. Max Planck Commentaries on World Trade Law, p 193

Van Den Bossche P, Zaouc W (2018) The law and policy of the World Trade Organization, 4th edn. Cambridge University Press, Cambridge, pp 544–613

Voon T (2019) The security exception in WTO law: entering a New Era. Am J Int Law Unbound, pp 45–50

Vranes E (2006) The definition of norm conflict in international law and legal theory. Eur J Int Law 17:395

Wang J (2017) India's policy toward Afghanistan: implications to the regional security governance. Asian J Middle East Israel Stud 11:119–120

Wilfred J (1953) The conflict of law-making treaties. Br Yearb Int Law 30:427

Wolfers A (1952) National security as an ambiguous symbol. Polit Sci Q 67:481–502

Wolfrum R(2010) Article XX GATT on general exceptions. In: Wolfrum R et al (eds) WTO – Trade in goods, Max Planck Commentaries on World Trade Law. Nijhoff, pp 455–478

Xinru L (2010) The Silk Road in World History, 1st edn. Oxford University Press

Yianopoulois AN, Paul ST (1983) Predial servitudes. West Publishing Company, p 520

Zhou Y (2003) History of international law. Foundation of international law. Source of international law. Law of treaties. Elsevier Science Publishing Company, Netherlands, pp 126–179

Official Documents and Reports

Afghanistan Pakistan Transit Trade Coordination Authority, Minutes of the 1st Afghanistan Pakistan Transit Trade Coordination Authority (Islamabad, February 11–12, 2011)

Afghanistan Pakistan Transit Trade Coordination Authority, Minutes of the 2nd Afghanistan Pakistan Transit Trade Coordination Authority (Kabul. May 31–June 1, 2012)

Afghanistan Pakistan Transit Trade Coordination Authority, Minutes of the 4th Afghanistan Pakistan Transit Trade Coordination Authority (Kabul, October 8–9, 2013)

Afghanistan Pakistan Transit Trade Coordination Authority, Minutes of the 5th Afghanistan Pakistan Transit Trade Coordination Authority (Islamabd, January 10, 2014)

Asian Development Bank, Turkmenistan–Afghanistan–Pakistan–India Natural Gas Pipeline Project, Phase 3, Completion Report, Project No. 44463-013 (March 2018)

Asian Development Bank, Afghanistan Joins Tajikistan Kyrgyz Republic Cross-Border Transport Accord (August 29, 2011)

Afghanistan Central Statistics Office Report (2008)

Chief of Staff's Office of the President, Media Directorate, The Unity Government: Three years Achievements at a Glance, 49 (February 2018) (Official Version. Dari), https://ocs.gov.af/uploads/documents_dr/17.pdf

Central Asia Regional Economic Cooperation, Secretariat, CAREC Corridor Performance Measurement and Monitoring – Annual Report 2016 (January 2018)

Central Asia Regional Economic Cooperation, CAREC Transport Corridors at Safely Connected: A Regional Road Safety Strategy for CAREC Countries 2017–2030 (2016), https://www.carecprogram.org/uploads/2016CAREC-Road-Safety.pdf

Council of the European Union, User's Guide to Council Common Position 2008/944/CFSP (2008)

Economic Cooperation Organization, ECO Vision 2025 and Implementation Framework (February 2017)

European Union Intellectual Property Office, 2019 Status Report on IPR Infringement (2019)

GATT Analytical Index, https://www.wto.org/english/res_e/booksp_e/gatt_ai_e/gatt_ai_e.htm

Government of Afghanistan, V Afghanistan National Development Strategy (2007). www.ands.gov.af

Government of Pakistan, Foreign Office Yearbook 2002–03 (Foreign Office of Pakistan, 2003)

Government of Pakistan, Foreign Office Yearbook 2005–06 (Foreign Office of Pakistan 2006)

Government of Pakistan, Development Authority of Pakistan, Country Report on Afghanistan: Executive Summary (2018)

I.C.J., Advisory Opinion, Legal Consequences for States of the Continued Presence of South Africa in Namibia (South West Africa) notwithstanding Security Council Resolution 276 (1970), REP. 16 (1971)

International Monetary Fund, Emergency Customs Modernization and Trade Facilitation Project (November 2003)

International Monetary Fund, World Economic Outlook (October 2016)

International Monetary Fund, Islamic Republic of Afghanistan, Country Report 18/127 (May 2018)

International Monetary Fund, World Economic Outlook (October, 2014)

Institute for the Study of War, Afghanistan and Pakistan, http://www.understandingwar.org/pakistan-andafghanistan

International Law Commission, Fragmentation of International Law: Difficulties Arising from the Diversification and Expansion of International Law, Report of the Study Group of the International Law Commission, A/CN.4/L.682 (April 13, 2006)

International Road Transport Union, Principles Governing International Transit – Drawn up by the International Road Transport Union based on the Opinion of a Panel Appointed by the World Trade Organization, https://www.iru.org/apps/cms-filesystem-action?file=Webnews2009/Gatt-transit.pdf

League of Nations, Treaty Series, VII Publication of Treaties and International Engagements Registered with the Secretariat of the League of Nations. 1921–1922

Ministry of Agriculture, Irrigation and Livestock of Afghanistan, National Comprehensive Agriculture Development Priority Program 2016-2020 (August 2016)

Ministry of Commerce and Industry of Afghanistan, Afghanistan National Export Strategy 2018–2022 (2018)

Ministry of Commerce and Industry of Afghanistan, Directorate of International Trade, Afghanistan 2009-2013 Trade Review (2013)

Ministry of Commerce and Industry of Afghanistan, Export Tariffs List of Goods (December, 2012), http://moci.gov.af/Content/files/%D8%AA%D8%B9%D8%B1%D9%81%D9%87% 20%D9%87%D8%A7%DB%8C%20%D8%B5%D8%A7%D8%AF%D8%B1%D8%A7% D8%AA%DB%8C.pdf

Ministry of Commerce and Industry of Afghanistan, Afghanistan National Standards Authority (ANSA), Standards Adopted by the Afghan National Standards Authority (December 2012), http://moci.gov.af/Content/files/ANSA%20standards%20EN.pdf

Ministry of Finance, Brief Report on Three Years 2015–2017 Main Activities and Achievements of Ministry of Finance (2018)

Ministry of Finance, Third Joint Economic and Trade Commission between Afghanistan and China and Signing Cooperation Agreements

Ministry of Finance of Afghanistan, Afghanistan Customs Department, Annual Progress Report 2016 (2016)

Ministry of Finance of Afghanistan, Afghanistan Customs Department, Five Year Strategic Plan 2014–2018 2014)

Ministry of Finance of Afghanistan, RECCA VII, Towards Regional Economic Growth and Stability: The Silk Road through Afghanistan (2015)

Organization for Economic Cooperation Development, Aid for Trade: Making it Effective in OECD, 8 Division for Cooperation Report (2007)

Organization for Economic Cooperation Development, Reducing Trade Cost for Least Developed Countries in OECD, Aid for Trade at a Glance 2015: Reducing Trade Costs for Inclusive, Sustainable Growth, 133 (2015)

Pakistan Afghanistan Joint Chamber of Commerce and Industries, Pak Afghan Trade (2018)

PAJCCI, Draft Annual report 2014 (2014)

Pakistan Bureau of Statistics, www.pbs.gov.pk/sites/default/files//external_trade/8_digitlevel/exp/5_exp_200809_to_2012-2013.pdf

Regional Economic Cooperation Conference on Afghanistan, VII Declaration, Deepening Connectivity and Expanding Trade through Investment Infrastructure and Improving Synergy, Annex II (Ashgabat, 2017)

Regional Economic Cooperation Conference on Afghanistan, Afghanistan–Centered Regional Cooperation: From Planning to Implementation (November 2018)

Special Inspector General for Afghanistan Reconstruction (SIGAR), Analysis of TAFA Final Report (April 2014)

Trade Development Authority of Pakistan, Ministry of Commerce of Government of Pakistan, Country Report on Afghanistan, Executive Summary, (Karachi 2018), https://www.tdap.gov.pk/word/AFGHANISTAN.pdf

The Asia Foundation, Afghanistan in 2019: A Survey of the Afghan People, 15th Annual Opinion Survey (December 2, 2019)

Third United Nations Conference on the Law of the Sea, 2nd Committee, Revised Draft Articles in keeping with the Declaration of Developing Land-Locked and other Geographically Disadvantaged States, Doc. A/CONF.62/C.2/97 (1974)

Third United Nations Conference on the Law of the Sea, Informal Single Negotiating Text, Official Records 137, 168, U.N. Doc. A/Conf.62WP.8/Part 11 (1975)

United Nations Conference on the Law of the Sea, U.N. GAOR, 29th Sess., 11th mtg, U.N.Doc. A/Conf. 13/43 (1958)

United Nations Security Council Resolution, U.N.S.C. RES. 38, U.N. Doc. S/RES/38 (January 17, 1948a)

United Nations Security Council Resolution, U.N.S.C. RES. 41, U.N. Doc. S/RES/41 (February 6, 1948b)

United Nations Security Council Resolution, U.N.S.C. RES. 47, U.N. Doc. S/RES/47 (April 21, 1948c

United Nations Security Council Resolution, U.N.S.C. RES. 51, U.N. Doc. S/RES/51 (June 3, 1948d)

United Nations Security Council Resolution, U.N. Doc. S/RES/90 (January 31, 1951)

United Nations Security Council Resolution, U.N.S.C. RES. 123, U.N. Doc. S/RES/123 (January 16, 1957)

United Nations Security Council, Letter dated 1 August 2019 from the Chargé d'affaires a.i. of the Permanent Mission of Pakistan to the United Nations addressed to the Secretary-General, S/2019/623 (August 1, 2019)

United Nations General Assembly, U.N. GA, 28th Sess., Supple No. 21 & corr.1 & 3, vol. II, annex VI, sect. 5, Draft Articles Relating to Land-locked States, U.N. Doc. A/AC. 138/93, A/CONF.62/C.2/L.29 (1973)

United Nations General Assembly, U.N. GAOR. No. 71/205, Situation of Human Rights in the Autonomous Republic of Crimea and the City of Sevastopol (Ukraine), GAOR. A/71/PV.65 (December 19, 2016)

United Nations Convention on the Law of the Sea, Question of Free Access to the Sea of Land-Locked Countries, A/CONF.13/29 and Add. 1 (Geneva, 1957)

United Nations, Preparatory Documents, I Extract from the Official Records of the United Nations Conference on the Law of the Sea (United Nations publication, 2009)

United Nations Economic and Social Council, Preparatory Committee of International Conference on Trade and Development, Second Committee, Report of the Technical Sub-Committee, U.N. Doc. E/PC/T/C. II/54/Rev/1 (1946)

United Nations Conference on Trade and Development, U.N. ESCOR, 35th plen. mtg. U.N. Doc. E/CONF. 46/141, Vol. VI (1964)

United Nations Conference on Trade and Development, The Way to the Ocean, Transport and Trade Facilitation Series 4, U.N. Secretariat (United Nations Statistics Division, 2017)

United Nations Committee on Development Policy (May 2016), http://www.un.org/en/development/desa/policy/cdp/ldc/ldc_list.pdf

United Nations Economic and Social Commission for Asia and Pacific, Transit Transport Issues in Landlocked and Transit Developing Countries, Landlocked Developing Countries Series 1, U.N. Doc. ST/ESCAP/2270 (2003)

United Nations Economic and Social Commission for Asia and Pacific, Fifth Technical Workshop on Afghanistan's Accession to the WTO (New Delhi. December 3, 2014)

United Nations Economic Commission for Asia and the Far East, Problems of Trade of Landlocked Countries in Asia and the Far East, Report by the Secretariat, U. N. Doc. ECAFE/I & T/Sub.4/2 (1956)

United Nations Conference on Trade and Employment, Final Act and Related Documents, U.N. Doc. E/CONF.2/78, U.N. Sales No. II.D.4 (1948)

United Nations Conference on Trade and Employment, Interpretive Note, Annex P to the U. N. Charter, U.N. Doc. E/CONF.2/78 (1948)

United Nations Economic Commission for Europe, Explanatory Note to Article 8, paragraph 3, The TIR Convention 1979a, 9 REV. 50, http://www.unece.org/fileadmin/DAM/tir/handbook/english/newtirhand/TIR6Rev9EN_Convention.pdf

United Nations Economic Commission for Europe, TIR Handbook, U.N. Doc. ECE/TRANS/TIR/6/REV.11 (2018)

United Nations Economic Commission for Europe, Explanatory Note to Article 8, paragraph 3, The TIR Convention 1979b, 9 REV. 50, http://www.unece.org/fileadmin/DAM/tir/handbook/english/newtirhand/TIR6Rev9EN_Convention.pdf

United Nations Economic Commission for Europe, Strengthening Regional Cooperation in Central Asia: A contribution to long-term stability and sustainable development of Afghanistan, SPECA Economic Forum (2010)

United Nations Office of the High Representative for the Least Developed Countries, Landlcoked Developing Countries and the Small Island Developing States (OHRLLS), UNCLOS and Landlocked Developing Countries: Practical Implications: Summary Report (2012)

United Nations, World Economic Situation and Prospects 2016 (2016)

United Nations, One UN for Afghanistan, (March 27, 2018)

United Nations Office on Drugs and Crime, Country Profile: Pakistan, https://www.unodc.org/pakistan/en/country-profile.html

United States Department of Commerce, Doing Business in Afghanistan: 2011 Country Commercial Guide for US Companies (2011)

United States Agency for International Development, Trade and Accession Facilitation for Afghanistan, Final Report (August 2013)

United States Agency for International Development, Response to the Inquiry Letter on Afghan Customs Revenue, United State Agency for International Development Memorandum (March 19, 2015)

United States Agency for International Development, Analysis of Afghanistan Pakistan Transit Trade Agreement (May 2014)

World Bank, Analysis of Afghanistan Pakistan Transit Trade Agreement (2014a)

World Bank, Islamic Republic of Afghanistan Agricultural Sector Review: Revitalizing Agriculture for Economic Growth, Job Creation and Good Security, AUS9779 (June 2014b).

World Bank, Afghanistan Economic Update (April 2014c)

World Bank, Afghanistan Economic Update, No. 96045 (April 2015)

World Bank Group, Doing Business 2019: Economy Profile 2019: Afghanistan, World Bank (16th edn. October 2018)

World Bank Group, Doing Business 2018: Economy Profile 2018: Afghanistan (15th edn. April 2018)

World Bank Group, Pakistan@100 Regional Connectivity, Policy Note (May 2019a)

World Bank, Second Customs Reform and Trade Facilitation Project: Implementation Status and Results Report, Project No. P112872 (December 7, 2017)

World Bank, Afghanistan-Second Customs Reform and Trade Facilitation Project: Restructuring, Report No. RES30675 (December 18, 2017)

World Bank Group, Afghanistan Development Update: Building Confidence Amid Uncertainty (WASH, D.C. July 2019b)

World Intellectual Property Organization [WIPO], Coordinating Intellectual Property Enforcement, WIPO/ACE/14/5 REV (August 22, 2019)

WTO Analytical Index (3d edn. 2011)

WTO, Fifth Meeting of Trade Ministers of Landlocked Developing Countries (2016a)

WTO, Committee on Trade and Environment. Trade & Environment, The Doha Mandate on Multilateral Environmental Agreements (MEAs)

WTO, General Council Decision on Doha Agenda Work Program, Annex D, WT/L/579 (August 2004)

WTO Secretariat, Speeding up Trade: Benefits and Challenges of Implementing the WTO Trade Facilitation Agreement, World Trade Report (2015)

WTO Secretariat, Article V of The GATT 1994 – Scope and Application, Note by the Secretariat, G/C/W/408

WTO, Working Party on the Accession of the Islamic Republic of Afghanistan, Report on Accession of the Islamic Republic of Afghanistan – Derestriction of Documents, WT/ACC/AFG/38 (November 13, 2015)

WTO, Negotiating Group on Trade Facilitation, Negotiations on Trade Facilitation–Compilation of Members' Textual Proposals TN/TF/W/43/Rev.19, part F-LDC Provisions (June 30, 2009)

WTO Negotiating Group on Trade Facilitation, Clarifying and Improving GATT Article V, TN/TF/W/176 (November 7, 2011)

WTO Secretariat, Harnessing Trade for Sustainable Development and a Green Economy (2011)

WTO, Fifth Meeting of Trade Ministers of Landlocked Developing Countries (2016b)

WTO, Committee on Trade and Development, Special and Differential Treatment for Least-Developed Countries, WT/COMTD/W/239 (October 12, 2018)

WTO Secretariat, Overview of Afghanistan's Commitments to the WTO (2018)

WTO, Report by the Secretariat, Quantitative Restrictions: Factual Information Notification Received, G/MA/W/114/Rev.2 (May 20, 2019)

Printed by Printforce, the Netherlands